A History of
English Literature

ALASTAIR FOWLER

A History of
English Literature

Harvard University Press
Cambridge, Massachusetts

First Harvard University Press paperback edition, 1991

Library of Congress Cataloging in Publication Data

Fowler, Alastair.
   A history of English literature.

   Includes index.
   1.   English literature—History and criticism.
   I. Title.
   PR83.F65   1987   820'.9   86-33525
   ISBN 0-674-39665-0 (alk. paper) (cloth)
   ISBN 0-674-39664-2 (paper)

To Marjorie and Alex

Contents

Preface to Paperback Edition

This new edition has given an opportunity for some corrections. I have also made additions to the last two chapters, and provided suggestions for further reading.

Alastair Fowler
April, 1989

Preface to First Edition

A history of English literature may well be thought too large a venture for one volume, let alone one historian. But this book may partly excuse itself by concentrating, less ambitiously, on literary forms. Literary contents have obviously changed profoundly, perhaps irrecoverably, over the centuries. Think of the gulf between the literature of medieval Christendom and the doubting, reforming, private literature of the Victorians. It is less obvious how far continuity has been maintained: how far the means of representing life have gradually changed throughout the history of literary forms. I mainly trace the second sort of changes, changes in kinds and forms. Sometimes these have social or economic causes; but more often they are developments internal to literature – shifts of fashion, deeper movements, growth cycles, effects of compensation.

My constant question has been, How have the proportions between the various elements of literature changed? For such changes affect the pleasures of reading more than is usually recognized. As far as possible, I have tried to explain how best to approach each writer: what obstacles to avoid, what allowances to make, what pleasures to expect. Whatever else it may sometimes be, experiencing literature is always an especial pleasure, distinct from others. But the pleasure of an individual author can be so distinct that it needs to be learned. My hope is to enlarge the reader's sense of the variety of literature.

In the present age, attempts to evade the past have led to neglect of older writing. But in creating the future we need access to the widest variety of past literature – not only for perspective, for benchmarks and for values and visions we lack, but also in order to grasp the literature of our own time.

While this book seldom avoids evaluation, it primarily describes. It is written for students coming to grips with unfamiliar parts of literature, or revising familiar ones; and I have had particularly in mind intelligent adults new to literary criticism. So technical terms are explained, and names and dates set out in full, but hard words are not avoided. Also, the 'schools' and 'movements' are discussed, although I am aware that good literature has hardly ever been written to overthrow (or to follow) a fashion.

Besides explicit evaluations, others can be inferred from the scale of the treatment. However, some *caveats* are called for in this regard. Necessities of exposition (particularly with difficult or neglected writers) have sometimes distorted relative scales. Besides, it needs to be remembered that important writing may not be of comparable interest formally; in a history constructed on other principles, George Orwell might have claimed a larger place. Similarly, popular kinds such as science fiction, in which words are comparatively insignificant, may have received less than their rightful wordage. Another source of distortion is temporal foreshortening. In the modern period names swarm, since posterity has yet to make its selection: here the treatment is inevitably cursory.

For coherence, I have focused on the literature of the British Isles, and specifically of England – although with many necessary side glances at Scotland and Ireland. I bring in US and Commonwealth writers only when they have a direct bearing on the argument; this has meant excluding some who are very considerable, like Mark Twain. In a temporal dimension, I have limited the horizon to works that can still be read with pleasure and without translation; so that I begin, in effect, with Chaucer.

The debts incurred in writing a book like this are many. Indeed, the personal influences are too many even to list. I might begin with C. S. Lewis and F. W. Bateson and E. D. Hirsch and J. F. Kermode; but where would I end? Colleagues and pupils at the Universities of Oxford and Edinburgh and Virginia – and extramural students, among them those in the dedication – will doubtless recognize the impress of their ideas in the pages that follow – indulgently, I hope. But I must thank in particular Wallace Robson and J. C. Levenson and Christopher Butler, whose conversation illuminated my thinking at crucial stages; E. M. Brown and R. D. S. Jack, who read parts of the manuscript; Stuart Gillespie and John V. Price, who drew my attention to some errors; and David Perkins, whose report for Harvard University Press made a number of invaluable corrections and suggestions. I am also grateful to Sheila Strathdee, who keyed and copied much of the book.

In one sense all is due to my wife's love and possibly endless patience. In another, the main debt is to John Davey, the editor, since the book was his idea. Writing it has been to me a privilege and – however challenging at times – a delectation. I hope that some of this will communicate itself.

Alastair Fowler

A History of
English Literature

A Note on Citations and Abbreviations

Explanations of technical terms are signalized by small capitals. In quotations, old spelling and punctuation have in general been retained – modernized only occasionally, when this was thought desirable; but *i/j*, *u/v*, ornamental italics and capitals, and italics for proper names have been normalized throughout. Occasional indications of scansion have been kept or introduced.

ABBREVIATIONS

a.	acted
ch.	chapter
ed.	edited by, edition
par.	paragraph
pt.	part
ptd.	printed
rev.	revised
s.d.	stage direction
st.	stanza
wr.	written

I

The Middle Ages:
From Oral to Written Literature

A HISTORY of literature can only begin in the middle. The earliest surviving works in Old English already present highly developed forms. Structurally, for example, the epic *Beowulf* (?eighth century; preserved in a tenth-century manuscript) is intricately wrought, while its allusions presuppose the existence of even earlier works now lost. And before writing there existed an oral literature, probably of great antiquity, whose tradition has to some extent continued down to the present, alongside our relatively belated written literature. The Celts and Saxons brought oral literature with them to England, and so did the Normans, Danes and Vikings. The Roman historian Tacitus wrote of a thriving oral tradition in ancient Germania. True, a post-Conquest starting point of English literature could be fixed on linguistic grounds: it is not literature in Primitive Germanic or Old Norse or Old English (Anglo-Saxon), but in English. (Indeed, even within Middle English literature – *c.*1100–1500 – much cannot now be read, but must be translated.) But one should never forget that such a beginning is arbitrary. We can deal with only a small part of literature; and the part's claim to completeness rests on fictions – like the true story that Chaucer and Gower invented English literature as we know it.

ORAL LITERATURE: BALLADS

Nowadays oral tradition is often underestimated, and assumed to be simple, limited, unambitious. Literature based on word-of-mouth tradition needs a comparatively restricted DICTION, or choice of words. Its syntax and texture have to be loose, with many repetitions, to ensure ease of uptake. And there is an economy of oral delivery, which calls for a high incidence of formulaic material. In the Middle Ages, this meant familiar narrative motifs; stock similes; TAGS or spacers, like 'as I you

say', 'wythoute fable [truly]', 'on day' and 'what nedeth wordes mo?';
and standard FORMULAS like 'the gude red wine', 'the tears blinded his
eie', 'gold and silver and precious stones' and 'by aventure or caas [by
chance or circumstance]'. These may indeed at first seem bald, even
otiose; but they could be used pleasurably with skilful variation, to give
a precise effect in performance. Rapport with an audience made
possible subtleties of tone that were exploited by literate authors such as
Chaucer — whose poems, although transmitted by manuscript, were
also performed at court. And even exclusively oral literature could be
sophisticated and ambitiously structured. An illiterate Russian of our
own time is said to have composed a poem of 40,000 lines.

Some idea of oral literature can be arrived at from the surviving
variety of BALLADS or narrative folk songs — popular versions of
romances, love tales, tales of devotion and betrayal, or laments based on
tragic historical events. Many English and Scottish popular ballads go
back to the Middle Ages. But, with few exceptions, they began to be
written down only in the fifteenth century. Most exist in seventeenth-
century or eighteenth-century texts (often popular versions of earlier
professional literature), having been preserved by collectors such as
Bishop Percy, Sir Walter Scott, F. J. Child and now The School of
Scottish Studies. And the tradition is a living one, as it was for the
Elizabethan Sir Philip Sidney, when he heard a blind fiddler sing: 'I
never heard the old song of Percy and Douglas that I found not my heart
moved more than with a trumpet.' It can still be a peak of one's literary
experience to hear a folk singer like Jeanie Robertson, perhaps perform-
ing a version of *The Battle of Harlaw* handed down to her by word of
mouth.

Much can be learnt by comparing numerous versions of a single
ballad, or versions of distinct but similar ballads such as *Edward,
Edward* and *Lord Randal*, in each of which a recent tragic event is
powerfully implied. One notices the abundant common fund of
architectonic devices that enable the singers to order their versions:

> Why dois your brand sae drop wi bluid,
>   Edward, Edward?
> Why dois your brand sae drop wi bluid?
>   And why sae sad gang [go] yee, O?
>
> O, I hae killed my hauke sae guid,
>   Mither, mither:
> O, I hae killed my hauke sae guid:
>   And I had nae mair bot hee, O.

Here, besides the repetition of line 1 as line 3, there is the appositional or
PARATACTIC structure whereby the last line is simply put alongside, with
no more connection than 'and'; the duologue pattern, with four lines
answering four; and the symmetry of the short lines, with 'Mither,
mither' exactly matching 'Edward, Edward'. On a larger scale, stanzas
answer stanzas in a similar way, or else cumulate by threes – as in the
sequence *hawk | horse | father* and the later (answering) sequence of
consequences: exile for Edward, poverty for his wife and children, but
for his mother a curse that opens a quite new perspective on the story.
The organization depends so heavily on such merely cumulative and
additive structures, in fact, that a fair amount of constructive work is left
to the audience to perform.

The additive and cumulative principles also combine in that commonest of medieval devices, the CATALOGUE. Modern readers are often
put off by the extent to which older literature consists of lists; for these
now seem dull and empty. But they had a vital function in oral
performance, being easy to follow and to carry in memory. They
usefully reviewed existing knowledge, and – since their syntax was so
easy – could make implicit points of some subtlety, for example by
varying familiar sets of famous names. Moreover, catalogues were often
ordered in a significant way, whether in some meaningful sequence (the
first, central and last places being of special dignity) or in relation to
schemes like that of the Seven Deadly Sins.

Often a list that seems artless proves to be ordered in an intricate or
even problematic way – as for example the haunting description of the
living dead in fairyland, in the early fourteenth-century *Sir Orfeo*, a short
fairy romance or BRETON LAY:

> Som stode withouten hade [head],
> And som non armes nade,
> And som thurgh the body hadde wounde,
> And som lay wode [mad] ybounde,
> And som armed on hors sete,
> And som astrangled as they ete,
> And som were in water adreint [drowned],
> And som with fire all forshreint [scorched].
> Wives there lay on childbedde,
> Som dede and som awedde [mad],
> And wonder fele [many] there lay besides
> Right as they slepe her undrentides [siesta].
> Ech was thus in this warld ynome [taken],
> With fairy thider ycome.

> There he seigh his owen wif,
> Dame Heurodis, his leef [dear] lif,
> Slepe under an impe-tree [grafted tree] . . .
>
> (lines 391–407)

Here the sets are perhaps to be arranged in pairs: two groups of the dismembered; two hurt in body and in mind; the armed sitting on horseback and the disarmed at table; the drowned and the burnt; two women in childbed (dead and mad); and two sleeping (noonday sleepers and Heurodis). Or are we to group by threes – three sets of wounded; three of unwounded; three of victims of sudden natural death (drowning, fire, childbirth); and finally three general categories: dead (l. 400), mad (l. 400) and sleeping (l. 402)? Some of the groupings further hint at sequences – like the progressions from head to arms, and from riding to eating. The net impression is of elusive multifariousness, blurred status. One gets a sense of comprehensive multiplicity far beyond what so short a list might have been expected to give.

Sir Orfeo was refashioned as a ballad with its own variant forms (*King Orfeo*, collected in the late nineteenth century); and so were *King Horn* and several other short ROMANCES, or chivalric narratives. In transmission by word of mouth there could be no completely fixed text at all, in fact, since there was no single order of words. Not the words, but the story, was the thing: if singers were true to that, to the inner shape, they had some degree of freedom to improvise words and in effect compose new versions. It was another world from that of manuscript transmission, in which firmer ideas of a text's detailed determinacy developed, and a scrivener could be blamed (as in 'Chancer's words unto Adam'), for inaccurate copying. Thus in oral literature transmission and composition overlapped. Each new teller's version, if not each performance, might be substantially different. In such a process, a repertoire of formulas and constructional schemes was indispensable. Singers were bound to rely on their memorial stores of well-tried expressions. But that was by no means altogether a disadvantage, since these often had a rugged force: 'Then up spake X . . . ', 'Y had not gone a mile but one . . .'.

From all this follow several large consequences, of import for the character of medieval literature as a whole. First, the reliance on formulaic language implies that from the earliest historical times poets made use of POETIC DICTION – that is to say, a choice of words different from that of ordinary speech. (Diction did not begin as colloquial or natural, and only later became artificial or literary.) Second, almost all medieval writing has the somewhat loose organization of oral literature;

it lacks the power to curtail accumulations, to subordinate elements syntactically, or to condense into complexity. Third, and perhaps the widest consequence of all, authorship itself was different from what it has since become. Instead of being conceived as an individual role, it merely supplemented an original divine authorship.

Few now believe that the people, rather than individuals, created oral literature (in James Grimm's phrase *das Volk dichtet*, 'the folk is the author'), but certainly medieval writers borrowed from one another freely, not only without any sense of plagiary, but even boasting their faithfulness to an admired predecessor. 'Book' commonly referred to a codex containing works by several authors; and there were no terms corresponding to our 'work' or 'poem'. Neither modern pseudonymity nor such oral tradition as survives offers more than a faint analogy of the confusion of authorship in the Middle Ages. Indeed, after the Saxons Alfred and Bede, Chaucer is the first individual figure of any great significance in our literature. Few earlier names, even, are secure, unless through circumstances of locality or anagram signature. On the other hand, for all this uncertainty of identity, medieval authors sometimes show a very accessible intimacy – perhaps because they wrote directly for a familiar audience.

The GENRES or kinds of writing in the Middle Ages naturally reflect the literature's oral character. Thus, much of the best work is in the form of sermons, or hymns, or stories meant for performance. And a favourite genre was the debate – as in *The Owl and the Nightingale* (*c.*1200) – a form closely related to the exercises of academic oral instruction. For if the Middle Ages were an age of faith, they were also a time of controversy, of Abelard's *Sic et Non*.

Another striking feature of oral literature was its fragmentation into many separate local traditions. These cannot be classified (like their modern equivalents) as metropolitan or provincial. Indeed, several areas had an equal claim to preeminence. Particularly in verse, Anglo-Norman (or French) domination continued into the fourteenth century; only towards the end of that century did an English dialect gradually begin to establish itself as central. This was the London–Essex dialect, in which Chaucer wrote. But even as he did so the north was producing a literature quite as sophisticated and varied – and arguably more accomplished. The tradition represented by works like *Sir Gawain and the Green Knight*, *Pearl* and *Cleanness* was by no means provincial. Indeed, its cultural connections with the south have been underestimated. Only the accident that linguistic development favoured Chaucer's dialect made the northern words come to seem difficult, and in consequence deprived the northern poems of any great influence on subsequent literature.

The court poetry of this so-called ALLITERATIVE REVIVAL was highly traditional; often employing or finessing on the alliterative formulas of oral literature. Some think, in fact, that its transmission was primarily oral; but the existence of false or 'eye' alliteration, like 'Quere-so-ever I jugged gemmes gaye' (*Pearl* 7) betray a manuscript tradition. The northern poems I have mentioned are unquestionably great works; yet they survive in only a single manuscript. Perhaps no other fact more forcibly brings home how precarious manuscript transmission could be – and how much of medieval literature may in fact have been lost. It is worth reflecting on its evanescent glories, of which only fragments or bare titles remain to us.

MEDIEVAL ROMANCES

In approaching medieval literature adjustment has to be made to the large fact that much of it is in verse – even storytelling and popular exposition, which are now regarded as prose functions. A main narrative kind, at first generally in verse, was the ROMANCE (Old French *romant*), an adventure story of chivalry or love. The romances were of course Christian – part of the great medieval response to the challenge of pagan classical literature. They need not be edifying in any obvious way; none the less, they usually have an inner *sens* or significance, and almost universally sustain an aspiring elevation.

This appears even in description, which is idealized. The *Gawain* poet proposes to tell 'an outtrage awenture of Arthurez wonderez [an exceedingly strange adventure from among the marvellous tales of Arthur]' (*Gawain and the Green Knight* 29), and is soon speaking of curtains 'beten wyth the best gemmes / That myght be preved of prys wyth penyes to bye, / in daye [embroidered with the best gems that money could buy]' (lines 78–80). Idealization also shows in extremes of emotion; as in Gawain's shame on his return to the court, or the joy at Orfeo's reunion with Heurodis ('For joye they wepe with her [their] eighe [eyes]', *Sir Orfeo* 591), or Lancelot's grief at parting from Guenivere:

> there was never so harde an herted man but he wold have wepte to see the dolour that they made, for there was laementacyon as they had be stungyn wyth sperys. And many tymes they swouned, and the ladyes bare the quenc to hir chambre.

And Syr Launcelot awok, and went and took his hors, and rode al that day and al nyght in a forest wepyng.

(Malory, *Morte Darthur* xxi.10)

Similarly idealized are the codes of chivalry (especially loyalty to a lord) and of love (especially 'courtly love', so called). In consequence, the romances have often been spoken of as unrealistic or wishful. It is true that they may explicitly contrast the less than ideal present with 'the olde custome and usage of this londe' (*Morte Darthur* xxi.1). Yet they are morally realistic, to the extent that they often test codes of conduct by probing contradictions within them or between them. And several of the romance writers, notably Sir Thomas Malory (d. 1471), even seem on the whole to lack a romantic sense of wonder. They evoke it, when they do, almost accidentally: not by leaving mysteries unexplained deliberately, but through being unable to make sense of stories they can only repeat.

Several fourteenth-century romances revived the alliterative tradition of Anglo-Saxon literature. In this tradition elaborate stanzas were sometimes used, like the ones in *Gawain and the Green Knight* and (parodied) in Chaucer's Tale of Sir Thopas. Versification was based not on syllable-counting metre but on patterns of stresses. Each line had to have four heavily stressed syllables, arranged in two pairs and so far as possible alliterating (beginning with the same sound, not necessarily the same letter):

> Than glíftis [looks] the gud kýng:
>   and glópyns [is sad] in hérte,
> Grónys full grisely [dreadfully]:
>   wyth grétande téris [tears of grief]
> Knélis down to the córs: and káught it in ármes . . .
> (*Morte Arthure* 3949–51)

The rhythmic patterns seem to have been those of speech – but speech regularized and reduced to system. Thus, many of the narrative formulas are alliterating phrases, half-lines in effect: 'on body and bones'; 'stif and stronge'. The requirements of alliterative verse promoted the development of a poetic diction of vaguely meaningful (or purely poetic) words like 'clene' (clean, pure, chaste, neat). Similar are the numerous synonyms (poetic or borrowed) for commonly recurring words, such as 'burne', 'freke', 'gome', 'carle' and many others for 'man'. Fragments of this diction survived into later literature; and alliteration itself became an occasional resource for many metrical poets from Chaucer onwards, until in the eighteenth century neoclassicism eventually made it taboo. Alliterative verse was capable of a great variety of effects; although it tended to be bold or grim rather than subtle.

The term 'romance', like the modern 'novel', covers a broad spectrum of types, from vast sprawling chronicles or chronicle–romances (Layamon's late twelfth-century *Brut*; John Barbour's fourteenth-century *Bruce* – 'A fredome is a noble thing!') through near-epics (the fourteenth-century alliterative *Morte Arthure*) to short romances or *lais* – some of them forerunners of the sort of concentrated short story later perfected by Heinrich von Kleist. Generally the romances reflected court values, and were French in orientation, if not actually drawn from French originals. Nevertheless, they might treat several 'matters' – not just the 'matter of France' (stories of Charlemagne) but also of Britain (Celtic myth and legend) and of Rome (including Theban or Trojan material; though not from Homer, whose poems were unknown).

The 'matter of Britain' included the Arthurian CYCLE, or group of stories centring on the court of King Arthur. This provided the storyteller with an available *mise en scène* – a world of forests, castles and strange customs, of fresh marvels and familiar characters. The alliterative *Morte Arthure*, *Gawain and the Green Knight*, the *Awntyrs of Arthur* (*c*.1400) and many similar works take up the same episodes, sometimes from French predecessors ('as the book telleth'), or make reference beyond themselves by easy invocation of a preexisting romance world – as when the *Gawain* poet refers casually to 'the Rounde Table' (*Gawain and the Green Knight* 39), or the stanzaic *Morte Arthur* begins 'In Arthur dayes, that noble kinge, / By-felle Aunturs ferly fele [Befell adventures wondrous many]' (lines 5–6).

Loose ends of this sort are characteristic of romance. They belong to a type of structure in which separate themes and adventures are interwoven in such a way as to preclude overview from any single perspective. INTERLACE or *entrelacement* ensures that no section is self-contained, and may even make the work as a whole depend on the cycle. On a post-Renaissance view all this is easily put down to lack of unity. (Already Chaucer favoured single-action romance of the Knight's Tale type; satirizing the interlaced form in his Squire's Tale.) But the romances are not classical works. Medieval audiences had their own aesthetic criteria: as in visual art, they generally preferred interwoven linear intricacy.

Medieval writers were not taught to aim at the Aristotelian unity of action that we take for granted as ideal. Instead they valued interlaced multiplicities of incident, such as might give an impression of unsearchability or secret interdependence – or else a sense of pure story.

Rhetoricians such as Geoffrey de Vinsauf (fl. 1210) gave enthusiastic directions to writers on how to digress: it was a standard way to develop a matter. All this could issue, so far as the romances were concerned, in a particular quality of sustained discontinuity, in which each thread was nevertheless indispensable. Thus, in Malory's *Morte Darthur*, Book xiv resumes the story of Sir Percival. In chapter 1 he consults a recluse and finds her to be his aunt, Queen of the Waste Lands. Chapter 2 breaks off to deal with Merlin's idea of the Round Table; and although chapter 3 returns to Percival (taking him to a monastery where he sees the wounded King Evelake of 300 winters), it immediately digresses to the story of Joseph of Arimathea. Furthermore, its concluding reference to blood of the ninth degree may be a link with xiii.7, where Gawain is of the ninth degree from Jesus Christ.

Malory's *Morte Darthur* (wr. 1470) was printed by Caxton in 1485, and also exists in a manuscript copy of about the same date, discovered in 1934. It continued the centuries-long process of compiling stories about Arthur, in which the enormous Vulgate Cycle represented an earlier stage of reordering. Malory followed the true story, but altered emphases and details, rearranging events to shape a narrative that was morally consistent in everything then considered important. (This did not include characterization, which might be varied freely or neglected.) There are few casual novelistic details, and these few (like Gawain's love of apples and pears) always serve a necessary purpose. The moral value of the story – and indeed its main interest – lies in analogies or other connections between its interwoven episodes. Thus, Guenivere's trial as poisoner in Book xviii foreshadows her later trial for adultery in xx, besides showing her as a figure of Discord, complete with fatal apple. Similarly, Book iii has a graded series of quests – Gawain's, Tor's and Pellinor's – in each of which the quester causes an unfortunate death, but does so in very different moral circumstances: by accident, setting obligation above mercy, and through hardness of heart. Such graded series are very common in romances: one might for example compare the temptations in *Gawain and the Green Knight*. The temptress begins with a direct offer of 'service'; proceeds indirectly through talk of love; and deviously entraps Gawain in breaking a promise so as to preserve his life.

Yet the quests in Malory seem not so much moral achievements as discoveries of personal truths already operative. They are 'aventures' (chances), exposing the quester to such confrontations with the unknown as will reveal his nature. 'But syr Launcelot rode overthwarte and endelonge a wylde foreyst and hylde no patthe but as wylde adventure lad hym' (xiii.17). For in romance the unknown turns out to be consistent, even if arbitrary in its heavy chains of consequences: Pellinor's callousness will indirectly lead to his betrayal and death, iii.15, just as Balin's failure to save a lady will lead to his striking 'a stroke most dolorous that ever man stroke'. At every turn the moral code is disconcertingly clarified. Malory's code (and the chivalric code generally) seems elusive now; because it was one of private virtue, unlike the public virtue of the Renaissance and after. Malory himself was aware that old ways were passing – that war, for example, was becoming more total – and, although innocent of any historical overview, he set in the past his story of partings and renunciations, of the 'grete angre and unhap that stynted not til the floure of chyvalry of alle the world was destroyed and slayn' (xx.1).

Malory's style can be deceptive. His paratactic syntax seems simple – designed for oral delivery and rapidity of narration. But the simple diction is highly selective or 'pure': sturdy venerable English words are preferred, long abstract French words and technical terms avoided. Circumstantial description is rare, apart from the marvels themselves, and what there is of it does not occur scattered through, but (as often in medieval literature) concentrated in set pieces for emphasis – for example in accounts of rituals accompanying climactic events. The narrator's part, like his words, limits itself to simplicity, so self-effacingly as to seem transparent. Yet in sum Malory actually achieves a distillation of earlier romance styles: one quintessentially imbued with values. These are embodied in often-repeated phrases and key words, such as 'worship' or honour, the desire to be 'the best knight of the world'. And they find powerful expression in the dignified, laconic restraint of the direct speech. Malory's is the first great prose style in English literature.

FRAMED NARRATIVES

Interlace was one great formal principle of medieval literature; another was FRAMING. Frames were conventional, for example, in dream poems, which became popular after the thirteenth-century French *Roman de la rose* (translated in part, perhaps by Geoffrey Chaucer, as *The Romaunt of the Rose*). Such poems begin and end with dreaming and waking, often in a pleasance, so that the intervening narrative section is presented as a dream or vision. It thus enjoys the freedoms of imaginative status and the advantages of a distancing perspective. The sometimes very elaborate frames may introduce the poet's professional concerns, or refer to specific literary contexts, like the tale of Ceyx and Alcyone in *The Book of the Duchess*. In this way analogies are brought in, which may be equivalent to those of interlace. More generally, the low-key frame serves to prepare the reader for the vision's heightened mood. Some of the pleasantest passages in medieval literature occur in such framing prologues – particularly with poets of the second rank, such as John Lydgate (*c.*1370–1449/50).

Most of Chaucer's poems of middle length – *The Parliament of Fowls*, *The Legend of Good Women* and the rest – are framed in this way. They use ordinary frame conventions, such as the seasonal setting in spring. But Chaucer's greatness at once shows in his historical mastery of commonplaces – in his urbane command of the ideas of the European *auctores* he brings into play, in his lightness of touch in penetrating to profundities. In *The House of Fame* a Dantean eagle (symbolic of philosophical or contemplative thought) elevates Chaucer in what must be a *somnium coeleste* or vision. Treating an abstraction via description of her allegorical 'house' was a classical device (found for example in Virgil's mythological places), and also one that had been used in the *Roman de la rose*. But it was original to treat Fame (and by implication poetic fame) as a subject for contemplation. Throughout, Chaucer's thought is corrosively sceptical – a scepticism directed even at poetry itself – as when the dreamer glances at the inadequacy of his own conventions:

> Loo! how shulde I now telle al thys?
> Ne [nor] of the halle eke [also] what nede is
> To tellen yow that every wal
> Of hit, and flor, and roof, and al
> Was plated half a foote thikke
> Of gold . . .
>
> (*The House of Fame* 1341–6)

The inevitable impossibilities are trotted out and easily transcended. This is not exactly the double meaning of later irony, but rather the sly tone of the humorous speaker.

Another kind of frame connected together many tales; either forming a mere container for them, or else – as in Gower and the Italian Boccaccio – combining them so that they interacted or implemented a scheme. In the frame narrative of Giovanni Boccaccio's *Decameron* (1349–50) fugitives from the plague tell stories to pass the time. They treat in turn several distinct themes, which have thus to be seen against a background of imminent mortality. And in *Confessio Amantis* (three recensions, ?1390, 1391, 1393), by Chaucer's contemporary John Gower (?1330–1408), a lover's confession to love's priest Genius, the natural self, constitutes a minutely developed allegorical frame, in which relatively undetailed, beautifully shaped tales are inserted as examples clarifying the deadly sins of love. In effect the tales survey a broad range of human experience in a rational, systematizing way, such that they almost anticipate the method of the Renaissance. Gower was a great intellectual, and his masterpiece communicates an impressive vision. It is a moving, terrible vision, of life as threatened by irresistible and irrational impulses. By the end of his life-long confession Gower's lover has become too old: 'the thing is torned into "was" . . .' (viii.2435). The individual tales, drawn from Ovid or the romances, are triumphs of *refacimento*, the art of stylish re-presentation.

Gower had the gift of selecting just what formed a spare, classic unity, logical rather than allegorical in coherence. Even his neat tetrameters (four-stressed lines) are balanced, divided often into equal halves. His easy plain style, clear even when dull, excludes all syntactic complications, yet so traces out the linear narrative as to reinforce its moral qualities (or sometimes its atmosphere) by little underlining arrangements. Thus, the story of poor Canace's incest is shaped to bring out the abruptness of consequences. Her brother's child is spoken of as if it might already be born; then at line 202 we hear it 'was noght delivered yit' – an afterthought that allows the immediate continuation to be economical and unexpectedly sudden: 'But riht sone after that sche was'. Although he wrote with moral fervour, 'moral Gower' was our first major poet of formal elegance in narrative – superior, in this regard, even to Chaucer.

The tales of Geoffrey Chaucer's (?1340–1400) *The Canterbury Tales* (probably unfinished at his death) are so realistic, and so rich in characterization and description, that their exemplary import *vis-à-vis* the frame is easily missed. Moreover, the frame itself is rumbustiously vivid enough to seem not to need a meaning. Nevertheless, realistic as it is, the journey through placeless sordid suburbs in the framing narrative of the prologues and endlinks has been shown to symbolize a pilgrimage of life. Within this didactic setting, each tale contributes its particular import to the 'ordering of parts' by Chaucer the compiler (*compilator*). But – and this is the great subtlety – it does so indirectly, through its relation to the other tales.

A striking feature of *The Canterbury Tales* is the encyclopedic diversity of its genres, from courtly romance (The Knight's Tale and Chaucer's own Tale of Sir Thopas) to bawdy FABLIAU or story (The Reeve's Tale,

The Merchant's Tale); from miraculous legend (The Prioress's Tale, The Second Nun's Tale) to sermon (The Pardoner's Tale, The Parson's Tale). Various as they are, the tales often suit their teller; although this aptness need not be dramatized psychologically. Sometimes the match of tale and teller is surprising; sometimes – as with the imperious Wife of Bath – it can be touching. Nevertheless, the tales also answer one another in their substance; which may concern aspects of marriage (The Merchant's Tale and The Franklin's Tale), or theological topics such as Providence (The Man of Law's Tale and The Nun's Priest's Tale). These exchanges work not only by explicit rebuttals, as when a tale is told to 'quite' or repay another, but also through more implicit responses – formal confrontations, or oblique returns to themes from new directions and in wider contexts. And always the implied tendency is sceptical: always human conclusions are undercut: always the ultimate outcome of the storytelling seems to be *contemptus mundi* or otherworldliness. The conclusion of the work is The Parson's Tale, which was preserved as a sermon in several medieval religious libraries.

Chaucer's comprehensive scepticism required that each storyteller's perspective should be offset by those of others in his immortal company, perhaps representing different social groups. The General Prologue introducing the pilgrims at the Tabard surveys a wide range of medieval society, including various 'degrees' (ranks) and – not quite the same thing – distinct pretensions to gentility. The three wholly respectable communal functions have ideal representatives in the Knight, the Parson and the Ploughman his brother. All the other pilgrims, including Chaucer's own persona, are mocked. But the mocking is comparatively light: it presents each individualized type in terms that draw on traditional 'estates satire', yet it acknowledges that specialization of work has made values more relative. Some have argued that even the Knight is satirized, as a ruthless mercenary. But Chaucer need not be automatically ironic; and the list of the Knight's battles (all against the heathen) argues his dedication in fighting for God.

The Monk's portrait is also apparently ambivalent:

> This ilke [same] Monk leet olde thynges pace,
> And heeld after the newe world the space.
> He yaf [gave] nat of that text a pullèd hen,
> That seith that hunters ben nat hooly men,
> Ne [nor] that a monk, whan he is recchelees [careless of discipline],
> Is likned til a fissh that is waterlees, –
> That is to seyn [say], a monk out of his cloystre.

But thilke [this] text heeld he nat worth an oystre;
And I seyde his opinion was good.
                    (*The Canterbury Tales* I(A)175–83)

His worldliness seems to be approved. Only, the approval takes a special stylistic form; interchanging divine and human standards: 'A *manly* man, to been an abbot able'. Chaucer puts 'How shal the world be served?' instead of 'how shall God be served?' In other words, we sense verbal IRONY, and see that what is said denies what is meant. It may be wrong, however, to make pilgrim-Chaucer into an entirely separate fictional character. Chaucer himself may be adopting a poker-faced *faux-naiveté*, and speaking in a distinct *persona* – a recognized strategy in medieval literary theory. In other words, there may be a single, poised *tone* of voice, rather than two separate voices or meanings. Doubt on such points commonly arises with half-oral literature.

At any rate, once the irony is seen, the Monk's portrait becomes delicious. It relishes his devoted gourmandizing at every turn – 'a pulled hen'; 'nat worth an oystre'. The details may seem randomly casual – merely keeping up the narrator's non-judgemental externality; but each makes its point, not so much psychologically as morally. For example, to mention that the Monk's palfrey is 'broun as is a berye' fixes in a single image (designed for the moral art of memory) both his aristocratic taste in horses and his love of food. Such a precise style makes almost every word count: it may be speech-derived, but it has entered far into the subtleties of which written literature will be capable. Chaucer needed every possible resource of style for his difficult purpose of pursuing 'gentilesse' – for that elusive internalizing of values which characterized his time.

The Canterbury Tales may ultimately be edifying, like most medieval literature; but this does not mean that it is anything but secular in many of its individual parts. The Miller's Tale, for example, has on the surface little serious point at all. It hardly persuades one to follow the carpenter in preparing for an imminent apocalypse. Nor is its reductive animality specially aimed at demolishing the idealizations of the Knight's Tale. Between these contiguous tales of contrasting genre there are certainly formal parallels, including a repeated line, which show that the Miller intends parody. And there are also forward connections, with tales about prediction and Providence. But what we are mostly aware of in the Miller's Tale is Chaucer's comic genius. Other fabliau writers might have been capable of the intrigue leading to Nicholas's hot kiss, or have managed the carpenter's fall in a waterless tub. Only Chaucer could combine these in a final cumulative catastrophe of hilarious images, enshrining for the memory a contrast between those who await the end of the world and those who burn in sin.

Chaucer is not, of course, writing a FABLIAU in the ordinary sense. To this relatively limited French genre – coarse, anticlerical popular farce, recounted in bare narrative – he has added a wealth of description and characterization. And he has also elaborated a relatively subsidiary feature: a certain rank-conscious relishing of the coarseness of imperfectly gentle people, such as one finds, much later, in Dutch genre painting:

> on a day this hende [gentle] Nicholas
> Fil with this yonge wyf to rage and pleye,
> Whil that hir housbonde was at Oseneye,
> As clerkes ben ful subtile and ful queynte [sly];
> And prively he caughte hire by the queynte [cunt],
> And seyde, 'Ywis [sure], but if ich [unless I] have my wille,
> For deerne [secret] love of thee, lemman [lover], I spille [perish].'
> And heeld hire harde by the haunchebones,
> And seyde, 'Lemman, love me al atones [right away],
> Or I wol dyen, also God me save!'
> And she sproong as a colt dooth in the trave [enclosure for unruly horses],
> And with hir heed she wryed [turned] faste awey,
> And seyde, 'I wol nat kisse thee, by my fey [faith]!
> Why, lat be,' quod she, 'lat be, Nicholas,
> Or I wol crie "out, harrow" [help] and "allas"!
> Do wey youre handes, for youre curteisye!'
>
> (*The Canterbury Tales* I (A) 3272–87)

The Miller may imagine he is showing the sort of courtesy lovers display in real life, outside the world of romance. But perhaps the better of the pilgrims find instead an illustration of just how ungentle carpenters' wives – and millers – can be. Chaucer realizes, in fact, the potentialities of the fabliau for refined literary subtlety.

As might be expected with a work in the courtly French tradition, most of *The Canterbury Tales* is not in native alliterative verse but in smooth METRE. Metrical verse, which has only occasional alliteration, depends for its structure on counting syllables. (Unstressed final -*e* is pronounced, unless ELIDED or dropped, for example before a vowel.) In Chaucer's practice, stressed and unstressed syllables alternate, not mechanically but with a rhythm regular enough to suggest the underlying abstract metre or measure. Chaucer's favourite metre was the HEROIC COUPLET, that is, five-stressed lines rhyming in pairs – a form that was to prove of great value and to go through many subsequent transformations.

Chaucer's finest romance is not any of *The Canterbury Tales*, but *Troilus and Criseyde* (?1386), a reworking of Boccaccio's *Il Filostrato* (*c.*1335). Some have understandably seen it as anticipating, in certain ways, the modern novel. In Book ii, for example, Chaucer departs from Boccaccio to follow a long bantering conversation between Criseyde and Pandarus. The passage establishes Criseyde as intelligent, sensitive, charming and modest – not by attributing these qualities, but by representing her actual speech in detail. There is even some 'unnecessary' realistic detail:

> Whan he was come unto his neces [niece's] place,
> 'Wher is my lady?' to hire [her] folk quod he;
> And they hym tolde, and he forth in gan pace,
> And fond two othere ladys sete, and she,
> Withinne a pavèd parlour, and they thre
> Herden a mayden reden hem the geste [romance]
> Of the siege of Thebes, while hem leste [for their pleasure].
>
> (ii.77–84)

The detail also functions, it is true, as a sophisticated version of interlaced allusion, with the seige of Thebes as an ominous analogy to that of Troy. (In literature, innovations usually overlap older structures.) Nevertheless, the poem's novelistic tendency so far seems strong. But then we meet great areas where details are vague or lacking – even such important matters (from a novelistic point of view) as the ages of the central characters.

It is not even certain that the main action of *Troilus and Criseyde* is MOTIVATED, or imagined as issuing from inner experience. Has Chaucer at all grounded Criseyde's betrayal of Troilus in emotional changes that make it intelligible psychologically? Her falling in love, although subtly gradual, is not accompanied by inner reflections. Nor do we receive such information as might help to make sense of the betrayal in terms of character. The end is not told from Criseyde's point of view; so that the love remains sweet in our minds, even if she does not. Troilus's 'double sorwe' consequently becomes heightened by thoughts of how much he has lost, how great was his prosperity in love. One need not even think of Criseyde as 'slydynge of corage' (v.825: ?'inconstant' ?'of melting disposition') in a very bad sense. The tragedy is greater than could lie merely in an obvious moral defect.

Chaucer may not exactly have written the first novel, but none the less, his *Troilus and Criseyde* represented a great achievement of fiction as well as of poetry. In its scale – its sustained imitation of life through a single unified narrative line – it initiated a development that would eventually lead to fiction as we know it.

ALLEGORIES

So far ALLEGORY has been referred to casually; now it is time to consider what the term implies. On a local scale, allegory or *allegoria* may be a figure of speech, defined as extended metaphor. 'The state is a ship' exemplifies metaphor; 'he is steering the ship of state into troubled waters', allegory. But works based on large-scale allegory are thought of as being allegorical in a broader sense. They are likely to introduce personified abstractions like 'Will', 'Wit' and 'Dowel', and to tell stories of conflict between virtues and vices, or of journeying between symbolic places. In such works, medieval people distinguished two elements: the 'outer story, called the FABLE and often likened to a husk, and the inner story or kernel, called the *SIGNIFICATIO*. A kernel could be found in any story, whether it grew there from the beginning or not. Medieval preachers and storytellers were accustomed to allegorize not just every verse of the Bible, but even the mythological stories of Ovid, full as these were of paganism. Indeed, it was largely from this ALLEGORESIS, or allegorical transformation of ancient classics, that a Christian literature emerged.

The modern reader may be more interested in stories than in their moralization; but adjustment to medieval literature involves recognizing that this was not the case with earlier writers and readers. For example *The Fables* by the Scottish poet Robert Henryson (b. before 1425; fl. 1480) are elaborately worked out in didactic terms. In 'The Preaching of the Swallow' everything has significance – even the precise description of the seasons. The 'heit and moysture stilland [distilling] from the sky' in summer (l. 1684), in spring the 'soft morning' (l. 1713) and 'the harrowis hoppand in the saweris trace' (l. 1724): these are not just conventional decoration, but part of a detailed argument developing the moral of the swallow's foresight. And that is not all. The highly moral Aesopian fable itself provides Henryson with the text for a sixty-three-line 'Moralitas' tracing additional theological allegories. In this the fowler scattering chaff is a figure of the devil poisoning man's soul.

Such allegorical interpretation often related a text to the Christian scheme of salvation by a system of fourfold 'senses': (1) literal

(Jerusalem the historical city); (2) allegorical, referring to the redemptive history (Jerusalem as the Church); (3) tropological or moral (Jerusalem as the individual soul); and (4) anagogical, referring to eternal matters (Jerusalem as the City of God). Thus, in 'The Preaching of the Swallow', the fable emphasizes the literal sense of the story of a swallow's practical foresight, whereas the 'Moralitas' identifies the swallow as the Christian preacher mindful of man's end – of the risk of 'everlestand pane' – and so supplies the anagogical sense.

The Old Testament had so often been allegorized to accommodate it to the New that the Church Fathers had evolved a regular system of typology, in which for example Moses' delivering the people of Israel from Egypt was a TYPE or FIGURE of Christ's delivering man from sin. A similar figural content underpinned the medieval MYSTERY PLAY cycles dramatizing sacred history in a series of pageants, often performed on Corpus Christi. For these were ordered according to ages of history in the divine plan of salvation. For example 'The Fall of Man', a pageant found in all the English cycles, prefigures Christ's temptation in the wilderness (the subject of a later pageant), while contrasting with it in outcome. Historians used to think that the fourteenth-century cycles developed from liturgical drama (short plays performed as part of the liturgy) through a process of secularization which took drama out of the church. But the development is now agreed to have depended rather on the recently established Corpus Christi festival, and on the growth of the craft guilds. (These were responsible for production: hence 'mystery' or craft play.) Even the comic element in the cycles cannot be seen as simply profane, since it is used to contrast the human and the divine, and in any case often contains allegory. Thus, in the Wakefield Second Shepherds' Pageant, Mak's concealment of a stolen sheep by swaddling it in a cradle travesties the incarnation of Christ the *agnus Dei*. Funny as this play is, it repeatedly brings out the blasphemousness of sin.

The mystery cycles can also be seen, however, as reflecting a broader change of style in religious art – the shift towards late gothic realism, with its reemphasis of Christ's humanity. The mystery plays generally portrayed the Passion in a far from idealized way. In the York Crucifixion, for example, the bore holes in the cross have been misplaced, and Jesus' body must be stretched:

    1 SOLDIER: . . . A roope schall rugge him doune
        If [even if] all his sinews go asoundre . . .
    2 SOLDIER: Lugge on, ye both, a litill yitt!

3 SOLDIER: I schalle nought cease, as I have seele [as I hope to have bliss].

(lines 131–2, 137–8)

Even here, however, realism is complicated by the special effect of anachronistic blasphemy. Such ironies are everywhere in the speeches of villains in the cycles; generating a characteristically grotesque, horrifying, black-comic quality. The mystery cycles were repressed as papist in the 1560s; but the principles of divine comedy continued to operate implicitly, at a deep level, in much Renaissance drama.

The greatest allegorical achievement of the English Middle Ages was without doubt William Langland's (?1330–?86) *Piers Plowman* (A-text ?1367–70; B-text after 1370; C-text ?1385–6). Its early reputation is reflected in the large number of surviving manuscripts – half as many as those of *The Canterbury Tales* itself. Langland's vast rambling allegorical quest exists in several partly independent versions or revisions, especially the so-called A-, B-, C- and Z-texts. Apart from descriptions of the Seven Deadly Sins (passus ii) and a few similar passages, *Piers Plowman* has little direct realism. Not only is everything in it allegorical, but the literal fable has not even much narrative continuity – nor, at times, much interest. But read the *allegoria* step by step, and you find yourself in an absorbing, unforgettable world. Modern nonsense about the certainties of an age of faith falls away, for the poet seems everywhere to be looking for his way in a wilderness of perplexities. *Piers Plowman* is contemporary with *The Canterbury Tales* (Langland lived in London within a mile of Chaucer) and shares its subject of pilgrimage; yet the two works could not be more different. They have, however, one striking resemblance. Like Chaucer, Langland's Piers – Everyman, Christ, Saint Peter, the responsible Christian – questions the basis of pilgrimage, and everything else with it. Good works are better than going on pilgrimage. Yet when, in a familiar passage, Piers receives a pardon that offers salvation to those only who (impossibly) do well, he tears it up: 'And Pieres for pure tene [vexation] · pulled it atweyne' (B.vii.116). There can be no salvation by mere good works. Long before the Reformation, Langland was grappling with the problem of Justification.

Piers's subsequent quest for Dowel, Dobet and Dobest (active, contemplative and mixed lives? allegorical, tropological and anagogical senses?) repeatedly leads him to theoretical formulations that he cannot understand. And these in turn involve him in more detailed explorations, for example of the part played by Knowledge. Beginners often content themselves with the early passus, or measures, of *Piers Plowman*; but it is better to plunge into the great visionary allegories – the Tree of Charity (B-text, passus xvi), or the jousting of Longinus and the debate of the four daughters of God (B.xviii). *Piers Plowman* is a moving work, of fundamental human interest. Its thought is deep, yet its language has remained relatively accessible – colloquial and undecorated, stripped to functional essentials, plain although northern:

> 'After sharpe shoures,' quod Pees · 'moste shene [bright] is the sonne;
> Is no weder warmer · than after watery cloudes.
> Ne [nor] no love levere [dearer] · ne lever frendes,
> Than after werre [war] and wo · whan Love and Pees be maistres.
> Was nevere werre in this worlde · ne wykkednesse so kene,
> That ne Love, and [if] hym luste · to laughynge ne broughte,
> And Pees thorw pacience · alle perilles stopped.'
> 'Truce,' quod Treuth · 'thow telles us soth, bi Iesus!
> Clippe [embrace] we in covenaunt · and each of us cusse other!'
> 'And lete no peple,' quod Pees · 'perceyve that we chydde!
> For inpossible is no thyng · to hym that is almyghty.'
> 'Thow seist soth,' seyde Ryghtwisnesse · and reverentlich hir kyste,
> Pees, and Pees here · *per secula seculorum* . . .
>
> (B-text xviii.409–20)

Langland had a great impact (especially among the clergy) in his own time, and has had an even greater since. He is the first of a line of intense writers – among them Spenser, Blake, Beckett – who seem to penetrate to the very bedrock of experience.

Nevertheless Langland's train of thought is not always easy to follow. What may give difficulty is the form of his allegory – the interlacing of visions, expositions, semi-liturgical passages and abrupt digressions. He likes to shift from one *allegoria* to another linked to the first by a connection in the fable, but not otherwise continuing the surface sense. Thus, B-text passus xvi has many allegories of trees (and fruit and props), and so may be regarded as continuously concerned with fruit-growing. But the fable is discontinuous. At first the tree stands for Patience, whose fruit is charity or 'Werkes / Of holynesse' (C-text xix.12–13):

> Pacience hatte [is called] the pure tre · and pore symple of herte,
> And so, thorw god and thorw good men · groweth the frute Charite' . . .
>
> (B-text xvi.8–9)

But then we are told, contradictorily it seems, that the tree 'groweth in a gardyne . . . Amyddes mannes body' (B xvi.13–14), farmed by *Liberum-*

Arbitrium (Free Will) under Piers Plowman; and, a little later (at l. 62), that the ground is goodness. Allegories of three props (corresponding to the Persons of the Trinity) intervene, prompting allusion to a legend of three roots of the Holy Rood. And soon the fruit will be Matrimony ('a moist fruit with-alle', l. 68), or Maidenhead, or – more bewildering still– 'Piers fruit the plowman' (B xviii.20: the new man is the fruit of human nature raised by Grace). Langland sustains no single continuous allegorical system. Instead he keeps us on an exalted plane of visionary coherence, where we move readily from image to image. Yet the ardent anguished thought generating the images is not dreamlike, but clear and crisp. Each individual allegory develops an earlier point in more detail, or turns to a related aspect of the same insight. Langland's method is a brilliantly effective one, simulating the actual process of thought as it improvises proliferating analogies in order to go further and further into a deep truth.

This last feature is not so remarkable as it may seem, for in the Middle Ages allegory was continually resorted to in ordering the emotions and in writing about them, even quite informally. It has to be considered not only as a form of composition, but as a means of perception, of arriving at thoughts. Allegorical perception could be traced in other religious allegories, such as Thomas Usk's *The Testament of Love* (?1387), an ambiguous philosophical allegory in highly wrought prose; or John Lydgate's translation of Deguileville's influential *The Pilgrimage of the Life of Man* (1426–30). But I turn instead to a comparatively artless secular allegory which nevertheless has emotional delicacy: *The Floure and the Leaf* (fifteenth century; probably, like *The Assembly of Ladies*, by a woman). In *The Floure and the Leaf*, as in many dream visions, aspects of emotion are represented by characters, and statements may be made through these characters' actions or descriptions – or even through their mere presence in a particular household. The personifications and descriptions are conventional, but need not be woodenly so. Here, the mysterious company of the Leaf – virgins and 'persevering' knights of honour, constant true lovers who

> Though that they shuld hir hertës al to-tere,
> Would never flit, but ever were stedfast,
> Til that their lyves there asunder brast.
>
> (lines 488–90)

– do not contend in any cut-and-dried way with the frivolous company of the Flower, but seem protective and charitable towards them. Indeed, the Flowers, though idle and withering, are portrayed less as evil than as 'simple of nature' (l. 559) and exposed to life's weather. In choosing her own allegiance the writer–dreamer meditates a practical choice beset by dangers like 'Male-Bouche [Slander], and al his crueltè', not an abstraction remote from ordinary social experience. Up to the sixteenth century – and in some cases later still – it was in the main through allegory that emotions were identified, clarified and talked about. They could also be *expressed* through allegory; but expression of feelings was not thought edifying, and counted as a very subsidiary concern.

FIFTEENTH-CENTURY DEVELOPMENTS

The Middle Ages were after all plural; and differences among them need to kept in mind. Thus, the last thirty years of the fourteenth century – in large part the reign of Richard II (1377–99) – saw the appearance of no fewer than four great writers: Chaucer, Langland, Gower and the *Gawain* poet. After this Ricardian efflorescence, how-ever, the literature of the politically disturbed fifteenth century seems rather low pressure. Nevertheless, far-reaching developments were at work. Perhaps the most fundamental of these grew out of the increasing use of English for official purposes and in ordinary affairs – out of the recovery, in short, from French domination. A plain English prose, based on speech, gradually emerged.

This prose was capable of graphic directness – as in certain of the *Paston Letters* (a voluminous family correspondence of 1420–1500). But either its writers were content with very short unconnected sentences, or else they relied heavily on chronicle-like parataxis, an uncommunica-tive, barely grammatical articulation by repeated 'and's:

> And John Marchall tolde me that there was a thryfty woman come forby [past] the watteryng [-place] and fond the wey stoppyde, and askyd hym [w]ho had stoppyd the weye; and he seyd they that had pore [power] to yeve it, and askyd here wat was freere than gyfte. And she seyd she sey [had seen] the day that Paston men wold not a sofferyd that.
>
> (Agnes to John Paston I, 8 Nov., ?1451)

When anything more than the simplest arrangements of subordinate clauses was attempted, the result was likely to be a labyrinthine sentence that never quite finished. This is true not only of a writer like Caxton, but even of formal religious prose – as also, indeed, of the Biblical translation by John Wycliffe (d. 1384) that gave it a new impulse. And, as we saw previously, Malory himself used a highly paratactic style to achieve effects of honourable simplicity.

Prose did not at first develop further in a syntactic direction, but through changes in diction. For, in their attempts to imitate the ancients stylistically, early HUMANISTS (students of classical antiquity) like John Tiptoft, Earl of Worcester and John Skelton began to introduce Latinate words ('ornate terms') and even Latin word order. The result was sometimes ludicrous enough; but the very effort of choosing words in relation to SUBTEXTS (or models) with specific proportions proved of value in the long run. In this endeavour William Caxton (?1422–91), the first printer and publisher, had considerable influence. Admiring Skelton's work, and himself having a European perspective on the shortcomings of English, Caxton kept trying to 'augment' prose with a more adequate vocabulary, although his attempts often failed through deficiencies of taste.

Much literature was in any case still in verse – even didactic treatises of a sort that would not nowadays be cast in memorable form. Poetic developments of the fifteenth century can mostly be referred to two fairly distinct tendencies. One is a movement towards realism, the other a programme of abstract rhetorical patterning and 'literariness'.

Realism is protean in its diversity; and there has been much confusion about its elusive medieval appearances. In the Middle Ages, most apparently realistic representations of experience – even those attempting to be more than brief *exempla* or moral anecdotes were strictly exemplary. Their details were always necessary or typical, and invariably made definite moral points. Unfunctional, merely realistic detail, of the sort we take for granted, hardly occurred. In this, even Chaucer's General Prologue to *The Canterbury Tales* is no exception. For example, the apparently random scrap of information that the Squire 'carf biforn his fader at the table' (l. 100) in actuality demonstrates the Knight's typical unostentatiousness, since it indicates that he employed no separate carver. More rarely, one finds a fuller 'picturing', as in Chaucer's characterization of the Wife of Bath, in which a few of the details may be, so to say, unnecessary. But in the fifteenth century (and beginning earlier) the proportion of physical detail in description increased, not just in low-style comic writing but in religious prose such as Julian of Norwich's (?1343–after 1413) meditations on the Passion, where it served the purpose of a deeply emotional piety.

Chaucerian precedents laid foundations for the relatively full detail in several autobiographical poems by Thomas Hoccleve (1368/9–c.1430). Hoccleve not only tells us that at the Paul's Head tavern in London they served 'wafres [spiced cakes] thikke' (this might be meant to illustrate that the company was 'sumwhat likerous'), but also that he used to blush at any mention of the act of love — 'For shame I wexe as reed as is the gleede [glowing coal]' ('La Male Regle' 159) — beyond question an unnecessarily particularized response. He often relies on conventions, or uses allegorical personification to search his melancholy experience (he suffered a breakdown); but that is by no means inconsistent with personal details. These he puts together in a manner immediately eloquent — as in his 'Complaint' (1421) in rhyme royal stanzas (*ababbcc*):

> Aftir that hervest inned [gathered] had hise sheves,
> And that the broun sesoun of Mihelmesse
> Was come, and gan the trees robbe of her leves
> That grene had ben and in lusty freisshenesse,
> And hem into colour of yelownesse
> Had died and doun thrown undir foote,
> That chaunge sanke into myn herte roote.
>
> (lines 1–7)

A COMPLAINT was meant to verbalize grief in a way that not only analysed but alleviated it; which the seasonal reverberation of the melancholy here begins to do. Hoccleve's autobiographical passages have the capacity to speak across the centuries in a surprisingly individual way.

The other, more 'literary', movement took several routes, of which one may have been pioneered by a disciple of Chaucer, the influential John Lydgate (*c.*1370–1449/50). Lydgate was one of the wordiest writers of a wordy century: even his short poems are gaudily caparisoned elephants. At his best, as in the *Troy Book* (1412–20) ii, he could be an agreeable narrative poet with a not very good ear. (His insensitive rhythms are mechanical, although at least free from the chaos that afflicted much verse of the time with a recrudescence of the old four-stress divided line.) Lydgate seems to have been content that literary events — passages of any aesthetic interest — should be distributed sparsely like currants in his copious pudding of conventional dough and cliché. Nevertheless devotion to his 'master Chaucer', that 'floure of Poetes', prompted Lydgate to add to *The Canterbury Tales* — and so to stumble upon an idea of some importance: the dependent or EPICYCLIC work. This should be distinguished from the cyclic work belonging merely to the same cycle with others. The epicyclic work attaches itself — parasitically if you like — to a specific previous work, whose imaginary world it extends (perhaps with quite different contents). In the event the *Siege of Thebes* (wr. 1421–2) disappoints, but Lydgate's prologue, presenting it as an additional

Canterbury Tale, introduced a fertile idea that was to be taken up by many subsequent writers, from Spenser and Shakespeare (in their continuations of Chaucer and Gower) to Stoppard and Enright (in *Rosencrantz and Guildenstern Are Dead* and *Paradise Illustrated*).

Sequel reached an altogether different degree of success and authority in the work of the Scottish poet Robert Henryson (b. before 1425, fl. 1477–8). Henryson begins *The Testament of Cresseid* where Chaucer left off *Troilus and Criseyde* – with the spheres through which Troilus left his mortal life – after which he returns to supply Criseyde's end. But the emphasis is very different. Whereas Chaucer mentions the 'erratik sterres' ironically, even perfunctorily, Henryson realizes them anthropomorphically, in a magnificent council of planetary deities, together unfolding the mind of God. The most powerful and fundamental of them, the god who pronounces sentence on Cresseid, is Saturn:

> Atouir [over] his belt his lyart [grey-streaked] lokkis lay
> Felterit [tangled] unfair, ouirfret with froistis hoir,
> His garmound [suit] and his gyte [cloak] full gay of gray,
> His widderit weid fra him the wind out woir [carried out],
> Ane busteous [strong] bow within his hand he boir,
> Under his girdill ane flasche [quiver] of felloun flanis [cruel arrows]
> Fedderit with ice and heidit with hailstanis.
>
> (lines 162–8)

When Troilus meets Cresseid again after her betrayal, and after a gap of years, Henryson imagines that they fail to recognize eath other. Literally, this is because she is half-blind, having suffered physical degeneration; in the allegorical or 'dark moralization', it is because virtue and vice cannot comprehend each other. Cresseid's allegorically significant leprosy arouses both horror and charity: especially when, in a moving final passage, she evinces – too late? – the stirrings of regeneration.

In all this Henryson depends on Chaucer's work for the antecedents of his story, for his characters' remembered past, and indeed largely for the characterization itself. But how independently he goes on, with a sustained seriousness quite outside his master's range, to look unflinchingly at the dark fates that threaten mankind. It is not Henryson's much-discussed pathos only, but his grandeur and depth of feeling that make for an early manifestation of tragedy, albeit in a bitter northern version.

Fifteenth-century literariness could also take the shape of various rhetorical refinements. One was *aureation*, or the heightening of diction with gorgeous Latinisms, often polysyllabic. The verbal equivalent of

ceremonial armour and ornate international gothic painting, this was a
diction full of words like 'conservatrix' and 'pawsacioun' and 'vinarye
envermailyd'. Lydgate popularized aureation, and later Dunbar
became its most adept practitioner.

Another possibility was the plainer, abstract style brilliantly adopted
by the French prisoner of war Charles d'Orleans (1394–1465), the finest
lyric poet of the century. (LYRIC is poetry intended as song, or at least to
suggest song.) The most valuable ransom d'Orleans brought may well
be counted his love poems. In these poised, lucidly constructed
masterpieces, abstract generalizing expressions abound ('In the forèst of
noyous hevynesse',), together with personifications drawn from literature, like Daunger (sexual reserve or obstacle) from the *Roman de la rose*.
D'Orleans will ask Fortune 'Why wyltow not wythstand myn hevynesse?' or wish on behalf of his mistress for 'Honure, ioy, helthe, and
plesaunce [pleasure] . . .'. One can see another sort of abstraction in his
rhetorical symmetry and patterning. Sometimes he divides the contents
of a line into balanced halves:

> Yond oon is small, and yond streight sides has,
> Hir foot is lite [small], and she hath eyen clere.
> ('O sely anker [fortunate anchorite]' 19–20)

Or he may take a preposterous argument through formally matching
aspects; as when he confesses to his spiritual father a kiss 'of gret swet-
nesse':

> Which don was out avisiness [without deliberation];
> But hit is don, not undon, now.
> My gostly fader, I me confess
> First to God and then to you.
>
> But I restore it shall doutless
> Again, if so be that I mow [may],
> And that God I make a vow,
> And elles I axe foryefness.
> ('My gostly fader . . . ' 5–12)

This *allegoria* of 'restitution' neatly answers the one denying premedita-
tion in the 'theft'. D'Orleans tightened the construction of love poetry in
a way that anticipated the closer textures of the Tudor lyrists Wyatt and
Surrey.

Poems like d'Orleans's may perplex a modern reader into asking
inappropriate questions about sincerity and seriousness. Medieval love
poems were not immediate expressions of individual feeling, so much as

songs, to be performed in the course of the game of love or some other ceremonious social activity. They addressed public, shared experience; although even their most traditional formulations were doubtless often felt personally, and might have had autobiographical correlates. Consequently, if a medieval lyric seems obscure, this is generally because some convention has not been recognized, whether through lack of shared context, or through modern ignorance of the convention itself.

In such cases, our best approach is likely in the first instance to be through formal artifice. This was often impressive. For, so far as lyric is concerned, the Middle Ages are one of the most productive and accomplished periods we know of. An astonishing number of songs have survived, to give an inkling of the number that must once have existed. Many of them, naturally, are from the fifteenth century. But they derive also from the earliest phase of our literature: the seasonal songs 'Sumer is icumen in' and 'Lenten [Lent] is come with love to toune' are probably both from the thirteenth century, for example. Medieval lyric embodies a great variety of kinds, many of them religious, like the Complaints of Christ (originally much quoted in sermons), in which Jesus will make a poignant appeal from the cross – as in 'Ye that pasen be [by] the weyye', or 'Wofully araide [afflicted; beaten]':

> Thus nakid am I nailid, O man, for thi sake . . .
> So rubbid, so bobbid [buffeted], so rufulle [pitiful], so red . . .
> What myght I suffer more . . .?

The religious lyrics drew on the whole tradition of European Latin hymnody; but they had their own dignity, as well as a certain grave, touching, homely simplicity – I am thinking of such lines as 'God be in my head, / And in myn understandynge . . .' – that would seldom be recaptured in later song.

One might expect the CAROL to have been another religious genre; but this expectation oversimplifies. The carol was originally secular – a merry song associated with seasonal feasting and with a particular dance, which indeed was often attacked from the pulpit. This ring dance with joined hands called for an accompanying song, usually in stanzas of four four-stressed lines (*aaab*) sung by the leader, alternating with a chorus couplet (*bb*). The carol was so popular as to be comparable to the modern pop song. Nevertheless, most of the 500 surviving carols are by clerics, and many contain scraps of Latin from hymns. There was only one medieval society.

Nativity carols, whether liturgical ('Lord and Prynce that he shuld be, / A solis ortus cardine [From the land of the rising sun]') or unpretentiously informal ('Swet Jhesus / Is cum to us'), accorded well with the Christmas season. Other carols might announce the service of a course in hall, like 'The borys hede that we bryng here', or relate to some ceremony or entertainment. Thus, 'Ho[l]ly stond in the hall' belonged to a game of contention between the sexes:

> Nay, Ivy, nay, hyt shal not be, iwys [certainly];
> Let Ho[l]ly hafe the maystry, as the maner ys.

Others again are of such obscure origin that they give an impression almost mysteriously strange:

> *Lully, lulley; lully, lulley;*
> *The fawcon hath born[e] my mak [mate] away.*
>
> He bare hym up, he bare hym down;
> He bare hym into an orchard brown.
>
> In that orchard ther was an hall,
> That was hangid with purpill and pall [rich hanging].
>
> And in that hall ther was a bed;
> Hit was hangid with gold so red.
>
> And yn that bed ther lythe a knyght,
> His wowndes bledyng day and nyght.
>
> By that bedes side ther kneleth a may [maid],
> And she wepeth both nyght and day.
>
> And by that beddes side ther stondith a ston,
> Corpus Christi wretyn theron.

This Corpus Christi carol has been taken to refer to the Grail legend, although some think it has a more recent subject – or, alternatively, a subsequent application – in the grief of the displaced queen Anne Boleyn (whose badge was a falcon). But the poem's mystery is not altogether accidental, not merely the obfuscating consequence of historicity. For the formal achievement of medieval song was already almost as fine as that of the late Tudor period. Simple as the carols seem, they are many of them also consummate flowers of art.

Medieval literature has an endless fascination. It lies at an extreme edge of our historical reach. And it opens a strange, ceremonious world

– hierarchically ordered, comprehensively meaningful – whose ideals, at least, are in some respects superior to those of the modern world. Or perhaps the attraction of medieval literature lies in this, that it offers a range of kinds, forms and aesthetic pleasures based on different principles from those of Renaissance and later literature. The model it takes for granted (nonunified composition, polyphonic interlacement, structures corresponding to the divine comedy pattern of history) is a quite distinct one. Consequently, when one turns to the literature of the Middle Ages, it is as if the scale of one's experience were enlarged by several notes.

2

Renaissance Prose and Verse

A MAIN theme of this chapter is renaissance, the revival of antiquity in literature which accompanied and led that in the other arts. This 'revival' or 'rebirth' – or perhaps, rather, this reconsideration of antiquity in a new way – had an underlying impulse in the Humanists' improved study of ancient classics. To some extent this enabled them to recover classical forms through imitation. But the Humanism of northern countries was unlike that of Italy. Far from displacing Scholasticism, Humanism in Britain at first offered an improvement of the old system. There was no immediate break with the past. Some expressions of Humanism, indeed, such as close lexical imitation of the classics, were only to develop much later, towards the end of the seventeenth century, with the Augustan phase of classicism. In consequence the northern Renaissance – the age of Henryson, Douglas and Dunbar in Scotland, More and Wyatt in England – abounds with misconceptions of periodization. The Scottish Renaissance poets are often called medieval, although they dealt with Renaissance material in distinctively Renaissance ways, long before any English poet achieved a comparable synthesis.

DOUGLAS AND DUNBAR

In spite of precise mythological details and suggestions of classical ideals, Gavin Douglas's *Palice of Honour* (1501) remains for the most part a medieval work – an epitome, in fact, of the traditional dream-vision genre. It resembles *The House of Fame* in treating conflict between the demands of life and of art. But it has none of Chaucer's elusiveness; and it is more comprehensive in summing the possibilities of the kind. In spite of a harder stanza (nine lines with only two rhymes), Douglas sustains a crisp particularity throughout; exuberantly accommodating specific details and technical information – rather too much of it for the modern taste. He shows similar virtuosity in mixing with native diction passages of aureation, a style he was one of the first to introduce into Scottish literature. This AUREATE style, the literary equivalent of International Gothic, uses a Latinate poetic diction of learned and often polysyllabic words like 'umbrate', 'obumbrate', 'illuminat', 'diurnall', 'vivificative'. This is often combined with glittering imagery of brilliance or of precious stones – as in the description of Honour's palace, all crystal and silver and ivory 'midlit [mingled] with gold anamilit all colouris'. Douglas's dreamer looking through a chink in the door can report only on a floor of amethyst and an enthroned god: the rest is too bright to see. Such brilliant scenes contrast starkly with infernal wastelands where 'na gers [grass] nor herbis wer visibill / Bot skauppis [bare stony banks] brint with blastis boriall [northern]'. Douglas's unusual care to keep the dreamer's standpoint in mind results in sharp visualizations and well-relished details. His brisk vigour makes the poem as enjoyable as any of its kind.

With the *Eneados* (completed 1513) we move to a new cultural phase and to a startlingly original work. In it, Douglas invented nothing less than verse translation itself. Moreover, his informed reverence for Virgil, his consequent scrupulosity about keeping to the original sense, and his care to preserve the proportions of the *Aeneid*: all these speak the man of the Renaissance. Douglas was quite unlike his predecessor Caxton, who worked as a medieval redactor, freely cutting a whole book of the poem when he thought it advisable. Douglas himself expanded his original by seventy per cent throughout, mainly through an effort to clarify by taking in details from the glosses of Ascensius and other editors.

By common consent, the *Eneados* is the best English translation of any epic. Ezra Pound goes so far as to call it 'better than the original, as Douglas had heard the sea'. Nautical and briskly energetic as he often is, Douglas comes closer to Virgil than any 'correct' neoclassical translator could and perhaps the more so for having no conception of intervening 'Middle Ages'. Yet his anachronisms – 'nuns of Bacchus', 'rekand chymnais' (*fumantia culmina*) and the like – are not all quaint effects of innocence. Douglas is already capable of deliberate modernizing (he almost anticipates Oldham); as notably in his use of contemporary military terminology. Seeking a Virgilian effect, he adopts various solutions in different places: an alliterative romance style for martial passages, but for the descent to Avernus, a more inventive diction:

> . . . Seir [Many] thingis drinchit [buried] in the erd [earth] full law,
> And deip envoluit in mirknes [darkness] and in mist.

Thai walkand furth, sa dirk uneth [scarcely] thai wist
Quhiddir [Whither] thai went, amyd dym schaddowis thair,
Quhair ever is nycht and never lycht dois repair,
Throwout the waist [desolate] dongeon of Pluto king,
Thai voyde boundis and that gousty [dismal] ring;
Siclyke as quha wald throw thik woddis wend
In obscure lycht, quhair mone [moon] may nocht be kend [known].

(VI.iv.64–72)

One critic has described Douglas's vigour as 'rough hewn'; but this is to confuse his courtly language with the present degraded state of Scots. In fact the style of the *Eneados* is intricately artificial, not only in its Virgilian use of archaism and its 'curyus castis [devices] poetical' suggesting Latin word order, but also in its syllable symmetries. The latter device (exemplified in the 111212111 pattern of 'Hard to the entre, in schynyng plait and mail',) was to influence Surrey. It could be seen as a continuation of fifteenth-century methods; but Douglas also anticipates what John Stevens has called 'the new sound' of postmedieval verse, in that he frequently adjusts rhythm and texture to sense. Consider his metaphorical suggestion of the elm of delusive dreams in the impenetrable texture of 'Undir ilk leif ful thik thai stik and hyng'. Douglas's deployment of his astonishing 'fowth' or abundance of language constantly reflects similar poetic judgements.

As if such a translation were not sufficient claim to greatness, Douglas added the first English language georgic, with some of the first detailed nature descriptions. (GEORGICS are instructional or descriptive works, written in the poet's own person.) For he prefaced the twelve books of the *Eneados* proper and the Thirteenth Book of Maphaeus Vegius' continuation with Prologues. Inspired by Virgil's *Georgics*, these Prologues treat a variety of topics, which they address in various metres (unlike the translation itself, which is heroic couplets throughout). Certain of the Prologues, such as i, iii and vi, initiate literary criticism in the vernacular, discussing the problems of translation, Virgil's art, or the poverty of English (i.e. Scots) in comparison with Latin; others, like ii or vi, relate to the Virgilian book they introduce; and others again are ethical or devotional. But the most original, and still the most popular, are the 'Nature' Prologues, vii, xii and xiii. No seasonal description in medieval literature, not even the *Gawain* poet's, compares for precise observation of landscape and weather with the georgic winter scene in Prologue vii:

Browne muris kythit [showed] thar wysnyt mossy hew,
Bank, bra [brae] and boddum blanchit wolx [became] and bar.

For gurl [stormy] weddir growit bestis hair.
The wynd maid waif the red wed [weed] on the dyke,
Bedowyn [immersed] in donkis deip was every sike [ditch].
Our [over] craggis and the front of rochis seir [separate]
Hang gret ische schouchlis [icicles] lang as ony speir.
The grond stud barrant, widderit, dosk or gray,
Herbis, flowris and gersis wallowyt [withered] away.

(Prologue vii. lines 56–64)

And we have to wait until the Augustan period for visual details like Douglas's comparison of trapped windlestraws to little hinges, or his fish 'Wyth fynnys schynand broun as synopar [cinnabar], / And chyssel talys, stowrand heir and thar'.

Whereas the aristocratic Douglas accommodated writing with the political involvements of a bishopric, William Dunbar (*c.*1460–*c.* 1530) was a professional poet at the sophisticated court of James IV. (His language was not a local dialect, but the court standard Scots, or, as it was called, 'English'.) As a court makar, Dunbar was necessarily accomplished in the poetic genres of his time – a variety of French, English and Scottish kinds that we now tend rather crudely to conceive of as falling into moral and allegorical, 'flyting' and satiric divisions. And within this cadre of craftsmen he early attained preeminence, achieving a finer technical finish than any Scottish poet, even if he never quite hit on Douglas's touches of enchantment. Dunbar has a style characterized by concerted power and minute precision, which moves into the Renaissance by virtue of its compression. He surpasses Douglas and all English examples in carrying aureation to *raffiné* extremes – 'Up sprang the goldyn candill matutyne / With clere depurit bemes cristallyne'. Some have seen his offsetting of aureate Latinism against a contrastingly earthy vernacular as determined by subject. But it is rather a matter of genre height. Thus, in 'The Tretis of the Tua Meriit Wemen and the Wedo', Dunbar plays the trick of starting with the aureate terms of romance and dropping to unexampled coarseness in the women's sexual reminiscences. His distinctive sense of humour is even more outrageous in the cursing match 'The Flyting of Dunbar and Kennedie', or in wild fantasies like the mock heroic 'Turnament' between a tailor and a soutar.

The old term 'Scottish Chaucerian' hardly applies to Dunbar, since he took up quite different options in the medieval repertoire (like the allegorical kinds), and never attempted Chaucer's subtlety of character or irony. In 'The Goldyn Targe', for example, he is content to enjoy brilliant manipulation of dream-vision conventions. He packs in literary

echoes (including some of Virgil), without, however, emulating the
depth or even the learned qualities of Douglas's *Palice of Honour*.
Dunbar's poem communicates emotional intensity – as in its insistence
on the perilous sensual power of Presence – but makes no personal
disclosure: we attend a performance rather than become confidants.
This is true even of such moving meditations as his 'In Winter' and
'Timor Mortis Conturbat Me'. The first of these enacts its train of
thought in an apparently intimate allegory, in which Age with sinister
friendliness urges 'cum neir / And be not strange, I the requeir' and
reminds that a reckoning has to be made, while Death casts open his
gates. But a sly conclusion has the speaker (not prepared even yet)
looking forward to summer. The meditation has not quite been the
poet's. 'Timor Mortis Conturbat Me' belongs, like many of Dunbar's
poems, to a medieval genre; nevertheless there is a new economy and
urgency in its review of dead makars, the fellowship he himself must
presently join.

EARLY TUDOR PROSE

In English literature, medieval and Humanist strands intermingled as
much as in Scottish, if not more so. John Bourchier, Lord Berners
(1467–1532/3), for example, was still in many ways a medieval translator, willing to abridge freely and content to have 'ensued [followed]
the right sentence [gist]'. His prefaces may speak of the new 'facondyous
arte of rethoryke' (rhetoric based on copiousness of invention), but
except for his *The Golden Boke of Marcus Aurelius* (1535) the works
themselves are transparently direct. Berners's reputation rests on his
1523–5 translation of Froissart, the fourteenth century French chron-
icler. Here his effortless style meets that of the original on easy terms of
shared ideals. Separated by a century as they are, the two works breathe
the same atmosphere of adolescent eagerness, heroic fervour, strong
emotion:

> 'Gentle king behold here we six who were burgesses of Calais and great
> merchants; we have brought to you the keys of the town and the castle;
> and we submit our self clearly into your will and pleasure, to save the
> residue of the people of Calais, who have suffered great pain. Sir, we
> beseech your grace to have mercy and pity on us through your high
> nobless': then all the earls and barons, and other that were there wept for
> pity. The king looked felly on them, for greatly he hated the people of
> Calais for the great damages and displeasures they had done him on the
> sea before. Then he commanded their heads to be stricken off.
>
> (*Froissart's Cronycles* cxlvi)

What could be simpler? There is little patterning beyond heroic alliteration, elegiac repetition and pairing of nouns for stateliness. Yet Froissart's distinctive tone sounds again.

And Berners is quite as good in parts of the erotic allegory *The Castell of Love* (1549) and in the fairy romance *Huon of Burdeux* (1534). These are full of marvellous romance details, such as Huon's difficulty when he decapitates the giant Angolafer: 'the head was so great and so heavy that he could not remove it nor turn his body.' Except for Malory, Berners is the only English prose writer to achieve the authentic simplicity of medieval romance.

With Sir Thomas More (1478–1535) we seem to move to a different, quite unchivalric milieu. In fact, however, the chivalric ideal would take a very long time indeed to die out; although it was effectively being displaced throughout Europe by a new ideal, centred on the peaceful life of the courtier or bureaucrat rather than on the martial life of the knight. This new ideal amounted to the pattern for a new society, complete with philosophical rationale (largely neo-Platonic). It was expounded in 'books of nurture' such as Sir Thomas Elyot's *The Governour* (1531) and Baldessar Castiglione's *Il Cortegiano* (1528), later translated by Sir Thomas Hoby as *The Courtyer of Count Baldessar Castilio* (1561).

More had a complex personality, strongly drawn to absolute positions (primitive Christian, Platonic) yet committed to office and the practical leverage it gave. These different sides of his personality are separately developed in two of the characters in his Utopia (1516): Morus, the compromising statesman, and Raphael Hythloday, the visionary who has lived in Utopia. More's neo-Latin masterpiece in the tradition of Plato's *Republic* is deeply felt and brilliantly written. (This does not always appear in Ralph Robinson's 1551 translation, which may be relatively vigorous, but now seems cumbrous and unsubtle.) A seminal work, the *Utopia* assembles many of the features of political science fiction and utopian satire – the traveller's tale frame, the element of vision, the enigmatic relation to real life in points of detail. By contrast with the shared ideals of Berners, it confronts us with ironies and ambiguities, which are only darkened further by the outspoken vehemence of its criticism of the condition of England – enclosure, unemployment, vagrancy.

It even remains uncertain whether the name 'Utopia' derives from Greek *ou-topos* (Noplace) or *eu-topos* (Wellplace). In many ways Utopia seems a good place; yet how ideal is a society that approves of war? Then, some have found contradictions between the Utopians' communism and More's Christianity, or between their diversity of religions and his persecution of heretics. But these contradictions are superficial only. The communism has to be seen in the light of primitive church practice – and of More's own monastic education. In any event, Utopia is not so much a perfect society as one obedient to natural reason, like that of Swift's Houyhnhnms. That is to say, *Utopia* puts an *a fortiori* argument. If such a system results from merely rational considerations, More implies, how much better ought Christians to order their lives. As things stand, however, Europeans are often irrational, and therefore unfit for alterations of religion – even though among the Utopians these could lead to acceptance of Christianity. But it would be a mistake to oversystematize More's sceptical satire, since it abounds in local ironies and agile changes of norm, designed to catch out different groups of readers. *Utopia* is a subtle work, not only passionate but deeply considered.

In his English works More seldom reaches such heights; and he descends to abysmal depths in his offensive controversy with the 'heretic' William Tyndale. The vernacular was not yet sufficiently developed to allow for many stylistic effects, or even much precision of meaning. But *A Dialogue of Comfort* (1553; wr. 1534) is an emotionally authentic and closely argued meditation, written in prison in preparation for martyrdom. It is one of the most moving of the many Tudor moral works. – For this was a period with a passion for morality, when the works written or translated were more likely than not to be edifying, and when even the decoration of houses was sometimes based on improving emblems or sententiae or moral sayings.

More's opponent William Tyndale (1494/5–1536) was a dedicated controversialist, an exile – and eventually a martyr – in the cause of Protestant reform. He gave his life to contending that the Bible should be made accessible, and to this end himself translated the New Testament (Cologne 1525 destroyed; rev. edn Antwerp 1534). In controversy Tyndale may perhaps be less witty than More. Yet he appears to better advantage: a reforming argument is easier to sustain rationally and singlemindedly. Tyndale's coherence belongs to a personality with little of More's interesting complexity; but it generates a far superior style – lucid, urgent, and unified, rhythmically compelling:

> Thou shalt understand, therefore, that the scripture hath but one sense, which is the literal sense. And that literal sense is the root and ground of all, and the anchor that never faileth, whereunto if thou cleave, thou canst never err or go out of the way. And if thou leave the literal sense,

thou canst not but go out of the way. Neverthelater, the scripture useth proverbs, similitudes, riddles, or allegories, as all other speeches do; but that which the proverb, similitude, riddle, or allegory signifieth, is ever the literal sense, which thou must seek out diligently . . . this literal sense is spiritual, and everlasting life unto as many as believe it.

(*The Obedience of a Christen Man*)

It may be that Tyndale has sometimes too simple a view of the Bible. Nevertheless his concentration on grasping the main tenor – so to say the narrative or dramatic meaning – was a sound one in a translator. Shared by later translators and interpreters of the Bible, it eventually brought about a profound change in interpretative practice – and even in ordinary reading.

It could also lead to clean prose and fine translations:

Come unto me all ye that labour/ and are laden/ and I wyll ease you. Take my yooke on you/ and lerne of me/ for y am meke/ and lowly in herte: and ye shall fynde ease unto youre soules for my yooke ys easy/ and my burthen ys lyght.

At least a third of the Authorized Version of the New Testament (1611) follows Tyndale's wording; and the rest often retains his rhetorical structure:

Come unto me all yee that labour, and are heavy laden, and I will give you rest. Take my yoke upon you, and learne of me, for I am meeke and lowly in heart: and yee shall finde rest unto your soules. For my yoke is easie, and my burden is light.

Biblical translation, which was important from many other points of view, was of the first importance stylistically, in that it established the loose trailing additive (i.e. PARATACTIC) style most congenial to the English language.

The flow of Bible translations had two fountainheads, one Humanist and the other Reforming. Advances in Greek and Hebrew scholarship were applied in such works as Erasmus's Greek New Testament (1516) and Latin translation; while the aims of the Reformers found embodiment in Luther's tendentious German translation of 1522. Tyndale himself might be burnt, but his 1534 translation issued in a surging flood of English Bibles, increasingly printed in England. The most notable were Coverdale's (1535, 1537), the Great Bible (1539), the Calvinist Geneva Version (Geneva 1560), the Bishops' Bible (1568), the Romanist Rheims New Testament (1582) and the King James Bible, the Authorized Version (1611). Coverdale's translation, without equalling Tyndale's in scholarship, maintained his homely raciness but made many local changes, sometimes to brilliant effect. Generally, the changes that eventuated in the familiar Authorized Version came gradually through advances in scholarship, and depended so much on improvements imitated from earlier translations (quite often across party lines) that individual authorship is unattributable. Thus 'Be of lyke affeccion one towardes another' (Tyndale) is corrected to 'Be of one mynde amonge youre selves' (Coverdale) and then to 'Be of the same mind one towards another' (King James). The literary value of the Authorized Version – very largely identical with that of Tyndale's – is debated; since much of its content and rhetoric belong to the original Greek or Hebrew. But at least we can be sure that the value should not be reduced to a matter of fine rhythms. The great, although indirect, influence of Biblical translations is to be put down less to its literal familiarity than to its deliberate finish. No structure of words has ever been so profoundly considered by so many of the nation's best minds over such a long period of revisions.

There is great literature also in the Book of Common Prayer, whose compilers were less innovative in their approach to the medieval inheritance. The older Latin *Use of Sarum* was already brilliant writing: compressed, antithetic, even epigrammatic in style, and elaborately rhythmic, with cadences based on the CURSUS. (The medieval Latin *cursus* was a set of prose metres, latterly simplified to the three modes 'plain', 'slow' and 'fast'.) The compilers of the 1549 Book of Common Prayer, however, seem to have devised an English *cursus* distinct from the Latin one. And they scrupulously avoided any suggestion of epigrammatic wittiness or obvious patterning, which in the curt vernacular would have been inappropriately obtrusive. So 'Te Deum laudamus: te Dominum confitemur' becomes 'We praise thee, O God, we knowlage thee to be the Lorde'. The aim is evidently a restrained, understated effect, of inevitability without cerebral display – a liturgy not for intellectuals alone but for the whole people. Yet an impressive rhetorical discretion has considered every syllable. Take (at random) the Third Collect at Matins: 'graunt that this daye wee fall into no synne, neyther runne into any kinde of daunger, but that al our doinges may be ordered by thy governaunce, to do alwaies that is righteous in thy sight . . . '. Here 'any kinde of daunger' varies the parallel 'no synne' in syllable length and number; the shift into the passive mimes submission to God's will; and 'do alwaies' echoes 'al our doinges' in a self-effacing CHIASMUS (*abba* pattern) that suggests, as often, obedient responsiveness. The English Bible and liturgy have undoubtedly had an extensive indirect influence on the whole subsequent development of prose style.

The practice of translation in general moulded the rhetoric of Tudor prose in a more immediate way. Translators had a device of using a pair of words to straddle the meaning of a single original word, and this fostered a taste for displaying superfluous copiousness of synonyms:

> in [Homer's] books be contained and most perfectly expressed, not only the documents martial and discipline of arms, but also incomparable wisdom, and instructions for politic governance of people, with the worthy commendation and laud of noble princes; wherewith the readers shall be so all inflamed that they most fervently shall desire and covet, by the imitation of their virtues, to acquire semblable glory.
>
> (Sir Thomas Elyot, *The Governour* I.x)

Some writers, not content with doublets, heaped up piles of near-synonymous words – like Richard Hyrd in the Preface to his *The Instruction of a Christian Woman* (1529): 'that I were able in our English tongue to give this book as much perspicuity, light, life, favour, grace, and quickness [liveliness], as Master Luis Vives hath given it in Latin . . .'. The result was a slightly cumbrous, heavy prose, sometimes quaint to posterity, but inwardly stiff to the point of inexpressiveness. Perhaps fortunately, there were others – like Sir John Cheke (1514–57) – who argued the contrary case for preferring 'pure' native words. In any event, both principles of composition called for stylistic choices, and so allowed writers to begin to develop the skills that would make possible the great prose of the seventeenth century.

EARLY TUDOR VERSE

So backward in development was Tudor verse that although John Skelton (?1460–1529) outlived Dunbar and probably borrowed from him, he reads like a medieval poet. His texture is loose, his sense of rhetorical proportion nonexistent. Often, as in his 'open' satires (direct invectives against church abuses and the new learning, indifferently), he uses the medieval short-lined satiric verse form called after him 'skeltonics':

> I purpose to shake oute
> All my connynge bagge,
> Lyke a clerkely hagge.
> For though my ryme be ragged,
> Tattered and jagged,

> Rudely rayne-beaten,
> Rusty and mothe-eaten,
> Yf ye take well therwith
> It hath in it some pyth.
>   (*Collyn Clout* 50–8)

Such verses may be doggerel; but they often show an accurate sense of rhythm that has made Skelton a favourite with poets – from de la Mare to W. H. Auden – to whom he has opened a treasury of audacities. His light dancing rapid Byronic style – 'lyke the penne / Of hym that wryteth too fast' – calls for an equally rapid reading that unfortunately is difficult to keep up now, because of his strangeness and obscurity. His meaning is often involved in Latin wit, or liturgical allusion, or topicalities of court life.

Nevertheless Skelton's boldly individual poetry still lives as much as any early Tudor writing. There is irresistible energy in his outrageous coups and his vivid fifteenth-century realism – the interminable coarsenesses of *Elynour Rummynge* (?1517), for example, or the Chaucerian vignettes of *The Bowge of Court* (?1498). Technically, Skelton may be inferior to Dunbar, whether at flyting or aureate sonorities: and he may rattle on with fatal Lydgatean fluency, shovelling rhymes in a manner at first astonishing and then appalling: but all the same he impresses with his originality in enlarging the topics of the poet's role. One of his finest achievements in this direction is the *Garlande of Laurell* (?1495), which has also a suite of exquisite lyric portraits of ladies – relatives and friends of the Howards – such as Margaret Hussey:

> Mirry Margaret,
> As mydsomer flowre,
> Jentill as fawcoun [falcon]
> Or hawke of the towre; . . .
>   (lines 1004–7)

These gentle poems, hard to reconcile with Skelton's roughness elsewhere, sound a new and tender strain of lyricism.

With his Humanist reading and his extensive travel on the Continent on diplomatic missions, Sir Thomas Wyatt (1503–42) was well equipped to urge English poetry in an Italianate direction, towards the Renaissance ideals of unity and clarity that it has since pursued. Wyatt is the earliest poet still quite widely read – although this confidence is sometimes insecurely based on the assumption that his words have their modern meanings. He wrote effective satires ('Mine own John Poins') and fine translations of the Psalms; but he is mostly read for his love lyrics.

Wyatt inherited a great tradition of medieval and Tudor song (for England led Europe in music at the time), even if there is no firm evidence that his poems were written for music. His songs show great accomplishment, for example in the astonishing diversity of metrical experiments, and in the modulated syntactical connections of refrains ('In eternum'). In the older view, Wyatt's rhythms were rough, at best just managing slavish regularity. But it has been shown that he not only introduced the strict counting of syllables but went on at times to revise towards deliberate irregularity, for the sake of expressiveness – as in the irresolute line end 'unstable, unsure and wavering', ('What No Perdy'). But how original are his love lyrics? Necessarily they use the language – even the clichés – of courtly love. Sometimes, however, these may be a disguise for more businesslike or more intimate emotions, or for sentiments too dangerous to voice directly at Henry VIII's autocratic court. But we need to beware of biographical assumptions: Wyatt's love complaints may not so much express injuries as promote obligations – or merely provide material for the performer. At all events, he was preeminent in the rendering of emotional intensity.

Many of Wyatt's poems are free translations from the Italian, especially from Petrarch and from Petrarchists such as Serafino Aquilano. For this strategic work he was fitted by his Humanist feeling for individual words, and consequently for rather closer texture. In sonnets like 'My galy chargèd with forgetfulnes', the first in English, he shows a preference for a more particularized and dramatic diction than that of his original, 'Passa la nave'; so that Petrarch's ship (the ship of love) becomes a punishment galley, and *sospiri* become '*forcèd* sighes'. (The SONNET is a short lyric poem of about fourteen lines, often divided rhetorically and metrically into an eight-line OCTET and a six-line SESTET.) Wyatt's success depends on his determination – surpassing even that of his Italian models – to subordinate everything to a single dominating poetic idea or CONCEIT. Sometimes, indeed, his passionate complaints are so dramatically consistent and concentated as to be difficult. (He was criticized for being 'too diffuse', that is, disordered.) But a poem like 'They fle from me that sometyme did me seke' communicates its powerful intensity, even while debate rages as to exactly what it means.

> It was no dreme: I lay brode waking.
> But all is torned thorough my gentilnes
> Into a straunge fasshion of forsaking;

And I have leve to goo of her goodeness,
And she also to use new fangilnes.
But syns that I so kyndely ame served,
I would fain knowe what she hath deserved.

(lines 15–21)

Wyatt's pursuit of unity of rhetorical effect did much to make possible poetry with the compression now taken for granted.

Henry Howard, Earl of Surrey (?1517–47) is a quieter poet than Wyatt, and has suffered from inappropriate comparison with him. He belongs rather, with Nicholas Grimald (1519–62), to a younger generation with quite different aesthetic aims. These aims included the reform of English prosody and the replacement of colloquial idioms and formulae by a closer textured, more literary, diction. Sometimes working in prison (the desk of not a few Renaissance writers), Surrey, Grimald and their associates devised canons and formulations eventually leading to the important anthology *Tottel's Miscellany* (1557), which included poems of Wyatt's recast on a smoother, regular basis. Surrey's own verse was strategically significant, in that it was more easily imitable than Wyatt's, and offered an attractive neoclassical patterning of syntax. It often foreshadows that of the Augustans in its radical inversion ('And kindled fynde his brest with secret flame'), its balance ('Whose chilling venume of repugnaunt kind'), its alternating possessive forms ('Upsprung the cry of men and trumpets' blast'). Surrey's range is greater than Wyatt's, extending beyond love poetry to autobiographical ELEGY (lament or complaint) – as in 'Laid in my quyett bedd', or the funeral elegy 'Wyatt resteth here', or 'So crewell prison', with its touching glimpses of court pleasures and relationships. This last poem has a fine spatial and temporal structure linking the griefs of loss and of imprisonment: 'And with remembraunce of the greater greif, / To bannishe the lesse I fynde my chief releif.'

Surrey also translated *Aeneid* ii and iv, often following Douglas closely, but patterning the diction more continuously and reshaping the metre to BLANK VERSE (unrhymed enjambed pentameters), the first in English. (PENTAMETERS are five-stress lines; ENJAMBED lines run on syntactically.) He even began naturalizing the classical EPIGRAM – a short, pointed, compressed form that well suited his terse style – as in the sonnet epitaph on Thomas Clere:

Norfolk sprang thee, Lambeth holds thee dead,
Clere of the County of Cleremont though hight [called];
Within the wombe of Ormondes race thou bread,

> And sawest thy cosine crowned in thy sight.
> Shelton for love, Surrey for Lord thou chase:
> Ay me, while life did last that league was tender;
> Tracing whose steps thou sawest Kelsall blaze,
> Laundersey burnt, and battered Bullen render.
> At Muttrell gates, hopeles of all recure,
> Thine Earle halfe dead gave in thy hand his Will;
> Which cause did thee this pining death procure,
> Ere Sommers four times seaven thou couldest fulfill.
> Ah Clere, if love had booted, care, or cost,
> Heaven had not wonn, nor Earth so timely lost.

Surrey was fond of this epigrammatic 'Shakespearean' form of the sonnet, which he invented: three quatrains rhyming alternately and closed with a pointed couplet. Each of these innovations, too, he worked out stylistically. Whatever else it may be, the pleasure Surrey offers is a pleasure of words, sustained throughout.

After Surrey, English poetry appears to decline again, as it enters the plain-style phase (*c.*1545–75) that C. S. Lewis called 'drab'. There were still good things, like Thomas Sackville's fine gloomy Induction to *The Mirror for Magistrates* (1559, enlarged 1563, 1578, 1587, 1610 etc.), or Arthur Golding's honest translation (1565) of Ovid's *Metamorphoses*, in which Shakespeare admired, among other passages, this description of a boar:

> His eies did glister blud and fire: right dreadfull was to see
> His brawned necke, right dredfull was his haire which grew as thicke
> With pricking points as one of them could well by other sticke.
> And like a front of armed Pikes set close in battell ray [array],
> The sturdie bristles on his back stoode staring up alway.
>
> (*Metamorphosis* vii. 376–80)

But it sometimes seems as if mid-century poetry was mostly dull moralizing, in clumsy FOURTEENERS or heptameter (seven-stressed) couplets.

This appearance of decline may in part be deceptive – an impression formed on the evidence of such down-market texts as suffered the indignity of publication. Much of the best poetry existed only in manuscript, and some of this may not have survived. It circulated privately – like the Egerton and Blage Manuscripts, which included many of Wyatt's poems – intended for a small circle of acquaintances, or even exclusively for patrons and their immediate friends. One fine surviving miscellany, the Arundel Harington Manuscript, gives a glimpse of what we may be missing. Among many delights, it contains lively hunting poems and a fragment 'The Black Ladie', beginning in a homely mode of Renaissance georgic:

> In autume when mynerves men
>   with Sythe and Sickell had shorne
> Suche frute as Ceares yelded then
>   of everye kynde of corne
> and when eache shock and sheafe was laide
>   in carte and home ycarried
> a brode to walke then I assaide
>   that longe in house had tarried.

But such exceptions hardly change the general picture. Nor does the course of events in Scotland, where mid-century drabness was offset by Sir David Lindsay's vigorous work. (His unconventional romance *Squire Meldrum* contains some surprising realism, as in its account of the heroine's decisive early-morning initiative in love.)

In prose, too, the vernacular was still a second language, over-shadowed by Latin. Latin, the father language, dominated the world of ideas. Most educated people used it, not only for writing of serious aspiration but for intimate communication and even private thought. The two greatest writers of the age – Sir Thomas More and the poet–historian George Buchanan – wrote in Latin almost entirely.

3

Elizabethan Mannerism

W HAT occasioned the great flowering of Elizabethan literature in the century's last two decades remains, as with other such efflorescences, largely obscure. Liberation from Marian persecution after 1558 was no immediate cause, even if the stability of the Elizabethan Settlement was a condition; for literature of quality scarcely appeared until the 1580s. Much may have been due to the increased availability of printed books, which fostered acceptance of a closer texture in writing. Sermon rhetoric must have had a great influence. And improvements in education took at last their long, slow effects. Every educated person was given a grounding in classical rhetoric, which taught him how to find matter (*inventio*), how to divide and organize it (*dispositio*), and how words might be put together stylistically for clarity or persuasion (*elocutio*). The reading public was equipped, in fact, to discern the unity of literary works and appreciate their craft. With a readership so sophisticated, the long-delayed Renaissance phase in the development of style could be passed through quickly; so that the distinctive Elizabethan rhetoric was not Renaissance, but already MANNERIST. Mannerist rhetoric is always stylish and self-conscious, showing relish for ornate or cleverly arranged words. In its Elizabethan version, it had a surface that depended on SCHEMES (patterns of arrangement) rather than on TROPES, or metaphorical figures of speech — although the latter are by no means lacking:

> Aye, but Euphues, hath she not heard also that the dry touchwood is kindled with lime, that the greatest mushroom groweth in one night? That the fire quickly burneth the flax? That love easily entreth into the sharp wit without resistance, and is harbored there without repentance?
>
> (*Euphues. The Anatomy of Wit*)

Such parallel arrangements and periphrases abound in *Euphues* (1578), John Lyly's popular didactic romance. It may use ordinary proverbial material, or make familiar allusions; but it gives a special stylistic *frisson* through the excess of their easily multiplied variation:

> to love and to live well is not granted to Jupiter. Who so is blinded with the caul of beauty discerneth no color of honesty. Did not Gyges cut Candaules a coat by his own measure? Did not Paris, though he were a welcome guest to Menelaus, serve his host a slippery prank?
>
> (*Euphues. The Anatomy of Wit*)

One of the striking features of Elizabethan rhetoric was its reliance on AMPLIFICATION, or exaggerated emphasis in the interest of persuasive effect. No prose work of the period illustrates this more obviously than Sir Philip Sidney's masterpiece, the *Arcadia*. Every image in this 'ocean of images' (as his friend Fulke Greville called it) is fully amplified. Sidney will not say that his heroines take off their clothes and go to bed, but that 'they impoverished their clothes to enrich their bed which for that night might well scorn the shrine of Venus'. In Elizabethan romances generally, the story was relatively unimportant, existing mainly to evoke the world of romance or to provide passionately charged occasions for rhetorical expression. In the *Arcadia*, this wordy emotionality is carried to an extreme by one of the greatest rhetoricians of his age. Sidney arranges exaggerated reversals of Fortune – who herself at Musidorus's rescue smiles to see 'that a scaffold of execution should grow to a scaffold of coronation'. Nevertheless the story also has substance: there is an overriding coherence, partly psychological (for example the contrast of Pyrocles and Musidorus), partly of a fairytale sort.

For Sidney produced a new form by combining the Renaissance pastoral romance of Sannazaro and Montemayor with the ancient heroic romance of Heliodorus, in which story was of more account. The *Old Arcadia* (1912; wr. 1577–80) was still pastoral and lyrical; but in the incomplete revision (wr. 1582–4) known as the 1590 or *New Arcadia*, Sidney dropped many of the songs and moved further into the Heliodorian world of wonder. The *Arcadia* has often been described as a forerunner of the modern novel; and there is truth in this, for Richardson and Fielding both used it extensively. But that does not make Sidney's work a fumbling attempt at novelistic realism. He aims less to write naturalistically about ordinary actions than rhetorically, about people at their best and worst – 'notable images of virtues, vices' (as he puts it in *An Apologie for poetrie*). His is not the spectator realism of modern fiction but an empathic or metaphoric or participant realism. It is rhetorically mimetic, involving the reader at every turn in the feelings of the characters. Thus when Basilius tries to escape and 'Each coffer or cupboard he met, one saluted his shinnes, another his elbowes, sometimes ready in revenge to strike them againe with his face', the narration itself shares Basilius's paranoid sense of an animistic hostility in inanimate objects – and involves us in it too. Similarly, PATHETIC FALLACIES (attributions of feelings to things) fill the work, and continually encourage participation by readers who are themselves, after all, part of nature – 'the cloudes gave place, that the heavens might more freshly smile upon her; at the le[a]st the cloudes of my thoughts quite vanished' (1590 I.xiii.3). Taken together, the interwoven stories of the *New Arcadia* constitute a penetratingly realistic exploration of different aspects of irresponsibility and self-deception. If you enter into its emotions and join in the searching debates that focus its issues, you will not remain the same. For its 'passionately delighted' moral fervour is infectious. Unfinished and imperfect it may be, but the *Arcadia* remains a great masterpiece – in Britain, for centuries one of only two fictional works generally admired, and in America accepted even by the Pilgrim Fathers.

In *An Apologie for poetrie* (1595) Sidney writes of poetry as 'a speaking picture', meaning the imaging of virtues. But the *Arcadia* is also in a more specific sense pictorial. Many passages are devoted to describing pictures like Philoclea's in Kalander's pleasure-house, or those carried in the procession at Phalantus's tournament. This pictorialism partly belongs to the Renaissance PARAGONE or theoretic contest between poetry and painting. But it is also meant to guide one in forming images of virtue in one's own mind. Sidney later returns to the pictures and applies them morally, when the action itself comes to be worked out in pictorial terms – 'this act painted at one instant redness in Philoclea's face and paleness in Gynecia's, but brought forth no other countenances but of admiration . . . ' (1590 I.xvii.5). One of the pleasures of the *Arcadia* lies in seeing its pictures come to life in a profuse variety of ways. Sometimes, Sidney realizes them in the action as if they were preliminary statements of themes. When Pamela wears a diamond in a dark setting, it emblemizes the stoic constancy that she will subsequently enact during her imprisonment.

The *Arcadia*'s rhetoric is far more flexible than that of Lyly, and has a wider range of style levels – descending, when contrast is required, to homely or ugly words like 'slubbered up'. In his schemes, Sidney avoids any hint of the mechanical by taking care to blur slightly the match between balanced phrases. Moreover, he uses style to mime meaning, as in the retarding effect of the repetition with lengthened variation in 'an eloquence as sweet in the uttering as slow to come to the uttering'. And he can make his artificiality seem natural by pretending to scramble a little to complete a pattern, perhaps by having to have recourse to a coinage or unusual word – the parts of Kalander's house are 'all more lasting than beautiful but that the consideration of the exceeding *lastingness* made the eye believe it was exceeding beautiful'. But the rhetoric of spontaneity was to be carried further by others.

Everything in the *Arcadia* is meant to confirm the DECORUM or thematic unity of the individual work, while decorously observing rhetoric's general conventions (unless its amplifications might be thought a shade extreme). But many Elizabethan works – including another of Sidney's – deliberately flouted conventional decorum. Prominent among writers practising this unconventional mannerism was Thomas Nashe (1567–1601). Imitating the Italian Pietro Aretino, Nashe developed a particular sort of deliberately 'incorrect' rhetoric; pursuing amplifications, extreme like Sidney's, through highly specific imagery drawn from low life – apparently for the sake of bizarre local effects. His grotesque 'base comparisons' seem arbitrarily irrelevant, but may at any moment present a knowing allusion or satiric edge; as when in *Lenten Stuffe* (1599) the beards of swaggerers back from the Cadiz expedition are 'broad as scullers' maples [mops] that they make clean their boats with' – implying not only their fringe-beard style but also their dirtiness. Nashe's comparisons may depend on the sense of touch (the Marignano battlefield is 'like a quagmire, overspred . . . with trampled dead bodies'); but this seems designed less to imitate a solid world, than to offset the primarily intellectual connections of his rhetoric.

In *The Unfortunate Traveller* (1594) Nashe relentlessly confines his register to the bathos, puns, low diction and erudite wit of satiric epigram writ large. A high-sounding tag like *Tendit ad sydera virtus* will lead to a pun on cider; the king will be said to have 'stood not long a-thrumming of buttons'. Nashe's anti-hero Jack Wilton is fundamental to the invention: in a wonderfully spontaneous way the whole farrago issues from this one clever rascally character. *The Unfortunate Traveller* is dear to the hearts of critics, who apparently mistake Nashe's conservative stylishness for modern unconventionality.

Nashe shared a taste for satiric and sordid particulars with Thomas Dekker (?1570–1632), whose *The Guls Horn-Booke* (1609) appealed to a contemporary interest in the criminal underworld. But both writers' styles are really as flowery as Lyly's, except that the flowers are stinkweed. In another direction, they resemble Dickens in energy and piquant flavour – but also in their tendency to go on too long. Nashe's *Pierce Penilesse* (1592) and Dekker's *Seven Deadly Sins of London* (1606) show how much they learnt from the schemes of sermon rhetoric and from other more obviously didactic writing. Tudor sermons could themselves be racy tirades. Hugh Latimer's famous *Sermon of the Plough* (1548) is an example:

> But nowe for the defaulte of unpreaching prelates me thinke I coulde gesse what myghte be sayed for excusyinge of them: They are so troubeled wyth Lordelye lyvynge, they be so placed in palacies, couched in courtes, ruffelynge [swaggering, behaving arrogantly] in theyr rentes [rags; property], daunceyinge in theyre dominions, burdened with ambassages [embassies], pamperynge of theyr paunches lyke a monke that maketh his Jubilie, mounchynge in their maungers, and moylynge [drudging] in their gaye manoures and mansions, and so troubeled wyth loyterynge in theyr Lordeshyppes: that they canne not attende it.

This belongs to an oral tradition. But formal religious prose was also in the forefront of development; for many of the best minds were occupied with theology or ecclesiastical controversy. Undoubtedly the finest intellectual prose of the sixteenth century is to be found in Richard Hooker's *Laws of Ecclesiastical Polity* (Books I–V, 1593–7; Books VI–VIII posthumously, 1648–62). Hooker (?1554–1600) wrote to defend the light of reason against a stark Puritan opposition between the things of God and the things of man – the latter including the Elizabethan Settlement. Particularly in the early books (as where he develops a broad conception of general grace), he conducts his argument with an impressive foresight that allows him to circumvent his opponents by preparing in advance a strategic ground of more generality and depth than theirs. His sober, Latinate style – cumbrous at times but richly musical – generally succeeds in being both functional and lucid; although he will not put clarity before precision. It is a style that impresses not by devices but by penetrating seriousness, by understanding.

> But now that we may lift up our eyes (as it were) from the footstool to the throne of God, and leaving these natural, consider a little the state of heavenly and divine creatures: touching Angels, which are spirits immaterial and intellectual, the glorious inhabitants of those sacred palaces, where nothing but light and blessed immortality, no shadow of matter for tears, discontentments, griefs, and uncomforable passions to

work upon, but all joy, tranquillity, and peace, even for ever and ever doth dwell: as in number and order they are huge, mighty, and royal armies, so likewise in perfection of obedience unto that law, which the Highest, whom they adore, love, and imitate, hath imposed upon them, such observants they are thereof, that our Saviour himself being to set down the perfect idea of that which we are to pray and wish for on earth, did not teach to pray or wish for more than only that here it might be with us, as with them it is in heaven.

(I.iv.1)

If Hooker's sentences are often long, we seldom lose our way, or sight of where the emphasis comes. He knows how to combine English repetitions and alliterations and even pairs of native English words ('immaterial and intellectual'; 'pray and wish for') with a Latin syntax that allows many ideas to be held in suspension or brought to bear together.

LYRIC FORMS

In poetry, too, classical and English strengths combined to good effect. The classics were beginning to exert an increasing influence, through the gradual effect of Humanist educational methods such as imitation. (Very close stylistic imitation was inculcated by means of repeated translation of the same passage from Latin into English and back.) This method was primarily used with rhetorical prose; but it could be extended to poetry, as in the exercise of composing Latin epigrams. And it was also extended to neo-Latin and Continental vernacular literatures – especially after Spenser's 1579 success showed something of the potentialities of English verse. By the 1580s there was a good deal of ostentatiously voguish academic verse, imitative of Italian, French and Spanish. All this brought a new sophistication and subtlety; as one can see for example by comparing Wyatt's direct satires with George Gascoigne's much more oblique 'Gascoignes woodmanship' of 1573. And at the same time new genres came in, which were either classical or Continental in origin. Among these the SONNET SEQUENCE, or series of sonnets arranged as a composite work, stands out: it enjoyed an astonishing vogue and became an important agency in the development of self-consciousness.

The sonnet sequence in English derived ultimately from Dante's *La Vita Nuova* and, more especially, from Petrarch's *Canzoniere*. This great masterpiece haunted Europe with its metaphysical vision of love's subjectivity as a hyperbolic, paradoxical state of contradicted being. 'I burne yet freeze' (Thomas Watson); 'Icie disdaine, is to my soule a fire, / And yet all these I contrary doe prove' (Michael Drayton). Typical Elizabethan sequences (and there are scores of them) consist of 100 or more sonnets, interspersed with other lyric genres – songs, in *Astrophil and Stella*. Often the array is rounded off with a long poem, such as Spenser's 'Epithalamion' or Shakespeare's 'A Lover's Complaint', the whole forming a numerological pattern in imitation of Petrarch's. The contents of the sequences have been obscured by the biographical assumptions of generations of novel-conditioned readers. These have taken it for granted that sonnets express the emotions of lovers and that sequences tell their stories. But for the most part the Elizabethan sequences are not arranged on a narrative basis; in a novelistic sense they tell no story at all. They can, indeed, identify and analyse phases of emotion. Only, the emotions are rather more general than we may expect. Love will serve perhaps as an instance in an argument about the largest terms of life – time, desire, satisfaction, change. In the best examples, a tight formal structure obliges rational contemplation, and opens a way to self-discovery.

The sonnet sequence became a highly self-conscious form. As we saw, individual sonnets appeared in English as early as Wyatt, but the first sequence was *The Hecatompathia or passionate Centurie of Love* (1580), by Thomas Watson – who had begun, significantly, by translating Petrarch into Latin. Sir Philip Sidney's brilliant sequence *Astrophil and Stella* (1591; wr. ?1582) set a new standard of achievement, and fully naturalized the genre. ('Apollo hath resigned his Ivory Harp unto Astrophel' wrote Thomas Nashe.) In a common modern view, Sidney overturned the Petrarchist convention of a helpless, submissive lover and a cruel fair – as when Astrophil falls in love 'Not at first sight' (ii), or rebels against Love and abuses Stella (Song v), or makes physical advances (Song viii). But the truth is far more complex, since *Astrophil and Stella* also amounts to a compendium of sonnet conventions. Astrophil ostentatiously rejects Petrarchism – 'I am no pick-purse of another's wit' (lxxiv) – but uses Petrarch's words to do so: 'love doth hold my hand, and makes me write (xc, from *Canzoniere* cli). In any event, the call 'looke in thy heart and write' (i) was more than a little ambiguous, in an age when the book of the heart was often regarded as a record of filth ('In libro cordis lege quicquid habes ibi sordis'). Despite the convincing portrayal of Astrophil, he is not to be associated very closely with Sidney. In fact, he offers a negative example, as came to be common in sonnet sequences ('All this I write, that others may beware': Watson lxxxix).

Nevertheless, Astrophil is a subtly attractive figure, easy to identify with in his attendance at the School of Love or his attempt at chaste Platonic love, in his joys at a kiss or his banishment to absence with the paradoxes of belief that that brings. These stages of the lover's progress can be traced through several interrupted subsequences. Thus, there is a group tracing 'psychomachias', or struggles between personified abstractions. In this group, Virtue at first sets up a conflict within Astrophil, between Will and Wit (iv); but later Virtue comes to be identified with Love (xiv, xlviii); and later still the conflict shifts to Stella (lii: 'Let Vertue have that Stella's selfe; yet thus, / That Vertue but that body graunt to us'); until in lxxi–lxxii Astrophil is on the point of abandoning ideal love altogether. He is guilty, in fact, of much that the finer Elizabethan lovers reprehended. For example, in xxxi, when he looks at the moon and asks 'Do they call Vertue there ungratefulnesse?' he in effect accuses Stella of ingratitude, and so betrays his self-pity and self-regard.

Astrophil's emotional imbalance finds a spectacular correlate in his deliberate stylistic indecorums. Most obviously there is an excessive frequency of the stylish TRADUCTIO, word play on different forms of the same word: 'Do they above love to be lov'd, and yet / Those Lovers scorne whom that Love doth possesse?' Less obviously, there is an indecorum in treating things 'too high for [his] low stile to show' (lxix). Astrophil often goes in for overbold mixtures of the three conventional style heights; addressing personifications (supposed to be treated in middle style) with intimate familiarity: 'Desire, though thou my old companion art' (lxxii). ('Thou' was then more familiar and intimate than 'you'.)

> But thou Desire, because thou wouldst have all,
> Now banisht art, but yet alas how shall?

The incomplete grammar of the closure, however touching in its incoherence, would have been considered unsuitably informal for a sonnet.

Most sonnet sequences are concerned with disappointed if not illicit passion. But one or two, like Edmund Spenser's and William Habington's, celebrate love consummated in marriage. Spenser's *Amoretti and Epithalamion* (1595) takes up the old Petrarchan woes with delicate irony, in order to question the nature of his own different, modern love. It has a formal accomplishment unsurpassed by any other sequence. Like the *Canzoniere*, its numerical composition is intricately calendrical, culminating in a triumphal wedding song whose 365 long lines mime the cyclic temporality marriage implements yet transcends. Spenser's sonnets are so closely connected – externally by rhyme links, internally by continued imagery – that the sequence almost becomes a poem in fourteen-line stanzas. Yet the individual sonnets are as finely structured as if each were a solitary achievement:

> Lyke as a huntsman after weary chace,
>> seeing the game from him escapt away,
>> sits downe to rest him in some shady place,
>> with panting hounds beguilèd of their pray:
>
> So after long pursuit and vaine assay,
>> when I all weary had the chace forsooke,
>> the gentle deare returnd the selfe-same way,
>> thinking to quench her thirst at the next brooke.
>
> There she beholding me with mylder looke,
>> sought not to fly, but fearelesse still did bide:
>> till I in hand her yet halfe trembling tooke,
>> and with her owne goodwill hir fyrmely tyde.
>
> Strange thing me seemd to see a beast so wyld,
>> so goodly wonne with her owne will beguyld.
>
> (lxvii)

This takes its departure from hunting conceits by Petrarch, Tasso and Wyatt ('Whoso list to hunt'), but has a tonality entirely its own. The first quatrain rehearses the traditional metaphor of the huntsman–lover exhausted by the chase; but the second introduces a deer–deare as thirsty as the hounds of desire are hungry. And in the sestet answering this octet reciprocity becomes union, as the TENOR and VEHICLE (literal and figurative) sides of the metaphor collapse into one another, and the fearless dear is tied with morally firm bands of love – 'with her owne goodwill'. (Tameness then regularly symbolized sexual submission.) Is the 'trembling' the lover's or the deer's, a sign of residual fear or of passion? The sonnet does not express feelings so much as meditate on the reciprocity of true love – on the 'strange thing' that separate individuality should be willingly beguiled.

In Shakespeare's *Sonnets* (1609) the impression of individual consciousness is so strong that many post-Romantic readers have understandably been unable to see anything but immediate expressions of love experiences. They have asked who is the 'man right fair' (the Earl of Southampton?) and who the 'dark lady' of Sonnets cxxvii–cliv. But such unanswerable questions distract from the poetry. It would almost be better to think of the *Sonnets* as addressed to the poet's own genius or 'better angel'. Many of them are concerned with large issues of time and love, death and truth, memory and fame. (In this they resemble Petrarch's *Canzoniere* and Spenser's *Ruines of Rome* (1591), now thought to be the closest model.) They explore the selflessness of love and the jealousy of desire – not only sexual jealousy but also that of rival poets competing for patronage. Shakespeare's sonnets are sometimes difficult because they have the unfamiliar privacy of manuscript literature, which in the Renaissance might be addressed to a single patron or at least a very select readership. But they can also puzzle us now by their highly traditional content; although Shakespeare treats this with an unparalleled largeness of thought. And the sonority of his language can satisfy even when its meaning is obscure – 'When to the Sessions of sweet silent thought'; 'For precious friends hid in deaths dateles night' (xxx); 'Time doth transfixe the florish set on youth' (lx). Few readers have felt the need to ask how a flourish is transfixed.

The romantic passionate TROPICAL (figurative) discourse of the *Sonnets* may at first seem much too vulnerable to misreading; but in actuality it is highly controlled and logical, as well as being resonant with its accompaniment of answerable diction. For example, Sonnet xxx is informed by a coherent allegory of a manorial court (hence the 'sessions'). And Sonnet lxxxi consistently compares different sorts of survival:

> Or I shall live your Epitaph to make,
> Or you survive when I in earth am rotten,
> From hence your memory death cannot take,
> Although in me each part will be forgotten.
> Your name from hence immortall life shall have,
> Though I (once gone) to all the world must die,
> The earth can yeeld me but a common grave,
> When you intombèd in mens eyes shall lie,
> Your monument shall be my gentle verse,
> Which eyes not yet created shall ore-read,
> And toungs to be, your beeing shall rehearse,
> When all the breathers of this world are dead,
>   You still shall live (such vertue hath my Pen)
>   Where breath most breathes, even in the mouths of men.

Here conviction is achieved through manifold fitnesses of language, all reinforcing the series of antitheses between exalted patron and humble poet. 'Each part' of the poet 'will be forgotten'; but the later mention of 'eyes' and 'tongues' in time to come shows (without its having to be said) that by contrast the parts of the celebrated patron will survive in rehearsal. Minute details contribute. Thus, the *traductio* in 'tongues to

be your *being* shall rehearse' mimes the repetition it refers to. 'Or . . . or'
in lines 1–2 is more expressive than 'either . . . or' would have been,
since the identical openings show it is immaterial which dies first. And
in 'From hence your memory death cannot take', the inversions enact
death's failure to separate 'your memory' from 'hence' by juxtaposing
them. The rich eloquence of the *Sonnets* is unsurpassed.

Shakespeare often tempers it, however, by intermingling low diction
or by using the witty closure of EPIGRAM. (The epigram was a short
poem usually leading up to a 'point' or penetrating turn of thought.
Modelled on examples in Martial or in the Greek Anthology, it was
established in England by More's neo-Latin *Epigrammata* (1518) and
had won an astonishing popularity by around 1600, the period of
Thomas Campion's *Poemata* (1595) and John Harington's English
attempts.) The Shakespearean sonnet – unlike the Petrarchan with its
octet| turn| sestet structure – consists of three quatrains and a conclud-
ing couplet. And the couplet is often crisply epigrammatic:

> Thus have I had thee as a dreame doth flatter,
> In sleepe a King, but waking no such matter.
>
> (lxxxvii)

Samuel Daniel's sweetly poignant but more ordinary sonnets *To Delia*
(1592) have the same structure, the same pointed closures. And the
tendency was carried further by Michael Drayton (1563–1631), who
explicitly rejected the lyric monotony of 'whyning Sonnets': 'Into these
Loves, who but for Passion lookes, / At this first sight, here let him lay
them by'. He preferred the variety of sonnet–epigram – 'the true image
of my Mind'. Thus *Idea* lxi is split into eight lines of epigram and six of
sonnet:

> Since ther's no helpe, Come let us kisse and part,
> Nay, I have done: You get no more of Me,
> And I am glad, yea glad with all my heart,
> That thus so cleanly, I my Selfe can free,
> Shake hands for ever, Cancell all our Vowes,
> And when We meet at any time againe,
> Be it not seene in either of our Browes,
> That We one jot of former Love reteyne;
> Now at the last gaspe, of Loves latest Breath,
> When his Pulse fayling, Passion speechlesse lies,
> When Faith is kneeling by his bed of Death,
> And Innocence is closing up his Eyes,
>   Now if thou would'st, when all have given him over,
>   From Death to Life, thou might'st him yet recover.

More satirically, Sir John Davies in his *Gullinge Sonnets* (?1594) sends up sonnet conventions by systematically translating them into epigram equivalents. His Cupid is clothed:

> His hose of hate, his Codpeece of conceite,
> His stockings of sterne strife, his shirte of shame;
> His garters of vaine glorie, gaye and slight,
> His patofels [overshoes] of passions I will frame;
> Pumpes of presumption shall adorne his feete,
> And Socks of sullennes excedinge sweete.
>
> (*Gullinge Sonnets* vi)

These are all instances of a widespread transformation of other kinds by epigram – a development that will continue to be a topic in later chapters.

The Elizabethans and Jacobeans also cultivated a contrary taste for pure lyric. Madrigal and lute song (the 'ayre' for a single voice) were as much in demand with them as pop music today, but had the standing of high art. Some of the greatest songs in the language were written by John Dowland (?1563–?1626), John Daniel (*c.*1565–1630), Thomas Campion (1567–1620) and others of their remarkable generation. Campion, who was more outstanding as a poet than a musician, interestingly thought of his airs as like 'quicke [living] and good Epigrammes' – presumably epigrams in the manner of Catullus or the Greek Anthology, with the 'difficulty' of serious compression. He wrote against automatic rhyme in his *Art of English Poesie* (1602), and himself composed in QUANTITATIVE METRE, a classicizing (and highly demanding) system whereby syllable length and accentual stress generally coincided:

Rōse-chēekt ' Lāwră, ' cōme

The result is ravishing. Like all songs, these need to be heard, since much of their pleasure lies in the interaction of words and music. But even as poems, Campion's airs have an enchanting quality. It seems to depend on their use of simple public imagery in which all that is commonplace has been transfigured by passion and by the intricate poetical workmanship of patterning and allusion. Often there is subtle variation from stanza to stanza – as with the intensifying denial in 'There is a Garden in her face'. Songs like 'Now winter nights enlarge' and 'Followe thy faire sunne, unhappy shaddowe' seem instantly lucid; but their patterning generates shifting implications that raise the mind far above conventional Petrarchism:

> Followe thy faire sunne, unhappy shaddowe:
> Though thou be blacke as night,
> And she made all of light,
> Yet follow thy faire sunne, unhappie shaddowe.

The shadow, at first 'blacke as night', turns out in a later stanza to be 'scorched' black; while night, from being the condition of the shadow, becomes a 'luckles night' that may also affect the disdainful sun. And the 'fair sunne' herself is 'made all of light', not in mere hyperbole, but in opposition to what will follow her fading.

Drayton, whom we met as an epigrammical sonneteer, could himself in another mood be intensely lyrical. Indeed, one of his principal contributions was to naturalize a major lyric form, the ODE. (Odes are long, ceremonious lyrics, often with a complex stanza structure.) Drayton's *Odes* (1606; 1619), an unusually decisive collection, offered native or invented equivalents for a wide range of lyric modes – not only those of Ronsard and Horace, but of Pindar and Anacreon, and even of heroic song, realized in an art ballad, the 'Ballad of Agincourt'. Drayton's aim was to reascend to the elevation of ancient lyric. Although he sometimes fell short of this, 'To the New Yeere' achieves a mysterious serenity and monumentality:

> Rich Statue, double-faced
> With Marble Temples graced,
>   To rayse thy God-head higher,
> In flames where Altars shining,
> Before thy Priests divining,
>   Doe od'rous Fumes expire.

Is the subject cosmic order, erotic exaltation, or poetic art? These questions also arise, if less obviously, with Drayton's greater rival, Edmund Spenser, author of 'Epithalamion' (1595) and *Prothalamion* (1596).

In 'Epithalamion' Spenser celebrates his own wedding day with an ode that is 'occasional' and personal yet traditional and general. It resembles some of the greatest Renaissance poems in being designed to relate uniquely to a single occasion (unlike modern poems, which make their effect in groups). As quite often, the occasion is commemorated not only by poeticized references to its events, but also by adjustments of the poem's numerical proportions, in such a way as to record the date or similar data. Much attention has focused on the NUMEROLOGY of 'Epithalamion', whereby details of the structure of its variable stanzas correspond numerically to the astronomy of the wedding day. For example, changes in the form of the refrain divide the stanza–hours between day and night in the right proportion for St Barnabas' day. But this is only one of the ways in which Spenser's visionary imagination brings all into accord.

> Ah when will this long weary day have end,
> And lende me leave to come unto my love?
> How slowly do the houres theyr numbers spend!
> How slowly does sad Time his feathers move!
> Haste thee O fayrest Planet to thy home
> Within the westerne fome:
> Thy tyred steedes long since have need of rest.
> Long though it be, at last I see it gloome,
> And the bright evening star with golden creast
> Appeare out of the West.

He effortlessly finds equivalents in the conventions of classical EPITH-ALAMIUM or wedding ode for his Christian ideas and homely realism. Angels and a 'holy priest' attend the antique rite, elevating rather than detracting from its high ceremonial. It may be hard now to appreciate the love of ceremonial order felt by many Elizabethans (even by Protestants like Spenser); but no reader of 'Epithalamion' can fail to sense its pure exultation, an unusual sentiment in literature.

LONGER POEMS

The longer poetic genres at first presented great difficulty, and were only after many attempts achieved. Before anything was written that still bears reading today in the way of pastoral, for example, much dull stuff by Googes and Turbervilles had to be worked through. PASTORAL ECLOGUE is a medium length form consisting of dialogue between shepherds (supposed to be simpler than the poet), often with an inset narrative or song. Its repertoire excludes exact knowledge, together with representation of the passage of time, of work, of difference of rank and of external details: all in the interest of concentration on essentials. By a tradition going back through Baptista Spagnuoli (Mantuanus, 1448–1516) to Petrarch, pastoral eclogue may conceal ecclesiastical and political allegories, based ultimately on the serious pun in *pastor*. Nevertheless, pastoral purports to realize an unhistorical, changeless world. That is why Sir Walter Ralegh's rebuttal of Marlowe's 'The Passionate Shepherd to his Love' insists on change: 'Time drives the flocks from field to fold . . . The flowers do fade . . . Had joys no date nor age no need, / Then these delights my mind might move'. Pastoral presupposes a Golden Age in stasis, in arrest.

By contrast GEORGIC – the mode in direct contradistinction to pastoral – concerns itself throughout with instruction and work, seasonal and geographical variety and historical change. Georgic took even longer than pastoral to establish itself in the vernacular; although, as we have partly seen, there were early attempts in Gavin Douglas's Prologues, in Elizabethan hunting poems and in praises of country life. Spenser's original departure was to mix these opposite modes deliberately. In *The Shepheardes Calender* (1579) he showed easy mastery of the pastoral genre up to his own time, and went on to finesse on it by blending in features of the contrasting georgic, in such a way as to create a more realistic rustic impression. Thus, the twelve monthly eclogues make the beautiful addition (as Alexander Pope was to call it) of a highly unpastoral calendar and proportionable seasonal round. Similarly, Spenser includes physical suffering and labour, and makes his shepherds use rough dialect words – 'My ragged rontes [small cows] all shiver and shake'; 'blowen bags' [swollen udders]; 'The rather [earlier] Lambes bene starved with cold' ('February', 5, 81, 83). The first considerable poem of the Elizabethan age, this was an epoch-making work. It has a remarkable variety, ranging from fiery politics of a militant Protestant cast to solemn ceremony – as in the elegy to 'Dido':

> The sonne of all the world is dimme and darke:
> The earth now lacks her wonted light,
> And all we dwell in deadly night,
>   O heavie herse.
> Breake we our pypes, that shrild as lowde as Larke,
>   O carefull verse.
>
> > ('November', 67–72)

The craft of *The Shepheardes Calender*, particularly in its textural modulation, is very fine. But it is too engaged a work to have survived as a whole.

Spenser went on to a more lasting pastoral achievement in *Colin Clout's Come Home Again* (1595), the greatest pastoral eclogue in the language. This is purer pastoral, carrying the sequestration of the green world to an extreme, indeed, through the arrangement of inset within inset narrations. Yet Spenser gently mocks the limits of the mode itself, for example by obliging his shepherd–poet Colin to paraphrase even such ordinary (but unpastoral) terms as 'sea' and 'ship':

> So to the sea we came; the sea? that is
> A world of waters heaped up on hie,

> Rolling like mountaines in wide wildernesse,
> Horrible, hideous, roaring with hoarse crie.
>
> (lines 196–9)

Nevertheless he can introduce such grim realities as 'bloody issues . . . grisly famine' and 'nightly bodrags [raids]', and can rise, in a georgic rather than pastoral way, to an exalted vision of cosmic love (lines 799– 894). Spenser was also great in other ways; but formally he occupies a strategic, even a unique, position in English literature. There is a sense in which he invented fully serious English poetry. He was a model for many that came after, as the first to achieve in English a complexity and refinement previously found only in the literature of antiquity.

So far we have considered long poems departing from Virgilian models; but a classical inspiration just as strong was the Ovidian. Read at school, Ovid's *Metamorphoses* stimulated a taste – avid during the Middle Ages and now revived – for digressive mythological narrative. The *Metamorphoses* itself was sturdily translated by Arthur Golding (1565) and finely by George Sandys (1626). And many original works aimed at the Ovidian tonality of erotic warmth intermittently cooled by 'artificial' (then a good word) digressions and allusions. From this neogothic vogue, three EPYLLIA or longish mythological narratives stand out: Shakespeare's *Venus and Adonis* (1593); Christopher Marlowe's unfinished *Hero and Leander* (1598, wr. before 1593); and its continuation by George Chapman (1598). The most enjoyably brilliant of these is Marlowe's. Intensely sensuous, it nevertheless remains controlled, within a stylish romantic diction modelled ultimately on that of the camp epicist Musaeus (fifth century). No sooner do we reach the lining of Hero's garment than description teasingly digresses into mythology:

> Her wide sleeves greene, and bordered with a grove,
> Where Venus in her naked glory strove
> To please the carelesse and disdainfull eies
> Of proud Adonis that before her lies . . .
>
> (i.11–14)

Or, what begins as simple visualization will swerve through simile into allusion –

> For everie street, like to a Firmament,
> Glistered with breathing stars, who where they went
> Frighted the melancholie earth, which deem'd
> Eternall heaven to burn, for so it seem'd,

As if another Phaethon had got
The guidance of the sunnes rich chariot.
(i.97–102)

– until the poem becomes a tissue of enhancing embroidery heightening the mood and taking everything ordinary up into poetry.

The visual clarity of Marlowe's pictorial effects is nevertheless striking. It can best be appreciated in the context of the Renaissance *paragone* between poetry and painting, in which, as their status changed, rival claims to superiority were pressed. Which art represented external nature with more liveliness? Which moved the feelings, or 'spoke' more eloquently? Which came closer to philosophical nature, to ideas? Marlowe was one of the first of a line of poets – among them Spenser, Crashaw, Milton and Pope – who attempted to overgo painting. He aimed to show that poets could equal the liveliest effects of the painters – and go on to do other things beyond them.

When critics say that epic became unwritable after Milton, they sometimes forget that it was very nearly so before him. Most Elizabethan and Jacobean attempts at long poems were dull failures. Some of the best of them approached the impossible goal by way of another impossibility, translation. Joshua Sylvester's translation of Du Bartas's French Biblical epic *Devine Weekes and Works* (1592–1605) at least cannot be called dull; but it is seldom better than quaint or flavoursome. Winter in Sylvester will 'perriwig with wool the bald-pate Woods' (II.i.4.176) and the world be divided by the sea's 'divers-brancht retorsions' (I.iii.89). Michael Drayton's and George Sandys's Biblical paraphrases are on another plane, and offer much more than the historical interest of pointing forward to *Paradise Lost*. There were also secular translations. Sir John Harington's version of Ariosto's *Orlando Furioso* (1591) has little more than energy. And the *Roland* of John Stewart of Baldyneiss (c.1540–c.1600) is too highly wrought rhetorically. But Edward Fairfax's Tasso – *Godfrey of Bulloigne* (1600) – was the greatest verse translation from a vernacular original until Sir Richard Fanshawe's Camoens (1655). Although stylistically important, however, Fairfax's masterpiece could not assist others in the mastery of large structures. Nor could George Chapman's great Homer, inventive though he was in finding equivalents for the diverse forms of his original. Here he has captured the epic simile's simple physicality:

All grave old men, and souldiers they had bene, but for age
Now left the warres; yet Counsellors they were exceeding sage.
And as in well-growne woods, on trees, cold spinie Grashoppers

Sit chirping and send voices out that scarce can pierce our eares
For softnesse and their weake faint sounds; so (talking on the towre)
These Seniors of the people sate, who, when they saw the powre
Of beautie in the Queene ascend, even those cold-spirited Peeres,
Those wise and almost witherd men, found this heate in their yeares
That they were forc't (though whispering) to say: 'What man can blame
The Greekes and Troyans to endure, for so admir'd a Dame,
So many miseries, and so long? . . . '

(*Homer's Iliads* iii.159–69)

Chapman's independent style has local difficulties, connected sometimes with convictions about Homer's hidden meaning. But in general the poetry is transparent, flexible and remarkably free from routine formulas.

So far as original verse is concerned, the only long works of any significance (with one exception that I shall return to shortly) are Drayton's. His *Mortimeriados* (1596; rev. as *The Barons Warres*, 1603) achieves a success far beyond that of Daniel's *Civil Wars between York and Lancaster* (1595). Daniel seems content to versify accurate history; whereas Drayton, who takes literature more seriously, gives his narrative a marvellously rich poetic texture. And *The Barons Warres* is not his only ambitious work. His georgic on an epic scale, *Poly-Olbion* (1612; wr. ?1598–1612), is a vast digressive life's work with everything in it somewhere, including fine poetry. Only its being tied to topographical sequence has debarred it from lasting greatness and consigned it to neglect. If not so influential as Donne and Jonson, Drayton like them had his own circle (Alexander, Drummond, Browne and others): he is in some sense a major figure.

SPENSER'S *THE FAERIE QUEENE*

The great exception among Elizabethan long works is Spenser's allegorical EPIC (heroic narrative), a poem apart, in some ways, from its immediate context. For many readers, *The Faerie Queene* (Books I–III, 1590; I–VI, 1596) lives with other great visionary works – although not without objection from critics sceptical of such survivals into the age of the novel. Undeniably a classic of the sort that is variously misinterpreted in different periods, it was quarried by the Augustans for diction or gothic atmosphere, misread by Romantics wanting visual images, and depended on for sermons or escapism by Victorians and Edwardians. It has come to be deeply interwoven with subsequent literary tradition, for whose understanding it is indispensable. And still it discloses new facets.

Often *The Faerie Queene* is taken for a ROMANTIC EPIC, or interlaced narrative like some of its models – say Ariosto's *Orlando Furioso* (1516; 1532). But romantic epic served Spenser merely as a vehicle or 'fable' for allegory. As he says himself, his poem is 'a continued Allegory, or darke conceit' in which the episodes, and even many details within them, are metaphors. True, *The Faerie Queene* resembles other romances – and excels almost all – in evoking the romantic mise-en-scène of 'wastefull wayes', 'wandering forests', supernatural powers, 'griesly monsters' and chivalrous knights with archaic accoutrements. And it has exciting fragments of narrative, interrupted and interlaced in such a way as to suggest endless extent. But the stories are not the simple external narratives they may at first seem. Everything is allegorical. Even a detail of posture may carry a metaphorical implication; as where standing signifies uprightness – the meaning it had through centuries of allegorical interpretation of the Bible. Similarly, taking off armour implies moral vulnerability. Thus, when the Red Cross Knight sits resting at I.vii.2 'Disarmed all of yron-coted Plate', Orgoglio surprises him not by a mere external accident, but by his own fault. Nevertheless, reading the allegory is not a matter of extracting occasional moral messages that Spenser for some reason felt obliged to disguise. Rather do the metaphors belong to a continuous representation of internal experience selected and generalized. In any case, the allegory's moral content, like its topical allusions, is itself an image of deeper, visionary, Christian–Platonic truth.

Modern critics insist on the poem's undramatic quality; and this is obviously right in the sense that it seldom offers a direct naturalistic representation of objective reality as it would appear to an observer. Nevertheless, Spenser's subjective narrative offers another sort of realism. In this, the reader is put through the represented experience not as a spectator but as a participant. When Phedon has told his appalling case history and Guyon briskly advises him 'all your hurts may soone through temperance be easd' (II.iv.33), a good reader will sense that the response is facile, and be ready to find an irony – particularly in the light of later developments of the main narrative. But an indolent reader will see the speech as authorial rather than dramatic, and be dismayed when his ideal hero Guyon later comes a cropper. In the House of Mammon, Guyon prepares to fight the Giant Disdayne but is deterred. Mammon counsels him that

> nothing might abash the villein bold,
> Ne mortall steele emperce his miscreated mould.

> So having him with reason pacifide,
> And the fiers Carle commaunding to forbeare,
> He brought him in.
>
> (II.vii.42–3)

This does not mean that Guyon has overcome disdain. In the romance tradition elsewhere followed by Spenser, heroes never shake hands with Giants; nor need they rely only on reason and be limited to 'mortal steele'. Mammon has 'brought . . . in' his visitor with a vengeance. Later, Guyon faints; which many have taken to mean that he is worn out by self-denial. But in fact his failure is spiritual. His virtue is of a disdainful sort; as appears in the scornful speeches that give Mammon his chance.

The passage, like many in *The Faerie Queene*, is more dramatic than the critics of spectator realism have supposed. In Elizabethan fiction such subtly ironic narrative was new. Much later, however, Fielding and other early novelists were to take it as their point of departure from Spenser. And in this they knew very well what they were doing.

The Faerie Queene offers its highest pleasures in extended descriptions of 'places' of the imagination, like the Garden of Adonis (III.vi), the House of Busirane (III.xi) or Isis Church (V.vii). These set out in symbolic terms the natures of principal virtues or vices, and in doing so turn out to have described aspects of life itself. This penetration to the bases of inner life is a feature of the ordinary world of romance; but in Spenser this tradition's psychological health is at its most robust. His symbolic beings are no mere personified abstractions: they have the force of profound archetypes, concentrated by art. Beyond that, they embody a vision. In the Garden of Adonis

> There wont faire Venus often to enioy
> Her deare Adonis joyous company,
> And reape sweet pleasure of the wanton boy;
> There yet, some say, in secret he does ly,
> Lapped in flowres and pretious spycery,
> By her hid from the world, and from the skill
> Of Stygian Gods, which doe her loue envy;
> But she her selfe, when ever that she will,
> Possesseth him, and of his sweetnesse takes her fill.
>
> (III.vi.46)

In Spenser's vision, the form-giver Venus still has access – as in art and in ordinary sexuality (III.vi.29) – to a paradisic sweetness whose potentiality remains unspoilt by all the knowledge and technique ('skill') of the gods of death. From this plane of philosophical myth Spenser easily moves through the more readily intelligible genealogy of Pleasure's descent from Cupid and Psyche, and the nurture of Amoret, to the Faery court and the resumed story. Such tactful transitions are the stuff of great art.

To enjoy *The Faerie Queene* the reader has to be alert for passages that illuminate each other. The information that when Amoret came to Faery court 'many one . . . found/ His feeble hart wide launched [wounded] with loves cruell wound' (III.vi.52) needs to be remembered in reading the episode of Busirane's masque, where Amoret herself (who embodies this vulnerability of love) is shown wounded by a 'cruel hand', with her 'trembling hart . . . drawne forth, and in silver basin layde,/ Quite through transfixed with a deadly dart' (III.xii.20–1). A similar interaction occurs even at the distance and on the scale of whole books. Each book treats a different virtue, and has an appropriate mode or tone; so that one book will often answer another with an effect of half-remembered tonality. In this way the moral schemes and harsh, clear-cut dénouements of Book V are followed by a different, almost contrasting style in the subtle and lingering accommodations of Book VI, even so far as outwardly similar episodes are concerned. And the socially responsible pastoral romance of VI complements the more abrupt Ariostan romance of III, with its landscape of private passion.

In descriptions and narrative allegories alike, Spenser returned to medieval traditions, rethinking and refashioning them for his more individualistic modern age. Under his hand, the older romances with their combats of prowess were reshaped into densely significant narratives symbolic of spiritual, moral or psychological conflict. It would hardly be an exaggeration to say that the very idea of symbolic description is a Spenserian legacy. Yet it was also through his work, as much as any, that the medieval traditions themselves came to be transmitted to the centuries that followed, as a basis for yet further symbolisms.

4
Elizabethan and Jacobean Drama

REALISM began earlier in drama than in the novel – a later form to mature. There were anticipations in the later romances, and faint parallel developments in early seventeenth-century fiction. But the great advances were in the theatre. The beginnings of realism were naturally very gradual, and proceeded by short steps: here an unusual realization of psychology, there a few specific details of a Vice's villainy. Dramatic forms altered in response, but went through rather more rapid changes. Formal novelties, generic mixtures and hybrids became characteristic of Elizabethan drama. The Morality continued, however, throughout the century (Thomas Dekker *Old Fortunatus*, a. 1599). It even reached new heights, notably in Skelton's sober *Magnyfycence* (?1515–18) and Lindsay's impassioned *Ane Satire of the Three Estaitis* (a. 1552). In the former, the density of sententious content is remarkable. Felicity's indeed magnificent speech has grave and subtle rhythms such as had not perhaps been heard before in English drama:

> Al thyngys contryvyd by mannys reason,
> The world envyronn [around], of hygh and low estate,
> Be it erly or late, welth hath a season.
> Welth is of wysdome the very trewe probate.
> A fole is he with welth that fallyth at debate.
> But men nowe a dayes so unhappely be uryd [disposed],
> That nothynge than welth may worse be enduryd.
>
> (*Magnyfycence* 1–7)

In the sixteenth century, if not before, the Morality was accompanied by another popular dramatic form, the INTERLUDE. This term has given a great deal of trouble, since it was applied to works of such diversity: in Scotland to farces, in England to moral allegory but also political allegory and coarse comedy. Probably 'interludes' – contrasted with outdoor 'stageplays' – meant simply indoor plays. They are usually short enough (about 1,000 lines) to have been played between the courses of a meal in a great house or college, as part of a festive occasion. Two kinds of interlude used to be imagined, aristocratic and 'popular'. But increasingly all are seen as related to great house auspices. Typically they were written for a small professional company (often four men and a boy) of resident or loaned or itinerant players. Such a troupe could not have performed open-air Moralities with their large casts. Indeed, the interlude troupe required to be matched by a special, more technical approach on the dramatist's part, to provide for doubling of parts. This feature has the odd corollary that characters tend to vanish disconcertingly half way through. (Such dwindling of parts continued in Shakespeare's time, when it seems not to have been felt as a defect: even in *King Lear*, arguably his greatest play, both Cordelia and the fool lack sustained presence and development.) The interlude's professional organization, very different from the guild organization of the mystery play, was a vital step in theatrical development.

But in substance the Tudor interludes can easily seem remote enough now. They are still close to their homiletic origins; so that they may convey the impression of being a series of short sermons. Characters are given to preaching to one another, or even to the audience:

> Nowe maie ye see all in this tide
> How the vice is taken, and vertue set aside.
> Yonder ye maye see Youth is not stable,
> But evermore chaungeable: . . .
>
> (*Youth* 542–5)

Moreover, simple as the action is, its events have no continuous sequence of cause and effect. In *Youth* (a. ?1513/14), the title personage is converted because the course of the argument requires it, not because any psychological change, whether gradual or sudden, provides motivation. True, the simplicity of the early Tudor interludes is a little deceptive. Direct address can be used with subtlety. Also, we have to think abstractly about personifications before they disclose the interlude's meaning. Charity's misfortunes, for example, make figural allusions to the sufferings of Christ; and the very fact that it is Charity rather than another virtue who persuades Youth to repent carries implications. Similarly in *Respublica* (a. 1554) there is a system of double personifications, whereby the vices disguise themselves as personified virtues: Avarice as Policy, Insolence as Authority, Oppression as

Reformation, and so forth. Nevertheless, the interludes are often simple to the point of dullness. Their direct realism, such as it is, appears in scattered satiric comments, and in locally graphic realizations of typical viciousness ('I shall lay thee on the ear'). Or, particulars of vice (a list of wines, or games of chance), originally homiletic in intention, may have acquired adventitious historical interest.

Tudor interludes and Moralities have almost no individual characterization, and no psychology at all in the naturalistic sense – no interest in personality, except as a moral instance. Their speakers preach what is proper for the virtue or vice each represents. Perhaps they may even act appropriately. But these actions spring from no feelings: they are predictable in terms of moral philosophy rather than of character. Even the plays of Christopher Marlowe (to jump to the 1590s) still have comparatively little naturalistic characterization. This makes them difficult for modern critics trained in character analysis. Until recently, much of *Tamberlaine* Part I (*c*.1587) seemed obscure – and was undervalued – because it lacked motivation. Now, questions about motive are seen as irrelevant to its form of representation, in which graded series of examples set out abstract ideas much like those in the Moralities. How far Marlowe uses Morality structures actively, and how far passively, becomes for us the question.

This is not in much doubt with *Doctor Faustus* (?1592), where the form is overtly and selectively deployed. Faustus is discovered at a spiritual crisis. Which field of study will he commit himself to? He considers the arts in turn, but finds a reason to despise each:

> Is to dispute well logic's chiefest end?
> Affords this art no greater miracle?
> Then read no more, thou hast attain'd that end;
> A greater subject fitteth Faustus' wit.
>
> (lines 8–11)

This greater subject Faustus hopes to find in magic and its 'omnipotence' – 'a sound magician is a demigod' (line 61). But to put this blasphemous plan into operation is to begin a Morality play: a good angel and an evil spirit promptly counsel him. In the opening and concluding scenes there is, however, some characterization. Faustus has the immature man's excessive shallow enthusiasms, for example. (This is not a trait much stressed in the criticism, which tends to be seduced by Faustus's boundless aspiration.) He is hardly a representative 'man of the Renaissance': Marlowe shows him despising the modern Ramus and the ancient Aristotle indifferently. Faustus' summary of the arts is really non-naturalistic – a medieval way of representing experience lasting over a period of time. Marlowe is writing, in fact, a modified form of Morality. And the genre was to remain available, with surprisingly little modification, for several decades. It must have received powerful reinforcement from habits of self-examination cultivated by the religious of the time, through works of casuistry and the procedures of the confessional.

INCREASES IN SCALE AND COMPLEXITY

During the sixteenth century, one of the main developments in dramatic representation – although one that has never been much discussed – was increase in scale. The changes leading to realistic representation as we know it can often be seen as scale changes. Increased detailing has been introduced into all aspects, except perhaps moral analysis. Nowhere is this more striking than in political drama. From early in the century there comes little in the way of detailed portrayal: only a few topical allusions in interludes (*Youth*; *Hick Scorner*) and summary emblems in pageants. In Scotland, to be sure, *Ane Satire of the Three Estaitis* (a. 1540, 1552) is comprehensive and packed with graphic details. But these have a local, immediately satiric, force; they are not articulated into any continuous realistic representation. In the later political interludes and Moralities (*Respublica*, a. 1553; *The Three Ladies of London*, ptd 1584), the characters become moral types rather than allegorical abstractions, with some corresponding elaboration of the exemplary action. And much the same is true of John Bale's half-allegorical chronicle play *King John* (a. 1539) or Thomas Norton's non-allegorical but very generalized political tragedy *Gorboduc* (a. 1562).

But move on to Shakespeare's *King John* (?1590–1) or *Richard III* (a. 1592), and you are at once struck by the increase in 'unnecessary' detail. (In the interval, of course, a beginning has been made on biography, in such works as More's *History of King Richard the Third*, Harpsfield's and Roper's lives of More, and Cavendish's life of Wolsey.) Thus, Bale has Cardinal's or Legate's formal speeches; but apart from these his realism extends no further than abuse and satire and Biblical quotation. There is no room for personal relations, for a King Philip or a Constance. In Shakespeare, there is still a good deal of summary presentation: emblematic scenes, representative events. But these features begin to be integrated with character and even to serve as further differentiation of it; as when telescoping Richard III's villainies expresses his versatility and opportunistic energy. With Shakespeare's

1 Henry IV (a. 1597), fully detailed action is arrived at. Again, Morality features persist. Schematic contrasts of Hal with Hotspur belong to an allegory of true and false honour, while the prince is beset by temptations to irascibility (Hotspur) and concupiscence (Falstaff, the Vice). Nevertheless, the sheer quantity of realistic detail and the subtlety of characterization this allows are of a different order altogether. The alteration of scale is most remarkable. In *Youth*, Riot introduces the prince to Lechery and persuades him to embrace loose life, all in 100 lines. But in *Henry IV* the tavern scenes between Hal and Falstaff, while covering similar moral issues, occupy many times that wordage. In the same way, *Youth* merely hints at Wolsey in a few allusions; whereas Shakespeare's *Henry VIII* (a. 1613) represents him talking at length in his own person and displaying contradictory traits of character. The difference is usually explained as a result of abandoning allegory. But it was due to something more positive than that: an enhanced interest in literal meaning, in the exemplary grain of history itself.

Plays also became very much more complex during the late sixteenth century. To be like life, they needed complication beyond mere enlargement and addition of detail. They needed for one thing complicated PLOTS or story patterns. In the interludes and late Moralities, plots were extremely simple: several plays could be adequately summarized as 'youth, led astray by plausible vices, is redeemed by grace'. It was a vital development, therefore, when intrigue plots were introduced, whether in imitation of classical comedy (Plautus, Terence) or of Italian (Machiavelli, Ariosto). One of the first to take this step was George Gascoigne, a highly innovative although minor writer, whose *Supposes* (a. 1566) translates Ariosto's *I Suppositi*. Here – almost without surviving precedent in English – we have a plot that is quite intricate. A young Sicilian studying at Ferrara changes places with his servant, to get access to his mistress: his rival, an elderly doctor, turns out to be the servant–master's father: and other false or mistaken identities complicate matters further. Gascoigne takes evident pleasure in the complications, for he signals them by punning side-notes that list the main 'supposes' or false suppositions. *Supposes* is a COMEDY OF INTRIGUE, which is to say that character in it is subordinated to complication of plot. (The genre was closely akin to the Italian *Commedia dell' arte*, in fact – a largely oral tradition of improvised comedy with predetermined, permanent characters.) Intrigues were to form a considerable element in most subsequent drama, by no means all of it comic. Our greatest master of plotting, Ben Jonson, achieves some sort of ultimate in *The Alchemist*

(a. 1610), which in some unencompassable fashion keeps several handfuls of con game intrigues going simultaneously. The brilliant quickening of pace that eventually makes their interdigitation impossible gives audiences a high pleasure.

Another source of creative complication – and one that has proved inexhaustibly rich – was to use a previous literary work as subject, or point of departure, or text for comment. The new work now involved two elements instead of one: the original and the response. Their relation might be that of parody or BURLESQUE (travesty); as in the mechanicals' play of Pyramus and Thisbe in *A Midsummer Night's Dream* (a. ?1596), which burlesques or sends up the sort of tragical heroics found in *Cambises*, together with poetic versions of the Pyramus story by such as Mouffet.

Alternatively, the dramatist might take up a more sympathetic, not to say dependent, stance. So George Peele's *Old Wives' Tale* (ptd 1595) is amiably ironic in its exaggeration of the popular romantic plays favoured by the adult companies. (Of these plays little more than titles has survived, but they seem to have been disjointed assemblages of romance motifs: full of marvellous novelties, empty of moral content. Their most valuable contribution was freedom of transition – the possibility of irrational sequence.) Peele's delicate burlesque brought together and composed all that was typically romantic: fairy magic, enchantments, talking statuary, famous heroes. But it was more than a quintessence. He also achieved detachment from the world of romance, and made audiences conscious of their taste for it. Robert Greene's *Orlando Furioso* (a. 1592) extended a similar, but Ariostan, world in a less critical and more heroical direction. And one of the finest works in this mocking genre is Marlowe's *Dido* (ptd 1594), with its graceful travesty of Virgil.

Peele's other plays proceed similarly: *The Arraignment of Paris* (ptd 1584) reworks Greek myth as courtly MASQUE (mixed media allegorical spectacle), while *David and Bethsabe* (ptd 1599) modulates the Bible story into a remote key of pagan sensuousness and passion:

> Now Jove, let forth the golden firmament,
> And look on him with all thy fiery eyes.

Dramatically Peele's work is defective; but it brings to the theatre poetry of a new intensity, and not a little of its strange lyric beauty comes from interplay of double contexts. I need hardly say that such dependence on previous literature is neither imitative nor secondary in any bad sense.

Indeed, by opening new possibilities of concision and complexity it raised literature to a higher power.

This line of development led to the complex type of comedy that we think of as Shakespearean. It was not the only type available around 1600. Jonson invented another. On the whole he preferred to pursue an abstract idea through many concrete examples (the idea of transmutation in *The Alchemist*, of self-deception in *Bartholomew Fair*). But Shakespeare generally started with a story, often a familiar one – 'the story is extant and writ in choice Italian'. He would take some fairy tale, or old play, or 'former fabulous story', and subject it to reinterpretation. Or he might allegorize the 'golden story' – as he did with Greene's romance in *The Winter's Tale* or the casket story in *The Merchant of Venice* – so that it became expressive of his individual doctrine.

Shakespeare's comedy is capable of as much moral seriousness and intellectual weight as Jonson's, but it finds room for them differently. Often it works subtly through a generic complication. Thus, the old story and Shakespeare's new treatment may be in tension with one another; as in *The Merchant of Venice* (?1597), where the sour comedy stands out in contrast with the light neatness of its narrative source *Il Pecorone*. In the tale, for example, the ring intrigue is merely a practical joke: the play's serious reflections are absent or, at most, potential. All is simple and sentimental: when Giannetto (Bassanio) is reproached for giving the ring to another he weeps, softening his lady to instant explanation. But Shakespeare makes a deeper statement about marital obligation precisely by delaying this anticipated resolution, while the significance of the rings is brought out: 'that doctor . . . hath got the jewel that I loved'; 'mine honour . . . is yet mine own'; 'by this ring the doctor lay with me'.

The Winter's Tale (a. 1611) similarly interacts with its source, Greene's romance *Pandosto*; as in Leontes's contrastingly long penance for jealousy. And other events in the romance are allegorized or reinterpreted with a complicating effect. Since the best minds were sharpened then on allegorical interpretation, Shakespeare's plan would tend to bring intellect effectively to bear on the familiar action. His use of obvious sources is not a sign of negligence (as used to be thought) but a way of achieving concentration of meaning. It was a method that made for communicating fine moral shades, and for a many-faceted complexity of alternative views such as the Biblical commentaries of the time cultivated. It opened the way to representation with symbolic overtones; and it brought profundity into secular drama.

FORMAL REALISM

Along these and other paths, drama had arrived at formal realism by the time of, say, Marlowe's *Massacre at Paris* (a. ?1593) and Shakespeare's *Comedy of Errors* (1593). From this point of view, indeed, there is something like a watershed in English drama in the 1590s – a much deeper division than any in 1642. Here we need to be rather particular. Realism did not begin with Marlowe. Indeed, local touches of it can be found almost from the origins of drama; certainly from the first miracle plays. More recent was the occurrence of whole scenes that could be regarded as transcriptions from life – as the actual words of individuals in real situations. And newer still was the innovation whereby comment on the action, such as earlier might have been choric or directly authorial, was incorporated as a character's thoughts, for example in the form of soliloquy. It is because of this – because meaning was now conveyed through an apparently free-standing, self-contained imitation of life – that the last decade of the century marks the beginning of literature that is still 'alive', that can speak directly to us without much intervention by critics. It is possible for a modern audience to respond to a performance of *Hamlet* (a. 1600) much as they would if it were the same kind of representation practised today. They ask what *Hamlet* is about, and give new answers, as if it were a modern play, or life itself. Of course, this involves misreading; since *Hamlet* is not actually quite in our idiom. But it is only with Marlowe and Jonson and Shakespeare that such misreading becomes possible.

They were not alone in achieving such natural effects. Thomas Middleton (1580–1627), in particular, soon displayed superlative skill in realizing the fine texture of emotions – always, however, in the interest of exemplifying the moral analysis that was their deeper purpose. He specialized in strong scenes covering a bold sweep of emotional ground. (The scene was by now the unitary form in drama of all kinds.) His scenes can move from one moral equilibrium to another utterly different; yet he manages everything with such plausibility that no break in the inevitable steps between appears. *Women Beware Women* (a. ?1621) Act II Scene i is a striking example. Before it, Isabella seems almost too innocent to understand her uncle's incestuous desires; by its end, she is making advances to him. Her corruption by Livia is brilliantly convincing; as it must be, if Middleton the Puritan moralist is to succeed in his didacticism. Even Shakespeare does not always supply so much gradated detail of a change of mind.

Natural as it often seems, however, Elizabethan and Jacobean realism is sometimes deceptive, arousing inappropriate expectations. Non-naturalistic representation was still very well understood; and when it is resorted to the naturalism can switch off with disconcerting abruptness – like Shakespeare's in *King Lear* Act IV Scene vi, for example, where Edgar convinces Gloucester that he has thrown himself off a cliff. Alternatively, what we take for expressions of character may in actual fact be something quite different – moral example, perhaps, or metaphysics; as with Edmund's rejection of deterministic astrology in the same play, at I.ii.124–40. Even Shakespeare, who could write naturalistically at will, never sustained naturalistic realism throughout a whole play. He would always strike a balance between the demands of representation and of drama as performance or occasion. For the dramatic occasion had come to be endowed with a rich panoply of conventions and formulas; and these Shakespeare immensely enjoyed using.

Shifts in and out of naturalism were favoured by the physical nature of the stage and by the theatrical conventions of the time. The popular theatres (such as the Globe and the Swan) had evolved out of inns and bearpits; they retained a polygonal form, with seating raised above a standing area that corresponded to the former innyard. The 'thrust' arrangement of the stage put elaborately naturalistic scenery out of the question. Indeed, the stage was by our standards quite bare of scenery; although on occasion ambitiously realistic special effects could be hazarded, with flames, traps, cisterns of water and the like. Costumes and props were sometimes elaborate enough to attract the admiration of European visitors.

TRAGEDY AND ITS MIXTURES

In the absence of a native tradition, tragedy was slow to develop. We take the familiar kinds for granted, perhaps, and think the difference between tragedy and comedy obvious. But it was not, then. Medieval tragedies were hardly tragic, in our sense. They were stories (not plays) of divine judgements upon the guilty – like those that make up Chaucer's The Monk's Tale. Their subject was the downfall of the fortunate or powerful; their theme, God's underlying justice. This is a far remove from what we call TRAGEDY, in which a hero's fault or error leads to suffering greater than itself by a terrible disproportion, and far from just in the ordinary sense. The medieval tradition persisted in *A Mirror for Magistrates* (1559, 1578), a collection of twenty-six narrative poems, almost all of them about the misfortune or divine punishment of the guilty.

When Elizabethan dramatists came to take up classical models, they did not at first turn to Greek tragedy. Apart from academic dramatists, Shakespeare seems to have been the first to learn from the Greek tragedians – as in his probable use of Euripides' *Hecuba* in *Titus Andronicus* (ptd 1594). To most Elizabethans, classical tragedy meant Seneca. Seneca was translated into English, acted on the academic stage, and imitated in English plays from *Gorboduc* (a. 1562) and *The Spanish Tragedy* (a. 1592) onwards. The choice of model was not in every way ideal. Senecan tragedy is a form of closet drama, with little action and only the crudest psychology. It presents extreme passions and sensational events (some blood-curdling, like the unwitting ingestion of children's flesh in *Thyestes*), but mostly does so in narrative or lyric form. Its staple is long declamatory speeches, full of patterned rhetoric: in its world, events are opportunities for eloquence.

Seneca's impress was deep in Elizabethan tragedies of villainy, such as Marlowe's *Massacre at Paris* and *The Jew of Malta* (a. 1592) or Shakespeare's *Titus Andronicus*. The Senecan tyrants were eminently suitable for adaptation as Machiavellian villains. Ancient avoidance of stage violence, however, had less appeal. English tragedy was in a more than verbal sense a tragedy of blood: it included sudden death almost by rule. Aristotle describes the distinctive tragic action as arousing pity and fear; Elizabethan tragedies seem more calculated to arouse disgust and horror. Still, they number among them so fine a play as Shakespeare's *Richard III* (ptd 1597). This combines pageant history with many of the features of Senecan tragedy: bloody deeds, narratives of villainy, patterned declamations. On the eve of the battle of Bosworth, a procession – or pageant – of ghosts disturbs Richard's sleep; he is a tyrant as evil as Seneca's.

Where is the satisfaction in a play so dark? To some extent we catch Richard's infectious glee at the brilliance of his own wrongdoing; as when he succeeds in his cynical wooing of Anne, whose husband he killed. Some of the scenes palpably offer moral holidays. And we can sense a new beginning in the wish to face the ugliness of political motivation for what it really is – as opposed to the medieval idealizations of it. All this is equally true of Marlowe's *The Jew of Malta*. But Shakespeare offers a more believable tyrant, who in the end breaks down in remorse:

> My conscience hath a thousand several tongues,
> And every tongue brings in a several tale,
> And every tale condemns me for a villain.
> (*Richard III* V.v.147–9)

All this might be thought a shade dangerous morally. But the Elizabethans were used to evil characters. Even the Jew's exposé of Christendom would be to them a recognizable form of didacticism.

Senecan imitation developed into a characteristically Jacobean form, REVENGE TRAGEDY. Here we come to a theatrical landmark; for revenge tragedy is the genre of many of the earliest plays still in the repertoire. *The Revenger's Tragedy*, *The Duchess of Malfi*, *The White Devil*: all are revenge tragedies. Shakespeare's *Titus Andonicus* and *Hamlet* are not unrepresentative; and *Macbeth* is an inverted example. Normally the hero or villain–hero revenges a wrong – often under the direction of a more or less Senecan ghost. 'Revenge his foul and most unnatural murder', commands the elder Hamlet. Difficulties or delays or complications intervene, however, so that the revenge usually comes at the end, perhaps as the bloody culmination of some spectacle, like the inset play in *The Spanish Tragedy* (a. 1592) by Thomas Kyd (1558–94). This masterpiece of Kyd's was a *succès fou*: directly or indirectly it influenced every revenge tragedy that followed. For its vogue crystallized into a conventional form, which lasted, although to be sure not without modifications, for half a century.

Yet the original popularity of revenge tragedy is something of a mystery. Adjustment has to be made, of course, for the different level of violence in a society with no adequate police force. All the same, how can revenge have been acceptably presented as a duty of Christians? Perhaps it was not. After all, the chief character or PROTAGONIST of an English tragedy was not expected to be an ideal figure like the Greek tragic hero. Moreover, revenge may have worked as a symbol of all hazardous duties and doubtful responsibilities, such as the new moral imperatives of the time imposed. The problems of revenge may *au fond* have been problems of reform. Political implications are not usually so clear, however, as in *The Revenge of Bussy d'Ambois* (a. 1610), where Chapman makes his republican ghost tell Clermont: 'What corrupted law/Leaves unperformed in kings, do thou supply'. But this conjecture may still be too literal. Exotic settings, often Italian, would distance the violence (as can still happen in a Western film), allowing it to be taken as a general symbol of evil justly punished. Again, Sidney speaks of tragedy as exposing hidden corruption ('the ulcers that are covered with tissue'); and this idea fits revenge tragedy very well. Particularly after *The Revenger's Tragedy* (ptd 1607), the protagonist tended more and more to be a villain, whose cruelties became increasingly devilish. The search for deeds capable of shocking seems to have led to an inflation of stage horror. Latterly, revenge plays flaunted sensational crimes and spectacles: torture, insanity and rape; perverse and incestuous adultery; bloody dismemberings and macabre charnel horrors. The mechanism of revenge continued to be set in motion by an initial crime or fault; but the revenge was now much worse than the crime itself, so that something like the moral disproportion of ancient tragedy returned.

Revenge tragedy's attraction partly lies in its macabre pungency: it seems to have the authentic touch of evil. John Webster is particularly flavoursome. *The White Devil* (a. 1612) can be almost naturalistic: in Vittoria and Brachiano contradictory traits of good and evil are seen blurred together. But its naturalism is one that treats the sinister as normal. The choric Flamineo, indeed, takes relish in images so macabre as to approach self-parody or camp:

> It would do well instead of looking-glasses
> To set one's face each morning by a saucer
> Of a witch's congealèd blood.
>
> (III.iii.88–90)

He discovers corruption and mortality even in an everyday culinary term like 'coffined in a baked meat' (IV.ii.20).

As a sardonic outsider, Flamineo is specially close to Webster the satirist. But throughout the play (and others of its kind), the dramatist's uncovering of corruption finds direct expression in the character's own diatribes and artful revenges. Lodovico says: 'I limned this night-piece and it was my best' (V.vi.297). True to type, his horrifyingly devious revenge plot leads up to an unnecessarily formalized murder – a work of art indeed. (Lodovico poisons Brachiano's helmet; then, disguised as a Capuchin friar, brings him the extreme unction, mocks, and finally strangles him.) With this costume killing at the tourney one might compare the intrigue leading to the catastrophe play-within-a-play in *The Spanish Tragedy*, or the revenge masques in *Antonio's Revenge*, *The Revenger's Tragedy* and *Women Beware Women*. Such rituals are said to have the function of mediating the violence, like the *nuntius* (messenger) speeches of ancient tragedy, in which narrative art mutes and distances the physical horrors. It may be so. But the fatal rituals of revenge tragedy can also have a very different effect, delaying and heightening the violence, winding it like a spring, until finally it is released for purgation in blood. 'When the bad bleeds, then is the tragedy good' (*Revenger's Tragedy* III.v.205).

From one standpoint, *Hamlet* (a. 1600) is a regular revenge tragedy. It too has an inset play, which arouses expectations of revenge and an immediate dénouement. But Shakespeare defers retribution, so that in the event it is a fencing display – another inset show – that brings the violent end. This delay lasts altogether longer than usual. To some extent that is because of Claudius' counter-intrigue. But it is also bound up with character – with inner problems of a different sort from those occupying Shakespeare's colleagues. The setting, moreover, far from the violent Italy of later convention, is convincingly realistic; and the ethics of revenge are scrutinized to an extent seldom attempted. For example, Hamlet questions the spiritual credentials of his father's ghost, and hesitates over his commission in a way that other Jacobean revengers seldom pause to do. Indeed, *Hamlet* has a moral refinement rare in any literary period or kind.

Among the English genres, revenge tragedy is nearest to tragedy in the classical sense. (Some ancient Greek tragedies, such as the *Oresteia*, drew their plots from stories of revenge.) No definition of tragedy is possible. But beyond question *Hamlet* shows many characteristic family resemblances. For example, its conflict is not between good and evil, but between opposed goods: between moral reform and moral delicacy, between honour and Christian obedience. Hamlet himself is an ideal but not a flawless prince. Like that of Aristotle's tragic protagonist, his character has minor but fatal defects. He is idealistic to a fault, and consequently exacting both towards others and towards himself. He is also infirm of purpose – or believes himself to be so. Nevertheless, audiences feel (and this is a frequent aspect of tragic experience) that Hamlet's and the many other deaths are consequences disproportionate to his fault. In ancient tragedy the catastrophe demonstrated the terrible power of Fate. But in English tragedy, what is revealed is the appalling severity of God himself. Hamlet, like Oedipus or Orestes, has a mission to uncover and reform evil – here the corruption and militarism of Denmark: 'The time is out of joint: O cursed spite,/That ever I was born to set it right!' (I.v.188). As usual in English tragedy (*King Lear* is a rare exception), the evil must be purged by the blood of violent death rather than by suffering.

In spite of its many deaths, *Hamlet* hardly seems violent. It is even comparatively reflective, since the action is largely one of emotions. Some of it, indeed, takes place in the very mind of the protagonist, being communicated in the great SOLILOQUIES that above all other parts distinguish the play. (Soliloquies are speeches in which a character alone on stage – or acting as if alone – externalizes his inner thoughts and feelings.) These introspective and intimate speeches cross new thresholds of self-revelation:

> O! what a rogue and peasant slave am I:
> Is it not monstrous that this player here,
> But [merely] in a fiction, in a dream of passion,
> Could force his soul . . .
>
> (II.ii.551–4)

to such an extent that he wept:

> . . . Yet I,
> A dull and muddy-mettled rascal, peak . . .
> And can say nothing – no, not for a king,
> Upon whose property and most dear life
> A damned defeat [ruin] was made. Am I a coward?
>
> (II.ii.567–72)

No one dares to insult Hamlet in the trivial ways he goes on to imagine; yet he should not vaunt his honour, for he has submitted to the far greater wrong inflicted by Claudius. At this he calls his father's murderer names: 'Remorseless, treacherous, lecherous, kindless [unnatural] villain!' But now self-condemnation takes a fresh turn, as he sees that this private and purely verbal violence is only a new evasion: 'Why, what an ass am I! This is most brave [finc]'. He blames himself for unpacking his heart, for cursing 'like a very drab'; then abruptly he turns to action (or at least planning): 'About [set about it], my brains!' We are not of course to take this quite as a series of actual thoughts – as if Hamlet went chameleon-like through all these emotional turns on a single occasion. Still, he is not merely speaking about previous self-recriminations, either. His words are exactly like thoughts – only thoughts edited, ordered and made to suggest motives that Hamlet would not himself be aware of, like the sexual disgust reflected in 'whore' and 'drab' as self-insults.

In dialogue, Shakespeare's tragedies realize the nature of moral choice with similar minuteness. One thinks of Hamlet's scenes with Ophelia, or Othello's with Iago, or Macbeth's with his wife. All the mature tragedies present plots fully worked out in scenes that are not only theatrically effective but also convincingly realistic, replete with detailed moral deliberations and exemplary emotions, and expressed in high, magnificent poetry. These proportions of Shakespearean tragedy are taken for granted. But no other dramatist of the period adopted them; for none shared all of Shakespeare's strengths. Fletcher's poetry and morality impress, but not his plot development. Middleton has the plots and moral sense, but not the poetry. In whole plays, Webster perhaps comes closest; but he lacks Shakespeare's unfolding of individual character.

Tragedy in its unmixed form calls for an exceedingly rare moral imagination. In fact much Renaissance tragedy was hybrid – satiric tragedy, or heroic, or tragicomedy. Satire and tragedy may seem odd partners now; but so long as 'satire' was etymologically derived from 'satyr', it must have been an obvious recourse to combine it with *tragodia* or goat-song. The two kinds came to be thought of in similar moral terms, as characterized by their exposing of evil. The appropriate speaker of satire of the diatribe kind was a 'satyr' type – unrestrained, free-speaking and given to harsh, coarse, pessimistic denunciation – perfect for the stage. First to combine the currently popular satiric form with tragedy was possibly John Marston in *The Malcontent* (a. ?1600), quickly followed (if not just preceded) by Shakespeare. Marston's malcontent duke began a vogue for the type – to which Shakespeare's Thersites belongs, together with Tourneur's Vindice and Webster's Flamineo.

In this mixture there is a tendency for the satire to dominate, so that the tragic action becomes mere pretext, void of weight. This happens in the somewhat overvalued *Revenger's Tragedy* (ptd 1607), previously attributed to Tourneur but now, more plausibly, to Middleton. As often in the genre, unity depends on a pivotal satiric figure – here Vindice. It is his vituperation, expressed in violent and rather monochromatic imagery, that establishes the moral viewpoint. And he makes very long speeches indeed, like the opening diatribe, or the famous address to his love's skull:

> Does the silk-worm expend her yellow labours
> For thee? For thee does she undo herself?
> Are lordships sold to maintain ladyships
> For the poor benefit of a bewitching minute?
> Why does yon fellow falsify high-ways,
> And put his life between the judge's lips,
> To refine such a thing? keep horse and men
> To beat their valours for her?
> Surely we are all mad people, and they
> Whom we think are, are not; we mistake those:
> 'Tis we are mad in sense, they but in clothes.
>   (III.v.72–82)

These speeches, passionate if sometimes awkwardly argued, delineate a powerful satiric stance, Swiftian in extremity and rigour: the stance of one who 'should be dead' (I.i.121). They are, however, essentially non-dramatic. And when so much 'dialogue' is given over like this to satire, hardly enough remains for plausible development of the action. The plot is exceedingly contrived, with multiple intrigues (Vindice has two separate disguises: in one, he is warned against the other). Indeed, its revenge machinations seem calculated to demonstrate moral theses as much as to punish crime. For example, Vindice's revenge on the lecherous duke takes the form of manipulating him into a further assignation and into kissing a poisoned skull. The symbolism *sub specie aeternitatis* continues when the virtually dead sinner is forced to watch his own bastard committing incest with the duchess – to witness, that is to say, the legacy of his evil. The satirist comments: 'I ne'er knew yet adulterer without horns'. Other intrigues expose evil's surprising ubiquity and variation in similar ways. The revenger is, so to speak, a practical or experimental satirist, bent on discovering the extent of the corruption of the worldly court. Vindice even tests (for 'policy') his own mother's resistance to it. His perfect disguises facilitate all-seeing judgement; but they do not much exploit the possibilities of tragic action.

Heroic tragedy is a much more workable mixture. It was tried in Marlowe's *Tamburlaine* (ptd 1590) and Shakespeare's early histories, and brought to consummate achievement in *Othello* (a. ?1604), *Antony and Cleopatra* (a. 1607) and *Coriolanus* (a. 1607). In Renaissance literary theory, epic and tragedy were thought of as closely akin – both being comparatively elevated. But in practice, heroic tragedy comes out distinctly more lofty than unmixed tragedy. It is also more occupied with nobility. Shakespeare's Antony embraces Cleopatra and says 'the nobleness of life/Is to do thus'. Hamlet wonders 'whether 'tis nobler in the mind to suffer . . .'.

A closely related value is fame: in their last speeches, both Hamlet and Othello are concerned about posthumous reputation. As for *Antony and Cleopatra*, it is full of its lovers' fame. One of the most consistently heroic of tragedies, its main action follows out stages in a hero's ruin. Yet it transcends the moral conflict between public responsibility and private love: Antony finds another heroic aspiration, and in death Cleopatra lifts him up – a symbolic elevation – to the height of a monument. The epic aim shows in the play's long action, in which it contrasts with other treatments of the story. Its many short scenes, too, and especially the geographical panorama of the first half, suggest a large and comprehensive view. But above all, it is the style that makes for a heroic impression. The quality of style is no mere grandeur: fineness, rather, against whose touchstone certain of the characters come to seem, by the highest standard, deficient. It prevails throughout like a bracing climate, dignifying everything beyond the ordinary. So Antony of Octavia:

> Her tongue will not obey her heart, nor can
> Her heart inform her tongue – the swan's down feather,
> That stands upon the swell at the full of tide,
> And neither way inclines.

$$\text{(III.ii.47–50)}$$

(It is almost an epic simile that hesitates between applications.) Even the satirical Enobarbus will say things like 'Age cannot wither her, nor custom stale . . .'. Allowing for the dry straight soldier's being at a loss among the windings of Cleopatra's magic, still the speech is more elevated than realism would have dictated. We are meant to imagine an action constantly glorious and monumental, as in some surpassingly beautiful painting of Veronese's. It is as if the playwright himself were ascending to the heroic plane.

Worth comparison with Shakespeare's, in some ways, are the heroic tragedies of George Chapman (?1559–1634). The best of these badly undervalued works is not *Bussy D'Ambois* (although it was once a popular success), but *The Conspiracy and Tragedy of Charles Duke of Byron* (ptd 1608), a ten-act tragedy based, like several of his others, on recent French history. It portrays the temptations besetting a powerful subject (not unlike Essex) in an increasingly absolute and centralized monarchy – an important topic, deeply meditated. Chapman's play has little action of the sort that fills most Jacobean tragedies; but it has not much development of character, either, nor even naturalistic consistency – Byron is an admired and honoured hero yet at the same time totally false. (Chapman seems to have been the first to put on stage a politically dangerous character who was not simply a villain.) *The Conspiracy and Tragedy* explores ideals of responsibility and freedom, mainly through verbal exchanges – conferences, audiences, intrigues, difficult interviews and soliloquies. It may be all talk; but what magnificently grave and passionate talk. It may not be good theatre (that has hardly been tested), but it is deeply impressive dramatic poetry. Perhaps its ideal medium is radio drama. At any rate, the vast scale of its speeches is justified in a way that is not true of the diatribes in *The Revenger's Tragedy*, which are mostly commonplaces tricked out in lurid rhetorical colours. In Chapman, passionate thought comes seriously to grips with stoic ideas, and length is a function of inherent difficulty. The achievement itself is larger than life. Edwin Muir says that Chapman's heroes 'exist in another dimension from the rest of the characters'. But the lesser characters are not exactly small: if King Henry, for example, is not enclosed in a 'dream of greatness', he none the less has his own sober dignified weight. Chapman, more than any other Jacobean dramatist, can convincingly imagine the passions associated with office and with moral largeness. In *The Conspiracy and Tragedy* his ambitious duke aspires beyond a subject's place, to the 'first royalty' of virtuous man as he ruled before the Fall. But he reaches up in a way tragically admirable:

> 'Tis immortality to die aspiring,
> As if a man were taken quick [living] to heaven;
> What will not hold perfection, let it burst . . .
> (*Byron's Conspiracy* I.ii.31–3)

He expresses, perhaps, Chapman's own fervent aspiration to greatness.

Chapman's style is the most elevated, after Shakespeare's, and in some ways the most consistently elevated of all. This is the quality Webster singled out in a famous reference to 'that full and heightened style' of Chapman. The translator of Homer shows in his easy recourse to epic similes, in his splendid orchestration of parts, but also at times in a certain noble simplicity, 'hearty, just and plain':

> men whom virtue
> Forms with the stuff of Fortune, great and gracious,
> Must needs partake with Fortune in her humour
> Of instability, and are like to shafts
> Grown crook'd with standing, which to rectify
> Must twice as much be bowed another way.
> (*Byron's Conspiracy* II.ii.26–31)

If angels wished to speak in English, Chapman's is the manner of English they might use.

Mixture of tragedy and comedy may seem impossible. How can the same play work towards both laughter and tears? The two are not invariably separated in life itself, however. And, as we have seen, COMEDY in medieval literature meant something quite different from classical comedy: namely, a story beginning in perplexity but ending in blessedness, and showing the pattern of divine providence. It is this older tradition of divine comedy that occasionally provided the allegorical structure of Renaissance tragedy at its most profound. Thus, in *King Lear* (ptd 1608), much of the catastrophe's terror depends on its almost negating the verities that medieval comedy would just at that point have upheld. Cordelia embodies everything that in a divine comedy would have triumphed. But in Shakespeare's vision her breath is not permitted quite to cloud the dark glass held by Lear. It need hardly be said that even features obviously comic in another sense – the Fool's nonsense and farce routines, and the grotesqueries associated with the blinded Gloucester (his farouche flax-tufted appearance; his leap from a non-existent cliff) – add further to the terror of the play. *King Lear* may be said to deepen, without controverting, the reach of divine comedy.

But this was not the only proportion the mixture of comedy and tragedy could maintain. From Attic tragedy onward, the possibility was envisaged that a serious play might end happily. In Renaissance Italy there were the *tragedie miste* or *tragedie con lieto fin* of Cinthio and Guarini; and Shakespeare took up the mixture in *Measure for Measure* (a. 1604) and his other misnamed 'problem plays'. But indeed it was already part of native English tradition. A common arrangement, continued in the more equally balanced tragicomedy of the seventeenth century, was for tragic and comic material to be distributed between distinct plots, serious and comic.

This fertile structural idea claims a digression. For more than a century, say from 1580 to 1690, it was quite usual for plays to have double or even multiple PLOTS – that is, patterns of events, causally and thematically connected. These would have linking characters, and perhaps an *ensemble* scene or two where the plots merged (as in the conclusion of Middleton's *The Changeling*). This convention had several origins. First, there was an ancient model in the comedies of Plautus and Terence – a more important factor than currently allowed. Secondly, the Moralities often contained contrasting exempla or rudimentary subplots, and moreover had groups of characters on different planes of existence – angels, men and vices. This model helps to explain why Jacobean plots and subplots tended to be in subtle moral relationship. For they were not necessarily linked in a causal way at all: their main connection was one of theme – often analogy, or contrast, or parody, or simply a scheme of shared coverage. Thus, the subsidiary intrigues in *The Alchemist* (a. 1610) treat various sorts of hypocrisy and illusion. And Shakespeare's *Troilus and Cressida* (a. 1600) draws a complex analogy between political and amorous plots of equal weight – between Hector's pursuit of true honour and Troilus's of true love – each Trojan being overcome by an efficient Greek opportunist of modern Tudor stamp. A third origin of multiple plots was an Italian doctrine that in all drama the social ranks should be segregated.

(Shakespeare generally avoids such segregation; yet *Much Ado About Nothing* (?1598) offers an example, with its three plots more or less corresponding to different levels of rank.) This explanation is the most relevant to tragicomedy. There, higher ranks were expected to receive more tragic, or at least more serious, treatment. The socially lower plot is commonly the more comic; although in the seventeenth century this was sometimes reversed for special effect by the more inventive (not necessarily more egalitarian) dramatists.

Much of the interest of tragicomedy lies in the interaction of its tragic and comic parts. Very different mixtures are possible, from the delicacies of Fletcher's *The Faithful Shepherdess* (a. 1608–9) to the grotesqueries of *The Changeling*, where bedlam humour actually darkens the horror. Francis Beaumont (1584–1616) and John Fletcher (1579–1625) crossed a significant threshold when they took up the ideas of Giovanni Battista Guarini (whose controversial *Il Pastor Fido* Fletcher imitated) and pursued an intermediate mood – a carefully judged nuance between comedy and tragedy. In their hands, tragicomedy became a highly sophisticated form, suited to the private theatres. There, artificiality was far from being counted a fault; and subtle theatrical effects could be cultivated for their own sake. Tragicomedy offered many such, for the intermediate mood was partly achieved by rapid oscillation between comedy and tragedy. (This was rather unreal; but then drama is not required to be always probable.) Astonishing switches of mood were cultivated – improbable *coups de théâtre* occasioning delicious *frissons* of sentiment. Such effects are not to be lightly dismissed: they include many valuable theatrical moments. After all, Shakespeare's last plays belong with this group. In Act V of *The Winter's Tale* (a. 1611), the mixture of contrary emotions becomes so exquisite that 'their joy waded in tears'.

Tragicomedy depended so much on the emotional effects of plot reversals that a congenial taste developed for subjectivism. Illusionistic effects were pursued, as if the theatrical experience itself was another emotional frame to be broken, detached from, reentered. Sudden switches of fictive status were by no means foreign to Jonson and the later Shakespeare ('Our revels now are ended. These our actors . . . were all spirits' (*The Tempest* IV.i.148–9)). But now they became a chief interest. The pioneer of this exploration had been John Marston, especially in his masterpiece *The Malcontent* (a. ?1600, ptd 1604).

The Malcontent is Altofront, a deposed duke, who, like Prospero in *The Tempest*, intrigues both to regain his dukedom and to convert his enemies. To that end he disguises himself as Malevole, a 'gross-jawed' satirist. But he sustains the persona so continuously (even when alone, as at III.ii.1–14) that an ambiguity seeps in. Is he only acting? Does the satire not 'really' emanate from Altofront? Or from the actor and dramatist? A still more brilliant effect – with Altofront acting Malevole acting a 'high-famed' former duke – flashes in the inset masque, that leads to the dropping of all the masks. In another passage, the reigning duke Pietro learns to play a hermit, and to test Mendoza's honesty by reporting his own death. Since he relates in direct speech what purport to be his dying words, he has the most taxing part of all – acting himself. Later, he makes his cell vividly real, as he describes 'the hollow murmur of the checkless winds' and 'the unquiet sea [that] Shakes the whole rock with foamy battery'. It may be something of a shock to reflect that the cell is an invention of Pietro's. In this play, illusion seems more palpable than fact.

Theatrical artifices of a related sort abound in the tragicomedies of Beaumont and Fletcher. Indeed, there is little in Fletcher's *The Faithful Shepherdess* (ptd ?1609; revived 1633) that can have been meant as direct imitation of life. What probability is there in Perigot's offering to commit suicide because his love Amoret expresses sexual feeling towards him (III.i.314)? The interest of the scene lies in the unexpectedly changing passions associated with different attitudes to chastity when they are physically acted out *au pied de la lettre*. Assembling so many variations and contrasts of sexual feeling partly reflects an interest in psychology – an interest diverted somewhat from moral character to emotion itself. Yet there is also a formal preoccupation, as if these ill-matched couples performed the figures of some poignant ballet. Their passions are so devalued and formalized that wounds and death come to function as ordinary ways of pledging faith. In *Philaster* (?1609) the eponymous hero is ready to kill Arathusa – or be killed by her (IV.v.61–70). And when a passing 'country fellow' objects to his wounding a woman, Arathusa herself scornfully replies: 'What ill-bred man art thou, to intrude thy self/Upon our private sports, our recreations?' The lover's rhetoric (as the rustic accurately calls it) expresses emotions that are not quite what they seem.

Beaumont and Fletcher's *The Maid's Tragedy* (?1610), although in the end purely tragic, also explores bizarre emotional territory. This finely polished work – one of the masterpieces, indeed, of the high mannerist or early baroque style – nevertheless has some puzzling discontinuities. Take, for example, the justly famous Act II, Scene i, already singled out in the seventeenth century. The wedding masque has been performed (not without deep reflections on the theatrical experience, likening the audience to 'gods'); and the bride Evadne has been prepared for bed by her maids, among them the bawdy Dula, whose jokes she obviously finds shocking. When her bridegroom Amintor invites her to bed she seems coyly disinclined, so that he concedes she may keep her maidenhead one night more. Her notorious reply – 'A maidenhead Amintor/At my years?' – initiates a series of PERIPETIES or reversals of expectation. She explains that she means never to sleep with him: she already has a lover. He demands the name, only to learn that his rival is the king himself. Amintor and Evadne soon agree to keep up appearances in. public – as she has been doing already. In fact, the audience has been deceived: the coy Evadne of the earlier scene never really existed. It is usual to speak here of protean or inconsistent characterization; but that may be to impose inappropriate naturalistic expectations. (A pardonable error, there is so much naturalism in Beaumont and Fletcher.) Perhaps the effect aimed at is more illusion-istic – startling the audience into a sample, as it were, of Amintor's shock. Such an impression would be a sort of realism, if not the sort usually expected in Jacobean drama. Nor, for that matter, does the static descriptive 'character' of grief in the following Scene ii fit the stereotype. Beaumont and Fletcher entertain many subtle doubts as to what parts of behaviour are acted and what 'real'; and – a different distinction, this – what parts authentic, what spurious.

Such questions hardly arise from the next phase of tragedy. During the seventeenth century's second decade the complex tragic form that we may call 'Shakespearean' underwent drastic simplification. Beau-mont and Fletcher, although their genius was not for tragedy at its darkest, more or less held together its dramatic and prosaic, literary and poetic elements – Fletcher contributing the latter. But John Webster and Thomas Middleton separated them widely; and in their hands tragedy became a less manifold form. Webster's *The White Devil* (a. 1612) and *The Duchess of Malfi* (a. ?1614) are still powerfully effective; but in the main their power is that of poetic tragedy. Their dramatic actions are improbable and not well constructed. Yet this hardly seems to matter, such is the symbolic validity of their poetic sequences. Speech after speech offers unforgettable poetry. The Duchess of Malfi, asked if the cord terrifies her, answers

> Not a whit:
> What would it pleasure me to have my throat cut
> With diamonds? or to be smothered
> With cassia? or to be shot to death with pearls?
> I know death hath ten thousand several doors

> For men to take their exits; and 'tis found
> They go on such strange geometrical hinges,
> You may open them both ways . . .
>
> (IV.ii.215–22)

It is in such poetic expression of sentiment or mood that the value of Webster's tragedies resides, rather than in any special fineness of moral action or turn of event.

Middleton presents almost the opposite development. In *The Changeling* (a. ?1622), hardly a speech is quotable; only technically in verse, it aims to observe the colloquial limits of diction. Or at least, its departures from them keep a low profile, avoiding anything much more stylish than de Flores's insistent black puns. And the characters are just as ordinary: convincing types, but types none the less. The situations, however, are strong; they could be called melodramatic – as when de Flores, claiming his reward, produces a severed finger. But even this is intelligibly motivated. It fits with the sexual meaning of the glove that he picked up for Beatrice in the very first scene, a symbol of her fascinated horror of him. He well knows how she would hate his fingers to be 'thrust . . . into her sockets'. Middleton's principal effort seems to go into arranging ironic echoes of this kind between widely separate passages. Every detail seems to have been analysed morally. And every symbolism (which is to say, each moral point) is not only lucidly expressed but underlined. In the subplot, the themes are acted out more literalistically: Antonio's and Franciscus's disguising as madmen in pursuit of a mistress shows that their love is a form of madness. Then, each firmness of Isabella in the subplot contrasts with a weakness of Beatrice's in the mainplot. And each loss of innocence on Beatrice's part brings its further intimacy with evil de Flores, the figure of sin. Middleton allows himself none of the morally ambiguous 'blurring' in which Webster indulges. Caroline drama (1625–42) is often called decadent; but this can hardly be said of Middleton. In fact, his tragedy is Puritan – continuously didactic, relentlessly moral. Like a Protestant equivalent of the old Morality, it develops a broad, obvious symbolism, confirmed in many sharp details but not dependent on any one of these. The elaborate tests of virginity, for example, belong with other contrasts in the play between simple faith and falsity's artificial contrivances.

Middleton's construction is brilliant – a perfect expression of his ironies of divine justice. But the moral content has a somewhat coarse grain. This shows in the style of *The Changeling*. Not that its language is at all crude or inert; indeed, it impresses as continually enlivened and sharp. But what continually enlivens it is always the same irony and point. It may be full of 'ambiguities', but they all serve the same unambiguous, conventional moral. There are few depths, no uncertainties, nothing problematic. Or at least, the problems can be worked out like puzzles.

One cannot but regret, a little, that Middleton and his contemporaries abandoned the deep questioning of character and psychology so boldly taken up in tragedy's preceding phase. The comparative interest of their female characters (morally anatomized though they are) is partial compensation.

DRAMATIC STYLE

These, then, are some of the individual forms of Elizabethan and Jacobean drama. It is natural to ask what characterized the period of greatest achievement, say from 1592 to 1622. Had it anything like a period style? One thing that stands out is how conscious of style the dramatists were – and how communicative about it. This consciousness of the *manner* of their art leads me to call it MANNERIST, adopting a term familiar from its use in art history. Dramatists of all the companies, both adult and children's (especially perhaps the latter), draw frequent attention to dramatic style – whether explicitly, like Shakespeare and Jonson, in passages of literary criticism, or implicitly through parody or variation of previous styles (for example, Peele's burlesque of the romantic play). Above all, they focus on the theatrical transaction itself, often returning to the fact of representation, its metaphysics, its morality, its style. We saw something of this in *The Malcontent* and *The Maid's Tragedy*, with their subtleties of fictive status.

There is more self-consciousness in Beaumont and Fletcher's *The Knight of the Burning Pestle* (ptd 1613), where a play (itself a parody of apprentice romance) is remade before our eyes in response to audience participation. Consciousness of representation also appears in implicit self-references, like Webster's 'I limned this night-piece'; as well as in such obvious analogies to drama as the puppet play in *Bartholomew Fair*. Or the audience may be so much involved, by direct address or reference, that the edge of the theatrical space becomes blurred, until they wonder where the acting stops. Well may Jaques in *As You Like It* (a. 1599) say that 'All the world's a stage/And all the men and women merely players', or the Host in *The New Inn* (a. 1629) that

> All the world's a play;
> The state, and men's affairs, all passages

Of life, to spring new scenes, come in, go out,
And shift, and vanish . . .

Such generalities belong to no particular age. But in this period there was a special disposition to toy with a play's framing or abutment on reality, in such a manner as to confuse (or sharpen) the audience's sense of where precisely the boundary lay. Thus, the Induction Webster added to *The Malcontent* calls for a stage audience – no doubt mixed with real spectators – who discuss the play with the actors. Who should the 'spectator' acted by Will Sly (a well-known actor) ask to see, but Will Sly? And in *A Mad World, My Masters* (a. ?1605), the props that the con man Follywit borrows for an inset play are 'real' valuables. Plays within plays themselves acquired new significance as a means of reflecting on the dramatist's art. *Love's Labour's Lost* (a. 1594), *A Midsummer Night's Dream* (a. ?1596) and *Bartholomew Fair* (a. 1614) have each an inset play at the climax – an unimpressive play, but one that nevertheless contains large implications. As for *The Taming of the Shrew*, it is itself an inset play, watched by Christopher Sly.

These features all appear in *Hamlet*, the supreme mannerist or early baroque play. Here long passages are given over to discussing dramatic style and instructing the players. There is a play within the play. And in this inset play of the murder of Gonzago (itself framed by dumb show and prologue), Hamlet arranges for the insertion of lines of his own, a further inset of 'non-fictional' material designed to establish the king's guilt. When the Gonzago play is acted before Claudius and his court, Hamlet and Horatio watch how Claudius himself 'acts', to see if he will drop his mask. Meanwhile the real audience is watching Hamlet watch his stepfather, and beyond, doubtless, 'the gods themselves [do] see' (II.ii.543). Such multiple inclusions, which appear in other plays of the period, constitute framing of a particular style. In visual art, too, very elaborate frames were then in vogue. But the complexity of framing can also pose uncomfortable paradoxes of moral authenticity – as if only conscious actors were authentic.

The comic possibilities of inset plays were endless. In Middleton's *A Mad World*, for example, Follywit cheats his uncle Sir Bounteous Progress by disguising himself as a travelling player. He borrows valuables as props, and while his accomplices ride off with these, he gains time by delivering a prologue to the nonexistent play they were supposed to act. But the gang is brought back under arrest by a constable, so that Follywit has to improvise a play to follow his prologue, after all. In it, he acts a nepotistic magistrate, perhaps not much unlike his uncle. He pronounces that the constable is wasting his time, has him bound and gagged, and exits with his friends. Reality does not easily break in on Sir Bounteous: a fair time elapses before he grasps that although the uniformed clown remains on stage, there is not going to be any more play: 'Art not thou the constable in the comedy?' – 'In the comedy? Why I am the constable in the commonwealth, sir.' The shifting frame of this inset play lets one glimpse how real life consists of similar dissimulation. Middleton's usual way is to work out a simple moral very fully, in a wealth of theatrically effective scenes.

The manneristic taste for self reference found special satisfaction in CITY COMEDY, the satirical genre that around 1598 was beginning to replace the romantic comedy of Shakespeare's middle period. From its beginning in Jonson's comical satire – as early as *The Case is Altered* (a. ?1597) – city comedy was full of dramatic theory and theatrical gossip. Its inductions theorized: its characters commented on the action or the spectators: and its authors used it for missiles in the war of the theatres. (In this half-serious war, Jonson – whose aggressive drives were such as to lead him into fatal duels – took a special delight.) *Eastward Ho* (a. 1605) is even smart enough to caricature the stock characters and uninventive situations of city comedy itself. The genre expressed London's growing self-consciousness. This was reflected especially in its keenly relished local settings, which became a regular feature: Jonson even rewrote *Every Men in His Humour* (a. 1598), giving it a detailed London *mise-en-scène*. The culmination of the tendency came with the *Alchemist* (a. 1610), which is set in Blackfriars, in the very building where Jonson's company, the King's Men, played. City comedy thus offered an extremely topical and colloquial, essentially prose form – a perfect vehicle for surveys of emergent social types, or for direct self-appraisal. If it sometimes gives a lurid impression of almost total corruption, this is partly because it regularly works by exaggeration and extrapolation. Middleton in particular has a genius for taking evil to its own entirely logical conclusions. And Jonson's *Bartholemew Fair*, like some dramatization of Brueghel, fairly teems with energetic common life, all of it unremittingly (although sometimes affectionately) caricatured.

Mannerism found expression in every dramatic element – even in disguise. Always a useful comic device, disguise was now a principal resource. Partly this reflected an actual court pastime; partly it turned to advantage the fact that female parts were played by boys – transvestite disguise, especially, making a virtue of necessity. At the same time, it had the effect of highlighting the theatrical fiction itself. As for its deeper motivation, that may have had to do with the increasing sense that personality hid inaccessibly behind façades. Some instances, like that of Follywit, prompt one to see disguise as implying a lack of authenticity. On the other hand, dissimulation might be only practical – recognition of the inevitable disparities between what is and what shows. Disguise might even indicate a component to be assimilated in character formation. Or it might represent a phase of the character, left behind at the resolution (Shakespeare's Viola and Perdita come to mind).

Disguises could, of course, be multiplied. Jonson's *The New Inn* (a. 1629), a deliberately old-fashioned, high mannerist work, carries the device to extremes that demand interpretation. Many of the characters are disguised, some in ways so complex and improbable as to defy disentanglement, calling into question the whole idea of disguise. Jonson emphasizes the fictionality of such resolutions. Thus, the Host's son Francis is disguised as a girl: to trick Lady Frampull's lovers he pretends to be her kinswoman Laetitia. But in the dénouement it turns out that he really *is* her sister, that his *true* name is Laetitia. Jonson carries to absurd lengths the disclosure of identity that typifies the romantic play. His ridicule, however, is nostalgic and gentle. Indeed, the romantic conclusion suggests thoughts about our profoundest motives for fiction – thoughts even more serious than those evoked by the earlier, more classical, part of the play. There, all the disguises have clear moral meanings; so that Beaufort, for example, makes love to the disguised Frank because he is always deceived by appearances in love. But in the end, the mistaken joys that captivate erring mortals turn out to be true joy in disguise.

EXTERNAL INTERACTIONS

In this chapter I have tried to find an internal logic in the development of Renaissance drama. Another approach might have dwelt more on interactions with neighbouring or contemporary forms. The vogue of verse satire in the 1590s, for example, had a clear reflection in the satiric comedy of Jonson and others (*Poetaster* III.i actually dramatizes a satire of Horace's). And it was the popularity of romantic fiction that led to romantic plays and to their burlesque in such works as *The Knight of the Burning Pestle*. Again, musical forms contributed to drama, in ways only now being appreciated. Or, one might have traced the mutual influences of drama and MASQUE. A mixed media form, masque depended mainly on music, stage architecture, semi-dramatic poetry, dance and costume for its effects, which were often spectacular. The texts that have survived, even those that resulted from Ben Jonson's and Inigo Jones's collaboration, are now often obscure; since the masques themselves relied extensively on mythology and iconography, systems that have become obsolete. Corresponding in some ways to the double plots of drama, masque had two components, called 'masque' and 'antimasque'. These offered independent treatments of the theme in high and low, serious and grotesque modes respectively. Stage plays often borrowed masque conventions; incorporated parts of a recent masque (like the rustic dance in *The Winter's Tale*); or even had fictional masques inset within their own structure. In part, then, masque had a parallel development. But, being as it were a high-life equivalent of pageant, it tended to be more used for propaganda purposes – not only in support of the regime, but by all factions. The development of masque was naturally much interrupted (although never quite ended) after the outbreak of the Civil War and removal of the court in 1642.

Drama underwent much the same external influences as the rest of literature, for example through patronage and intellectual movements. But in addition it had to contend with contingencies like restraints upon acting for months at a time because of plague; and it had to fit in with the Church year. (It has emerged that Renaissance drama was inherently occasional, being adjusted in content and form to the great festivals.) There were also restraints of moral and political censorship, as is well known. However, one should not think of the Puritans as being invariably opposed to theatrical entertainment *per se*. Several of the patrons and even of the dramatists (Middleton, Massinger, Davenport and others) were of the Puritan tendency. However that may be, external political events overtook internal developments decisively when the public theatres were closed altogether in 1642. It is debated how far, even then, the Interregnum meant a break in dramatic tradition. For publication, private performances and the careers of dramatists (Davenant, Shirley) continued throughout.

It is remarkable that a form of literature so popular, with so much topical involvement, and open to so many external influences, could reach heights of literary achievement. One explanation may lie in the extent to which drama still belonged to oral tradition. Book learning had a lesser part in comprehending its depths, and convention a greater. However that may be, there is no doubt that in the hands of Shakespeare and Jonson at least, and of the best of their successors, Renaissance dramatic forms could serve as instruments of creative power.

5

The Earlier Seventeenth Century

By 1600 Sidney and Spenser, Marlowe and Peele, Hooker and Nashe were dead. Chapman and the temporarily neglected Drayton maintained some continuity; and the latter would have a revival in the 1630s. But a new literary movement was gathering way, which took its direction from two contrasting major figures, John Donne and Ben Jonson, both of them twenty-seven at the turn of the century. It was a movement away from the flowing amplitude of the Elizabethans to a style compressed, concise, even charged. To understand it one has to know something about epigram: of its special place in Renaissance education and of its European vogue – a vogue now further stimulated by growing knowledge of the Greek Anthology. In schools and universities a series of genres of epigram were taught, much like the formulations of elegy, satire and other classical kinds on a larger scale. All writers of any education learned to write these miniature kinds; in that sense all became partly classical – although, as we shall see, they were so in very different ways. What they all shared, however, was brevity. Wit no longer showed itself in copiousness or piquant incident, but in compression.

DONNE AND THE METAPHYSICAL POETS

John Donne (1572–1631) was not a professional poet like Drayton or Jonson. His poems were never published in his lifetime, even if many were written before he was twenty-five and circulated in manuscript. Yet he made a lasting mark with his satires and love ELEGIES (short thoughtful love poems), and to a lesser extent with his divine poems. Taking up Sidney's and Drayton's strategy of a passionate speaker, he made it more powerfully convincing. The narrator in Donne's *Satires* may recall Horace's. But no recent poet had kept up a dramatic voice so believable, so forceful, with such spontaneous and superior vitality:

Sir; though (I thank God for it) I do hate
Perfectly all this town, yet there's one state
In all ill things so excellently best,
That hate, towards them, breeds pity towards the rest.

(Satires ii.1–4)

It is actable monologue – even, in places, dialogue. The mention of acting may serve as a reminder not to confuse the voice with Donne's own. (He takes up several incompatible roles; and whereas he has poetic feeling to a high degree, the same cannot quite be said of his sincerity.) The vehemence and apparent ease of transcription from emotional life were in Donne's own time, as they are still, almost irresistibly influential. Many of the qualities of the so-called Metaphysical school – George Herbert (1593–1633), Henry King (1592–1669), John Cleveland (1613–58), Henry Vaughan (1622–95) and the rest – have to do with this choice of a dramatic voice that is intellectually acute, or quick to impart intimate thoughts. For example, intimate speech entailed a rhetorically 'low' or plain diction. Contrary to a usual view, the Metaphysicals do not differ from Jonson in that respect.

This plainness need not make them easy to read. Their rhetorical innovations militate against that. Poets can concentrate their effort on meanings stated syntactically; or (what often leads to greater difficulty) on meanings implied by extra-syntactic connections. When Donne wrote, one of those periodic swings was in progress that help to bring in changes in literary taste. Interest was shifting away from schemes – rhetorical arrangements dependent on ordinary syntax – to tropes, or figures affecting and supplementing syntax. The difference can be brought out by taking an extreme instance of the earlier schematic style such as these lines from a 'reporting sonnet' attributed to Ralegh:

Her face, her tongue, her wit, so fair, so sweet, so sharp,
First bent, then drew, now hit, mine eye, mine ear, my heart: . . .

The syntax is much like that of prose, only complicated by the permutational arrangement. Contrast this from Donne:

The world's whole sap is sunk:
The general balm th'hydroptic earth hath drunk,
Whither, as to the bed's-feet, life is shrunk,
Dead and interred . . .

('A Nocturnal Upon S. Lucy's Day' 5–8)

The main statement is about the diseased earth drinking up life's vital fluid. But it is supplemented by others expressed through poetic or 'lexical syntax', in which much of the interest lies. Implicitly, 'bed's feet' is linked not only with human feet but also with the plant stems (conduits of 'sap') that the ornamental legs of beds sometimes resembled. Poems with meaning so unobvious, and moreover compressed, could easily become difficult. (Too difficult, Dryden was to think.) As Donne's contemporary Jasper Mayne put it, 'we are thought wits, when 'tis understood'. What carries the difficulty off is partly singleness of thrust. For by comparison with Shakespeare's poetic logic, for example, Donne's is relatively simple. (Of course, his prominent argumentation – which was imitated and became common in seventeenth-century poetry – can make his logic seem complex, even when it is only intricate.)

In fact it is one of the chief features of Donne's poetry, and that of his best imitators, that the figures are organized around a single dominating idea or CONCEIT (*concetto*; 'device'). These conceits are, however, very different from the Spenserian or Shakespearean type. In the first place, they bring together things that are primarily unlike, such as fleas and marriage temples; so that the comparison seems 'far-fetched', 'unpoetic', novel. (The train of thought may be erudite or pseudo-erudite; but seldom scientific.) Second, the Metaphysical conceit has a distinctive, relatively simple metaphoric structure. Characteristically, a single set of tenor items matches a single set of vehicle items. Thus in Donne's 'The Flea', the 'blood' that is 'sucked' by the 'flea' and 'mingled' within its black body corresponds to the blood that would be mingled during the sexual act (according to current belief) by spouses in a 'marriage temple' with 'walls of jet'. Throughout, this misunderstood poem's purpose is to diminish casual sex by portraying it as a travesty of marriage.

After Donne, those who imitated him or who have been grouped with him did very different things with the conceit. Some used it for gallantry and preposterous wit: Suckling likened love to a fart; Marvell drew it into comparison with a pair of parallel lines. Others made the new poetry serve religious ends. Crashaw devised conceits that, while emblematic, are also sensuous and sensational, in a baroque, rather un-English way. In 'The Weeper' he strings many such together in a rosary-like catena of stanza–epigrams. Vaughan and Traherne preferred quieter figures. But all are overshadowed now by George Herbert, the dominating figure of the group, and a finer religious poet even than Donne. Herbert drew his comparisons from the Bible and the liturgy; so that they were involved in the subtleties of commentary and allegory and pious epigram. To the latter form of wit he was indeed no stranger: besides *The Temple* (1633), he wrote a Latin sacred epigram sequence *Lucus*. His greatest English poems, however, are deeply rather than cleverly meditated. He likes conceits based on homely or familiar things – as when he compares Divine Love to a human host: 'You must sit down, says Love, and taste my meat'. The unostentatious quietness is deceptive; disguising a horrific word play in 'my meat'. Herbert modestly sinks a substructure of great art and a wealth of emblematic images.

In a poem like 'Virtue', he will characteristically seem to have moved quietly through a series of ordinary, even commonplace metaphors:

> Sweet spring, full of sweet days and roses,
>   A box where sweets compacted lie;
> My music shows ye have your closes [cadences],
>   And all must die.
>
> Only a sweet and virtuous soul,
>   Like seasoned timber, never gives;
> But though the whole world turn to coal,
>   Then chiefly lives.
>
> ('Virtue' 9–16)

But each facet of each metaphor reflects with another, in such a way that successive readings gradually build to a composition of parts, until all is interconnected and resonant. Here, the 'sweet rose' of an earlier stanza was a regular emblem of mortal flesh; but its hue of 'angry' virtue connects it also with the 'sweet and virtuous soul', while its petals lie in a box as 'sweets compacted'. 'Compacted', however, being a musical term, refers to the moral harmony of the virtuous soul, often thought of then as like the diapason or unison of 'closes'. The soul turns out to be like the contents of the box (musical box? coffin?) in more ways than can at first easily be grasped. Here, as in 'Aaron', in 'The Collar', in 'Affliction (1)' and in many other poems, Herbert achieves religious poetry that has never been surpassed.

The Metaphysical poets are not finally to be characterized by their spoken, colloquial diction (that, they shared with the Cavalier lyrists), but rather by a crisp pointed wit that may find its focus in conceits of a special type. As for the scientific material that was once supposed to be a Metaphysical feature, only Cowley made much use of it. For the movement was not new in the sense of using new material. Indeed, its religious wing, in particular, often returned – for example in intricate typology – to medieval ways of thinking. The whole movement was intelligibly regarded as 'gothic' by critics of the Augustan period to follow. From the point of view of immediate development, it was the new classicism of Jonson and his disciples that faced forward.

Ben Jonson (1572–1637), a great and thoroughly professional poet, had a wide range of strengths, on which he was able to draw at will for very various purposes. Except on a few occasions, however, he rejected the Metaphysical way of pretending to think aloud 'spontaneously', preferring the sincerer fiction of one who openly makes a poem.

> Make not thyself a page
> To that strumpet the stage;
> But sing high and aloof . . .
> ('An Ode. To Himself')

He is not less witty than Donne, but his wit condenses in a quite dissimilar way. For the sense is worked out in the interest of clarity, and couched in such a manner that the form – often the very sound – rests in agreement with it. Even the surface meaning (always lucid in Jonson) is a good pointer to what his poems mean. Deeper meanings may lie hidden, but they are generally in accord with the obvious ones. Jonson says everything several times, simultaneously, in different ways; and this consonance, this mutual confirmation of elements, earns for his poetry an effect of integrity and weight. It has roundness, rightness and outrightness; so that, even when spoken rather than sung, it seems fuller than ordinary speech.

These are classical qualities; and to some extent the entire so-called 'Tribe' or 'Sons of Ben', the largest literary group of the early seventeenth century, including – either by allegiance or resemblance – Herrick, Carew, Suckling, Lovelace and Aytoun, can be associated with a classicizing tendency. Earlier, Spenser and Drayton had done much to establish classical kinds: Drayton's odes, in particular, had a fresh and authentic classical firmness. But the Tribe of Ben, besides turning on occasion to rather smarter models (Lucan, Seneca, Philostratus), did more to realize classical forms in their true proportions. Not infrequently they practised the ancient kinds with something of their original variety and precision.

Literary kinds have a vital significance, quite independently of any question of 'correctness'. They assist imitative outreaching, whether explicit in the finished form or hidden in the genesis of the work. And they offer a matrix within which poems can be conceived, far beyond the capacity of a single writer. This happens on the smallest scale; as when a pastoral motif, introduced by Jonson in *The Sad Shepherd* from Persius and Claudian, is developed by Edmund Waller ('At Penshurst'),

George Granville, Lord Lansdowne ('To Flavia') and Charles Hopkins (*White-hall*, 1698); and culminates in Pope's great line 'Where'er you tread, the blushing Flowers shall rise' ('Summer' 75). On the larger scale of complete works, the same obtains. Garden poems by Joseph Beaumont, James Shirley and others make a group from which Marvell's 'The Garden' stands out. Jonson's 'Inviting a Friend to Supper', based on Martial, is itself imitated in Herrick's satirical 'The Invitation' – a tradition that forms an important part of the context of Pope's Imitation of Horace's *Satires* II.ii. And a long pastoral and georgic tradition combining Virgil's with Isaiah's Messianic visions lifts Pope to one of the heights of *Windsor Forest*. In such cases, the shared expectations formed by the kinds make possible rapid uptake of the subtlest implications. Such imitation, far from being slavish, can constitute a means of communicating highly original effects. In the seventeenth century it was the basis of a public style whose easiness was reconcilable with depth.

Much of the period's poetry celebrated social occasions like weddings (of which an epithalamium might form an actual part), or contributed to relations with patrons or friends. Such OCCASIONAL VERSE has sometimes been disparaged. It has seemed too consciously willed to be inspired, its smart exaggerated compliments too obviously motivated. But that view hardly makes allowance for an older readiness to recognize obligation, and to work within temporal limits. Nor does it allow for the power of occasional verse to civilize social life. Such poetry can be at least as fine as the relations it celebrates.

In most periods literature depends on some form of patronage. Although in the seventeenth century the munificence of the great declined, much was owed to such patrons as Charles I and Prince Henry; the earls of Pembroke, Southampton and Newcastle; Sir Lucius Cary; Fulke Greville; Charles Cotton; Endymion Porter and Katherine Philips (the 'Matchless Orinda'). Women figure prominently in this register of greatness. The Countess of Pembroke – Sidney's sister and herself a poet – was a patron of Daniel, Breton, Jonson and others. Certain great houses became important centres of literary production. Great Tew, the seat of Sir Lucius Cary, Second Viscount Falkland, was 'like a college' (Aubrey), 'a university bound in a lesser volume' (Clarendon); Jonson resorted there, and Sandys and Waller and Hobbes. Other such 'colleges' included Wilton (the seat of the earls of Pembroke) and the Sidneys' Penshurst. Sir Philip Sidney's brother, sister, daughter and niece were all writers hospitable to writers. In such cases, relations between patron and clients could be close and good.

This is reflected in many poems of patronage: most especially in
ESTATE POEMS or country-house poems, which characterize the patron
by allegorizing his possessions. The best known is Jonson's 'To
Penshurst', a firmly constructed encomiastic epigram–ode in fifty-one
couplets. It catalogues amenities of the estate of Lord Lisle (Sir Philip
Sidney's brother), first outside the house and then inside; treating
several of them as moral emblems – like the silver eel, which signified
the slipperiness a magistrate had to control with firm grip:

> Bright eels, that emulate them, and leap on land
> Before the fisher, or into his hand.
>
> ('To Penshurst' 37–8)

Implicitly, the poem recommends Lisle to be content with his house's
relatively unostentatious and unimproved state. But throughout it
expresses evident respect for the Sidneys, and appreciation of the
freedom of their hospitality from consciousness of rank:

> Where comes no guest but is allowed to eat
> Without his fear, and of thy lord's own meat;
> Where the same beer and bread and self-same wine
> That is his lordship's shall be also mine.
>
> (lines 61–4)

Carew's imitation of this influential poem follows its topics closely,
but lays very different emphases. Scrupulous distinction of rank is what
he admires in Wrest's hospitality:

> Some of that ranke, spun of a finer thred
> Are with the Women, Steward and Chaplaine fed
> With daintier cates; Others of better note
> Whom wealth, parts, office, or the Heralds coate
> Have severed from the common, freely sit
> At the Lords Table . . .
>
> ('To my friend G. N. from Wrest' 37–42)

Herrick, by contrast, in his fine panegyric to 'princely Pemberton', is as
near-egalitarian as Jonson. And he presses in more content; holding
more surely to the genre's characteristic emblematic strand. In all these
poems – and in others besides, like Andrew Marvell's 'Upon Appleton
House' – the existence of kindred works allows the poet to convey much
by implication. Indeed, a special theme can be stressed merely by its
comparative prominence. With the Puritan Marvell it is the historical
dimension of General Fairfax's lordship and political responsibilities
that stands out in this way.

The estate poem was not a genre recognized by seventeenth-century critics: they would have been more likely to think of such writing as georgic. For it was one of the great innovations of the century to revive georgic, a mode neglected by the Elizabethans and sometimes not even considered poetry. The new idea of GEORGIC, by no means based exclusively on Virgil's *Georgics*, derived also from Hesiod's *Works and Days* and other didactic classics. It was a loose conception of digressive poetry in the poet's own voice, instructing in arts or morals, describing landscape, or recommending the good life of retirement (as in *Georgics* ii). English georgics were likely to be country poems, but not pastoral so much as rustic. Sometimes general and contemplative, they were as often concerned with particulars of work and the seasonal round – the 'greeny calendar', as Herrick puts it. One strand of topographical poetry led from Drayton's great *Poly-Olbion* through poems like Waller's 'To Penshurst' and Cotton's *The Wonders of the Peak* (1681), with its description of Chatsworth. Elsewhere, Cotton's neat transcriptions of nature in his quatrains on the seasons and times of day have the fresh *simplesse* of a van Goyen:

> Each one has had his Supping Mess,
> The Cheese is put into the Press,
> The Pans and Bowls clean scalded all,
> Reared up against the Milk-house Wall.

Another strand, which was to exert an even stronger pull on the Augustans, connected prospective poems and celebrations of building construction. Waller, for example, mingled Virgilian patriotism with description of architectural work in 'On St James's Park'. But perhaps it was John Denham who offered the most decisive mediation of Virgil's *Georgics*, in his prospective poem *Cooper's Hill* (1642; 1655; 1668) – particularly in the fine passage on the Thames, combining a vision of world trade with patriotic enthusiasm. Denham's firm construction and abstract patterns of balance may not be altogether to the modern taste; but there is no doubt of their appeal to the Augustans. And far more than generalized abstraction energizes his famous couplet, which will serve the next generation as a universal model:

> Though deep, yet clear, though gentle, yet not dull,
> Strong without rage, without o'er-flowing full.
>
> (*Cooper's Hill* (1655) 191–2)

Here are marvellously compressed parallels and contrasts in content and in form (of depth; perspicuity; movement; containment; assonances; phrase length; word length, order and repetition). But there is also a new complexity in the subject. The river may seem a natural one, or political, or one altogether symbolic of poetry. ('Smooth' and 'strong' were respectively terms for Jonsonian and Metaphysical qualities of poetic style.) Such implicit, even oblique, subjects became, during this period, quite common. Another example is Lovelace's 'The Grass-hopper', which is far from being merely about a chirping insect.

With these georgic groupings the estate poems obviously belong. Their descriptive and digressive method, to say nothing of their topics of improvement, hunting, feasting and the happy life, all make this clear. Marvell's 'Upon Appleton House', indeed, is a full-scale georgic poem: to the generic topics I have mentioned, it adds historical retrospection, retirement, and the description of agricultural labour. Many other works of the period that have been difficult to place should probably also be seen as georgic. Milton's *L'Allegro and Il Penseroso*, which describes the happy life in two contrasting moods, is pure georgic in its digressive sequence, its temporal organization and its sharp descriptive detail:

> When the gust hath blown his fill,
> Ending on the rustling leaves,
> With minute-drops from off the eaves.
> 　　　　　(*Il Penseroso* 128–30)

To georgic belongs some of the century's finest poetry – and the most typical of a period occupied with new subjects and the adaptation of classical conventions to treat them.

THE EPIGRAMMATIC TRANSFORMATION

Donne's characteristically complete unification, together with his quick wit, strongly suggests epigram; which makes it seem strange at first that he did so little in that kind (for his epigrams are few and poor). But then one sees how it is. Actually epigram appears everywhere in his work. The so-called *Songs and Sonnets* are, of course, love ELEGIES – erotic, figurative, often thoughtful in their prolonged movement to discoveries and illuminations. Yet they have something of epigram too. Look at their closures: ' . . . Being double dead, going, and bidding go' ('The Expiration'); 'Just so much honour, when thou yield'st to me, / Will waste, as this flea's death took life from thee' ('The Flea'); 'That since you would save none of me, I bury some of you' ('The Funeral'); 'Racked carcases make ill anatomies' ('Love's Exchange'). As often as not they are pointed, or witty, rather than simply passionate. And similar POINTS are to be found throughout; although the tone they presuppose was not thought particularly suitable for love elegies. In fact, one has to think of Donne's *Songs and Sonnets* as epigrammatic transformations of elegy – elegies compressed and sharpened. When Dryden and Dr Johnson censured Metaphysical love poems, what they ultimately disliked may have been this 'impurity' of kinds. For Donne's style is a mixture. Its diction must once have seemed too ordinary – too 'low' – for its figures. And its epigrammatic compression could be thought to put too much pressure on the syntax for poems meant to move the emotions. About 1732, Spence wrote that 'the majority of [Donne's] pieces are nothing but a tissue of epigrams'.

Many of Ben Jonson's poems show a comparable tendency. However much they may contrast with Donne's, in this respect they are little different. True, Jonson avoids flamboyant effects of mixture. It is in a consistently plain style that he pursues epigrammaticism:

> Farewell, thou child of my right hand, and joy;
> My sin was too much hope of thee, loved boy . . .
> (*Epigrams* xlv, 'On My First Son')

Many of Jonson's poems are pure epigrams, as their great compression and their sharp, hard definition show. But they are epigrams with new emotional (and indeed, physical) dimensions.

Drayton's later poems also became epigrammatic. But to give instances is misleading. It was an almost universal change, affecting most of the literature of the earlier seventeenth century. And it was as comprehensive in its effects: it cannot be understood merely in terms of imagery or style height (as used to be attempted). It was a sweeping generic transformation, affecting every literary element and most kinds. For example, mythology, which was not in general part of the epigram repertoire, came to be limited severely to special purposes. Significant works marking phases of the transformation include Marlowe's *Hero and Leander* (posthumous, 1598); Sir John Davies's 'Gulling Sonnets' and *Epigrams and Elegies* (1590?); Spenser's anacreontics (1595); Chapman's Homeric epigrams (1616); Bacon's *Essays* (1597, 1612, 1625); and Joseph Hall's 'Characters of Virtues and Vices' (1608). Kind after kind was modulated into an epigrammatical key. And meanwhile epigram itself kept extending its territory by mixture, aggregation, or simple enlargement; until Dryden (translating Boileau) could write that epigrammatic points had 'overwhelmed Parnassus with their Tide', and found their way into prose as well. The tide turned only with the century. Then the Augustans were to think of points as 'little gothic ornaments of epigrammatical conceits'. Conceited poetry, especially that of the late Metaphysicals, would be dismissed as false wit.

In the meantime, epigram had a long run, and a chance to show its varied potentialities. Along one line of development, the Metaphysical conceit could be compressed into ever smaller compass, until an extreme was reached in Clevelandism. John Cleveland's conceits, often contained within a couplet, are so brief as to be initially difficult, as in this from 'The Antiplatonic':

> Love's Votaries enthral each other's soul,
> Till both of them live but upon Parole.

(Besides its modern sense, 'parole' could mean a declaration.) Or take Cleveland's elegy 'On the Archbishop of Canterbury':

> There's nothing lives, life is, since he is gone,
> But a Nocturnall Lucubration.

This is epigrammatic brevity indeed. Along another line, epigram itself could be promoted in importance. So, from one point of view, Andrew Marvell's 'Upon Appleton House' can almost be seen as an enlarged estate epigram: a georgic epigram on a grand scale. For, however largely it aspires, its individual stanzas remain rigorously economical and nimble-witted – as in the gentle burlesque of the house's history: 'A Nunnery first gave it birth. / For Virgin Buildings oft brought forth.'

The culmination of epigram came with Robert Herrick (1591–1674), who best exploited the genre's freedom of subject and power of cumulative effect. After apprenticeship as a goldsmith, and Cambridge, Herrick achieved reputation as a poet in London, where he knew Jonson; but from 1629 (except when dispossessed) he was Vicar of Dean Prior in Devonshire. Although hardly a Cavalier, he showed the Cavalier poet's adventurousness in genre. *Hesperides and Noble Numbers* (1648), his double volume of 1,400 epigrams, miniaturizes kind after kind: lyric, sonnet, satire, eclogue, funeral elegy, love elegy (a sequence of them blazon Julia's several features), ode, epithalamium, and many others – even epic. Some are exalted, some ugly or obscene. Anthologists pick out the sweet flower-pieces; but even these argue mortality. And together with the compliments and satires they compose a complete Hesperides garden of elect flowers facing reprobate weeds. It is Herrick's western world in microcosm, illuminated by a georgic vision of human variety and growth regulated by a 'greeny calendar'. This calendrical metaphor relates almost everything in the collection, with a continuity that T. S. Eliot ('What is Minor Poetry?') seems to have missed. What changes and what lasts is Herrick's great subject: 'Time's transshifting'.

That coinage is one of many haunting words in Herrick; for he was almost the first poet to make single words tell. So 'Upon Julia's Clothes' uses a polysyllabic word to devastating effect:

> When as in silks my Julia goes,
> Then, then (me thinks) how sweetly flows
> That liquefaction of her clothes.

'Li-que-fac-tion' – the rhythm dissolves it, pausing exquisitely yet flowing easily too, like the fashionably loose silks themselves. Figuratively, 'liquefaction' meant a melting of the soul. So Herrick will often throw new weight on individual words, making them do more work and more sorts of work. In the same poem, Julia's 'brave Vibration' has more to it than the obvious sensuality: 'vibration' was a scientific term for the oscillatory movement that made *heavenly* spheres gleam with light. As often in Herrick, cool exalted ideas raise sensuousness to an ideal plane, in such a way as to evoke a strange poetic world, far from the usual range of epigram. (It is a world that will appeal to the Romantics.) Sometimes he creates mysterious Keatsian death-rites that reach out from this life into the next ('The Funeral Rites of the Rose') until we can no longer say on which side of death the fiction lies. The Hesperidean garden was among other things a land of the dead. But Herrick's poetry also addressed itself to present life. Even his antiquarian classicism served an ideal of civility that he pursued in response to the challenge of his own time – the engulfing of traditions in disorder and change. The ancient world offered hope of an uncontroversial social model.

The epigrammatic transformation amounted to a fundamental change: a revolution in literature. Although it was a passing stylistic fashion, it was also much more – if only because it left a lasting inheritance of far-reaching significance. For it achieved a new closeness of texture and economy of language, setting benchmarks for all subsequent literature. The new scale is one we take for granted. It is simply the scale of literature as we know it, the density we expect. Yet before the seventeenth century the close attention now given quite generally was confined to the Bible, the ancient classics, and a few neo-Latin and vernacular poets (notably Dante and Spenser). This change in the scale of attention is reflected in overall proportions. Thus *Paradise Lost*, although quite as ambitious a poem as *The Faerie Queene*, could be completed in a third of the length; and subsequently no great poem has been much longer than Milton's. Other lasting effects of the epigrammatic shift include the idea of a single, flexible style that can be applied to almost any subject. Before the seventeenth century only the epigram was subject-free; since, almost all poetry has come to be so.

SENECAN PROSE

Epigrammatic transformation affected prose nearly as much. Here too it showed in sprinklings of inset epigrams, particularly at the closures of paragraphs and chapters. And, more pervasively, it compressed prose style. Tudor prose now seems by comparison rather wordy. The epigrammatic modulation also assisted a new plainness. Those who see literature as progressive will surely count among the century's great achievements a simple lucid style capable of exposition or argument. Natural and spontaneous rhythms were set free, and for the first time there was a possibility of fully individual styles.

Changes in genre and in style were involved with a deeper change in the very aims of prose. This was thought of, and argued over, as one might expect, in terms of classical models. In a sense only the models changed, from Cicero to the silver-age Seneca and Tacitus. The Ciceronian rhetoric of longwinded superfluity and affected ornament was displaced by the gravity of SENECAN PROSE: terse, pregnant, majestic, oracular. Or (another point of view) copiousness and pure round neat composition were threatened by a fashionably abrupt 'hopping style', crabbed, portentous, incoherent and obscure. But again the anti-Ciceronian movement was more than a fashion. Its advent, notably in Bacon, signalled a change of attitude towards style itself − or, rather, away from it. This was conveyed perforce by stylistic means. All the same, the emphasis now fell on things rather than words. The shape of writing had to follow the content directly, not by way of formal symmetries or symbolic patterns. But when this programme was carried out, the content itself seems often in the event to have been found to be patterned. The style of Senecan authors, which used to be described as asymmetrical, is now thought to have its own symmetries, only less obvious than the older ones.

Senecan or Attic prose has actually two contrasting styles, the CURT and the LOOSE. The loose keeps the fluency of Ciceronian style, but adds naturalness and spontaneous changes of direction. It is easy and colloquial, and simplifies towards the plainness of epigram − just as the curt style might be regarded as taking up epigram's point and compression. From the counterpoint of the two Senecan styles (to say nothing of occasional reversions to Ciceronian periods) sprang many of the individual effects we admire in seventeenth century prose.

Several prose kinds were adapted to suit these styles – or invented, it almost seems, to accommodate them. Writing is responsive to criticism; and some of the finest seventeenth century achievements were in the sermon, a genre specially well provided for in rhetorical theory. A large part of medieval rhetoric had been concerned with sermon composition. To this, a new infusion of classical rhetoric was added, so that sermons had every chance of being sophisticated literary productions. Besides their homiletic and spiritual value, they often had the intellectual excitement – sometimes the intense relevance – of doctrinal or political controversy. And they offered a main form, in some places the only form, of public entertainment. Congregations took satisfaction in a sermon's structure, which was usually elaborate, with intricate 'divisions'. (Something of this, but no more than a vestige, survived within living memory in the Scottish Presbyterian - sermon.) Firmness of structure invaluably countered the tendency of the Senecan style to fall into unsuccessive choppiness. In this, the set subjects of the church year also helped – Advent, Nativity, Easter and their key Biblical texts. Many of Donne's sermons draw matter from the Psalms; many of Lancelot Andrewes's treat aspects of the Nativity.

Andrewes is perhaps the finest of all the sermon writers from a formal point of view. So lucid is he, and so integrated in his discourse, that he is able to impart a conception of structure on the scale of the whole sermon:

> Now to *venimus*, their coming itself. And it follows well. For it is not a star only, but a lode-star; and whither should *stella Ejus ducere*, but *ad Eum*? 'Whither lead us, but to Him Whose the star is?' The star to the star's Master . . . Last we consider the time of their coming, the season of the year. It was no summer progress. A cold coming they had of it at this time of the year, just the worst time of the year to take a journey, and especially a long journey in. The ways deep, the weather sharp, the days short, the sun furthest off, *in solstitio brumali*, 'the very dead of winter'. *Venimus*, 'we are come', if that be one [word], *venimus*, 'we are now come', come at this time, that sure is another.
>
> (Preached 25 Dec. 1622, from *XCVI Sermons*, 1629)

But brief quotation misleads: the entire sermon is Andrewes's unit. He progresses steadily, from compressed summary, through unfolded and clear development – always surely, always with an assuring calm – to a quietly inevitable conclusion.

Donne's sermons, although sufficiently acute, are less consistently rational. Their often passionate appeal is not primarily to the reason; their syntactic progressions may be elliptical, or abandoned altogether. The sustained emotional pressure, however, carries one over suspensions of meaning – which indeed in delivery may have been unnoticed. A related feature is the method of interpreting the texts that were generally both foundation and reinforcement of a sermon. Unlike most Protestant interpreters, Donne did not concentrate on the historical or literal sense. More than some other *via media* Anglicans, he revived the Augustinian tradition of typological interpretation. In such rehearsing of the correspondences of types and antitypes, some curiosity of reasoning was felt appropriate. Thus, in his solemn final sermon 'Death's Duel', Donne takes the link between Eve and Moses silently for granted, and freshens it with the almost throwaway remark that whereas the ark of bulrushes Moses was delivered from may not have been the first vessel, Eve certainly 'had no midwife when she was delivered of Cain'. We are reminded that the Metaphysical conceit had one source in the pious wit of the Middle Ages. Time and again a typological connection underlies Donne's thought – as in the great series of types of the Crucifixion:

> That the Red Sea could be dry, that the sun could stand still, that an oven could be seven times heat [heated] and not burn, that lions could be hungry and not bite, is strange, miraculously strange, but super-miraculous that God could die; but that God would die is an exaltation of that.

(The Old Testament miracles were regularly taken as prefiguring Christ's deliverance.)

Less oblique are the relentless amplifications of death's hold, in the same sermon ('the death of the womb, is an entrance, a delivering over to another death, the manifold deaths of this world'); or the tremendous answering negations of death:

> As the first part of a sentence pieces well with the last, and never respects, never hearkens after the parenthesis that comes between, so doth a good life here flow into an eternal life, without any consideration what manner of death we die: But whether the gate of my prison be opened with an oiled key (by a gentle and preparing sickness) or the gate be hewen down by a violent death, or the gate be burnt down by a raging and frantic fever, a gate into heaven I shall have, for from the Lord is the cause of my life, and with God the Lord are the issues of death.

Here, Donne's parallels and contrasts find brilliant reinforcements in matching alliterations, assonances, grammatical functions and rhythms. But they are not always so emphatic; for he sometimes mutes or relieves them with reversals or asymmetries. Repetitions, necessary to the economy of the sermon, he uses to great effect; as in the incessant returns to Biblical words. So 'issues' in the quotation is subsequently filled with meaning after meaning, until it seems the central word in the universe. Donne is excellent at choosing the ineluctably exact single word, whether prominent (like 'super-exaltation'), or self-effacing (like 'flow' in 'flow into an eternal life'). And he is a master of the cumulative rhythms of urgency.

No prose more dynamic had been achieved in English. But from a literary standpoint the sermon was a form that had nowhere to go. Aesthetically its limitations were crippling, because of the conflict between homiletic purpose and thematic unity. In all but a few of even Donne's sermons, directed meditation keeps giving way to pious irrelevances. But then, in a sermon the literary point of view is not the point.

Future development in prose was not to come in oratory but in more compressed meditative forms – of written rather than of spoken language. A pioneering figure was William Drummond of Hawthorn-den (1585–1649), who anticipated Browne by many years in exploring the essay as eloquent meditation. Drummond's *A Cypress Grove* (1630) is like Montaigne dressed up in splendid finery. Its thoughts on death may be unoriginal, but they are often penetratingly expressed: 'Who being admitted to see the exquisite Rarities of some Antiquary's Cabinet is grieved, all viewed, to have the Curtain drawn, and give place to new Pilgrims?' Only an overrelaxed, too comfortable quality prevents Drummond from reaching, on similar topics to Browne's, the Browne-ian heights of performance.

Sir Thomas Browne (1605–82) had a number of quite distinct styles. In fact, his two interlinked prose meditations, *Urn-Burial* and *The Garden of Cyrus* (1658), both range from a seemingly informal middle style in their earlier chapters to the spacious and elevated flights of their famous perorations. Here for the first time – with partial exceptions such as Sidney and Nashe – was a recognizable individual style achieved. I do not merely mean that Browne's style has distinctive features. These he has in plenty, such as his fondness for bold surprising brevities ('Oblivion is not to be hired'), or for suppressing connections until the sequence resolves into a succession of compressed epigrams:

Who can but pity the founder of the Pyramids? Herostratus lives that burnt the Temple of Diana, he is almost lost that built it; Time hath spared the Epitaph of Adrian's horse, confounded that of himself.

(*Hydriotaphia* v)

Browne is our earliest master in prose of the exact but unexpected word: one page finds '*Superannuated* piece of folly' and 'to *eye* the remaining particle of futurity'. Like the lively words, his sudden turns and digressions work to engage a reader's interest. Or there are his preposterously curious speculations, so frequent as to call for formulaic expression: whether such-and-such is so 'cannot escape some doubt' or 'were a query too sad to insist on'. But it is not these idiosyncrasies that make Browne's marvellous style. His style rather depends on his so evidently relishing the deployment of words that he seems present in them. This is often so with his stylish antitheses and lists of examples: they amount to a theme-and-variations form, in which meditated expression is foregrounded, without detriment to the content, which seems the more pregnant for the care taken over its expression – 'Adversity stretcheth our days, misery makes Alcmena's nights, and time hath no wings unto it'. Browne finds a way to communicate experience rather than its abstract label; and such eloquence takes us close to the man.

Browne took from Ciceronian rhetoric whatever was useful to him. For example his rhythm, particularly in cadences, makes use of the Latin CURSUS, or types of rhythmic pattern. Thus 'antiquates antiquity' and 'embryon philosophers' are examples of the type known as *tardus* ('measured'). The *cursus* accounts for something in Browne's style, but not very much.

The work of Browne the antiquary and botanist has justly been related to the contemporary enthusiasm for *nova reperta* or discoveries. He is at times the Neo-Platonic scientist collecting information or sceptically considering it. He feels also free, however, to take up gothic forms such as digression, or scholastic speculation. And in his matter (again Spenser-like) he cares more about what is true than what is new. Even his youngest work, *Religio Medici* ('The Faith of a Doctor', 1642) constantly takes the most agreed, the common ground. It may be a mistake to link it at all with modern oppositions of religion and science. For Browne, although discernibly a tolerant Christian Platonist, is hardly a systematic philosopher or theologian. He advances ideas less by argument than by persuasive lateral means like paraphrase, parallel expression, association, or undulating movement between opposites:

> Life is a pure flame, and we live by an invisible Sun within us. A small fire
> sufficeth for life, great flames seemed too little after death . . .
>
> *(Hydriotaphia* v)

He loves inescapable paradoxes – contradictions that stretch the reason.
These his marvelling curiosity holds together, ultimately, by stance;
almost by tone. Yet each point is made with so many judicious
considerations and formal confirmations that they become 'delightful
Truths' indeed.

It is in his perorations, however, that Browne is supreme:

> But the Quincunx of Heaven runs low, and 'tis time to close the five ports
> of knowledge; We are unwilling to spin out our awaking thoughts into
> the phantasmes of sleep, which too often continueth praecogitations;
> making Cables of Cobwebbes and Wildernesses of handsome Groves . . .
>
> Though Somnus in Homer be sent to rowse up Agamemnon, I find no
> such effects in the drowsy approaches of sleep. To keep our eyes open
> longer were but to act our Antipodes. The Huntsmen are up in America,
> and they are already past their first sleep in Persia. But who can be
> drowsie at that howr which freed us from everlasting sleep? or have
> slumbring thoughts at that time, when sleep it self must end, and as some
> conjecture all shall awake again?
>
> *(The Garden of Cyrus* v)

Some have wondered whether any stance could unite the disparities of
The Garden of Cyrus; suspecting Browne of the frivolity of merely
emptying a cornucopia of fives. But from a scientific perspective the
digressiveness is in a sense the point; reflecting as it does the embarrassment of new empirical observations – the multitude of facts not yet
ordered. In approaching Browne's work there are two contrary adjustments to be made: one for the genuine wonder that discoveries through
microscopy aroused in that age; another for the tradition of serious play,
whereby the work became a *tour de force* in imitation of a playful creator.
Browne would think himself to be tracing a significant 'character' that
was at least in the style of the divine author. In any case, his collection
may not be altogether alien to a generation that admires Pynchon's
amassment of posthorns, or Beckett's permutations of pebbles.

Browne's greatness is to build diversities of material into meditative
structures that satisfy the larger reason. His persistent meditations
remount in longer and longer flights, to fresh departures; and in each
new flight the ellipses and assumptions cover more ground – take more
for granted – until compression and speed of communication become
cumulative. From this point of view, the unfinished and now neglected

Christian Morals might well have become Browne's finest work. By means of allusion and abstraction, it takes compression furthest. Yet its style is Biblical – modelled especially on the epigrammatic Book of Proverbs (then highly esteemed) – and its drift always clear. It must be the most enjoyable moral philosophy ever written.

ESSAYS AND CHARACTERS

Much in Browne's work presupposes the essay and similar forms. The English originator of these was a greater writer – a greater mind, indeed, than almost any who finds a place in this book – Francis Bacon. Bacon, in turn, had Montaigne's essays to build on. But he reacted against the French writer; answering his personal assemblages of examples with something more intellectually formidable and (perhaps in consequence) impersonal. With this and the need for compression in view, Bacon chose to rely on short forms: MAXIMS, APHORISMS and the moral 'SENTENCES' (*sententiae*) popularly used as inscriptions. These succinct generalizations he shaped rhetorically, and concentrated to a weighty definitiveness only attainable by a very acute thinker. 'Dissimilation invites dissimulation' – notice how the repeated word reflects the immediate imitative response of the dissimilator, and how the precise 'invites' requires careful thought. In large-scale ordonnance – especially in division or *partitio* – Bacon demonstrates greater powers still. He applies them to very various subjects, but mostly to ones of public interest: marriage, friendship, atheism, great place, and the like. His aim is to add to the store of wisdom regarding practical ethics – to give advice as useful as Macchiavelli's, but sounder:

> as in Nature, Things move violently to their Place, and calmly in their Place: So Virtue in Ambition is violent, in Authority settled and calm. All Rising to Great Place, is by a winding Stair: And if there be Factions, it is good, to side a Man's self [join a party], whilst he is in the Rising; and to balance Himself, when he is placed.

To call such advice cynical would be a shallow view: in Jacobean society, the essays would scarcely have had influence for good, without their hard realism. Bacon offers the pleasure of distinguished reflections expressed with intensity and wit. Why then has he few constant readers? It need not be due to any failing on his part: he may be too far sighted for many to benefit from his wisdom. Or he may communicate repugnant truths.

Bacon greatly raised the aspiration of the essay, while at the same time tightening its form. The latter process is impressively demonstrated in the radical revision of his essays from 1597 to 1625; although eventually there was also adding of connections and examples, and even a discernible modicum of informality. Meanwhile others were going much further in that direction. Sir William Cornwallis (1579?–1614) and Owen Felltham (1602?–68), for example, returned to the informal exploratory essays of Montaigne, which in 1603 and 1632 were translated by John Florio.

The tone of Felltham's *Resolves* (?1623; 1628) is so personal that you are surprised when you recognize the substance as a traditional commonplace. By comparison with Bacon, at least, Felltham prefers to be on a positively intimate footing with his reader. When gift-giving in friendship slackens, he says,

> what a thorn it is to an affectionate mind, I desire rather to know by judicious observations, than by real experience: but sure I am, it no way can be small.
>
> ('Of purchasing Frends with large Gifts')

The informality can at times sag to mere chat; but generally Felltham is in a good sense serious. Yet he takes up paradoxical stances. These often serve as an opening: 'Though an enemy be not a thing necessary, yet is there much good use to be made of him'; 'Nothing hath spoiled truth more than the invention of Logic'. And many essays conclude with the formal 'resolves' of Felltham's title – exact prose equivalents of epigram closure. Two features of the *Resolves* were to be of future importance for the essay: an element of self-estimation, different from anything in Bacon; and a structure that on occasion mimes the theme. Appropriate structure is not easy to illustrate briefly, but 'Of Logic' will be found an obvious example. Its last part shifts ground in such a way as to show that the main argument against logic has really been a use of logic itself as a 'countermine' against its misuse. (Felltham's keen sense of relevance is always guided by theme rather than ostensible subject.) The image of mine and countermine is one of many fine surprising similes in the *Resolves*, of a type at which Hazlitt will later excel.

Two other essayists should be mentioned, for opposite reasons. Jonson's posthumous *Timber: or, Discoveries* illustrates the essay's close kinship with the commonplace book – a genre most intellectuals gave much of their time to, in the absence of cardfiles and photocopying. Jonson professed to despise essays as undigested; and in fact the material in his mere notebook is conspicuously well assimilated. It gives

an impressive glimpse of the processes of analysis and condensation –
habitual with Jonson – whereby he sublimed the thought of others to
gold; sometimes striking an epigram or aphorism ('A Prince without
Letters, is a Pilot without eyes'), sometimes adding his own reflections
or instances. The notes, all in separate paragraphs, amount on occasion
to powerful essays in brief. Had Jonson wished, he could have passed
even Bacon as an essayist. As it is, English literary criticism in the
modern sense could be said to begin with *Timber*.

By contrast, Abraham Cowley's essays, which appeared after the
Restoration in *Several Discourses by way of Essays, in Verse and Prose* (1668),
combined the elements of the familiar essay into its pure form. Here at
last was the genre that would be practised, without radical alteration, by
Lamb and Hazlitt. As Hazlitt was to discover, Cowley's easy talk is
entirely pleasant, whether he speaks (with astonishing precocity) 'Of
Myself', or on a less explicitly personal topic. Unfortunately, he does not
sustain the effort beyond a handful of essays. A pity; there is much to be
learned from him. Slight as a butterfly he may be; but he sometimes
goes, surprisingly, where Bacon's great battering ram of reason fails to
reach.

> The first Minister of State has not so much business in publique, as a
> wise man has in private; if the one have little leasure to be alone, the other
> has less leasure to be in company; the one has but part of the affairs of
> one Nation, the other all the works of God and Nature under his
> consideration. There is no saying shocks me so much as that which I hear
> very often, That a man does not know how to pass his Time. 'Twould
> have been but ill spoken by Methusalem in the Nine hundred sixty ninth
> year of his Life, so far it is from us, who have not time enough to attain to
> the utmost perfection of any part of any Science, to have cause to
> complain that we are forced to be idle for want of work. But this you'l say
> is work only for the Learned, others are not capable either of the
> employments or divertisements that arrive from Letters; I know they are
> not; and therefore cannot much recommend Solitude to a man totally
> illiterate. But if any man be so unlearned as to want entertainment of the
> little Intervals of accidental Solitude, which frequently occurr in almost
> all conditions ... it is truly a great shame both to his Parents and
> Himself, for a very small portion of any Ingenious Art will stop up all
> those gaps of our Time, either Musique, or Painting, or Designing, or
> Chymistry, or History, or Gardening, or twenty other things will do it
> usefully and pleasantly; and if he happen to set his affections upon Poetry
> (which I do not advise him too immoderately) that will overdo it; no
> wood will be thick enough to hide him from the importunities of
> company or business, which would abstract him from his Beloved.
>
>   ('Of Solitude')

All is easy, with particularities coming in just often enough, objections quietly met, and persuasions and enthusiasms advanced under cover of modestly humorous hyperboles.

More thoroughly epigrammatic than the essay was the CHARACTER, or brief description of a social or moral type. Pioneered by Joseph Hall, and by Jonson in his plays, its full popularity only came with Thomas Overbury's brilliant *Characters* (1614; ninth edition by 1616), to which Webster, Dekker and Donne contributed. The group have wit and shrewd observation (the satire of a scholar can still strike home); but they are limited by facile dependence on stereotypes – the Horatian characters, the types of medieval estates satire, and of course the *Characters* of Theophrastus (translated 1616). The *Characters* tend to consist of disconnected epigrams, or else to follow out some obvious metaphorical plan – as when punning terms of venery are used to hound 'A Whore' through the schematic years of maturation of a beast of chase. In every way Overbury's panorama of abuses and fashions is itself fashionable. No purer example of mannerist self-reference could be wished for than his concluding character, a character of itself:

> To square out a character by our English level, it is a picture (real or personal) quaintly drawn, in various colours, all of them heightened by one shadowing.
> It is a quick and soft touch of many strings, all shutting up in one musical close; it is wit's descant on any plain song.
>
> ('What a Character Is')

On a more popular level, Nicholas Breton's *Fantastics* (1626) show the same tendencies. In these georgic descriptions of the times of day or months – delicious essays in little – each sentence is a separate epigram:

> The currier [harquebus] and the lime-rod are the death of the fowl, and the falcon's bells ring the death of the mallard. The trotting gelding makes a way through the mire, and the hare and the hound put the huntsman to his horn.
>
> ('January')

The genre's atomistic tendency, together with Breton's lack of intellect, limit his achievement; but the copious particulars, besides being delightful, represent in their way an impressive sureness of purpose.

But it is the *Microcosmography* (1628) of John Earle that lives and continues to charm. His less satiric, less strenuously brilliant, more contemplative characters are elusively conducted along paths of lateral thought. He excels at the seemingly casual addition, which turns out to make a thematic link. Or an obvious connection will cover others at a greater depth, as in 'A Child':

> We laugh at his foolish sports, but his game is our earnest; and his drums, rattles, and hobby-horses, but the emblems and mocking of man's business. His father hath writ him as his own little story, wherein he reads those days of his life that he cannot remember, and sighs to see what innocence he hath out-lived.

Earle's portrait miniatures all conceal philosophical truths; even his actor is an emblem of life's changes and appearances. In his compassion for the human condition, he is ever alive to paradoxes: like his own 'contemplative man', we may say 'Nature admits him as a partaker of her sports'.

Essays and characters – and through them epigrams – were formative components of seventeenth-century literature, in that they merged with other genres. This was more than a matter of rhetorical fashion: it reflected new psychological observation, as well as a readiness to think freshly, to engage in speculation. In this sense the character became a main ingredient of biographies and histories.

NEW PROSE FORMS: BIOGRAPHY AND HISTORY

There were several late Tudor and early Stuart expressions of the commemorative impulses that underlie biography. Many felt, with Browne, that ''Tis time to observe occurrences, and let nothing remarkable escape us'. But Izaak Walton was the originator who assembled the form more or less as we know it – factual information, personal anecdotes, telling details and discussion of writings: all selected with a view to the characteristic and deployed within a solid chronological frame, in such a way as to unfold the life story, or at least give a perspective. He successfully began to loosen biography's dependence on the formal 'character'. This component, which often provided the closure, had tended to limit biography to illustration of explicit moral formulations. Yet it had seemed necessary all the same, to draw together what might otherwise have been inchoate ramblings (such as we actually find in Aubrey's unstructured gossip). Walton's brilliant artistry enables him to arrange his materials so as to bring his subjects – Donne, Herbert, Hooker, Wotton and Sanderson – immediately to life.

> It is observed that a desire of glory or commendation is rooted in the very nature of man, and that those of the severest and most mortified lives, though they may become so humble as to banish self-flattery and such

weeds as naturally grow there, yet they have not been able to kill this desire of glory, but that, like our radical heat, it will both live and die with us ... Several charcoal fires being first made in his large study, he brought with him into that place his winding-sheet in his hand and, having put off all his clothes, had this sheet put on him and so tied with knots at his head and feet, and his hands so placed, as dead bodies are usually fitted to be shrouded and put into their coffin or grave. Upon this urn he thus stood with his eyes shut and with so much of the sheet turned aside as might show his lean, pale, and death-like face, which was purposely turned toward the East, from whence he expected the second coming of his and our Saviour, Jesus. In this posture he was drawn at his just height; and when the picture was fully finished, he caused it to be set by his bed-side, where it continued, and became his hourly object till his death ...

(Life of Dr John Donne)

The biographer's own presence is another distinctive feature in Walton, often described as irony, and restrained enough for it. Actually the tone is more various: it is more like that of scrupulously fair appraisal, or comment consciously withheld.

The still newer and more difficult genre of autobiography is almost visibly conjured up, out of chronicle, memoirs, courtesy book and treatise, by the underestimated skill of Edward Herbert, brother of the poet. Herbert's work can easily be taken for naive swashbuckling and vanity; but the duels have a way of not eventuating, and beneath the panache and the splendid adventures runs a story of the composition of a humane and eirenic maturity. Herbert in actuality selects with the greatest care 'those Passages of my Life, which I conceive may best declare me, and be most useful'. He is a deliberate artist.

The novelty of Stuart autobiography is hard to exaggerate. It implied a new consciousness of individual identity. And the expression of this consciousness implied much more – something amounting to a mutation of sensibility. For this was a period of vivid personal memoirs – Lucy Hutchinson's and Sir Kenelm Digby's come to mind – as well as of special histories like Thomas Sprat's *History of the Royal Society* (1667). Memorial responsibility was keenly and widely felt. And antiquarian research issued in some great literature – notably William Camden's *Britannia* (1586, translated 1610), a work of astonishing scope, which in turn created an intense further interest in antiquarianism. Meanwhile, the form of general histories was changing fundamentally. The Augustinian–providential model came increasingly to be supplemented by a Tacitean–analytic, or even a mechanistic, model. And the

mythic element, the tracing of British history back to Brut, the founder
of New Troy, was gradually abandoned; even if constitutional disputes
(like the question whether Parliament antedated the Norman Conquest) gave a new political edge to national legend. History began to
begin in historical times.

These changes find reflection in two great histories, Ralegh's and
Clarendon's. In spite of its historiographic preface and its up-to-date
population dynamics (perhaps based on Harriot's calculations), Sir
Walter Ralegh's (1552?–1618) is in many ways a medieval universal
history – a 'mirror' for the advice of princes. Serious recollections of the
ends of human life inform his work; and his view is often sombre – as
when he surveys the fall of Rome:

> We have left it flourishing in the middle of the field; having rooted up, or
> cut down, all that kept it from the eyes and admiration of the World. But
> after some continuance, it shall begin to lose the beauty it had; the
> storms of ambition shall beat her great boughs and branches one against
> another; her leaves shall fall off, her limbs wither, and a rabble of
> barbarous Nations enter the field, and cut her down.
>
> (*History of the World* v.6)

As with other great works, the style of Ralegh's *History* belongs to no
one school exclusively: it can be fully symmetrical, expansive and
Ciceronian in sentence structure; but in diction it can also be simple
and sudden and varied. Its boldness only stops castigating princely
'troublers of the world' in order to confront the universal conqueror
Death. From begining to end, Ralegh is magnificent.

Clarendon's *History of the Rebellion* (wr. 1646–8, 1671–4) presents a
distinct contrast. For one thing, it is very much a participant's, an
insider's, account of the exercise of power – at times almost a memoir.
The Earl of Clarendon (1609–74) may sink his rank with exquisite
modesty; but his history none the less has all the advantages of his
having been Charles I's Lord Chancellor, and after the Restoration,
virtual ruler. Then, Clarendon's is very much a contemporary record,
evoking its period freshly yet also with finality. (Our own seventeenth
century is still peopled by the characters of his suave 'aftergame of
reputations'). Magisterially he wields his diverse elements – theme,
analysis, flavoursome detail, telling anecdote, impartial assessment of
character, swift irresistible narrative – and combines them, yet all the
time with informality and ease, into an ironic totality. The line of wit is
never slack: anecdote or analysis will always draw together to an
unobtrusively pointed closure. Sardonic about the less adequate

Royalists, Clarendon has an almost godlike magnanimity towards opponents (witness how he admires Cromwell's courage in face of the Levellers). Very occasionally scorn breaks out. But generally he is moderate, if sombre. He lets 'facts' speak effectively for themselves; how can he help it if they sometimes speak with a scathing deadpan irony? Broad as Clarendon's vision extends, where it now seems defective is in his blindness to emergent political movements. Of all our histories, this is the one that offers the greatest variety of literary qualities; and it is certainly the most readable. Here is Clarendon on the death of Viscount Falkland, the Cary of Jonson's Cary–Morison Ode:

> In the morning before the battle, as always upon action, he was very cheerful, and put himself into the first rank of the Lord Byron's regiment, who was then advancing upon the enemy, who had lined the hedges on both sides with musketeers; from whence he was shot with a musket on the lower part of the belly, and in the instant falling from his horse, his body was not found till the next morning; till when there was some hope he might have been a prisoner; though his nearest friends, who knew his temper, received small comfort from that imagination. Thus fell that incomparable young man in the four and thirtieth year of his age, having so much dispatched the business of life that the oldest rarely attain to that immense knowledge and the youngest enter not into the world with more innocence: whosoever leads such a life need not care upon how short warning it be taken from him.
>
> (*The History of the Rebellion* vii)

Clarendon's ease partly depended on exceptional command over his material (as with other great minds like Bacon and Hobbes). But it also depended on emergence of the PLAIN STYLE – a rapid, lucid, unambiguous medium of communication and self-communication, relatively unfigurative and direct. Such a style may seem a simple, natural thing; in actuality, it was one of the most difficult achievements of the century, and called for prolonged study of classical models. And the anti-Ciceronian movement made its contribution. Nevertheless, the plain style cannot be understood merely in terms of the victory of a critical school. It had more to do with the functional needs of the increasing torrent of expository works, in which most of the prose literature of the time has been found to float. The discoveries and accumulated knowledge of the previous century now issued in systematic works. These explanatory syntheses, embodied in forms such as the anatomy, the dialogue and the essay–treatise, necessitated something approaching a plain style. Whether the new style answered to needs generated by the information explosion or was itself a triggering mechanism that set the explosion off would be hard to decide; such situations are organic or reciprocal. But one factor, at least, is beyond doubt. Most early scientific writers were vociferously hostile to figurative language, and indeed to philological study generally (which they believed to focus attention on words rather than real things). Like Thomas Sprat, the historian of the Royal Society, they pursued the ideal – or perhaps one should say, chimera – of a language corresponding to particulars of matter and motion in a simple way. They wanted to reduce style to 'a mathematical plainness'. Separation of cultures had begun with a vengeance.

The new plain prose found innumerable applications. In philosophy, Thomas Hobbes's (1588–1679) sturdy rigour and determined lucidity would have been mute without it; and the same is true of much of the work of Bacon, the 'secretary of nature' and presiding genius of the new science – even if one recalls more readily his ornamented periods with their rich orchestration of metaphors. The plain style also opened up a north-west passage to travel literature, such as the vivid *Voyages* (1699) of the ex-buccaneer William Dampier. Then, its transparency made possible the allegory of Bunyan (where the inner narration must show through both fable and style), as well as the slow beginnings, at last, of realistic prose narrative. And the aptness of the new medium for introspection appears in many moral and psychological treatises.

Robert Burton's loose Senecan prose in *The Anatomy of Melancholy* (1621, with subsequent enlargements) shows one of the pitfalls in the way of achieving an expository plain style: it is simple and colloquial; but it lacks an adequate structural model. Burton has chosen to return to the learned meanderings of antiquity: of Macrobius' *Saturnalia* or Martianus Capella's *De Nuptiis*. And he carries this method so far as to adopt a digressive style, which can frustrate almost as much as it delights. Nevertheless, the *The Anatomy of Melancholy* is perhaps the earliest learned work still widely enjoyed. At the 'dividing line' (as John Middleton Murry put it) between the ages of superstition and science, Burton amassed an encyclopedia of ancient and modern learning about depression, together with related (or possibly related) psychological curiosities. As an ANATOMY it is arranged in systematic partitions, sections, members and subsections, progressively minute; while simultaneously and paradoxically it becomes in aggregate more and more universal, as the subject is related to everything. Everything offers an occasion of melancholy, the general or microcosmic human condition. The highly original result of the dis-covering, anatomizing process is that Burton not only turns 'his inside outward', but also turns the larger world outside in, as it were, and restructures it from a subjective standpoint. His view – and this is one of the great pleasures of reading *The Anatomy* – is very often ironic (perhaps always: one never quite knows). If the irony were merely destructive, it would perhaps tire through its prolonged uncertainty. As it is, the compassionate irony of this 'Democritus junior', this calm 'laughing philosopher', has made his book for many a sad oasis of sanity. Here, it seems, every oddity and flaw, every paradox of human nature and of nature herself, will at some point come up, and into perspective.

> As a long-winged hawk, when he is first whistled off the fist, mounts aloft, and for his pleasure fetcheth many a circuit in the air, still soaring higher and higher till he be come to his full pitch, and in the end, when the game is sprung, comes down amain and stoops upon a sudden: so will I, having now come at last into these ample fields of air, wherein I may freely expatiate and exercise myself for my recreation, a while rove, wander round about the world, mount aloft to those ethereal orbs and celestial spheres, and so descend to my former elements again. In which progress I will first see whether that relation of the friar of Oxford be true, concerning those northern parts under the Pole (if I meet *obiter* with the Wandering Jew, Elias Artifex, or Lucian's Icaromenippus, they shall be my guides) whether there be such, four Euripuses [straits], and a great rock of loadstones, which may cause the needle in the compass still [continually] to bend that way, and what should be the true cause of the variation of the compass . . .
>
> (II.ii.3)

Like many works of the century, Burton's georgic *Anatomy* is mixed in genre. Utopia, consolation, educational treatise and many admixtures of satire (another form using low and latterly plain style): all these kinds may be come upon among its labyrinthine *culs-de-sac*.

Plain style had applications still more informal. The seventeenth century, which brought extreme fashions in costume of loose informality – 'A sweet disorder in the dress' (Herrick) – saw also a new informality in epistolary style. Late Tudor correspondence, even between husband and wife, was often stiffly formal; and much that remains of it falls in any case into an official category. But a feature of Stuart literature is the quantity of informal letters, ranging from innumerable verse epistles of friendship or letter–essays (such as James Howells's, full of chat and anecdotes) to what may be called 'natural' letters, written without thought of publication.

> I was, since I came hither, in Murano, a little island about the distance of Lambeth from London, where crystal glass is made, and it is a rare

sight to see a whole street, where on the one side there are twenty
furnaces together at work. They say here that although one should
transplant a glass-furnace from Murano to Venice herself, . . . and use
the same materials, the same workmen, the same fuel, the self-same
ingredients every way, yet they cannot make crystal glass in that
perfection, for beauty and lustre, as in Murano. Some impute it to the
quality of the circumambient air that hangs over the place, which is
purified and attenuated by the concurrence of so many fires that are in
those furnaces night and day perpetually, for they are like the vestal fire
which never goes out.

(James Howell *Epistolae Ho-Elianae*, 30 May 1621)

The withdrawal of many gentlemen to their estates during the troubled
periods after 1630 may have contributed to this development of the
letter – which however is larger in scope, amounting to a new estimate
of private life. If a single correspondence were to be singled out, it would
have to be Dorothy Osborne's with Sir William Temple. Often
concerned, as often playful, these well judged letters are always loving
and thoughtful and utterly unaffected; so that they form one of the most
engaging series in the history of letter writing. Dorothy's every word
shows the presence of a mind one should love to have known.

A word should be said about translation; for the seventeenth century
was one of its great periods. With a larger, more educated readership,
the appetite for classical and European works in the vernacular was
insatiable. The activity of verse translators was correspondingly intense:
almost every poet attempted something in this line. Joshua Sylvester's
Bartas his Devine Weekes (1592–9, collected 1605) is no more than
quaint and flavoursome; but George Sandys's *Ovids Metamorphosis*
(1621–6) and *Paraphrase upon the Psalms* (1636) are good enough to have
prompted emulation in Milton himself. And Edward Fairfax's (1580?–
1635) *Godfrey of Bulloigne* (1600), a translation of Tasso's *Gerusalemme
Liberata*, has classic status. Although often less close to its original than
to *The Faerie Queene*, it achieves a fine texture:

> Her breasts were naked, for the day was hot,
> Her lockes unbound, waved in the wanton winde;
> Somedeale she swet (tired with the game you wot)
> Her sweat-drops bright, white, round, like pearles of Inde,
> Her humide eies a firie smile foorth shot,
> That like sunne-beames in silver fountaines shinde,
>   Ore him her lookes she hung, and her soft breast
>   The pillow was, where he and love tooke rest.
>
> (*Godfrey of Bulloigne* xvi.18)

It has not the same monumentality as Tasso's poem, but at times it is quite as interesting.

The harnessing of the new prose to translation produced the most permanent achievements. In 1611 came the great landmark, the King James version of the Bible, which was to establish itself with such incalculable pervasiveness that almost all literary prose after it owed debts to its diction and rhythms. But, as earlier chapters have shown, this Authorized Version was far from being the work of a single generation. And the development of secular translation was equally gradual. John Florio's (1553?–1626) *The Essayes of Montaigne* (1603), the version preferred by many, still seems quaint in a Tudor way. It is downright but unsubtle, stirring in rhythm (it stirred Shakespeare) but superficial, vividly concrete but overconcrete. Florio has energy and flavour; sometimes he seems to have learnt his English from Nashe. Yet, like North in his Plutarch's *Lives* (translated via the French version of Amyot), Florio obscures many of the qualities of his original. Philemon Holland's (1552–1637) translations of Livy (1600), Pliny's *Natural History* (1601), Plutarch's *Moralia* (1603), Suetonius (1606) and Camden (1610) are another matter altogether. For Holland was linguistically brilliant; so that although his vivid versions are too massive, enlarged as they are with doublets and details, they somehow reserve the spirit of their originals:

> Then casting all about in menacing manner his fierie and terrible eies, towards the captaines and principals of the Tuskanes, one while he challenged them one by one to single fight: otherwhiles he rated them all in general, calling them the hirelings and slaves of proud kings and tyrants . . . All this while bare he off their shot which light upon his target, and there stucke, and nath'lesse with full resolution kept the bridge still, walking his stations, and staulking like a giant.
>
> (*The Romane Historie* (1600) 50)

And when one comes to the translations of Fernando de Rojas's *Celestina* as *The Spanish Bawd* (1631) or of Cervantes's *Exemplarie Novells* (1640) by James Mabbe (1572–1642?), the Spanish proportions seem to be effectively retained and the English to be transparent. Easily readable translation had been achieved.

How did it come about that the seventeenth century produced such an exceptional amount of fine prose? No single answer is likely to satisfy everyone. Something must be due to the momentous issues of the time, with which thought and feeling deeply engaged. And there were many new subjects to be written about. But prose had also its own internal development, shaped for example by habits of classical imitation and of increasing compression. In this development the effects of improved education were paramount. What I take to be the chief factor of all tends to be left out of account: namely that the best minds were now for the first time finding expression in the vernacular almost as much as in Latin. Thus English prose was from one point of view a side effect of the Reformation.

6

Restoration Literature

THE Restoration brought relief for a majority of Charles II's subjects. But relief was not the only mood, nor was relaxation – nor yet overrelaxation and riot. There was also, at first, a darker mood of anxiety and tension, recrimination and score-settling. At such a time, writers who could make themselves heard by a broad range of social groups were invaluable – writers like Marvell, who said that the Parliamentary cause was 'too good to have been fought for', or George Savile, Marquis of Halifax, who wrote *The Character of a Trimmer* (1688), or Dryden, 'We have been so long together bad Englishmen'.

JOHN DRYDEN

Although not himself well off, John Dryden (1631–1700) became used to the company of fashionable gentlemen, and eventually arrived – not without difficulties and failures – at a poise that allowed him to address men of different status with equal dignity. By his boldness in crossing lines of rank and allegiance he was enabled to mediate to middle class readers a European tradition of larger values, which had previously been accessible only to the educated and privileged. He did not achieve this by his personal qualities alone, nor by tact and tactics in selecting just the tone that would appeal – now Biblical, now polite. In large part his success was due to the special ease of his style, which took the reader more fully into account than had that of any previous English writer.

At the same time, Dryden's achievement may be seen as part of a late seventeenth-century triumph of the lucid plain style over the Senecan style with its significant darkness. The Earl of Shaftesbury's famous announcement of the new taste went so far as to describe the style of the Senecan essayists as a monotonous 'common amble' – an atomistic succession of independent short sentences, witty without variation. The new style, as Dryden came to practise it, used more variety of models, in accordance with the subject matter. For with him style followed the line of thought in a highly functional way. Only, he took the greatest care to hide the art of this; so that it appears, if at all, only in a certain hypernatural quality. He avoids obvious patterning where he can. And where something like it is inevitable, as in parallel clauses (ISOCOLON) of comparison or contrast, he carefully mutes the effect – an effort diametrically opposite to that with which Dr Johnson, in a later period with a different taste, will underline his parallelisms. Thus Dryden's Shakespeare 'was naturally learn'd; he needed not the spectacles of books to read Nature; he looked inwards, and found her there'. The contrast finds plain and full statement; but it is not balanced out weightily, word against word. Dryden's effect has much to do with the way in which he carefully anticipates the reader, pacing him through the difficulties – and providing for these in the rhythms and proportions of the sentence structure. Yet all this is only part of an integral address towards his imagined reader, which is just as much expressed in the ease, in the tone of equal footing. And Dryden's ease is no mere imitation of breeding: he unites grace of manner with reason and robust morality in a firm, challenging way. He is perhaps the earliest critic still capable of persuading.

Dryden's criticism amounts to a substantial body of work, much of it occasional: between forty and fifty prologues, epilogues and letters, besides the formal *Essay Of Dramatic Poesy* (1668) and *A Parallel Betwixt Poetry and Painting* (1695). Yet it is not at first obvious where the importance or lasting value of these miscellaneous pieces resides. Excellent critics have valued Dryden as the first to venture at length into descriptive criticism – the *Essay* contains a long account of Jonson's *Epicoene*. But sharp descriptiveness hardly seems the main impression his work gives. There is more of that in his neglected near-contemporary John Dennis; although for description in English on the modern scale one has to wait for Addison on Milton (1712), Joseph Warton *On the Genius and Writings of Pope* (1756) and Hugh Blair's *Lectures on Rhetoric* (1762; not published until 1783).

The significance of Dryden's criticism lies in the fact that he was the first to address anything like a full range of critical topics. He displays an astonishing variety of interests, including speculations about genre or genesis; appreciations of Shakespeare's greatness; and judicial assessments – many of them thrown out casually, yet lasting to this day. His views are distinguished by breadth and soundness of taste, by intellectual acuity and independence. He set a benchmark for all subsequent criticism.

Dryden's essays reflect the multifarious concerns of a practising poet and dramatist, deeply involved in the politics of his difficult craft, and therefore prudently cautious in his pronouncements. There were precedents in French – in prefaces like Corneille's – for a writer's discussing his ideas. But Dryden's preference for particular issues derived primarily from the exploratory, sceptical cast of his own mind. His freedom is wonderfully engaging. Big names do not overawe him – 'Neither am I much concerned at Mr Cowley's verses before *Gondibert* (though his authority is almost sacred to me) . . .'. Sidney and Jonson and their immediate successors had on the whole treated fixed rules, and were in any case constricted by their authorities and by the rhetorical forms they used (forms of controversy or praise like the epideictic oration). But Dryden ranged wherever his interest led, among the various questions of his time – French versus English dramatic styles; rhyme versus blank verse; and the rest – illuminating them all and adumbrating, cumulatively, a whole aggregate of literature. He was the first to express an adequate idea, in English, of what literature is. For, like his great contemporary Sir Christopher Wren, Dryden was free from slavery to theoretical rules.

Among Dryden's exploratory speculations, some of the most interesting concern the operation of rhyme as a beneficial constraint in composition, a means of generating poetic ideas. 'Imagination in a poet is a faculty so wild and lawless that like an high-ranging spaniel it must have clogs tied to it, lest it outrun the judgment': the writing process needs to be slowed, to allow time for more creative choices. A similarly interesting topic is the genesis of wit. Again the imagination is 'like a nimble spaniel' and

> beats over and ranges through the field of memory, till it springs the quarry it hunted after . . . the first happiness of the poet's imagination is properly invention, or finding of the thought; the second is fancy, or the variation, driving, or moulding of that thought, as the judgment represents it proper to the subject . . .
>
> (*An Account of the Ensuing Poem*)

The analogy of the dog was a stock one in European criticism. But it was a newer idea, characteristic of Dryden, to use it to introspect on the experience of composition. He substitutes a phase of psychological action ('the variation, driving, or moulding of that thought') for the one of rhetorical arrangement that usually followed invention in such contexts.

Some of Dryden's best writing is in his occasional works, particularly

prologues and epilogues to plays. He was the unrivalled master of this
genre, and he brought it to a height never approached since. Often the
prologues and epilogues are panegyric; which need not at all mean that
they flatter. In fact, they can be belligerent. Dryden opted for society;
but he never ceased trying to bully or coax or shame it into a bit of sense.
Thus the Prologue to *Oedipus* anticipates an unfavourable reception,
and advises the audience that in such an event they should 'Damn it in
silence, lest the world should hear'. Dryden's authority allowed him to
say anything – so long as he judged his tone to perfection:

> See twice! Do not pell-mell to damning fall,
> Like true born Britons, who ne'er think at all:
> Pray be advised; and though at Mons you won,
> On pointed cannon do not always run.
> (Prologue from *Oedipus* 23–6)

Dryden's dispraises, as in his satires *The Medal* and *MacFlecknoe* (both
1682), have become more famous. And they are brilliant and funny, if
not always very just. *Absalom and Achitophel* (1681), written at the request
of Charles II against Shaftesbury's party, has a Biblical allegory with a
useful distancing effect. In this the king is King David, who 'wide as his
command / Scattered his Maker's image through the land' in the shape
of natural sons (implying that Monmouth is only one of many). The
meat of the satire is found by Dryden's lash in a series of characters: the
best are those of Shaftesbury (Achitophel), Monmouth (Absalom) and
Buckingham (Zimri). This transportation of the entire satiric prose
character form into verse – as distinct from Butler's use of its materials
on a different scale – set a pattern for much satire in the succeeding age.
To this pattern, in fact, Edward Young's 'The Love of Fame' (1725) and
Pope's 'Of the Characters of Women' (1735) conform, as much as to the
ultimate model in the Latin satirists. Dryden's Achitophel is

> For close Designs, and crooked Counsels fit;
> Sagacious, Bold, and Turbulent of wit:
> Restless, unfixt in Principles and Place;
> In Power unpleas'd, impatient of Disgrace.
> A fiery Soul, which working out its way,
> Fretted the Pigmy Body to decay:
> And o'er inform'd the Tenement of Clay.
> A daring Pilot in extremity;
> Pleas'd with the Danger, when the Waves went high
> He sought the Storms; but for a Calm unfit,
> Would Steer too nigh the Sands, to boast his Wit.

Great Wits are sure to Madness near ally'd;
And thin Partitions do their Bounds divide:
Else, why should he, with Wealth and Honour blest,
Refuse his Age the needful hours of Rest?

(lines 152–66)

The ambivalent epithets and concessions of positive qualities, together with the high dignified tone, combine to create a believable great figure, with a presumption of justice on the satirist's part. Respectfulness makes criticism all the more telling. We are as far as possible, here, from the style of Donne or Cleveland. Normal proportions of imagery, easy development of the natural metaphor of a pilot, judicious impersonality: such are the features in Dryden that prepare one to accept as reasonable even his later insinuations about Shaftesbury's Satanic role.

The critical *oeuvre* of a lifetime is not without its connecting themes. In Dryden's case – and indeed in the Restoration generally – perhaps the most prominent was pursuit of the heroic ideal, both in the sense of literary EPIC (grand narrative) and of social nobility. Even a metre could be chosen because it was 'more noble'. In Dryden's writing, the epic *Aeneis* (1697), as we shall see, constitutes the *chef d'oeuvre*; while *Absalom and Achitophel* is heroic satire *par excellence*. In it, even the most adverse characterizations, such as those of Shaftesbury and Buckingham, have considerable dignity. But *Annus Mirabilis* (1667) was already a strenuously heroic poem. And, more obviously still, the aspiration to epic actuated Dryden's repeated attempts at heroic drama. Again and again he tried to emulate the grandeur of Shakespeare's heroic tragedies – to achieve a purified form that would maintain elevation in diction, character and social decorum more consistently. These attempts were never wholly successful. Nevertheless *All for Love* (1678), ostensibly a *rifacimento* or remake of *Antony and Cleopatra*, can stand as an independent achievement of real force, capable of arousing excitement on the modern stage.

Many other writers, too, were fascinated by the epic ideal. Some, such as Abraham Cowley, attempted the epic poem itself. Others translated ancient epics, or, like Clarendon, gave epic shape to works in quite other genres. The tendency may have had something to do with the heroic nature of recent history, and surely had much to do with the sovereign place of epic in Restoration literary theory. Dryden considered it 'undoubtedly the greatest work which the soul of man is capable to perform'. Yet epics of real quality failed to materialize; the old aristocratic values of the genre had lost their cosmic validity, and new validation was wanting. This failure was not because of any indistinctness of aim. The idea of epic was all too sharply defined; only its implementation eluded the poets. – All of them, paradoxically, except the republican John Milton (1608–74).

EPIC was a continuous narration celebrating heroic figures of history or tradition. ('Continuous' is important; since it excludes medieval interlace and neo-gothic romantic epic.) Classical epic was supposed to attempt a comprehensive conspective view, on the highest level of seriousness; to convey a sense of moral height; and to build an impression of the larger context of noble action. An idea of it is best formed now from Homer, or from Virgil's *Aeneid*. Indeed that approach is almost mandatory, since each work belonging to the epic tradition alludes to and rivals its predecessors – particularly in expected set pieces such as the descent to the underworld (*Odyssey* xi, *Aeneid* vi), the great building operation (*Aeneid* i, *Paradise Lost* i, x) or the roll-call of leaders (*Iliad* ii, *Paradise Lost* i, xi). From one point of view, *Paradise Lost* (1667; 1674) follows epic conventions fairly scrupulously. From another, it is one of the most original works ever composed.

In Renaissance theory, the encyclopedic epic included within itself many different generic forms. Milton took up this idea enthusiastically – took it indeed to manneristic extremes. But he also gave it a subtle turn by including several distinct variants of epic itself. Thus, Books i and ii are a pagan classical epic, with Satan as its stoic hero. Some have taken this part to be a fair sample of the whole. But the poem is not uniform throughout, like a cheese; more like the cow, it is articulated into distinct members or parts. The next of these parts, beginning with Book iii, is Christian epic. Its hero is Messiah; and it has an EPISODE, or inset narration, Raphael's Christian but very martial epic. Books ix and x, however, modulate to tragedy, with man as protagonist. And Books xi and xii approximate to the Biblical epic form popularized by Du Bartas. Naturally all the heroes – Satan, Messiah and Adam–Eve – have virtues; but in each the virtues are differently rank-ordered, and only Messiah gives obedience to God the place Milton believed it should occupy, above love itself. It need hardly be said that the various modes and moral standpoints are nevertheless all meant to be effective locally. Even Satan's rhetoric should seem impresssive:

> Farewell happy Fields
> Where Joy for ever dwells: Hail horrors, hail

> Infernal world, and thou profoundest Hell
> Receive thy new Possessor: One who brings
> A mind not to be chang'd by Place or Time.
> The mind is its own place, and in it self
> Can make a Heav'n of Hell, a Hell of Heav'n.
> What matter where, if I be still the same,
> And what I should be, all but less than he
> Whom Thunder hath made greater? Here at least
> We shall be free . . .
>
> (*Paradise Lost* i.249–59)

– until, that is, you recollect that it is not really 'Thunder' that makes Messiah great. Satan is courageous but false – and self-deceiving, as the confused idiom of 'all but less than' betrays.

The profound influence of *Paradise Lost* largely depended on its being the first modern epic to rival the ancient classics stylistically. It has an astonishing compression of texture, a simultaneous lucidity and rich variety, made possible by Milton's intellectual command. In fact, the Miltonic style may best be understood as a form of thinking – as developing the soliloquy on an epic scale. The effect is one of exhilarating speed in apprehension. Milton achieves this above all through a syntax that hurries on from one sketched construction to another, through immensely long loose paragraphs which if read at speed are not difficult to follow, in spite of locally ambiguous connections. Then, the imagery is richly orchestrated like the thought. Consider the account of Pandemonium's architect, later known to the Greeks, Milton tells us, as

> Mulciber; and how he fell
> From Heav'n, they fabl'd, thrown by angry Jove
> Sheer o're the Chrystal Battlements; from Morn
> To Noon he fell, from Noon to dewy Eve,
> A Summers day; and with the setting Sun
> Dropt from the Zenith like a falling Star,
> On Lemnos th' Aegaean Ile: thus they relate,
> Erring . . .
>
> (i.740–7)

How many strands are woven here – the angry deity, the crystal hint of heaven, the height of a summer's day (with dew so remote from hell), a visual glimpse of a tiny falling brightness, suggestions of relative scale, allusions to Homer – until the whole fabric is abruptly crumpled up and casually thrown aside as 'erring' mythology. As for the diction, while generally elevated, it combines Latinate phrasing (as familiar then as English, to educated men) with colloquial immediacy, in a way that makes us feel Milton to be using the best part of language. *Paradise Lost* achieves a style that poets have aimed at ever since – or, at least, until a decade or two ago.

It is a style that hardly lends itself to brief analysis, so much is happening in it. Even a phrase or two, such as the description of the tree of life, 'High eminent, blooming Ambrosial Fruit / Of vegetable Gold' (iv.219–20), might easily give rise to many pages of explanation, on such points as the epic diction of 'High eminent', with its modified adjective following the noun 'tree' – but also looking forward to 'Fruit'; or the transitive use of 'blooming', rare and therefore suggesting not only the verbal sense ('bearing') but also the adjectival ('flowering, flourishing'), so that the plant as it were matures from flower to fruit within the phrase; or the famous paradox 'vegetable Gold', with its reference to the alchemic vegetable stone, a form of the elixir – one of many forward glances to a Fallen world where such purifications and remedies will become necessary; or the golden fruit's many analogues in paintings of the Fall – a sort of visual precision frequent with Milton, blind though he was. A supremely intellectual style, it nevertheless satisfies sensuously at every point.

Throughout the fictive world of *Paradise Lost*, creative originality scintillates. Milton's world is an astonishing, almost science-fictional construction, based on extrapolation of one great premise, unfallen nature – a presupposition worked out in every particular, from the psychological and zoological to the astronomical and gastronomical. The idea gives him *carte blanche* to make an implicit anthology of tradition and contemporary thought, dignifying what he believes best in them by using it for the basis of his unfallen world. Other materials for paradise come from the Biblical account, subjected afresh to minute scientific as well as theological reinterpretation. And finally the contemporary passion for gardening makes the whole illusion possible, since it allows Milton's new epic mixture – georgic instead of pastoral epic – to seem at once immediate and serious and desirable.

Paradise Lost was to have a unique value for the period that followed. Did it not rival the greatest achievements of the ancients in the most prestigious of genres? Ostentatious formal originality could be found in earlier attempts at epic, for example Spenser's. What made *Paradise Lost* an example to be followed was the brilliance of Milton's performance, and its accessibility to imitation. And besides having an influence on poets, thanks to Addison it came to enjoy a popular reception as well. It is, in fact, the most important of our vernacular classics; and as such it belongs both to its own time and to subsequent tradition. Its theology, its georgic enthusiasm, its multigeneric – almost operatic – form: these are of the seventeenth century. But the interpretation of georgic as a distinct mode was to be a major task of the eighteenth century; generic mixture in emulation of Milton's became a Victorian, and later a modernist, habit; and the moral issues of his poem remain live enough in our own time to excite many deliberate misreadings. Almost every ambitious writer from Pope to Joyce has in a sense written within the specific tradition of this one work.

The relevance and yet timelessness of a great work come out sharply when one compares *Paradise Lost* with Abraham Cowley's recently discovered epic *The Civil War*. Overtly, Cowley's serious, vivid poem is far more relevant to the events of his time, which it sometimes follows in more or less literal detail. But Milton's poem does not even make obvious whether the rebellion of fallen angels corresponds to the Great Rebellion against Charles I. Charles II's licensers are said to have found an allusion to the king in Milton's highly monarchic Satan; and in Parliamentary eyes, indeed, the Civil War was begun by Charles's rebelling against 'the Crown', in the sense of the king's office or notional 'true body'. But this antimonarchic thrust of *Paradise Lost* is not unqualified by less partisan reflections, which have allowed readers to see revolutionary traits in its Satan.

Some have even recast Satan as the poem's hero and their own; thinking it a deep thing to do to penetrate beyond Milton's official purpose of justifying the ways of God. But in fact this approach arrives only at archetypal symbolisms that could have been drawn equally well from other more superficial poems. These symbolisms have little to do with Milton's meaning – which incidentally contains its own critique of the aggressive drives underlying satanic pretension. Interpretation of *Paradise Lost* hardly begins unless it comes to grips with comparison between the differently rank-ordered virtues of Messiah and Adam–Eve, angels and devils. Milton was able to write an original epic because he had a new myth of virtue to offer – a morality of individual responsibility to God ('obedience') which he believed to be superior to the aristocratic honour of hierarchy. It is no exaggeration to speak of Milton as redefining honour. To idealize Satan, therefore, is to negate one of Milton's central affirmations.

The 'brief epic' *Paradise Regained* (1671) combines the Christian epic form found in numerous Christiads and episodic Biblical epics (Du Bartas, Drayton, Sandys) with the georgic mode, as well as with more internal cerebral genres like dialogue, colloquy and meditation. The admixtures are decisive. Epics such as Drayton's *Noah's Flood* (1630) had simply ornamented narratives from the Bible – often very enjoyably. But Milton followed out in detail the intellectual implications of a few strategic situations, to austerely magnificent effect. Yet, although it is currently under revaluation, *Paradise Regained* has never so far been rightly valued. Critics have required it to repeat the pleasures of *Paradise Lost*; and missing these have convicted it of bareness, overemphasis or repetitious prolixity. But in actual fact Milton seems to have been reaching out to a new style – one less compressed, ambiguous and epigrammatic than that of his first epic, but more lucid, unfolded and precise. It is a mistake to see this style as merely emphatic (or overemphatic): Milton's energies go as much, if not more, into the experiment of acting out the sense through local variations in syntax and diction. An obvious instance, occurring quite frequently, is the unnecessary accumulation of alternative constructions, in order to mime the act of choosing – or sometimes the temptation's exhaustiveness:

> beasts of chase, or fowl of game,
> In pastry built, or from the spit, or boiled.
> (*Paradise Regained* ii. 342–3)

Another, probably more frequent still, is appositional reiteration, used to imitate the process of thought. Thus, Milton's stringing together of near synonyms does not spring from careless lack of concision, but simulates the mind's error-correction in arriving progressively at the *mot juste*, or covering omitted shades of meaning; hence such lines as 'His Honour, Virtue, Merit, and chief Praise', and 'Get Riches first, get Wealth, and Treasure heap . . .' (the latter also miming the accumulation it refers to). This georgic device, which we now take for granted, was rarely used before Spenser and Shakespeare. Milton was exploring a new world of stylistic possibility, a world that the poets of the eighteenth century were to open up and settle. Then, miming the shape of thought – making the sound seem an echo of the sense – would become a main, even a programmatic, objective.

REVALUATIONS, EXPERIMENTS AND SURVIVALS

One of the strongest impressions imparted by Milton's writings is of intellectual edge. This is of course a personal quality; but it also amounts to more than that. In one way or another rationality seems ubiquitous in Restoration society – even in the wit of rakes like Rochester. Thus, the literature is characterized by scepticism and experiment, and especially by radical (often ruthless) revaluation. In much of this, the effects of scientific interests and new discoveries are evident. A more dubious factor seems to have been demoralizing relativisms fostered by repeated changes of regime. Certainly literature is not free from the period's negative features – from spiritual agonizing, moral scepticism, libertinism, intellectual superficiality and heartlessness. But its tendencies are contradictory to an extent even greater than with most periods; and those who slip into thinking of the Restoration as dissolute should remind themselves of the austere rationality of the Cambridge Platonists. These philosophers of Emmanuel College reasserted the intellectual order of the universe; and managed, unusually, to combine ecstatic mystical strains with a wide rational tolerance. 'Vitals in religion', Benjamin Whichcote believed, 'are few.'

Every age can be seen as transitional, mingling the old with the new, the experimental with the venerable. But in Restoration literature such contradictions are particularly obvious; perhaps because of political interruptions of tradition, or the extraneous nature of French cultural influences (which intensified with the return of the court). The contradictions were partly recognized at the time – as will appear in the next chapter from the controversy between Ancients and Moderns. There were still those who wrote within the forms and conventions of the Reformation period, or even of the Middle Ages, like John Bunyan (1628–88). Bunyan none the less created at least one enduring work. As often, it is the late contribution to a kind that achieves the status of classic.

The Pilgrim's Progress (1678; 1684) stands firmly in the tradition of medieval pilgrim allegory – of Langland, Deguileville and (less directly) Spenser. As usual in that genre, the fable or outward story is told with proverbial imagery, in colloquial language:

> And the more drink he hath in his crown, the more of these things he hath in his mouth: Religion hath no place in his heart, or house, or conversation; all he hath lieth in his tongue, and his Religion is to make a noise therewith . . . His house is as empty of Religion, 'as the white of an Egg is of savour'.

Bunyan has none of the difficulty or subtlety of Spenser; his allegory sets out familiar dogmas of the theology of Election in a harsh and fairly crude version. Yet even so he leaves nothing to chance. He spells everything out and works in at every point step-by-step interpretations in the medieval didactic manner. These are spoken by figures like Evangelist or Interpreter or Help: 'It is the descent whither the scum and filth that attends conviction for sin doth continually run, and therefore it is called the Slough of Dispond.' The earnestness – the compelling intensity of Christian's spiritual tribulations – has left a deep impress on the national imagination; so that the Delectable Montains, the Palace Beautiful, the Slough of Despond, Vanity Fair and the rest have become features of our mental landscape – to say nothing of Bunyan's powerful influence on other writers, from Swift and Thackeray to T. F. Powys.

In one sense, little in Bunyan is original. He borrows his large-scale imagery from pious emblem literature, or directly from the Bible (as side notes testify). Even the style, which many have praised, usually depends on the Authorized Version, by paraphrase or pastiche of its cadences – except that that is a misleading way to put it, since Biblical language was the language of Bunyan's own thought. The narrative must be called bare rather than spare, laborious rather than detailed. But somehow Bunyan turns even clumsinesses to account, so that they become warrants of seriousness, or help to communicate an infectious terror:

> In this Combat no man can imagine, unless he had seen and heard as I did, what yelling, and hideous roaring Apollyon made all the time of the fight, he spake like a Dragon: and on the other side, what sighs and groans brast [burst] from Christians heart. I never saw him all the while give so much as one pleasant look, till he perceived he had wounded Apollyon with his two-edg'd sword, then indeed he did smile, and look upward: but twas the dreadfullest sight that ever I saw.

The power and the pleasure of the book lie in its utter singleness of intention. Its consistency is absolute. *Grace Abounding* (1665), Bunyan's spiritual autobiography, is equally single-minded, and has more formal originality and economy; but evidences in it of abnormal psychology are more obvious and limiting.

One historian has identified the special savour of Restoration verse as its fascination with power. There is much in this: the panegyric verse of the period may be seen as poets' celebration of power in others, its satire as exercise of their own. But power was not yet commonly recognized as a category so fundamental as Hobbes argued it to be. A truer generalization might describe Restoration verse as fascinated with valuation and revaluation. Not only did changes of regime bring home relativities of value, but the cultural revolution that had broken up the Renaissance world picture necessitated a great deal of subsequent rethinking. Earlier, value had often been assigned according to place in the scheme of things; now, it had to be decided by fresh thought. From this point of view, literary criticism was a natural activity of the age, while panegyric and satire were opposite faces of a single coin.

Many new forms emerged from the age's chaotic yet creative bustle. However, its intellectuality found epigrammatic verse satire particularly congenial. In this grouping one of the most interesting works is Samuel Butler's *Hudibras* (1662; 1663; 1678), which used to be taken as a burlesque of Spenserian epic, satirizing Puritan hypocrisy. In reality Butler was repelled by every sect. His satire is far more extensive than at first appears; taking in not only every party and hypocrisy, but every high intention – indeed, every serious human activity whatsoever:

> 'Tis not Antiquity, nor Author,
> That makes truth truth, altho time's daughter;
> 'Twas he that put her in the Pit,
> Before he pull'd her out of it.
> And as he eats his Sons, just so
> He feeds upon his Daughters too.
> (*Hudibras* II.iii.663–8)

Such scepticism is rather un-English in its extreme persistence, however quintessentially English it may be in other ways. Its engaging movement is a series of darting associational side-steps – sometimes learned similitudes so far-fetched as to amount to Metaphysical conceits. In this use of associational sequence, Butler occupies an important place in the filiation extending from Rabelais through Nashe to Sterne and Joyce. But *Hudibras* has also a single connecting theme: namely, the unrelenting reduction of everything high or heroic. Its doggerel verse is very free and irregular, and may seem crude. But the roughness is deliberate, and, read carefully, can be heard as a flexible rhythm expressing the turns of an interesting, ironic mind. Butler contributed to the formal repertoire a particular variety of 'bad' or scrambling near-rhyme, known – like the verse itself – as HUDIBRASTIC:

> When . . . Pulpit, Drum Ecclesiastick,
> Was beat with fist, instead of a stick:
> Then did Sir Knight abandon dwelling,
> And out he rode a Colonelling.
> (*Hudibras* I.i.11–12)

Butler's exuberant octosyllabics could not be more different from the covertly ironic verses of Andrew Marvell (1621–78). 'An Horatian Ode upon Cromwell's Return from Ireland' (1650) is exquisitely smooth

panegyric, cut and undercut by razor-sharp ironies. Cromwell blasted
Charles like lightning, for:

> 'Tis Madness to resist or blame
> The force of angry Heaven's flame:
> And, if we would speak true,
> Much to the man is due . . .
>
>   (lines 25–8)

These lines are perfectly clear; yet some implication eludes you. It is not
that you want to know whether to stress 'much' ('To be honest, we do
owe Cromwell a lot') or 'man' ('Besides Providence's lightning, much is
attributable to the ambitious *man* who "urged" his own star'). The
meaning might hover between these possibilities and others. Rather do
you want to know what tone of voice to imagine the lines said in. That
would catch the shade of irony. Is it reluctant ironic resignation, or
privately mordant acquiescence? Ambivalence or ambiguity? In such
cases (and they come up often in Marvell's poetry), everything seems to
depend on the TONE or vocal reflection of attitude. The element of tone
acquires, in fact, new subtlety and importance through his work. Satiric
irony such as his must be thought far from the 'ritual of aggression'
found by some in Jacobean satire.

Many Restoration satires were IMITATIONS, that is, recreations of
older, often classical works. The satires of the Latin poets Horace and
Juvenal, especially, were recultivated in this way, and yielded late fruits
in the shape of some of the most striking poems of the period. Opinion
differed as to how close to its original an imitation ought to be, and in
what ways. But when John Oldham hit on thorough modernization –
transposing classics to new situations altogether – he produced what by
any account are sparklingly fresh poems. At the same time, imitations
incorporated great quantities of poetic ideas and structural sequences
from the literature of the first Augustan age; and thus laid an essential
foundation for the English Augustan movement to come. Among the
best were those by Oldham (1653–83), Sir Charles Sedley (1639–1701)
and John Wilmot, Earl of Rochester (1647–80). Oldham's were the
closest in thought to their originals, yet also the most varied and
technically ambitious. A new degree of smooth ease – learnt from in
turn by Pope – was reached in Oldham's imitation of Horace, *Satires*
I.ix (1681), where the bore tells us

> None has a greater gift in poetry,
> Or writes more verses with more ease than I;

> I'm grown the envy of the men of wit,
> I killed even Rochester with grief and spite . . .
>> (lines 65–8)

Oldham's Juvenal xiii (1682) is less even, but more distinctive and powerful:

> No shame, nor loss of ears, can frighten these,
> Were every street a grove of pillories.
>> (lines 137–8)

He is fond of soaring hyperboles, which however sometimes disintegrate into overemphatic rant.

Rochester strikes out more sparks of brilliance than Oldham – or any other satirist before Pope. But tremendous gusts of passion pour irresistibly through his verse paragraphs and give him no chance to qualify feelings or develop subtleties. He is extremely fluent with personas and their speech, and tends in consequence to rattle on in a way that lacks weight. Nevertheless, in spite of his own character as a debauchee, and his choice of unpromising subjects (dildos, perhaps, or nothing at all), he can often be worth reading for his moral content. He is quick-witted in making points – as when he says that wretched man is always arming himself out of fear: 'For fear he arms, and is of arms afraid, / By fear, to fear, successively betrayed . . .' And his imagery shifts and adroitly transforms itself as rapidly:

> Reason, an Ignis fatuus, in the Mind,
> Which leaving light of Nature, sense behind;
> Pathless and dang'rous wandring ways it takes,
> Through errors Fenny – Boggs, and Thorny Brakes;
> Whilst the misguided follower, climbs with pain,
> Mountains of Whimseys, heap'd in his own Brain:
> Stumbling from thought to thought, falls headlong down,
> Into doubt's boundless Sea, where like to drown,
> Books bear him up awhile, and make him try,
> To swim with Bladders of Philosophy;
> In hopes still t'oretake th'escaping light,
> The Vapour dances in his dazzling sight,
> Till spent, it leaves him to eternal Night.
>> ('Satyr', 12–24)

But the same speed can make for obscurity when he does not wait to be clear. Perhaps also from impatience, he has left many phrases of uncertain rhythm, jerky or even stiff in movement – as in 'They act Adultery with their own Wives'. These faults show up against the work of his contemporaries and immediate successors. For imitation was a very competitive form (the originals and other imitations of them were known to all); so that it reached a high standard of craft. Rochester wrote an especially fine free imitation of Horace *Satires* I.x; but his best is agreed to be the general 'Satyr' (or 'Satire') 'Were I (who to my cost already am' (1679).

In the metrical craft of the Restoration (to digress) we can observe two very different developments. One was the smoothing of the pentameter line, which had begun earlier under Jonson's direction, and which was to issue in the Augustan couplet. Edmund Waller (1606–87) was perhaps the principal craftsman of this smooth flexible line. He used such devices as parallelism, inversion and delay of the verb, in order to secure strong internal and final pauses – 'And Judges grave on high Tribunals frown'. (Compare Pope's 'And wretches hang that jurymen may dine'.) This type of line excluded rough emphatic rhythms. But within its limitations it had the advantages of eloquence and sensitivity to small rhythmic variations, as well as of accessibility to the amateur ear. The other development was the PINDARIC ODE, a lofty, often celebratory genre in irregular stanzas, modelled ultimately on the practice of the ancient Greek poet Pindar. Abraham Cowley (1618–67) – followed and surpassed by Dryden – established the form, in such bold flights as 'The Ecstasy', 'The Muse' and 'Brutus' (all ptd 1656). These odes expressed exuberant heated ideas and passionate feelings in appropriately loose and (relatively) free rhythms. Their variation of line length was a feature of particular importance for the future of poetic form.

But to return to imitations. They may seem to be in effect translations, and indeed the dividing line is sometimes faint. But we have to allow for different concepts of translation: especially for an earlier, Jonsonian, phrase-by-phrase method, by contrast with which imitation stood out as a distinct alternative. The freer Chapmanian (and French) method of translation – paraphrase rather than metaphrase – only gradually took hold in Britain; but, when it did, it gave a great impulse to literature. The intellectual curiosity of the age made it eager for translations that communicated the spirit of their originals. And enthusiasm for the new approach now brought on some of our greatest translations, not only from ancient, but also from modern vernacular, literatures. In such a movement, to be early was much. Among many fine translations that established themselves as classics, it is almost invidious to select but some for brief mention. Pace-setting imitations included Robert Herrick's and Thomas Stanley's (1625–78) from the convivial Anacreon, the ancient and reputedly profound Greek epigrammatist – extremely smooth, polite and private. And possibly the best of all the verse translators was Sir Richard Fanshawe (1608–66), whose version of Camoens's *Lusiadas* combines weight and energy with an exotic strangeness that comports well with the subject of exploration:

> Replied Veloso: 'tis not fit, not just,
> To treat soft subjects in so hard extremes.
> For a Sea-life (replenisht with disgust)
> Permits not love, permits not melting Themes.
> Our Story be of War, bloody, Robust;
> For we (the Wefts and Pilgrims of the streams)
>   Are only born to horror and distress:
>   Our future dangers whisper me no less.
>
>   (*The Lusiad* vi.41)

In an apostrophe to Fanshawe, John Denham contrasted him with earlier line-by-line translators: they 'but preserve the ashes, thou the flame'.

Prose translation was no less flourishing. The outstanding achievement – and indeed it still finds readers – is an incomplete version (1653) of Rabelais's works by Sir Thomas Urquhart, the Scottish exponent of universal (i.e. international) language. With superb confidence Urquhart often excels his French original. His word plays are more preposterous, his lists of synonyms longer, his excesses wilder and more reprehensible. Such overreaching would ruin the proportions of most originals; but with Rabelais it is just the tactic to communicate his extravagant spirit. Urquhart has flair in rendering non-semantic effects – effects of rhythm and texture and irony. Yet he also knows when to be simple and literal:

> None did awake them, none did offer to constrain them to eat, drink, nor to do any other thing; for so had Gargantua established it. In all their rule, and strictest tie of their order, there was but this one clause to be observed, DO WHAT THOU WILT. Because men that are free, well-born, well-bred, and conversant in honest companies, have naturally an instinct and spur that prompteth them unto virtuous actions, and withdraws them from vice, which is called honour.
>
>   (*Gargantua and Pantagruel* i.57)

Urquhart's Rabelais was a considerable achievement; it captured for our literature a domain that Sterne and Joyce and others have since inhabited without noticeably exhausting its resources. To turn to Charles Cotton's translation of Montaigne's *Essais* (1685) is to meet almost a contrast in style. Here the proportions of the original are faithfully sustained in every way (Florio's earlier translation is crude beside it); and Cotton's self-effacing style makes a limpid, seemingly natural medium, through which Montaigne speaks English easily. To some, Cotton's translation seems too 'polite', or smooth. They cannot have pondered the degree of Montaigne's own sophistication.

If translations and imitations are peripheral to literature in one direction, diaries and journals and special histories depart from it in another. The period was immensely rich in such writings; as if the dire public events had positively stimulated not only formal histories but private memorials of every kind. Samuel Pepys's Diary (1659–69), John Evelyn's Diary (1641–1706), Celia Fiennes's Diary (1685–1703), the Brief Lives of John Aubrey (1626–97), Anthony Wood's Diary and *Athenae Oxonienses* (1691–2) and Richard Gough's *The History of Myddle* (1700–2): all are of engrossing interest. They fall short of literature, however, in some sense; in that their contents are not always very thoughtfully selected, nor their syntax finely ordered, nor their words chosen with care to avoid inert expressions. Indeed, the very miscellaneousness of Pepys's Diary is partly what makes it appeal to readers of another age. And his unguarded stylistic casualness – even the abbreviations and improvised grammar – add to the immediacy; so that we seem to be with him in his office as he brings his diary up to date, or paginates his Navy Manuscript, or busies himself about another of his many projects. Some of us are never more secure and delighted than when following the busy vicissitudes of such as Pepys, the bustling official in the Navy Office. Others may take an interest in the unwitting evidence he offers of values that have passed away from our own society – as in expressions of satisfaction that no modern diarist would conceivably use. Or we may be engaged by the complex developing personality, given to business and pleasure and detached recording; to habits and irregularities; to weaknesses of the flesh and oaths (sometimes effectual) of reform. Does the document's appeal lie in our sense of security by contrary; or in emancipation from our own time and place; or in its honesty beyond – and yet in some ways beneath – ours? No one could be happy with an idea of literature that excluded such writings.

RESTORATION DRAMA

The various qualities of the Restoration – its experimentation and scepticism, its cynicism and satiric investigation, its trimming accommodation and its reexamination of the social contract, its moral acuity and shallow intellectualizing – all are reflected in its drama; although this used to be denied by those who saw the drama as escapist. Nevertheless, a remarkable group of plays, by Dryden, Shadwell, Etherege, Wycherley and Otway, followed after a pause by those of Congreve, Vanbrugh and Farquhar, stand out. These are distinguished by their sheer brilliance, without necessarily being representative of the full range of styles and topics that characterize the productive half century from 1660. This activity is the more remarkable in view of the fact that all the writing was for only two theatre companies – the Duke's, expertly managed by Sir William Davenant; and the King's, under Thomas Killigrew. Indeed, after the unrest connected with the Popish Plot (1678) theatre-going declined, the King's Company failed and a single United Company was formed (1682). The correspondingly minute audience for Restoration drama used to be described as a dissolute court coterie; but that idea is now exploded. In the earlier period, court patronage was naturally influential. Throughout, however, the audience was socially varied, and towards the end of the century it became distinctly bourgeois – and much worse behaved. Its tastes seem to have been homogeneously various.

Remarkably, in spite of the closing of the public theatres during the Commonwealth, continuity between Caroline and Carolean (Restoration) drama was unbroken. For one thing, the entire repertory at the outset was inherited. For another, during the first decade the influence of Fletcher's prose comedy was supreme. (Plays like *The Scornful Lady* were in a sense ahead of their time – and still seem astonishingly 'modern'.) John Shirley, too, can be seen as a pre-Restoration dramatist. In many ways, in fact, the break in dramatic tradition came not at the Interregnum but much earlier, through the development of naturalistic dramatic style. On the other hand, the introduction of female actors after the Restoration, and the increased use of scenery – to say nothing of the proscenium arch imported from the masque stage – were radical departures. In any event, the rapid turnover of the repertory (runs were less than a week) encouraged production of new plays and quick changes of style. The new plays embodied such types as heroic drama, romance, intrigue comedy, refined comedy and *précieuse* tragicomedy. They might concentrate on plot or on personality, on negative or on positive example, on wit or on humour (that is, satiric character). When critics discuss Restoration drama, however, it is most often the 1670s fashion for sex comedies that they are concerned with.

William Wycherley's *The Country-Wife* (1675) is now the most acted of these. The genre was one that had always to keep going further in new flagrancies of wish-fulfilling naughtiness. In this instance, Horner is a stud – and correspondingly a focus of strong or complex feelings. He is supposed to have suffered surgery in connection with the pox, and passes as impotent, so far as the husbands choose to know (the wives are better informed). In the sustained *double entendre* of the notorious 'china scene' (IV.iii), 'the filthiest thing in that play', as a character in *The Plain-Dealer* has it, the wives lubriciously compare Horner's services to them, under the pretence of discussing his china. Lady Fidget says 'To my certain knowledge he has no more left', but Mrs Squeamish feels sure 'he may have some you could not find'. Acted shamelessly enough, the scene can still give offence to many and great delight to many more. It is meant to be outrageous, and has not surprisingly prompted questions about Wycherley's moral purpose. But there can be little doubt of his anatomizing various types of jealousy, deception and hypocrisy, brought together by the turns of an ingenious and wildly improbable plot. *The Country-Wife* is not profound satire; but its underlying attitudes are consistent enough, and its art sustained enough, to validate the fun. Of all the Restoration dramatists, Wycherley has most ability to unsettle the sensitive. Vigour disguises his moral purposes effectively; but if his deeply implicit arguments do not persuade audiences, they can always admire how exhaustively his searching comedy squeezes new mileage out of stock jokes.

Moral questions have similarly attached to Sir George Etherege's *The Man of Mode* (1676), in its own time as now a controversial yet acknowledged masterpiece. The false Dorimant epitomizes all that is reprehensible in the fashionable man of pleasure – 'next to the coming to a good understanding with a new mistress, I love a quarrel with an old one'. All the same, he is portrayed attractively, and, far from meeting cautionary desserts in the dénouement, appears to succeed – overcoming Lady Woodvil's objections and marrying the delectable Harriet. The plot is simple to vacuity; but Etherege's wit has brilliance, his persiflage fantasy, and his descriptions poetry, while his characters present complexity enough to have puzzled many. A good deal turns on how Harriet's eventual lot is envisaged. We may think her easily able to look after herself and Dorimant too; in which case she cannot be counted as another of his triumphs. Although explicit moralizing is not to be looked for in this subtle play, we may nevertheless conclude that it nudges the feelings on towards a more marital disposition. All is a matter of delicate balances between characters – and between the audience's poised feelings for them.

In *Marriage A-la-Mode* (a. 1672), Dryden openly set out to raise the tone of comedy. The play's manners were professedly modelled on court gallantry – and specifically on the conversational style of the dedicatee, Rochester – as shows in the fineness of its compliments. The crude sexual stereotypes of cuckoldry are still relied on; but Dryden has found ways of hinting at them, without always pursuing *doubles entendres* quite to the hilt (even though he had a name for being able to do so). The grandiloquent main plot is heroic or high romantic. This relates thematically to the antiromantic minor plot through a shared metaphor of 'dying', in its sexual and literal senses. Dryden advances the complicated, undetailed action economically. This he does by means of a system of very frequent asides, which can reveal character quickly, and which almost amount to an additional plane of reality. The plotting is so tight and symmetrical – Rhodophil and Palamede both love the other's wife – that it may give the impression of an abstract art or game, 'a pretty odd kind of game' (III.ii.156). But there is more to the play than that. The true prince Leonidas may for a time express such a sentiment as 'Duty's a Name; and Love's a Real thing' (IV.iv.46), but in total effect *Marriage A-la-Mode* offers a defence of sensible behaviour between husbands and wives. It is striking (and quite funny) that however libertine the private 'league' finally arrived at by Rhodophil and Pala-mede (V.i) may seem in its wording, in substance it merely reformulates the institution of marriage.

In his Epilogue, Dryden appealed for moral support to the City – perhaps not altogether ingenuously. And before many years elapsed, theatre audiences would in fact become largely bourgeois; Jeremy Collier would make his notorious attack on *The Immorality and Profaneness of the English Stage* (1698); and the tense bravura of Restoration drama would relax, giving place to sentimental drama with unreal, exemplary characters. Congreve, it is true, responded to the moral challenge with *The Way of the World* (1700), a finely constructed and in part a brilliant play. (In the sparkling 'proviso scene', IV.v, where Millamant and Mirabell set out their satirical conditions for happiness, Congreve updates the marriage contract yet again, inviting a comparison with Dryden that is not to his own disadvantage.) But any argument based on *The Way of the World* would be double-edged. It is a complex, over-subtle play, perhaps impossible to appreciate to the full in the theatre. Nevertheless Congreve's small *oeuvre* is the most impressive of the period. In a play such as *Love for Love* (1695) he achieves a human variety and depth of insight beyond the usual range of Dryden.

The earlier, more thorough-going sex comedies currently attract more interest. Wycherley's, especially, can have impressive thematic development – as with his analysis of the moral and manly man's reluctant adjustment to society in *The Plain-Dealer* (1676) – although excitement there springs more from violent unsettling of sympathies with the hero. Manly is a problematic character – touchstone-sure in detecting hypocrisy, yet slow to see his own interest; morally lucid, yet deluded and ruthless in love.

How are we to estimate Restoration comedy? From Macaulay onwards, opinion has alternated between moral disapproval, on the one hand, and, on the other, something like Charles Lamb's only half-serious view that the form is unreal, artificial and therefore immune from moral considerations – which has given rise, in turn, to charges of triviality and emptiness. But the point of the comedy begins to be seen as lying more in display of manners expressing scepticism, or exploring ambiguous moral concepts. The improbable moral holidays now appear as deliberately false premises, which allow science-fictional treatment of everyday realities. Serious and intellectual as Restoration comedy may be, however, it is clever rather than profound. It is not indeed trivial; but that does not mean it has many deep thoughts. Thought-provoking would be a better description. It is a literature of entertainment – and why not? At the same time, there are things to learn from presentations of intelligent vice in full swing (if sharply observed), which could not be learnt from virtuous precepts. They may not exactly be lessons of virtue; but they feed the moral life none the less.

7
Augustan Classicism

THE term AUGUSTAN is used in very different ways: sometimes descriptively for the period of Queen Anne's reign (1702–14), sometimes for an ideal that was formative during the much longer period from about 1660 until the middle of the eighteenth century. Its basis was the analogy between Charles II, restored to the throne after the Interregnum, and Octavius Caesar, whose imperial establishment also ended a period of civil war. This analogy regularly implied certain convictions or hopes, of mythic proportion, concerning Britain's universal role, heaven's favour and a new age of enlightened patronage in which arts of peace would flourish. So Dryden hopefully welcomed Charles with the exclamation

> Oh Happy Age! Oh times like those alone
> By Fate reserved for Great Augustus' Throne!
> *(Astraea Redux* 320–1)

Gradually the emphasis altered, however, so that by the time of Pope and Swift – and still more that of Joseph Warton and David Hume – the analogy tended rather to stress the Augustan era's reforming character. Now the Restoration became a time of licence and corruption; and Charles was no longer quite an Augustus. He might be the friend of wits, but he lacked the true generosity of a patron: Otway had starved, Rochester's loose genius had gone unchastened. Increasingly, the value of classical civility was given a moral turn.

The analogy also progressively changed its focus in chronological terms. Retrospection worked its way through successive stages of Roman history, from the civil war period treated by Lucan (a favourite model in the early seventeenth century), through the Augustan peace, to the later fall of Rome, which was to possess Edward Gibbon and the British admirers of Piranesi). But to understand Augustan classicism, one has first to see how much it was impelled by prophetic ideas of reform – how much it looked towards a new age of enlarged possibilities.

AUGUSTAN CRITICISM

A gently reforming moral tone pervades the essays of Joseph Addison (1672–1719) and Sir Richard Steele (1672–1729), muted, however, and underplayed with a studiously informal style:

> It is my design in this paper to deliver down to posterity a faithful account of the Italian opera, and of the gradual progress which it has made upon the English stage: for there is no question but our great grand-children will be very curious to know the reason why their forefathers used to sit together like an audience of foreigners in their own country, and to hear whole plays acted before them in a tongue which they did not understand.
>
> ([Addison] *The Spectator* No. 18, 21 March 1711)

Even so, Addison's style is hardly so easy or relaxed as Dryden's. It is notable, therefore, that the persuasive power of *The Spectator* was much more widespread. Assisted by Steele and later by others, Addison produced *The Spectator* essays daily at first, besides organizing monthly sets and bound collections (1711–12, 1714). The essays went to over 400 subscribers (including some women, middle class as well as aristocratic): probably 4,000 copies in all were printed, and each was claimed to have twenty readers. Some essays purported to be written by members of a club, fictive personas like the sensible Whig Sir Andrew Freeport and the idealistic (but rather out-of-touch) Tory Sir Roger de Coverley. And of course Addison himself was the eponymous observer – an early instance in literature of the spectator attitude. *The Spectator* partly succeeded because it made few demands on its well-judged audience. It broached relatively few ideas, and conveyed them with unnecessarily abundant examples. In the multiplication of these there is a noticeable element of game – a device that was to be taken up by nineteenth-century essayists.

But one should not underestimate Addison: behind his good sense subtle persuasive strategies are at work in the Whig cause. Luckily these seem beneficient to modern inheritors of Whiggery. And if others can despise Addison's modest, liberal, non-doctrinal moderation, this is only because something like it has been established as a general standard, through his influence. In any case, his supposedly comfortable lukewarm mediocrity (with its correspondingly middle style) in actual fact ranges widely. It stoops to coffee houses and candlesticks; extends to an astonishing variety of social and literary topics; and rises to the sublimity – a new concept, this – of 'all the depths of eternity'. (Vast features of nature like mountains and spatial immensities, previously regarded as ugly monstrosities or objects of horror, were just beginning to be appreciated as SUBLIME, awe-inspiring, pleasurable.) The illusion that a single easy style can do all this without loss counts as a chief limitation of Addison's. Nevertheless the random element in the variety of *The Spectator* now has a distinct time-machine effect: through its pages eighteenth-century England seems to be rerun before us. One paper is about a perspective glass that allows a person to

> take a view of another, without the impertinence of staring; at the same time it shall not be possible to know whom or what he is looking at . . . This is set forth at large in the printed proposals for the sale of these glasses, to be had at Mr. Dillon's, in Long-Acre, next door to the White Hart . . . The inventor desires your admonitions, concerning the decent use of it . . .
>
> (*The Spectator* No. 250, 17 December 1711)

In the next, Addison writes on the Cries of London:

> Vocal cries are of a much larger extent, and indeed so full of incongruities and barbarisms, that we appear a distracted city, to foreigners, who do not comprehend the meaning of such enormous outcries. Milk is generally sold in a note above *Elah* [high E], and in sounds so exceedingly shrill, that it often sets our teeth on edge. The chimney sweeper is confined to no certain pitch; he sometimes utters himself in the deepest base, and sometimes in the sharpest treble; sometimes in the highest, and sometimes in the lowest note of the gamut. The same observation might be made on the retailers of small-coal, not to mention broken glasses or brick-dust.
>
> (*The Spectator* No. 251, 18 December 1711)

This effect should not be thrown away (as it sometimes is in selections) by picking out one ingredient, like the Coverley papers. It is certainly tempting to do this, though, with the eighteen papers on *Paradise Lost*, which did much to establish Milton's strategic position in Augustan literature. Together they make up, in effect, the earliest instance of a critical monograph meant for the general reader.

Addison's excellent taste, based on a sound rather than merely fashionable classicism, could appreciate a wide range of texts – even including some earlier popular literature. And he had enough originality to reach out towards emergent aesthetic ideas like that of the sublime (which was to be of central importance to the Romantic movement).

But much Augustan criticism tended to be narrower in conception. Often it was based on the assumption that ancient authors had already scaled all the heights, so that these were now best approached by correctly realizing classical forms, or recreating an earlier writer's tone or style. Such IMITATION worked tolerably well, where appropriate precedents existed: models are indispensable in serious art; and the familiar classics sometimes provided them effectively. Close emulation of Horace, for example, could have a tonic effect, as Rochester's or Pope's highly original 'imitations' suggest – to say nothing of the mass of lesser but still decent attempts (imitations of a single ode fill a considerable volume).

There were also, however, extensive tracts of literary endeavour with little or nothing by way of classical precedent. Classically minded critics tended to neglect these vernacular forms altogether, or else, what was worse, to apply to them inappropriate classical criteria such as unity. Then they could be savagely rigorous. Even the acute John Dennis (1657–1734), although in general a champion of Shakespeare, writes that 'the Faults of Shakespeare, which are rather those of the Age in which he lived, are his perpetual Rambles, and his apparent Duplicity in some of his Plays, or Triplicity of Action . . .'. Such wrongheadedness is often blamed on rules – neoclassical criticism was 'prescriptive'. But all judicial criticism, even the best, must apply rules. Dennis's comment goes wrong not because it is prescriptive, but because the rule it applies – the rule of single action – is irrelevant to Shakespeare's English genres.

Neoclassical criticism took for granted the possibility of describing, in quite a definite and minute way, each genre of classical origin: epic, tragedy, georgic and satire – even epigram, epitaph and lesser kinds. Such descriptions or rules covered not only formal structure but topics, tone, diction and every other constituent then recognized. In theory, the rules were not immutable:

> Great Wits sometimes may *gloriously offend*,
> And *rise* to *Faults* true Critics *dare not mend*; . . .
> (Pope, *An Essay on Criticism* 152–3)

But the extent to which modern examples might be regarded as having modified classical rules was controversial. This issue related to the controversy between Ancients and Moderns (the substance of Swift's *Battle of the Books*), and ultimately to the widening split between philological scholarship and science. One might suppose that all the writers would be Moderns, on the side of Robert Boyle, the Royal

Society and progress. But almost the reverse is true. Certainly Sir
William Temple was an Ancient, and so were Swift (his secretary for a
time) and Pope:

> Learn hence for Ancient *Rules* a just Esteem;
> To copy *Nature* is to copy *Them*.
> > (*An Essay on Criticism* 139–40)

EPIC TRANSLATIONS

The rules show no sign of having constrained Milton in *Paradise Lost*, a
more or less classical epic. His conception of them had been formed in
an earlier, freer period. After *Paradise Regained* (1671), however, there
was something of a crisis in the history of epic. An obvious (although
neglected) cause must be the personal difficulty faced by any poet
emulating a masterpiece such as Milton's. But that is not the whole
story. The challenge of epic had become overformidable for other
reasons, such as increasing difficulties in its mythological parts, and the
information explosion that had ended epitomization of learning in
traditional schemes of thought, thus making the responsibility of
encyclopedic completeness impossibly onerous. After the Reformation
and Counter-Reformation, moreover, the element of supernatural
agencies (known as epic MACHINERY) could no longer be treated in the
old Renaissance ways, accommodating pagan images as symbols of
Christian ideas. (Indeed, Christian belief itself was now under pressure.) Milton was the last to meet all the challenges of epic with success
– and even so he broke the rule that excluded Christian doctrine, by
often alluding to central verities of the Faith such as Christ's sacrifice for
the sins of mankind. After Milton, Sir Richard Blackmore's *Creation*
(1712) is remembered (if at all) by only a few passages. For the rest,
would-be epicists either merged epic with other genres (satire, georgic)
or else turned to particular predecessors and imitated them, now in the
parody and pastiche of MOCK EPIC, now in translation.

Supreme among verse translations of the period was Dryden's *Aeneis*
(1697), the crowning achievement of his strategic career, in which a
great innovator repeatedly returned to imitations of the classics. It
represents, too, the culmination of a century of effort by previous
translators of Virgil – lesser figures such as John Ogilby and the Earl of
Lauderdale – on whom Dryden drew very generously. One critic says
that certain passages 'can only be called Dryden's by the same figure of
speech which we use when we call cow's milk by the name of the

milkman who distributes it'. But this mistakes Dryden's intention, which was to use previous translations as materials for work of another, and more interesting, kind. He was not merely a more tasteful competitor in the same field. In a century of great translations he aimed – freely adding or subtracting particulars – at an imitation that would live with the spirit of the original: an English poem that would yet breathe with the Latin's vitality. Dryden may have failed to realize the stillness and economy of the *Aeneid*; but he marvellously rendered its various texture. This he pursued in a variety of ways. He went to immense pains to simulate individual sounds or actions mimetically, by devices learnt from Spenser and from Virgil himself. Thus, rhythm can be made to express length, as in

> Gold are their Vests: Long Alpine Spears they wield:
> And their left Arm sustains a length of Shield.
> (viii.877–8)

And there are many balanced and patterned lines similar to Virgil's: 'Who fights finds Death, and Death finds him who flies' (ii.450) (the inversion is expressive of Death's contrasting activity). Elsewhere Dryden sharpens lines to a modern edge. He will add enhancing allusions, political or literary, like 'And Acts and Monuments of Ancient Kings' (viii.415), which echoes Foxe's title. Or else he will enrich his verses with English spoils – as when he adds a Jonsonian epithet, to give Alecto her wonderfully sinister 'wicker wings' (vii.478).

But the greatest thing about the *Aeneis* is of a different order. When Pope called it 'the most noble and spirited translation I know in any language', and when Dr Johnson wrote of its 'sprightliness', what they had in mind was surely its strong momentum of forward movement. A reader is hardly inclined to linger over words, so great is the motive power – greater at times even than Milton's. And there is an irresistible *plein air* quality of direct nobility. Yet Johnson's famous phrase 'the hurry of delight' is not altogether right; for Dryden gives no sense of haste. His robust vigour aims at the main thing, and accomplishes this by according it a broad treatment. But then there is time to work in a sufficiency of sensitive details and to ensure that all contributes to the main effect. Dryden may not have Virgil's concentration, but he can convey the experience of epic – the sense of how a great authentic epicist might write in English.

In pursuing similar aims in his Homer translations – *Iliad* (1715–20); *Odyssey* (1725–6) – Pope had an advantage over Dryden. His predecessors were of superior quality – especially Chapman, Denham and

Dryden himself, to whom in a sense we must add Milton, since the latter imitated many Homeric passages, as well as providing a conveniently imitable epic diction. Yet although Pope often outdid the *Aeneis* locally, his Homer is not so delightful as a whole. It lacks Dryden's heroic singleness. In cultivating a more refined moral seriousness Pope introduces crowds of abstractions that tend to slow and confuse the reader, and make the narrative vague. Visually, however, he is precise and observant; so that careful selection can easily make him seem more brilliant than Dryden. Here is a sample, from Achilles' slaughter of Hector:

> Proud on his Car th'insulting Victor stood,
> And bore aloft his Arms, distilling [dripping] Blood.
> He smites the Steeds; the rapid Chariot flies;
> The sudden Clouds of circling Dust arise.
> Now lost is all that formidable Air;
> The Face divine, and long-descending Hair
> Purple the Ground, and streak the sable Sand;
> Deform'd, dishonour'd, in his native Land!
> Giv'n to the Rage of an insulting Throng!
> And, in his Parents' Sight, now dragg'd along!
>
> (*Iliad* 22.501–10)

The abstractions are not too confusing, the speedy violent alliterations not especially crude, the onomatopoetic dark consonants in lines 507–8 pretty fair. And the delicate colours exemplify a special contribution of Pope's: an individual painterly quality. But it is applied out of scale, in too much detail, until he comes to seem a miniaturist of wounds.

Pope's formidable problems arose in part from the height of his literary ambition. (The Homer was a great collective enterprise, whereby an atelier of assistants, Parnell, Broome, Fenton and others, prepared the canvas for Pope's virtuoso work.) He meant nothing less than revivification of the past – and a past, moreover, that would provide moral ideals for the present. With this in view, he felt obliged to interpolate analogies for heroic behaviour in contemporary aristocratic life. He made an identification – or what amounts to that – of the epic hero's hospitality with the English country gentleman's. A hyperconsciousness of rank crept in, a sense of insolent elevation that was quite foreign to Dryden, let alone Homer. At the same time Pope unfortunately rejected the ironies of Dryden's half-comic tone; opting instead for consistent seriousness and height. In consequence the antiquity he realized was pure but remote. Correctness, a virtue with

Dryden, had become deleterious – the limitation that notoriously made Fenton go through the contortions to avoid writing 'cow-heel':

> He said; and of the steer before him placed,
> That sinewy fragment at Ulysses cast,
> Where to the pastern-bone by nerves combined,
> The well-horned foot indissolubly joined . . .
>
> (*Odyssey* 20.365–8)

In such matters Pope had an enormous influence on his contemporaries, for good and ill. Yet he is hardly to blame if people sometimes failed to respond to the moral challenges of his Homer, but took up its more easily imitable poetic diction with enthusiasm. The generalized Latinate diction that F. R. Leavis saw as Miltonic is much more Pope's responsibility. One notes in particular a fondness for paired nouns and epithets in the same line: 'To shameful Bondage and unworthy Toils'; 'the hoar Head of unresisting Age'. The epithets are themselves a feature – sometimes concentrated and precise, as in 'hoarse-resounding shores', but often routine abstractions, or Latinisms designed to elevate ('eternal Hate'; 'meditated Blow'). But then, some of the pleasure of Pope's Homer comes from seeing how easily it maintains gravity and height.

MOCK EPIC

The Augustans may have found it no longer possible to produce original epics; but they had a keen appetite for the genre none the less. When this could not be satisfied by translations and scholarly editions, it took up epic as a vehicle for parody or satire.

Such a work is Pope's *Dunciad* (1728), a mock epic (or perhaps one should say satiric burlesque epic), ridiculing authors not to the poet's liking – notably Lewis Theobald the Shakespearean scholar, who had criticized Pope's edition of Shakespeare. The *Dunciad* exhibits many features of classical epic, some of them noticed for us by the 'editor' Martinus Scriblerus. There are invocations, divine interventions, games, visits to the underworld and visions of the future. But it has also another generic model – Renaissance epic. From the opening vision of the Cave of Poverty and Poetry and the Chaos where whimsical fancies or 'maggots' 'learn to crawl upon poetic feet' to the final vision of Dulness's cosmic yawn, the allegorical places often suggest Spenserian rather than Virgilian archetypes. One sees this in their pictorial quality and their fluidity. Again, allusion to individual contemporaries was a feature of Renaissance epic.

Not, of course, that Pope was satirizing Virgil or Spenser, who were both very much heroes of his. The epic features merely offer a vehicle; largely emptied of value, they serve in the main as a structural convenience for organizing satiric material. Nevertheless, they retain hints of their original force, and the memory of this former seriousness has a way of informing the poem so as to make the shortcomings of those it satirizes seem all the shorter. Thus, the Cave of Poetry (or nursery of bad poetry) alludes to the Garden of Adonis, and so half reminds the reader of what is travestied: of Spenser's symbol of great creating Nature. As for the object of Pope's satire – in effect, English society under Walpole's corrupt administration – it may seem impossibly large (heroically large?). In a first reading, one's heart may sink before the myriads of topical allusions to be mastered. But Pope treats the individuals as types – often types only too easily recognizable in present-day society. What matters is how he generalizes their errors as manifestations specifically of Dulness, or mindless insensitivity. Naturally, who criticizes Dulness must not himself be dull. And it is a pleasure to see how ingeniously Pope avoids this in the *Dunciad*, while always relating the objects of his satire to this very head. With grotesque yet composed inventiveness he makes the most unpromising material brilliantly poetic, from vomit and faeces to Theobald and Cibber. The action has endless vitality – dances, competitions, busy allegorical places, list after list, all commented on by the tirelessly tiresome editor – yet continually Pope insists on a single theme. It is the poet's command, in the end, that obviates boredom and saves the day. Mankind is not totally given over to Dulness after all.

The *Dunciad* went through several versions, principally those now called *Dunciad A* (1728) and *Dunciad B* (1742). The first had Theobald as its hero; with a full panoply of mock scholarship added, this became the *Dunciad Variorum* (1729). Then the *New Dunciad* or *Dunciad B* replaced Theobald by Colley Cibber, broadened the scope of the satire and adopted a graver, more Miltonic tone. Yet from the earliest beginnings to the final (and still imperfect) version, the *Dunciad* is to be valued for singleness of satiric vision. Its consistent indignation energetically gathers the impulses of a whole group of satires on dullness or nonsense, like Dryden's *Mac Flecknoe* ('The rest to some faint meaning make pretence,/But *Sh*---- never deviates into sense'), directing them into a comprehensive work on a heroic scale. Pope's is our first visionary or apocalyptic satire. Its prophecies of the doom of civilization stand at the beginning of a tradition that includes not only Blake's visions and MacDiarmid's longer diatribes, but also modern prose satires like those of Pynchon and Heller and West. As if this were not enough, the *Dunciad* is also the main conduit by which Renaissance devices of self-annotation and mock scholarship were transmitted to the present age. On the example of this one work – only a little supported by Swift's *A Tale of a Tub* – depend the complex forms of Nabokov's *Pale Fire*, Barth's *Giles Goatboy* and a crowd of other modernist, avant-gardist and 'experimental' works.

The *Dunciad* then is indisputably a seminal work. If we ask whether it is also a very great one, the answer is not so clear. It can, I think, be defended against the usual criticisms. For example, it has little in the way of epic action, but this is because of an eloquent decorum; it is Dulness's character to be supine, or do only what is trivial. All the same, the poem has its longueurs – passages that make one ask whether it is not all too much, whether it quite escapes the satirist's besetting fault of going on too long – the compulsiveness, in fact, of the censorious man.

Pope had already carried mock epic to perfection in a poem of more grace and charm – *The Rape of the Lock* (1712; enlarged 1714). Satire is but a part of this exquisite work, which can be enjoyed throughout as a true epic diminished to contemporary proportions – the epic quint-essence, so to say, realized in feminine miniature. Both for diminution and miniaturization there were traditions: one from an ancient parody of the *Iliad* through Nicolas Boileau's *Le Lutrin* (1674–83) and Samuel Garth's *Dispensary* (1699); another from popular mythology through Renaissance works such as *A Midsummer Night's Dream* and the fairy poems of William Browne, Robert Herrick and others. Besides, Pope was himself a very small man and had like Swift a special passion for tiny things (as witness his miniature landscape garden at Twickenham).

The Rape of the Lock subjects epic to a diminishing metamorphosis so complete that miraculously few of its features seem to be lost. This is the culmination, in a way, of the baroque pursuit of 'much in little'; but already one senses also a rococo delicacy. The compression works chiefly by ALLUSION (implicit reference) of a particular sort. Hardly a line has not a literary lineage; but Pope is not content with mere epic commonplaces, and selects – this is what gives much of the freshness – just those particular stock periphrases or classic phrases that are susceptible to delicacy ('th' Etherial Plain', 'the Finny Prey') or that can be revivified by their new context. In the latter group come 'verdant Field' (reused of a card table) and 'hoary Majesty' (the King of Spades). Naturally, small feminine things are selected for particular amplification: 'little Engine', 'glitt'ring *Forfex*' (scissors); 'shining Altars of Japan' (lacquered tables). Pope has an elegiac fondness not only for the epic world but for the world itself, whose mutability is focused in the domain of beautiful feminine décor – 'alas! frail Beauty must decay,/Curled or uncurled, since Locks will turn to grey . . .'. Yet he is also at his best in realizing and juxtaposing disparate worlds like the boudoir, the salon and the larger ambience of business and law.

In fact *The Rape of the Lock* is one of Pope's fullest responses to the *beau monde*. Ostensibly its tone conveys an Ovidian eroticism, as in Renaissance heroic epyllia. But this masks an uncertain number of ulterior suggestions, some gently satiric, some rather sharper:

> On her white Breast a sparkling *Cross* she wore,
> Which *Jews* might kiss, and Infidels adore.
>
> (ii.7–8)

Such a cross would present few difficulties of belief. The excursion on the bosom of the Thames is one of a series of luxurious scenes representative of high society, described with the utmost poise. Pope sometimes allows epic allusion to work half-seriously; and in Clarissa's advocacy of a sense of proportion the parody of Homer's strategic Sarpedon speech is very serious indeed. Implications about the littleness of fashionable life pervade the poem: the satire censures Belinda's entire kind. On her dressing table

> The Tortoise here and Elephant unite,
> Transformed to Combs, the speckled and the white.
> Here Files of Pins extend their shining Rows,
> Puffs, Powders, Patches, Bibles, Billet-doux.
>
> (i.135–8)

Symbols of Indian empire and cosmetic trivia, large black patches and modishly small black Bibles: the jumbled confusion of objects sets out a thorough confusion of values. Such descriptions are managed throughout with a disarming subtlety that was quite new. But perhaps the most original feature of all is to be found in the minute flimsy MACHINERY or mythological apparatus of spirits recruited from the Rosicrucian system. Pope manages to combine these half Christian, half psychologized spirits with a more elusively adumbrated machinery of pagan mythological roles, some of them taken by human agents. The result is shimmering brilliance that cannot possibly (can it?) give offence.

For his satires and epics alike, Pope adopted the HEROIC COUPLET. This metre was so indispensable for public poetry that it calls for special notice: no other metrical form – unless it be blank verse – has been a source of more poetic pleasure. A couplet, or pair of successive rhyming lines, is heroic when the lines are decasyllabic – a traditional metre for heroic verse from the time of Chaucer. But in the seventeenth century a specially 'closed' or end-stopped couplet was cultivated. Drayton, Jonson, Waller, Denham and Rochester (to name a few of the main figures) gradually discovered what irregularities were workable if the couplet was to be reasonably smooth and readable; and finally Dryden, and then Pope, brought it to completion. The detached couplet lent itself to satiric epigram, for which indeed it became a principal metre. But much effort also went into the attempt to sustain flexible continuous movement through verse paragraphs of many couplets. Even in Rochester the movement was still occasionally stiff; only with Dryden did it become dependably muscular. Ultimate refinement came with Pope's easy but less pronounced action. He perfected the system of CAESURAS or pauses within the line. A standard pause after the fourth syllable allowed for countless effects of significant variation, like the very early caesura and long succeeding flight of 'Oh! could I mount on the Maeonian wing . . .'. But Pope's metrical system has to be related to the rhetorical organization bound up with it. This allowed very free inversion of word order, in the interest of antithesis, parellelism, or similar patterns making for rhythmic emphasis. To take a simple example:

> One *Science* only will one *Genius* fit;
> So *vast* is Art, so *narrow* Human Wit . . .
> (*An Essay on Criticism* 60–1)

Here the undivided line renders singleness, whereas the caesura in the second line separates antithetic clauses in which contrasted words occupy equivalent positions.

OTHER FORMS OF SATIRE

This then is the metrical system Pope used for his satires – as, to a large extent, did Young and Gay – not only in mock epic but in formal satires. FORMAL SATIRE does not use any extraneous genre as vehicle; instead, it returns to an ancient monologue form of medium length, in which the satirist adopts a tone either of indignation or of raillery, and attacks vice through direct moral observations made more or less in his own person. It was a familiar genre in the eighteenth century both from the examples of Horace, Juvenal and Persius, and from the analyses of

Renaissance theorists. Its features included an abrupt opening ('Shut, shut the door, good John!'), free variation of style height, and absence of formal transitions or signposts between its parts. With this genre, imitation worked particularly well; since the discipline imposed a valuable distance from the poet's feelings that had previously been lacking. Distance could also be achieved by adopting a special pose or *persona*, such as the plain man or the innocent. The targets of satire, meanwhile, could be typified in a similar way, perhaps under a class name covering many individuals – 'A hundred smart in Timon and in Balaam'.

Pope's satires are all beyond compare for subtlety, brilliance, seriousness. The Epistles *To Arbuthnot*, *To Augustus* and *To Burlington* must be mentioned; yet they hardly stand out from their group. Are his epistles more in the vein of Horace (comic satire) or of Juvenal (tragic or heroic satire)? It has been said that Pope lived a Horatian myth; and his satiric epistles are often Horatian too, both in their tone and their ostensibly open-minded dialogue. They have all the swift variety of conversation and the half-conversation of internal monologue. Yet often, too, they rise to heights of indignation or praise of virtue – heights as lofty as anything in his epics –

> Oh Impudence of wealth! with all thy store,
> How dar'st thou let one worthy man be poor?
> *(Satires* II.ii.117–18)

Such height was not incongruous, so much had satire risen through the hierarchy of kinds. It flourished in a prescriptive age, when it had a natural audience in the coteries of coffee house society (Pope, Swift and Gay were friends; Addison, Steele, Garth and Congreve all belonged to the Kit-Cat Club). It would be a mistake to think of satire as merely censorious or (with Matthew Arnold) to dismiss it as unpoetic. It was a growing point of Augustan poetry, on which the most creative imaginations exercised their powers. They devised for it new forms such as the TOWN ECLOGUE (a scene with satiric monologue); they reintroduced old ones from Horace and Juvenal; or they borrowed existing vehicles – like Young, when he adapted the 'character' form to satiric poetry.

In prose, too, many genres were taken up as vehicles for satire – pamphlet and fable, scholarly edition and popular almanac. The last was put to use in a ferocious hoax whereby Swift predicted the astrologer Partridge's death; the joke being taken up by Congreve, Gay and so many others that Partridge was treated as dead, even in court. Augustan prose satire obviously had need of ironic disguise. Whereas verse satirists tended to look back to Ariosto, therefore, prose satirists turned to masterworks of irony – Rabelais' *Pantagruel* and *Gargantua*, Erasmus's *Encomium moriae* and More's elusive *Utopia*. Their satiric qualities were combined and intensified in the work of Jonathan Swift, from *A Tale of a Tub* (1704) onward.

For structure *A Table of a Tub* partly relies on parodic vehicles. Thus, it is introduced with a flurry of spoof preliminaries: author's apology, bookseller's dedication, bookseller's preface, dedication, preface, and analytical table. But it also belongs to the classical genre known as MENIPPEAN SATIRE, the principal satiric prose kind. Menippean or Varronian satire originally alternated prose and verse; but subsequently its alternating components became dialogue, narration and extreme digression. Swift renders the form – not it must be said with complete success – by interchanging a narrative allegory of denominational differences with 'digressions' or satiric essays that purport to explain such matters as the psychological basis of sectarian views. In these digressions some of his best work is already to be found.

Much of the interest of Swift's satire – and to some extent this is true of other Augustan satire – lies in a specially complex form of continued irony. (We see this also, for example, in Arbuthnot's *The History of John Bull* (1712), with its telling allegories of international politics under a fable of domestic or local affairs.) Swift's surface meaning is lucid, with all the crispness and strength that characterize the period's style. Like some calm lake of vitriol it gives no sign of the corrosive intensity beneath. IRONY is often said to be a figure in which the true sense contradicts the literal meaning. But in Swift's subtler irony the meaning need not be opposite exactly, and can be very elusive. Indeed, this is so much the case that his coherence, even his sanity, have been questioned. Needlessly – there is an inner consistency to his work, for those who can find it. Far from being mad, he might be thought unusually lucid in following out moral and spiritual implications. Only, he mixes proximate and ultimate matters in a way that makes his integrity uncomfortable – something easily thought abnormal. Often the charge means no more than that his clarity extends to analysis of the dishonesties underlying so-called Christian society. Appreciation of his greatness has come principally from those who, like Hazlitt, have been able to regard their own society with a little detachment, and Swift's with a great deal.

The consistency of Swift is beyond question, whenever his satiric strategy is grasped. Often he works out society's compromises in a matter-of-fact way, making their unenvisaged details and logical implications revealingly explicit. His tone will be gentle, even through the slight exaggerations and surprises.

> I grant this food will be somewhat dear, and therefore very proper for landlords, who, as they have already devoured most of the parents seem to have the best title to the children ... I have already computed the charge of nursing a beggar's child (in which list I reckon all cottagers, labourers, and four fifths of the farmers) to be about two shillings per annum, rags included; and I believe no gentleman would repine to give ten shillings for the carcass of a good fat child ...
>
> (*A Modest Proposal*, 1729)

Or, another of Swift's strategies is to hid his own views behind those of divisions of the target group. Thus, *An Argument Against Abolishing Christianity* (1710) purports to be the view of a politic nominal believer, arguing against radical atheism. 'Nor do I think it wholly groundless,' he reasonably warns, 'or my Fears altogether imaginary, that the Abolishing of Christianity may perhaps bring the Church in Danger ...'. That is, he thinks the proposal to abolish dangerous to the establishment – a main issue with him. So Swift persuades us to see what he thinks the motives of many users of the church really amount to. In such arguments (*A Modest Proposal* is another) there are generally one or two places where the satirist's mask half drops. At the end of *An Argument*, for example, it is calculated that abolishment would mean a fall of one per cent in East India stock: 'And since that is fifty times more than ever the wisdom of our age thought fit to venture for the preservation of Christianity, there is no reason we should be at so great a Loss, merely for the sake of destroying it.' That makes all plain enough, up to a point. But elsewhere there are more ambiguous, and perhaps ambivalent, passages. There the mask almost seems to conceal – and betray – pessimism as to whether true Christianity is compatible with civilization.

Swift's masterpiece, *Gulliver's Travels* (1726), comes to grips with the nature of man as political animal. It is again Menippean satire (alternating narrative and dialogue), and it uses as vehicle a recent kind of travel narration exemplified by William Dampier's *Voyages* (1697). As a story, the account of Gulliver's experiences among little people and giants won immediate acclaim, in spite of Swift's anxieties about its reception. But when some notion of the satire penetrated, misinterpretation succeeded, and charges of misanthropy. Not all of the work is easy to interpret. In particular, Gulliver's attitudes to the different value systems he meets change puzzlingly. Thus, he is sensible in comparison to the Lilliputians with their petty politics. Yet the Brobdingnagians represent a natural humanity which shows up his boasting to their king about civilized inhumanities. And the natural is itself shown to be an inadequate standard in the Fourth Book. The land of the Houyhnhnms (perfectly rational horses) is hardly a utopia: it seems that rationalism, when not subordinated to higher values, leads to pathological disgust. Are these shifts of perspective to be seen as evidence of eighteenth-century relativity of values? Much more likely they are a device of Swift's to surprise his reader into uncertainty and spiritual consciousness. *Gulliver's Travels* has tended to be interpreted in psychological terms – as if that offered the only basis of understanding. But in fact Swift sets out a completely consistent moral position. This is implied ironically in the dialogue parts, on which discussion has naturally concentrated. The story also requires attention, however, being vital for an understanding. It is in the story – in the Portuguese captain – that one finds an embodiment of the work's ruling value, *caritas*, Christian love.

Swift's treatment of the narrative was without precedent in satire. Instead of treating it perfunctorily, as a mere instrument, he developed it at least in part for its own sake – realizing it in detail with comprehensive imagination and ingenuity. This innovation was to be of seminal importance for the subsequent history not only of science fiction and fantasy, but of the novel. For example, after describing an execution Gulliver tells of his diversion in a Brobdingnagian model boat. It is not just that dimensions have been precisely worked out, but that we are given details: the trough 'had a cock near the bottom to let out the water when it began to grow stale' (Gulliver characteristically noticed that the cock was not quite at the bottom). It is all so plausible, so consistent, that we come to trust the traveller's veracity – and are correspondingly involved when his conceptions of moral reality break down.

GEORGIC AND MOCK GEORGIC

Satire was not the only genre to be revalued in the Augustan period. GEORGIC, or descriptive and instructional poetry, was another. It rose from being only questionably considered literature to occupy a high place in the hierarchy of kinds: in Addison's *Essay on the Georgics* (1697) these became 'the most complete, elaborate and finished piece of all antiquity'. Among many factors in the revaluation, the chief was perhaps a new phase in the dialogue between religion and science. With the founding (1645; 1662) of the Royal Society and the growth of scientific observation, especially microscopy, it had become necessary to describe God's presence in nature in new ways. Although this meant implementation and realization of old ideals as often as their disintegration, the emblematic world schemes were replaced by more detailed accounts and more discriminating classifications. Problems of a potentially disharmonious and dark or random nature were causing anxiety, and called for frequent affirmations of the 'preestablished harmony' of the cosmos. Then, from the 1580s onward, there had been advances in applied science, for example horticulture and farming. And the retirement of gentry to their estates during the Civil War encouraged contemplation and led to revaluation of ideas such as the georgic 'happy husbandman'. Among literary factors, the crisis in epic allowed the neighbouring kind to take over its encyclopedic and nationalistic functions. Finally, the excellence of certain instructional works in prose did as much as anything to raise the status of the didactic. Among these, two that represent opposite ends of the scale of systematic formality are John Locke's important philosophical *Essay in Human Understanding* (1690) and Izaak Walton's gently digressive *The Compleat Angler* (1653).

Some of these factors were of long standing, so that the question is asked why English georgic should have been delayed in comparison with European. One answer is that close imitation of Virgil's *Georgics* was not possible until imitation itself had developed as a genre. And that in turn had to await the increased closeness of texture brought by seventeenth-century extensions of epigram.

Many strands, in fact, went into the georgic web. One was verse essays, neo-Latin and English, on a whole gamut of topics, from syphilis and silkworms to angling and gardening. Another led from Drayton's seminal *Poly-Olbion* through topographical poems like Cotton's *The Wonders of the Peak* and Denham's *Cooper's Hill*. In these looser types of georgic, Hesiod was almost as important a model as Virgil. Then with Dryden's 1697 translation of the *Georgics* (and Addison's Preface) a new phase began, of direct emulations of Virgil: the so-called 'formal georgics' – works like John Philips's slightly stiff *Cider* (1708), in Miltonic blank verse, and Pope's superb local-descriptive *Windsor-Forest* (1713), a more essential yet freer imitation. They followed the formulas, structure, dispositional proportions and stylish transitions, even the themes, of the Virgilian model. But they searched out points of departure for their own treatments of nature.

Virgil's poem was in no sense the impulse; although certain of its features proved extremly useful, and were to be important for future developments. For example, its style height is neither consistently

elevated like epic nor abased like pastoral. It oscillates, in accordance
with the poet's own voice, between the mundane and the heroic – a
possibility grasped by Pope with brilliant assurance. The *Georgics* also
offered a type of digression, perhaps introducing exotic material, or
rising to mock heroic, or even to serious political reflections. Pope takes
up the last option in *Windsor-Forest*, in the passages on Norman
devastations and on London's imagined trade with a world at peace.
Georgic often mingles the prosperity of its work ethic ('Quicken your
labours, brace your slackening nerves,/Ye Britons' says Dyer) with a
sense of civilization's fragility. From one point of view, in fact, it is a
poem about peace. Yet this complexity does not arise from allegory, as
can happen in pastoral. These two modes are sometimes treated as
similar. As we have seen, however, they are in contrast throughout their
thematic gamut. The pastoral shepherd enjoys ease in a timeless golden
world; whereas a round of seasonal tasks occupies the life of the georgic
labourer. Factual knowledge must seem to be excluded from pastoral;
georgic ostensibly exists to instruct. Even Pope's descriptive version of
georgic explains a landscape saturated with historical and political
implications. And hunting, which is taboo in pastoral, belongs to the
georgic round (as witness the vivid pheasant shoot in *Windsor-Forest*),
and can even be its main subject, as in William Somerville's *The Chase*
(1735).

To extend the domain of poetry into a field of experience either quite
new or not previously poeticized is a considerable achievement. And
this – although we now ignore it – was accomplished by many of the
georgics and 'arts', such as William King's *The Art of Cookery* (1708),
James Grainger's *The Sugar Cane* (1764) and (best of all) John
Armstrong's *The Art of Preserving Health* (1744). Pope does something
similar for modern philosophical ideas in his *An Essay on Man* (1733).
This magisterial imitation of (and answer to) Lucretius is less com-
placent and more serious than some suppose. It can take in the
perspective of the 'poor Indian', untutored and exploited, without
poetic inconsistency. And in its demonstration of providential design it
succeeds in accommodating a wide range of ideas about man:

> Plac'd on this isthmus of a middle state,
> A being darkly wise, and rudely great:
> With too much knowledge for the Sceptic side,
> With too much weakness for the Stoic's pride,
> He hangs between; in doubt to act, or rest,
> In doubt to deem himself a God, or Beast;

> In doubt his Mind or Body to prefer,
> Born but to die, and reas'ning but to err; . . .
>
>   *   *   *
>
> Sole judge of Truth, in endless Error hurl'd:
> The glory, jest, and riddle of the world!
>
>   (Epistle ii.3–18)

Critics like to discuss contradictions in the poem; but it has few of a literary character. Its contradictions are such as hindsight easily finds in the literature of previous ages.

One of the most interesting of the formal georgics, John Dyer's blank-verse *The Fleece* (1757), did the same for technology. It can enter into details of Mr Paul's 'circular machine', telling how 'the carded wool'

> Is smoothly lapped around those cylinders,
> Which, gently turning, yield it to yon cirque
> Of upright spindles which, with rapid whirl,
> Spin out in long extent an even twine.
>
>   (iii.299–302)

Elsewhere Dyer invites his Muse to 'extend [her] daring wing' and survey the wool trade in America, where 'The Iroquese, Cheroques, and Oubacks, come' to the 'growing marts' of Virginia, 'And quit their feathery ornaments uncouth/For woolly garments'. Bringing such material into poetry presented many problems. (Dr Johnson exclaimed of *The Fleece* 'How can a man write poetically of serges and druggets!') The factual or commonplace had continually to be raised – now by careful selection avoiding the low; now by rhetorical embellishment ('Fleecy shuttle'); now by literariness of idea; now by very slight strangeness or unobviousness of expression ('his plough *divides* the glebe'); now by sensuous precision ('the *glistening* fleece'). The aim of all this effort was to show the work as part of a larger pattern, natural or moral. It may seem ridiculous, or even objectionable, that poets should have felt a need to dignify labour in this way. But where have we a comparable poetry of turbines or nuclear reactors? Eighteenth-century georgics served a valuable function by combining poetic pleasure with enough information to allow intelligent readers to take an interest in manufacture and trade, and enter into their aims with patriotic enthusiasm.

Almost anywhere in the formal georgics a shading of irony could steal in. Ater all, there was a Virgilian precedent in the mock heroic bees of the Fourth Georgic, 'unknowing how to fly,/And obstinately bent to win or die . . .' (Dryden's translation); and interaction of style heights made for complex, self-distancing perspectives. In John Gay's *Trivia* (1716) this possibility was developed at large; so that one has to speak of mock georgic. There had been a mock georgic opening to Thomas Dekker's *The Gull's Hornbook* (1609); and Gay possibly knew Henry Peacham's *The Art of Living in London* (1642) or Thomas D'Urfey's *Collin's Walk Through London and Westminster* (1690). His decisive innovation is to use the *Georgics* as a consistent mock form or vehicle. Virgilian allusion serves him as a poetic language, in which he is able to describe features of London that otherwise would be too commonplace to notice: 'When to assert the Wall, and when resign,/I sing: Thou Trivia, Goddess, aid my Song . . .'. As a result, he seems to see the city for the first time, with a startling freshness:

> Red-speckled Trouts, the Salmon's silver Jowl
> The jointed Lobster, and unscaly Sole . . .
> Walnuts the Fruit'rer's Hand, in Autumn, stain . . .
>   (*Trivia*, ii.415–16; 433)

As one reads, one looks from a time module at the Great Frost:

> Wheels o'er the hardened Waters smoothly glide,
> And raze with whitened Tracks the slipp'ry Tide.
>   (ii.365–6)

Gay's tone is neither satiric nor (like Swift in his London poems) disgusted. He relishes what he sees – although he can be sly, as in his description of street football: 'The dextrous Glazier strong returns the Bound,/And jingling Sashes on the Pent-house sound' (ii.355–6). As for the famous digressions (on the Frost, a fire, a street ballad), they are well judged, and arise easily out of the main sequence. Perhaps because of them, some have found *Trivia* lacking in compression. To me this is incomprehensible, for extension is part of its achievement and its pleasure. *Trivia* is one of the most wholly delightful poems in the language, and I can only wish it longer. The ugliness, dangers and horrors of city life are here satisfactorily contained within literary conventions that seem to have a place for everything:

> When dirty Waters from Balcónies drop,
> And dextrous Damsels twirl the sprinkling Mop,
> And cleanse the spattered Sash, and scrub the Stairs;
> Know Saturday's conclusive Morn appears.
>   (ii.421–4)

The convention of indicators of times and seasons is Virgilian; but these sights are of the here and now.

Augustan georgic evinced several developments that were to be of unforeseen consequence. One resulted from the fact that the subject matter of preceptive poems was comparatively laborious, so that poetic virtuosity tended rather to go into the formal aspects of the performance. Expected levels of finish soon became very high. And there flourished a vigorous tradition of imitative form – expressive adaptation of sound to sense. Milton, following Virgil, had pointed the way in his sublime account of creation in *Paradise Lost* vii, a favourite model for eighteenth-century nature poetry. There a line like 'Wallowing unwieldy, enormous in their gait' mimes, as well as states, its meaning (the first phrase being a huge mouthful). Another seminal work was Pope's georgic *An Essay on Criticism* (1711). He delivers and exemplifies many of his precepts simultaneously:

> When Ajax strives, some Rock's vast Weight to throw,
> The Line too *labours*, and the Words move *slow*; . . .
> > (lines 370–1)

(Note the first line's awkward clusters of consonants, and the second's long vowels in unstressed positions – 'too', 'move' – working against the metrical rhythm.) There could be no better way to prepare for the delights of preceptive poetry than to study Pope's illustrations in the *Essay*. He can accommodate rhythm and texture to sense with the ease of a virtuoso accompanist. And most of the other georgic poets attempt similar effects. Gay, too, mimes slow and laborious movement:

> When late their miry Sides Stage-Coaches show,
> And their stiff Horses through the Town move slow;
> > (*Trivia* i.25–6)

and so does Dyer: 'The heavy ox, vain-struggling, to engulf' – or, more steadily: 'On the long tinkling train of slow-paced steeds'. But enactment of meaning can also be of a subtler order. To take a familar instance: in Pope's line 'Here waving Groves a chequered Scene display', delay of the verb lengthens the caesural pause after 'Groves' until one feels a gap like those interrupting the groves themselves.

Naturally such effects were not confined to georgic poetry. One should rather think of a tradition centred in georgic but extending to other poetry about nature and creation. The *ne plus ultra* of one line of experiment was surely reached with Christopher Smart's magnificently eccentric *A Song to David* (1763), which characterizes scores of creatures through variation in syntax, verbal texture and rhythm:

The nectarine his strong tint imbibes,
And apples of ten thousand tribes,
And quick peculiar quince.
(Stanza lix)

The precise sounds of the last line, for example, render the quince's firm particularity of shape.

A little later, and the fashion had changed. Poetic structure loosened (like that of visual art) until it was less differentiated from prose and less amenable to mimetic shaping. Then Dr Johnson could become sceptical about the value – and even the actual extent – of adaptation of sound to sense. It was 'nugatory, not to be rejected, and not to be solicited'. Later still, however, in our own century, mimetic variation has become a potential strength in many kinds of poetry.

The other georgic development that proved of permanent value was the cultivation of indirection. Preceptive poets made a special aim of imparting their precepts obliquely – otherwise, indeed, the result would have been altogether too prosaic. This obliquity was not a matter simply of digression; although that could be one devious way of introducing unannounced contents. (The expansive pressure in hunting-poem digressions seems to have been irresistible; and much of Dyer's *The Fleece* is in effect geography.) It had more to do with implicitness – the attempt to teach without readers quite noticing. In the seemingly casual *An Essay on Criticism* this goes so far that the argument (a deeply thought and highly original theoretical statement) has largely been passed over. In much other georgic and georgic-related poetry, similarly, there are additional contents besides the obvious subject matter. Nature will be presented, perhaps, as a mirror of moral qualities in man (Denham; Parnell) or else of sublime verities (Thomson). Sometimes one is tempted to find, prematurely, a suggestion of something that has only emerged more recently – poetry with a deliberately obscured subject.

Many new or challengingly 'low' subjects, then, were treated in the georgic mode, and had to be raised stylistically to be suitable for poetry as that was conceived. At the same time, throughout the age informed by the Augustan idea attempts to reach the heights of epic continued. As we have seen, however, the strongly prescriptive character of Augustan classicism had more than aesthetic concerns. It also produced a great deal of moral reflection and moral satire – some of it of brilliant quality. This need not be thought of as negative or aggressive in impulse. In its political context it can be understood as springing from a positive aspiration: an Augustan society identifies abuses through satire, and reforms them.

To the Augustan age in large measure we owe the enduring heritage of classical values – balance, harmony, clarity, naturalness and beauty of style. Of course these were in a sense an inheritance from antiquity. But in Augustan England and (as we shall see) in the Scottish Enlightenment they were fully appropriated for the modern world, and first grasped in their relation to psychological normality and integration.

8

Later Classicism and the Enlightenment

SOME of the works mentioned in the last chapter could be regarded as manifestations of an intellectual movement known as the ENLIGHTENMENT. This had an international scope: in Germany it was the *Aufklärung* of Kant; in France, the movement of the *philosophes*, of Voltaire, Diderot, Rousseau and the other contributors to the *Encyclopédie* (1751–72). In England, where it began as early perhaps as the founding of the Royal Society (1660) and continued until the 1770s and beyond, it was partly philosophical and scientific (Locke, Berkeley, Newton), partly literary (Pope, Johnson). What characterized it everywhere was a commitment to clarity. This it achieved by a distinctively analytic, empirical method. It studied the causes of change by analysing them within a broad context of interrelated factors. Adam Smith praised Berkeley's *Essay Towards a New Theory of Vision* as 'one of the finest examples of philosophical analysis that is to be found'. Putting great faith in reason (the movement often amounted to secular humanism), writers of the Enlightenment were not afraid of large perspectives and bold simplifications. Naturally they had criticisms to make of existing systems of thought, which seemed to them less than rational. But they tended to be reformist, if not meliorist, in attitude. Their writing communicates a positive sense of liberation and excitement.

HUME AND THE ENLIGHTENMENT

Enlightenment writers determined to address the generality of men: indeed, they were the first ever to aim at a readership so various. With this in view, even the philosophers presented much of their work as essays, recommended by elegance of style. The Earl of Shaftesbury's *Characteristics* (1711), and even John Locke's *Human Understanding* (1690), are eminently readable; giving pleasure by sheer lucidity, by the ease with which they communicate ideas. From the first, the Enlightenment philosophers showed a deep interest in human nature as the basis not only of morality but of perceived reality itself. They approached every topic accordingly; treating it on a human scale and with merely natural presuppositions.

By the later eighteenth century the focus of the British Enlightenment had moved to Scotland, which then was intellectually the dominant partner of the Union. The work was carried forward by Henry Home (Lord Kames) (1696–82) in the field of aesthetics; by James (1730–94) and Robert Adam (1728–92) in architecture; by Adam Smith (1723–90) in economics; by Hugh Blair (1718–1800) in literary criticism; by David Hume (1711–76), William Robertson (1721–93) and Adam Ferguson (1723–1816) in history; and by Hume and Duguld Stewart (1753–1828) in philosophy. Few societies can ever have achieved so rapid and comprehensive an efflorescence.

One side of the Enlightenment showed a strain of scepticism (Locke, for example, questioned the existence of the material reality supposed to cause sensation); and this was taken a great deal further by Hume, the most penetrating of the Scottish Enlightenment philosophers. Hume went beyond Locke and Berkeley in denying the necessity of causation itself; allowing it little more than psychological force. The full extremity of his early *Treatise of Human Nature* (1739) was probably not grasped. Even so, it was not well received; and Hume adopted a more disarming approach in *Essays Moral and Political* (1741). He gave these essays larger themes than Addison's or Steele's: 'Of the Dignity or Meanness of Human Nature'; 'Of Civil Liberty'; 'Of Passive Obedience'. In this they reflect not only the form's new status, but the largeness of Enlightenment thinking – the same that appears in Pope's projected *magnum opus* of systematic essays. On political topics, Hume's *Essays* put forward generous ideas of man's potentiality. In exact contrast to what Edmund Burke will assert, Hume holds that 'the world is still too young to fix many general truths in politics, which will remain true to the latest posterity'. Empiricism tells him, not unhopefully, that

> It is not fully known what degree of refinement, either in virtue or vice, human nature is susceptible of, nor what may be expected of mankind from any great revolution in their education, customs, or principles.
>
> ('Of Civil Liberty')

Often Hume's address to the generality of men recalls the informality taken for granted in modern philosophy. He broke new formal ground, as regards closeness of reasoning. As for his style, it is in many ways attractive; yet its mildness lacks the wit Johnson will supply, and that the essay will require to sustain life beyond its first age.

Hume's finest work is the *Dialogues Concerning Natural Religion* (1779), which he suppressed during his lifetime, probably from motives of prudence. He laboured over its style, and the fruit is extraordinarily pure, smoothly rounded. It perfectly represents the writer's cool, amused irony – an irony towards mankind at large, not altogether excluding himself. The local ironies are sometimes far from obvious; as when Philo–Hume remarks to Cleanthes:

> you are sensible that, notwithstanding the freedom of my conversation, and my love of singular arguments, no-one has a deeper sense of religion impressed on his mind, or pays more profound adoration to the divine being, as he discovers himself to reason, in the inexplicable contrivance and artifice of nature. A purpose, an intention, a design strikes every where the most careless, the most stupid thinker; and no man can be so hardened in absurd systems, as at all times to reject it.
>
> (Part xii)

These ambiguities are inexhaustible. If the argument from design is only intermittently convincing, can it be sound? If the 'contrivance . . . of nature' is 'inexplicable', how does the divine being discover himself to reason in it? Yet is Philo completely 'hardened' to the rejection of design? Hume's work represents a terminus for the Enlightenment – a limit to the possibility of rational explanation in terms of causality.

JOHNSON AND BOSWELL

In turning to Samuel Johnson (1709–84), we approach one of our greatest prose stylists – and one who has had remarkable influence on writers as different as Edward Gibbon and Joshua Reynolds, Jane Austen and William Hazlitt. Johnson's is an easily imitable style, at least superficially; and it has had many imitators. It uses obvious parallelisms of many sorts:

> [Addison's] prose is the model of the middle style; on grave subjects not formal, on light occasions not grovelling; pure without scrupulosity, and exact without apparent elaboration; always equable, and always easy, without glowing words or pointed sentences.
>
> (Life of Addison; ed. Hill ii.149)

All writers use parallel phrases; but Johnson multiplies them, and underlines them rhetorically: in the quotation, 'on', 'grave', 'subjects', 'not' and 'formal' have each a grammatically equivalent word in the next phrase. This unison ensures that as the phrases go two by two into a predictable ark, the sentence structure always seems clear – no small adantage where many of the sentences are abstract in content and PERIODIC in syntax (i.e., delay their main verb). But there is a certain illusion in this; for although Johnson's phrases match grammatically, this is not always true of their meaning. In the last quotation, 'subjects' and 'occasions' hardly belong to the same category. The antitheses, in particular, tend to be reduced to a non-functional status – to be merely grammatical or 'verbal'. Such superficial patterns are like the reduced, low-relief ornaments of English Palladian architecture, to which indeed Johnson's clear style has rightly been compared.

Johnson would have described his own as a medium style. But if it is not high, it is very grand, and carries the weight we associate with prose's loftiest efforts. Some of this weight it gathers from the habit of assigning pairs of overlapping words to a single object – 'the constituent and fundamental principle' – a feature that has been disliked as heavily emphatic, although its aim was to assist clarity. Then, the diction is weighty from being always considered, never low: Johnson avoids 'accidental and colloquial senses', and often prefers philosophical terms and abstractions of classical derivation (as many of them Greek as Latin). He has been thoughtlessly criticized for his difficult words – words like 'annuitant', 'adscititious', or 'alexipharmic'. These can mostly be defended as economical discriminations of exact ideas. But there is no question that Johnson makes large demands on his reader, especially by his sustained abstractness. Yet even this is bound up with belief in the truth of general ideas. And one is usually carried through the difficulties by Johnson's exhilarating energy of address. To one of his large intellect, accuracy and pithiness come naturally: he can concentrate effort on the real problem, and so achieve a unity of effect that has the power of an avalanche. Locally, he matches his matter with endlessly noble and resonant phrases – 'the passes of the mind'; 'the blunders and ignorance of wit'. The writing seems large, like the man: an early biographer spoke of his 'bow wow way'. It is a style hard to disagree with, impossible to ignore.

Johnson's endlesssly bifurcating style is best known – and most often imitated – from his *Rambler* essays (1750–2). These have the penetration of thought that Hume's *Essays* had recently displayed, combined with a far greater stylistic interest. (Competition challenged Johnson.) The wit is not exactly scintillating (when an elephant dances, it will not charleston); but the acute thought gives constant pleasure by being fully expressed. The *Ramblers* represent the essay's highest point of abstraction. They are at their best when they treat broad generalities of human nature, as in 'An Allegory on Wit and Learning':

> Novelty was the darling of Wit, and antiquity of Learning. To Wit, all that was new, was specious [attractive]; to Learning, whatever was ancient, was venerable . . . Learning always supported her opinion with so many collateral truths, that, when the cause [case] was decided against her, her arguments were remembered with admiration.
>
> (No.22)

Johnson's *Idler* essays (1758–9) are sometimes more oblique, in a way that is liable to surprise by its turns –

> a parrot, indeed, is as fine as a colonel, and if he has been much used to good company, is not wholly without conversation; but a parrot, after all, is a poor little creature, and has neither sword nor shoulder-knot, can neither dance nor play at cards.
>
> (No.5)

Both series of essays may seem a little heavy to a modern reader. All the same, anyone who wanted to clarify his moral ideas could follow worse plans than reading a Johnson essay a day.

Rasselas (1759) continues Johnson's search for happiness (already begun in the eastern tales of the *Rambler*), adding narrative illustration and a larger sequence that at times – as with the rising waters of the Nile – approaches symbolism or myth. This austere narrative is paradoxically more confessional than the essays. Perhaps narrative displacement allowed Johnson to approach his fears and despairs more closely.

Johnson's English *Dictionary* (1755) was the first on a historical plan; although there had been larger general dictionaries, besides specialized ones. It achieves greatness on several counts. First, there is the magisterial clarity of the definitions, which in best Enlightenment style took a great leap forward lexicographically. Second, Johnson introduced the idea of illustrating his definitions, and assembled a brilliant anthology of passages from authors as early as Spenser and Ralegh, as recent as just before his own time. In making this period 'classic', Johnson is openly prescriptive; as too in his valuable information about acceptability and distribution. 'Bamboozle' is 'a cant word not used in pure or in grave writings'; 'Anotherguess . . . though rarely used in writing, is somewhat frequent in colloquial language'. In the course of his vast labour Johnson will very occasionally strike a personal note. Or, his pungency will become irrepressible, so that he anticipates Bierce in exploiting the possibility of humorous or epigrammatic definition – as in 'Pension . . . pay given to a state hireling for treason to his country' (a brickbat that will boomerang when he himself accepts a royal pension). The *Dictionary* is a book to browse in: it will be found educative in a rich diversity of ways – not only in the history of the language, but in that of ideas; in literature; and in style.

As the Augustan age opened with a great critic, Dryden, so it closed with another; for it was in literary criticism that Johnson's powers found their proper arena. There is some criticism already in the *Rambler*, and more in the 1765 edition of Shakespeare – whom its preface powerfully defends against unintelligent application of the rules of unity of time and place. But the bulk of Johnson's criticism comes late, in *Lives of the English Poets* (1779–81; 1783), indisputably his finest work, although begun in his sixty-eighth year and written very rapidly – fifty-two lives in four years. The title's 'English poets' are really the English Augustans. The commissioning booksellers anticipated more public interest in these, and the biographer found more affinity. Indeed, Johnson's criticism did much to establish the grouping: a task for which, as a scholar–critic, he was well fitted. Dryden, although he identified many of criticism's topics, was too occupied, as professional poet and dramatist, to do much with them; Johnson went deeper, and made contributions that are still valued.

The *Lives* consist each of three sections, biography (the longest), character and criticism, on a plan, seldom varied, that Johnson perhaps took from Bertrand de Fontenelle. It has been said that few connections link the biographical and critical parts; and certainly Johnson is not a biographical critic in the modern sense, for he seldom traces psychological causes. But his Enlightenment interest in biography takes countless literary-critical turns, as he traces the poets' education and reading, their models and heroes; their associations and quarrels; even (where he can) their methods of composition. Every mention of a poem in the biographical part carries implications of value. And there are frequent critical digressions, such as the famous identification, introduced between biography and criticism of Cowley, of the Metaphysical school.

Such groupings had never been marked out for English literature; yet Johnson went beyond naming to describe the Metaphysicals' manner of poetic thought (their WIT) with a remarkable breadth of understanding. Considered from an Augustan reader's point of view, the Metaphysicals may be deficient in the power to move or astonish; but

Johnson's general ideas show him how to think of wit differently, in a Lockeian or Burkeian way. It

> may be more rigorously and philosophically considered as a kind of *discordia concors* [concordant discord]; a combination of dissimilar images, or discovery of occult resemblances in things apparently unlike. Of wit, thus defined, they have more than enough. The most hetero-geneous ideas are yoked by violence together; nature and art are ransacked for illustrations, comparisons, and allusions . . .
>
> ('Life of Cowley'; ed. Hill i.20)

And he adds a wealth of examples, including several still regarded as of key significance. All this anticipates the historical adjustment we now take for granted. Johnson's scholarship enables him to supply a context of criticism and to arrive at judgements that are principled rather than merely prejudiced: knowledge of Cowley's association with the Meta-physicals allows appropriate allowances to be made in estimating his poetry. But the judgement itself is, as it should be, largely moral. Thus, the Metaphysicals 'wrote rather as beholders than partakers of human nature; as beings looking upon good and evil, impassive and at leisure . . . without interest and without emotion'.

This is Johnson's usual judicial pattern: measurement of perfor-mance first against ordinary or classical proportions, and then, more fundamentally, against those of human nature. For example, the reader is delighted, then astonished, by Butler: 'But astonishment is a toilsome pleasure, he is soon weary of wondering, and longs to be diverted.' In the lives of Dryden and Pope, whose work is most normal, Johnson's sceptical criticism has to detect the subtlest departures from the norm, and arrive at the finest distinctions. Moreover, his judgements appeal to human nature in another way, in that he values the public's long-term preference ('the common sense of readers') above temporary critical fashions ('literary prejudices'). This may seem more egalitarian than it was: Johnson meant the *informed* public.

A great figure cannot be subsumed within a movement. Johnson's conservative pessimism, to go no further, diverged sharply from the progressivism of the Enlightenment. His complex individuality, as well as his ideas, form the subject of James Boswell's *Life of Johnson* (1791), the most renowned biography in English. Indeed, the Johnson of popular tradition is the creature of Boswell as much as the creator of *Lives of the English Poets*. This is not quite to question the truth of Boswell's *Life*. For his largely unrecognized shaping of the Johnson legend went to the length of stage managing real events that might show his subject in a desired light – whether by arranging encounters or by bringing grist to Johnson's conversational mill and coaxing him to grind out memorabilia. He extended Johnson's mind – and sometimes manipulated him, like an unscrupulous journalist. True, the shaping continued in composition: surviving drafts show Boswell altering Johnson's words. But this was to make them more, not less, characteristic. It was a reporting convention to remould speech in the interest of rhetorical smoothness and symmetry; Boswell's changes, however, pursued the personal, the authentic.

Boswell made two innovations of consequence in the *Life*. First, he introduced overriding themes or preoccupations, which structure much of the material. Time and again, for example, he casts Johnson in sovereign roles, or connects him with the king. He makes Goldsmith complain of Johnson's being respected as monarch of the club; he compares Johnson's compliment to the grants of kings; he shows Johnson not merely laying down the law but, as it were, legislating on constitutional matters, or assessing the king's powers. His Johnson even suffers from the king's evil. Sometimes he himself plays Whig to Johnson's Tory; but that is to bring out the extent of their agreement on political principles shared by all in a constitutional monarchy. (It was a period of radical agitation.) The theme of the monarchic commoner has much explanatory power: details that seem digressive may be found to relate to it.

Second, many passages in Boswell express a new sensibility, an intuitive sympathy (however inadequate) for his subject's inner life. When he nearly arouses Johnson's 'dismal apprehensions' of death, he admits 'Here I am sensible I was in the wrong, to bring before his view what he ever looked upon with horror'. By including Johnson's flaws and weaknesses – something he was much criticized for in his own time – Boswell moves decisively away from the tradition of idealized panegyric. He prefers details of living actuality. With this in view he will switch into a dramatic mode, so that direct speech sounds across the centuries – 'conversation alone, or what led to it, or was interwoven with it, is the business of this work'. In fact, Johnson's voice gives the *Life* much of its special distinction. He is a great talker and an unforgettable aphorist: 'He who does not mind his belly will hardly mind anything else'; 'Sir, people may come to do anything almost, by talking of it'; 'All censure of a man's self is oblique praise. It is in order to show how much he can spare'; 'The wretched have no compassion'.

Preservation of Johnson's voice depended on a compositional method that Boswell developed for his journals. He may have jotted down very brief notes while in company; but those that have survived were written subsequently, sometimes late at night on the same day, sometimes – thanks to his unusual power of memory – in arrears by as much as a fortnight. Boswell's accurate recording impressed even the outstanding scholar of his time, Edmund Malone. From one point of view, it shows his discipline as an advocate; from another, it suggests journalistic ability. Boswell certainly operated effectively as a journalist when he paid an arduous visit to Corsica to interview the freedom-fighter General Paoli.

Boswell's stature has grown since the publication (only in the second half of this century) of his voluminous journals, which come close to composing an enormous autobiography. They were written in an age of memorial activity, when journal-keeping was a Scottish tradition. Nevertheless, the amplitude of their vivid, tenacious recording dumbfounds one. Boswell was a compulsive diarist. However, he also intended the detail: although not a deep thinker, he moved in intellectual circles, and his intelligent realism has the Dutch School minuteness characteristic of the late Enlightenment. The contrast is instructive with Pepys, whose details are fewer, more random and less clear. Another contrast lies in the extent of self-analysis. Pepys occasionally worries about his wife's jealousy; but Boswell, in a period of sensibility and Scottish puritanism, continually agonizes about his sexual promiscuities, puzzles over the identity of his greatness, grapples with his melancholy, or takes his moral or emotional temperature (which, especially in Holland, is often low). Boswell's coarseness can be repulsive. Yet all is saved by the truth, honesty and charm of the character whose emergence makes a main fascination of the journals. It is a difficult character to fix – mercurial, contradictory. The writing reflects an artlessly vain, sincere, manipulating tuft-hunter. He is passionate in the Scottish way, yet disciplined in observing himself; intelligent, yet shallow and self-deceiving; impulsive yet calculating; insecure yet unsnubbable; outstandingly gregarious in an intensely social age, yet able to stand apart from the group and record its speech. Boswell attached himself for a time to Johnson (as Spence had done, to Pope); but he had other interests – politics, landowning, his career as an advocate. This many-sidedness may be one cause of the journals' success.

Everyone should know at least the early *London Journal* (1762–3). It bustles with youthful excitement, as Boswell listens to coffee house conversation, enjoys social meals, is frightened climbing the Monument, has pasages of arms with prostitutes, or meets with James Mac-

Pherson, Hugh Blair, John Wilkes and Charles Churchill, all four on the same page. Yet even here the 'foul fiend' of melancholy can seize him: 'I hated all things. I almost hated London.' For all Boswell's faults, the frail humanity of the journals is strongly sympathetic. They record an immature sensitive man's long search for integrity: a search with which a reader can scarcely help becoming identified.

EDWARD GIBBON

Hume's ambitiously impartial eight-volume *History of England from the Invasion of Julius Caesar to the Revolution of 1688* (1754–62) was an admirable Enlightenment enterprise. Yet for vast erudition and philosophical seriousness it bears no comparison with Edward Gibbon's *The History of the Decline and Fall of the Roman Empire* (1776–88). Gibbon's great work, the issue of more than twenty years of research – entailing archeological, numismatic, chronological and other ancillary studies – has the scope of a world history. In its command over detail and its freedom of movement over wide tracts of time and space, the *History* displays intimidatingly powerful organization. And it has a single bold perspective: something very much of its age, yet almost without parallel in previous histories on such a scale. Throughout it traces certain specific causes of the Roman empire's degeneration. Among these, notoriously, the Christian religion is supposed to figure. And certainly Gibbon exercises both scorn and quiet irony at the expense of the Church, which he portrays as inimical to civilization. But he has also Christian heroes. It might be more accurate to describe his scorn as directed against the Church's irrational enthusiasms.

Gibbon offers perspectives in another sense, in that his *History* is consistently picturesque. The narrative parts come to dramatic focuses; and the descriptions are visually realized in crisp, telling detail:

The pomp was opened by twenty elephants, four royal tigers, and above two hundred of the most curious animals from every climate of the north, the east, and the south . . . The victories of Aurelian were attested by the long train of captives who reluctantly attended his triumph, Goths, Vandals, Sarmatians, Alemanni, Franks, Gauls, Syrians and Egyptians. Each people was distinguished by its peculiar inscription, and the title of Amazons was bestowed on ten martial heroines of the Gothic nation who had been taken in arms. But every eye, disregarding the crowd of captives, was fixed on the emperor Tetricus and the queen of the east. The former, as well as his son, whom he had created Augustus, was dressed in Gallic trousers, a saffron tunic, and a robe of purple. The beauteous figure of Zenobia was confined by fetters of gold; a slave supported the gold chain which encircled her neck, and she almost fainted under the intolerable weight of jewels. She preceded on foot the magnificent chariot in which she once hoped to enter the gates of Rome.

(chapter xi)

Each perspective is also drawn, however, to a point. And this often depends on a contrast measuring the effect of some change. Thus, the end of the senate 'suggests an awful lesson of the vicissitude of human affairs'; and is followed, after atrocities against patricians, by an exhortation: 'Ascend six hundred years, and contemplate the kings of the earth soliciting an audience as the slaves or freedmen of the Roman senate!' There are naturally passages of general reflection. But these are outweighed by specifics, 'circumstantial and animated': scenes, anecdotes and even accounts of surviving objects like buildings and medals. This concreteness makes Gibbon's *History* one of the most readable of all great classics. The movement is easy, varied, rapid, yet unhurried; so that its conclusions emerge naturally, with a force suggesting inevitability.

Understandably in so long a work, the *History* has a detectable pattern of style: a steadily sedate rhythmical sonority, neither high nor low. There are some stereotyped formulas, particularly in analysis of motive (the weakest element), or in characterization of the rather unindividual minor figures. But for the most part Gibbon varies his style brilliantly. In consequence, although certainly a big style, it is quite a self-effacing one, and may only be noticed in its wicked slynesses. The narrative seems to carry all fluently along on its own. A secret of this lies in Gibbon's method of composition, whereby he shaped whole paragraphs inwardly: 'It has always been my practice to cast a long paragraph in a single mould, to try it by my ear, to deposit it in my memory, but to suspend the action of the pen till I had given the last polish to my work.' For the rest, Gibbon's style is the man, and has the man's limitations. It reflects his love of truth, his devotion to the task – but also his rigidity and occasional unworthiness.

To anyone who has sensed the greatness of the *History*, Gibbon's *Autobiography* (1827,1896) is obligatory reading. This consists of no fewer than six memoirs, which were anthologized by Lord Sheffield and composed into a single comfortable narrative. It bears the stamp of the Enlightenment, no less in the boldness of Gibbon's renewed attempts to solve the autobiographical problem, than in his difficulties with internal material. A scholar's life might be thought a dry subject; but Gibbon enjoys his vocation with such relish, and is so unhesitant an egoist, that he secures one's identification. Besides, he is truthful in what he chooses to write – occasionally to the point of painful self-censure. And a careful reading will find hints – in fears and anxieties – of dangers that surrounded Gibbon's steady work so threateningly as to call for a kind of heroism. His account of finishing the *History* at Lausanne on a June evening of 1787 is famous. He laid down his pen and took several turns in his acacia walk:

> I will not dissemble the first emotions of joy on the recovery of my freedom, and, perhaps, the establishment of my fame. But my pride was soon humbled, and a sober melancholy was spread over my mind, by the idea that I had taken an everlasting leave of an old and agreeable companion, and that whatsoever might be the future date of my History, the life of the historian must be short and precarious.
>
> (*Memoirs of My Life*, 1787)

But Gibbon's struggles with autobiography do not in the end avail. His largely external method is inadequate; so that the work lacks intimacy of introspection. It engages, but cannot satisfy.

After Johnson and Gibbon, high style prose tended to deteriorate. It is as if writers wandered on the wrong side of a vast park wall enclosing the fertile antitheses and inaccessible periods of the great Cham. To write like Johnson one had to think like Johnson. Already in Gibbon there are ominous signs of the difficulty – half-automatic suavities, generalized phrases. True, the prose of the Irishman Edmund Burke (1729–97) achieves more flexibility of movement than Johnson's; but at the cost of superficiality and opportunistic meretriciousness. Burke was a great orator of generous feeling, whose unrigorous thought is unfortunately expressed in repetitious inflated rhetoric. His style never uses one word where two can be inserted instead. (It is a measure of the inferior general level of nineteenth century prose that the Victorians accorded Burke's blowsy amplifications the highest place.) The best late classical prose was content to aim at a lower style height – the height of an Austen or a Peacock – and to abandon logical connection on a Johnsonian scale, remaining content with easy progressions of thought from one local epigrammatic effect to another. Coleridge hated this 'short-witted' popular prose: he saw it as dangerously influenced by French models, and labelled it in *The Friend* 'fashionable Anglo-Gallican'. In Scotland, meanwhile, the virtue of the Enlightenment lasted longer. There, writers like Boswell, Hogg and Galt continued to achieve prose with an admirable clarity of structure.

MOOD AND SENSIBILITY

The Enlightenment dominated intellectual life throughout the century in Scotland, and all but its concluding years in England. In both countries, a literature of empirical description and satiric analysis flourished profusely. Late Augustan poetry, far from being exhausted (as is sometimes said), was so vigorous that even its mediocre productions remain recognizable – vertebrate, never merely miscellaneous. Besides the two grave moral essays of Johnson (*London*, 1738; *The Vanity of Human Wishes*, 1749), the period can offer the interminably rumbustious satires of Charles Churchill (1731–64) and the deadlier observations of Peter Pindar (i.e. John Wolcot, 1738–1819). Even within the Enlightenment itself, however, there were occasional darker tones – when all its bold vistas seemed only to disclose, in the end, more of man's frailty. In poetry, this darker, not at all optimistic mood can receive surprisingly full expression:

> Life protracted is protracted Woe.
> Time hovers o'er, impatient to destroy,
> And shuts up all the Passages of Joy.
> (Johnson, *The Vanity of Human Wishes*
> 228–30)

It is a mood that relaxes or perhaps shrinks from energetic striving, and accepts instead the weakness of depression. Here we have the very obverse of the century's bright and resolute boldness.

At its extreme, the dark mood dwells on death. Such poems as Thomas Parnell's 'A Night-Piece on Death' (1722) or Robert Blair's ambitious *The Grave* (1743) thrill with charnel horrors in the *memento mori* tradition. And countless funeral elegies contribute topics to Edward Young's once popular but now disappointing *Night Thoughts* (1742–5), a book-length blank verse meditation on bereavement, full of familiar ideas in commonplace words. The graveyard school of poets was fascinated by a certain range of vivid, physical images of horror: a 'lone churchyard' with a 'new opened grave', shaded by 'deep pendent cypress' and 'black and funereal yew' ('cheerless, unsocial plant'), where 'night's foul bird' screams, 'grisly spectres' flit through 'gloomy aisles' and 'far-winding vaults', and groans are 'Laden with heavier airs from the low vaults'. Among the 'arms, angels, epitaphs and bones' everything reverberates with dark resonances – 'hollow groans', 'hollow charnel', 'hollow tombs'. In themselves repellent, these images were developed and varied through the genre until they acquired pleasures of familiarity and poetic association. Are such graveyard topics morbid? Perhaps; or it may be we who morbidly avoid the subject of death. At any rate, melancholy contemplation of the tomb was regularly practised in the eighteenth century, and with practice became less anguished and more agreeable – a relaxed entertainment of dark emotions.

Three themes are usual: retirement; *memento mori* (the reminder that the grave awaits poet and reader); and the vanity of human pretensions ('names once famed, now dubious or forgot'). All three combine in Gray's *Elegy in a Country Churchyard* (1751), one of the greatest poems of the century. Its quatrains select the purer elements of the repertoire, and bring the whole tradition to a culmination. Gray chooses to explore the greater pathos in the death of ordinary men:

> Far from the madding crowd's ignoble strife,
> Their sober wishes never learned to stray;
> Along the cool sequestered vale of life
> They kept the noiseless tenor of their way.
>
> (lines 73–6)

The noble strength of the *Elegy*'s calm resigned feelings set it off from earlier poems of shallower melancholy. It still has power to move.

At a less extreme pitch, poetry of melancholy was fashionable – a fashion apparently peculiar to Britain – throughout the period. The melancholy should be distinguished from pathological afflictions: it was most often a benign variant taking such forms as resignation or gentle sadness. At first contained, even impersonal, the emotion grew more enthusiastic and more unreal, until at last it intensified into the Romantic melancholy of the next century. At the middle stage of this development, the poems of William Shenstone (1714–63) are full of mild placid exclamations of sensibility. But sometimes they relax into expression of actual feeling, such as it is. Shenstone modifies elegy to express sentiments of retirement, personalized by location at his landscaped estate The Leasowes, or else by autobiographical details 'I saw my friends in evening circles meet'; 'On listening Cherwell's osier banks reclined'. He readily submits to gloomy weather, 'black ideas', or thoughts of solitary withdrawal into adjacency to nature:

> Bear me ye winds, indulgent to my pains,
> Near some sad ruin's ghastly shade to dwell!
> There let me fondly eye the rude remains,
> And from the mould'ring refuse, build my cell!
>
> (Elegy xvii)

Mark Akenside's (1721–70) 'solitary prospect' in *The Pleasures of Imagination* (1744) is wilder but just as dark:

> 'Twas a horrid pile
> Of hills with many a shaggy forest mixed,
> With many a sable cliff and glittering stream.
> Aloft, recumbent o'er the hanging ridge,
> The brown woods waved . . .
>   and still at every fall
> Down the steep windings of the channeled rock,
> Remurmuring rushed the congregated floods
> With hoarser inundation . . .
>
> (ii.274–83)

Akenside's book-length poem represents a far more ambitious effort than anything in Shenstone. But in the event it disappoints by its slackness of thought – by an inflated verbosity from which sense seems to peter out. As an early attempt at the subject of Wordsworth's *The Prelude* it makes one marvell at how many pitfalls the later poet was able to avoid.

The poetry of retirement and melancholy meditation led on, by clear lines of development, to the Romantic discovery of self. This is perhaps the place, then, to ask when the self was discovered in literature. For medieval literature knew almost nothing of individual personality: its introspection proceeded along rigidly casuistic lines. During the Renaissance subjectivity began to stir, particularly in dramatic literature, where the feelings associated with decisions were displayed, and in sonnets, which did much to explore one range of private emotions. The seventeenth century epigram did more. And the inquiries of Burton and Browne (in their very different ways) enlarged the possibility of self-consciousness. But it was only in the eighteenth century that literature made a sustained attempt to express the individual feelings of those with the leisure to discover themselves. Paradoxically, this attempt often had the appearance of taking part in the Enlightenment's pursuit of general ideas. Perhaps generality of language offered a type of disguise, by making individual feelings seem safely distanced – as if they were mankind's rather than the poet's. Yet consciousness awakened; and with it awoke sympathetic identification on the reader's part – the feeling of one sentient individual for another.

One of the ways of achieving inwardness was by exploration of moods refined from the feelings associated with literature. The poetry of Shenstone, Gray and Collins is extremely literary; evoking mood, as it does, from an accumulation of recognizable allusions or (more often) of fainter, languishing half-echoes, not only of Augustan predecessors but also – and especially – of Spenser and Milton. *Comus* and *Il Penseroso* are vital contexts. The genre is often the private ode or meditative poem of elaborate stanza structure and stately, ceremonious movement. William Collins (1721–59) is now the most interesting of the group, for his delicate art and his first, hesitating adumbration of a new sphere of mental being: one that has occupied a succession of poets, from Wordsworth in his own century down to Wallace Stevens in ours.

Collins's landscape of the imagination – much unlike the everyday world of the satirists – is conjured into being from abstractions that draw their substance purely from memories of literature and nature. His personifications nevertheless have mythic reality, and he addresses them with exclamatory, emotional warmth. Instead of talking about inner feelings, he invokes them as if they were external. In 'Ode to Evening' (1746), Eve – the evening – mythologizes the transient moment of creativity itself. The opening lines' elaborate art, counter-pointed against Eve's simple pastoral conception, gives place to looser expression as Collins's ideas become progressively larger – but also more inward with the creative imagination. With intense sympathy the ode evokes natural images, as if to replace the forms dying into darkness. Meanwhile the syntax drifts and takes on an uncertainty that allows several beautiful effects:

> Then lead, calm vot'ress, where some sheety lake
> Cheers the lone heath, or some time-hallowed pile,
>   Or up-land fallows grey
>   Reflect its last cool gleam.
>
> (lines 29–32)

The 'gleam' of Eve's car is fainter than it would have been if it had come directly after 'sheety lake', instead of being dimmed, as it were, by coming over the 'up-land fallows grey'. Beneath the slight logical incoherence, however, there continues a cogent imaginative sequence. Such effects in Collins are of great intimacy. And in some of his other odes, too – even in the 'Ode to Liberty' – poetry is similarly a subject, obvious or concealed.

From the poetry of self-reflective mood there emerged a new idea of the imagination, and a new stance for poets. This was a time of poems about the pleasures of melancholy and the imagination, many of them centred on a distanced persona of the poet himself, portrayed as 'enthusiast' or 'pilgrim' or 'votary'. (ENTHUSIASM, which often meant religious inspiration, was viewed with a certain suspicion in the aftermath of the Civil War; but after Shaftesbury's qualified defence in *Characteristics* it gradually regained favour, particularly in unecclesiastical versions.) But now the religious note was heard noticeably and rather unexpectedly – almost as if the poets of imagination meant to offer a substitute for orthodox religious belief, or at least a supplementation. Meanwhile the imagination itself was undergoing a hesitant revaluation, which had begun with Shaftesbury, and led on through such passages as Joseph Warton's praise of the 'ecstatic eye' in *The Enthusiast: or the Lover of Nature* (1744) to the awakened sensibility of the late eighteenth century.

A typical form for this development to take was meandering reflections of the idealized enthusiast – during his 'wild wanderings' among the beauties of nature – as in James Beattie's *The Minstrel* (1771–4). The rambling, desultory movement, although it can prove an obstacle to modern readers, none the less made a significant innovation, and would continue to shape much Romantic poetry. It provided a formal resonance with the 'deliberate purposelessness' that according to Emmanual Kant distinguished aesthetic experience. The literature this receptiveness generated has been undervalued by moral critics, from Dr Johnson to Dr Leavis. Leavis has little time for a poetry of weakness: he treats the 'meditative–melancholic' tradition as a 'by-line'. But in reality it is nearer to being the main line. The Wordsworth of *The Prelude* found his point of departure in Warton and Beattie and Thomson; and although he went much further in testing and attesting the powers of the imagination, he could hardly have done so without assuming their mantle of sensitive enthusiast. Many of his most famous poems introduce the aimless wanderer who, like the enthusiasts of Thomson or the averted figures in Friedrich's paintings, embodies consciousness of self.

A similar tendency towards self-reflection can be detected in prose and drama. The main action of Sterne's *Tristram Shandy* (1760–7) is writing itself: its chronology repeatedly draws attention to autobiography's limitations of proportion. And Richard Cumberland's more essayistic *Henry* (1795) pursues the same reflexive end. Dramatic examples were more superficial. An outworn comedy of manners had grounded among shallows of sentiment and artificiality. But Henry Fielding was inventive in his burlesques, some of them based on the idea of rehearsals (with interpolated criticism) of bad plays – as in *Pasquin* (1736). And Richard Brinsley Sheridan's *The Critic* (1781), still actable in spite of its topical caricatures, achieved an outstanding success, against the run in terms of quality. Even so, one has to admit that Sheridan more often reflects on his theatrical rivals than on any deep truths of dramatic art or of human nature.

As I have said, the melancholy of most late eighteenth-century landscape poetry was associated with normality and health, if not exactly rude health; although, being then peculiar to Britain, it might be miscalled 'the English disease'. But there was also a strain of pathological melancholy, perhaps attributable to depression caused by rapid social change. William Cowper (1731–1800), who was troubled by religious guilt, suffered from bouts of insanity and could never look at wild scenery without depression. Quiet, innocent, domestic nature cheered him; but although he was 'enamoured of the sequestered scene' his enjoyment even of it yielded to intermittent guilt at his involvement in society's corruptions. This morbidity now impairs the reputation of his masterpiece, the six-book georgic *The Task* (1785). But Cowper is excellent at recording impressions of ordinary Buckinghamshire or Bedfordshire landscapes – 'sullen skies/ And fields without a flower' – that have the comfort of familiarity. The details are subdued; yet being scrupulously faithful to the scene as subjectively apprehended by a solitary walker, they give pleasure: 'The distant plough slow moving'; 'the sound of cheerful bells/ Just undulates upon the listening ear ...'. In this way Cowper transcribes many faint, unobtrusive beauties – not, as in previous nature poetry, from an external spectator's standpoint, but intimately, as sensed by one who feels.

And *The Task* is more than a series of landscapes: its reflections offer an astonishing variety. Cowper conveys with intelligence a whole world of impressions, some of them new in poetry: greenhouse gardening and civil rights; prison graffiti and embroidery; a female vagrant and a returning mariner –

> At his waist
> A girdle of half-wither'd shrubs he shows,
> And at his feet the baffled billows die.
>
> (i.523–5)

Now he will redefine the status of poetry against a background of changing attitudes to work; now he will 'crack the satiric thong'. Or the arrival of the post with a newspaper will widen the range, in georgic fashion, to 'vast concerns' (iv.56). To most of these Cowper responds with humane, uninflated feelings. He keeps always to a domestic scale, and sometimes shows, with touching honesty, the difficulty of maintaining large Enlightenment perspectives. His voice is level, with a serious humility that engages one's sympathy. Cowper is too respectful of his reader to offer unrestrained confession: only occasionally, as in the famous passage comparing his breakdown to the wound of the 'stricken deer', does the intimacy become deeply private. Just as his retirement barred sociability, so his privacy debars self-expression.

In Virgilian georgics of the late eighteenth century, the process – learning and appreciating beauties – came to matter more than the ostensible subject matter. Meanwhile the appetite for novelty led to ever more rapid reading. Consequently logical connection grew less important; a modern reader may even be impeded by the sense of its absence:

> Thus fare the shiv'ring natives of the north,
> And thus the rangers of the western world,
> Where it advances far into the deep,
> Towards th'antarctic. Ev'n the favour'd isles,
> So lately found, although the constant sun
> Cheer all their seasons with a grateful smile,
> Can boast but little virtue; and, inert
> Through plenty, lose in morals what they gain
> In manners – victims of luxurious ease.
> These therefore I can pity, plac'd remote
> From all that science traces, art invents,
> Or inspiration teaches; and enclosed
> In boundless oceans, never to be pass'd
> By navigators uninform'd as they,
> Or plough'd perhaps by British bark again:
> But, far beyond the rest, and with most cause,
> Thee, gentle savage! whom no love of thee
> Or thine, but curiosity perhaps,
> Or else vain glory, prompted us to draw
> Forth from thy native bow'rs, to show thee here
> With what superior skill we can abuse
> The gifts of Providence, and squander life.
>
> (i.617–38)

This large change tended to give the mere sequence of images a significance it has since retained.

Many of the georgics used blank verse. This, from its association with the exemplary Milton, came to be an 'alternative' form, appropriate for experimental subjects and for serious (especially dark) themes. It is really a very different blank verse from Milton's. Meandering in movement – even if less haphazard, sometimes, than it seems – it lacks any compelling forward impulse lasting longer than a sentence.

In style, the touch became broader; so that distinctions between poetry and prose diminished – just as, during the same period, architectural ornament was reduced. On the whole, poetic diction grew less precise, more suggestive; so that only a habit of unfelt generalization, one almost fancies, prevented an immediate evolution in poets such as Shenstone and Akenside and Beattie into the language of the Romantics. Against this background, it is not surprising that Cowper's plain, specific observations and his sincerities – mild as they are – should have been admired by the next generation.

By such changes poetry, which earlier in the century had had the crispness of woodcut, came to assume the softer washes of introspection and mood. Meanwhile subjectivism found similar expression in prose. The fashionable cult of sensibility, which measured eminence by warmth of social feeling, found its liturgy in Laurence Sterne's *Sentimental Journey* (1768), with its calendar of exquisitely interesting situations – satirized, however, in Sheridan's *School for Scandal* (a.1777), in Joseph Surface. Works of sensibility are not easy to appreciate now, since they depend on an answering warmth that the modern reader tends to withhold. The blood of a novel like Henry Mackenzie's *The Man of Feeling* (1771) pulses mainly through its operations on the reader's sentiments. There is little attempt to plumb depths of personality or motive – little attempt, even, at naturalistic coherence of character. The question you have to ask is not why Mackenzie's Harley or Sterne's Yorick feels so warmly or so contradictorily. The question is rather what sentiments you may be able to sympathize with, yourself.

NEW TYPES OF NOVEL

By far the largest literary counterpart of the Enlightenment could be regarded as the early novel; for there seems little doubt that the empiricist climate was favourable to the development of realistic fiction. The 'rise' of the novel is often – and understandably – connected with the individualism of the emergent bourgeois class. But that emergence took place a good deal earlier, so that it could hardly provide an immediate correlative – unless, perhaps, the slow effects of educational change were to be stressed. The novel attempted to explore emotions of family life, and relations between social groups, at a deeper level than previous realistic genres. Once its thrust is put in such terms, one is inevitably reminded of the Enlightenment's bold exploration of social contexts.

It is hard now to imagine a literature without novels. And it is harder still to conceive a time when other forms were preferred for their higher development. But of course the novel did not spring fully formed from the head of Daniel Defoe (1660?–1731). Satire was an important antecedent – especially the satiric drama of the Restoration and early eighteenth century. Drama had an obvious contribution to make in the rendering of dialogue. Then, the romance, the dominant form of fiction (which was already relying less on extreme or marvellous situations) contributed structures, themes and countless sentimental motives. And other elements derived from other genres – individual histories, journals, memoirs, letters, and spiritual allegory in the Puritan tradition. Two earlier kinds were particuarly valuable to Defoe: EXEMPLARY or didactic fiction, and picaresque.

Defoe's *Moll Flanders* (1722) may be labelled a PICARESQUE novel; that is to say, it tells the episodic story of a rogue's progress, without much detail of description or sentiment. The narrative is episodic in order to present a linear series of graded instances, usually of crime and sexual liaison. *Moll Flanders* seems now to lack an obvious overall plot; and so, even, does the superior, more psychological *Roxana* (1724). Both have their concealed moral structures, however, which are easily recovered by comparing episodes, places, dates, identities, social ranks, sums of money. Such contents are no longer generally appreciated, and may not ever have been – even if many early readers were shopkeepers with a keen interest in money and status. It was a profane society that Defoe addressed, portrayed and disapproved of. His moral ideas might be thought too arbitrarily signified – or perhaps one should say, insufficiently realized in the action. Nevertheless, it is ultimately the pressure of Defoe's unrelenting moral urgency that gives his narratives momentum. And gives clarity too. Roxana pursues a moral (or immoral) course that is implicitly clarified at each stage; although the details whereby Defoe manages this are not yet fully psychological.

What raises problems of interpretation is solely his rigorous effacement of authorial comment. Both novels are narrated entirely from the rogue's aberrant point of view. When the reader has to construct an author's story indirectly like this, one speaks of UNRELIABLE NARRATION. The method came to have great importance for the novel's development. It was not original with Defoe (it goes back to Nashe and beyond); but he grasped its moral potentiality as never before, even if he never quite mastered its technical difficulties. It goes without saying that he had little idea of the complex aesthetic potentialities that unreliable narration gave access to.

Robinson Crusoe (1719), although cast as spiritual autobiography, shows many of the same qualities. Here Defoe outlines, in diagrammatically simple terms, a hard-pastoral world of unremitting effort and divine judgement. There are only meagre traces of anything beyond individualism (*one* glimpse of a ship, *one* footprint). Such details seem very realistic, and so they are; although several are also emblematic. For example, the goats Crusoe keeps would once have been recognized as reprobate; while the footprint signified common human mortality. Such points remind one that allegory still worked easily in Defoe's time. In this respect he was a transitional figure, looking back to Spenser and Bunyan as well as forward to the parables of Hawthorne. *Robinson Crusoe* has more to offer than a myth of capitalism. The acquisition of scarce resources is there; but so are explorations of the individual's experience of cultural change, and of his relations with God and his fellow men (including members of another race).

The story has a compelling authenticity, remarkable in view of the unfamiliar setting. In this documentary reality, which can beguile far from thoughts of fiction, lies Defoe's main contribution. Stylistically he achieves it by a plain style concentrating on unsensuous factual denotation. He has countless matter-of-fact inventories of things, which every now and then conceal a local point – 'some Portugueze Books also, and among them two or three Popish Prayer-Books, and several other Books, all which I carefully secured'. But always the narrative links these things snugly to the end of self-sufficiency. Defoe imagines Crusoe's predicament so vividly that he makes involvement easy. And today the story continues to be resonant: it has been supplemented in many works appropriating its imagined world – whether by poets re-allegorizing it, or by pornographers bent on filling a notable gap in Crusoe's activities.

At an opposite extreme of fictional possibility from Defoe lay the older form that Samuel Richardson's (1689–1761) novels in some ways relate to: the romance. This had been the dominant form of fiction, and was still very popular, especially with women. It accentuated fine sentiments rather than story. Richardson, however, hit on the important innovation of working out both story and emotions in very full detail, all within strict limits of probability. In this, his *Clarissa Harlowe* (1740) and *Sir Charles Grandison* (1754) were to set norms for the central development of the novel, which may be traced through Jane Austen, William Thackeray and Anthony Trollope to Henry James.

Richardson selects details in accordance with his vision. Even so, the sheer amount of them can sometimes make one aware how arbitrary, how much a matter of convention, normative realism is:

> He is constantly accusing me of over-scrupulousness. He says I am always out of humour with him. That I could not have behaved more

reservedly to Mr Solmes: and that it is contrary to all his hopes and notions, that he should not, in so long a time, find himself able to inspire the person whom he hoped so soon to have the honour to call his, with the least distinguishing tenderness for him beforehand.

Silly and partial encroacher! not to know to what to attribute the reserve I am forced to treat him with. But his pride has eaten up his prudence . . .

You will say, that I am very grave: and so I am. Mr Lovelace is extremely sunk in my opinion since Monday night: nor see I before me anything that can afford me a pleasing hope. For what, with a mind so unequal as his, can be my best hope?

I think I mentioned to you, in my former, that my clothes were brought me. You fluttered me so, that I am not sure I did. But I know I designed it. They were brought me on Thursday; but neither my few guineas with them, nor any of my books, except a *Drexelius on Eternity*, the good old *Practice of Piety*, and a *Francis Spira*. My brother's wit, I suppose. He thinks he does well to point out death and despair to me. I wish for the one, and every now and then, am on the brink of the other.

(Clarissa, Letter 173)

Yet Johnson was right to defend Richardson against charges of tediousness: 'if you were to read Richardson for the story, your impatience would be so much fretted that you would hang yourself. But you must read him for the sentiment, and consider the story as only giving occasion to the sentiment.' Eleven letters intervene between Clarissa's agreement to accept the protection of the ladies of Lovelace's family and her actual elopement; 225 between her rape and pining death. Yet almost every minute step of the action has the excitement of believable virtuous emotions superior to one's own ordinary feelings.

The unwavering focus is on endangered integrity, defended, inch by inch, to the death. Clarissa's individual principles are traced through intricate conflict with the social code, as interpreted by her family and later by her subtle betrayer Lovelace. No more recent heroine has come near to equalling Richardson's full realization of a loving, fiercely independent woman in her struggle for personal wholeness. The earliest of novels is already in some ways the greatest. What praise suffices for an author who not only grasped the novel's main possibilities, but carried it to a lasting benchmark? In spite of a certain remorseless didacticism, *Clarissa* is still our most moving tragic novel.

Richardson's novels are EPISTOLARY: they are presented as series of letters supposed to be edited, merely, by the novelist. Telling a story in this way inevitably imposes certain constraints. But it also makes possible an extreme form of realism, since the letters purport to be actual documents. Moreover, the epistolary novel (an important form that has served writers as diverse as Fanny Burney and John Barth) was at first less formal and artificial than it may seem now. Changes in letter writing have to be allowed for. In Richardson's time long narrative letters were common, so that an epistolary novel could plausibly consist of a series of first person narratives. Again, letter writing was then a far more intimate means of communication. It could even at times be more intimate – certainly more convenient – than speech: Richardson himself wrote notes to his family within his own house. Intimacy, indeed, is a special feature of his fiction; Smollett writes of his 'surprising Intimacy with the human Heart'. In this regard there is a subtle interplay between Clarissa's correspondence with her friend Anna Howe and Lovelace's with Belford. Richardson's invention grew out of a different project, a set of model letters (he was a printer, or publisher) meant as a systematic guide to correspondence and conduct. But he learnt so well to write 'to the moment' that his fictional letters often influence the action and may even enter it physically. In his *Pamela* (1740), the heroine notoriously keeps her letter-journal stitched into her petticoat, next to her hips.

Henry Fielding (1707–54), who brought to novel-writing the very different experience of a dramatist, journalist, barrister and magistrate, comprehensively rejected Richardson's conception of life as continual moral striving towards a tragic outcome. Fielding's own larger, and predominantly comic, world has room within its serene and mysterious order for much besides social aspiration and moral testing. And in a sense his enlargement of the novel into Christian comedy has been validated by history; since nineteenth-century novelistic developments were largely in a comic direction (Austen, Thackeray, Trollope, Meredith). In *Joseph Andrews* (1742) and *Tom Jones* (1749) Fielding also reacted against Richardson by drawing back from minutely realized, intensely subjective viewpoints. Instead he advanced Enlightenment generalities about human goodness, and reasserted other facets of realism – judicious 'realism of assessment'; celebratory realism attempting to comprehend the whole nature of life; and the sophisticated realism that takes in storytelling itself. Fielding was something of a theorist (he had studied under Burmannus at Leyden), so that he had a sharp awareness of fiction's status. He often seems in his novels to grapple with a question that never troubles Richardson: what true realism might be.

This has many consequences for Fielding's art. Most obviously, it means a great deal of intervention: not only authorial comments in passing, but literary-critical chapters on subjects like the novel's genre ('comic–epic in prose'). Even the characters discuss ideas: especially Parson Adams, who sketches a theory about the *Iliad* that still bears thinking about. Thus Fielding originated both the novel of ideas and the type in which authorial mediation is noticeably intrusive:

> Thus far the Muse hath with her usual Dignity related this prodigious Battle, a Battle we apprehend never equalled by any Poet, Romance or Life-writer whatever, and having brought it to a Conclusion she ceased; we shall therefore proceed in our ordinary Style with the Continuation of this History.
>
> *(Joseph Andrews* III.vi)

Less obviously, he invented (or at least transferred from Spenser and romantic epic) the important idea of a narrative that draws attention to its own fictionality:

> Suppose a Stranger, who entered the Chambers of a Lawyer, being imagined a Client, when the Lawyer was preparing his Palm for the Fee, should pull out a Writ against him. Suppose an Apothecary, at the Door of a Chariot containing some great Doctor of eminent Skill, should, instead of Directions to a Patient, present him with a Potion for himself . . . In short – suppose what you will, you never can nor will suppose any thing equal to the Astonishment which seiz'd on Trulliber, as soon as Adams had ended his Speech.
>
> *(Joseph Andrews* II.xiv)

For good measure, Fielding was also the first novelist to achieve detailed third-person narration *in extenso*. And he began the use of fiction in controversial or dialectic or generically experimental ways, so as to present ideas of society. Thus, *Joseph Andrews* partly makes its statement by departure from previous novels. It begins with burlesque of Richardson's characters, then takes them out on exemplary excursions into a more adventurous world, where they must grow to meet the challenge of other values – now those of epic, now of Cervantes, now of the New Testament latitudinously interpreted. This larger world includes vignettes of colloquial life, ranging far lower than Richardson ever cares to go. Fielding prefers to keep his distance from characters – discontinuing episodes before proportion is lost in involvement. The minor characters, indeed, are satiric and almost allegorical. But he increasingly inclines to comic characterization: he may delineate individual incorrigibles with Hogarthian severity, but his overall representation is amiable and sane – as society itself could be, he persuades us.

The novels of Tobias Smollett break less new ground: his *Roderick Random* (1748) and *Peregrine Pickle* (1751) return to the picaresque form, even if he enriches it with the observations of a seasoned traveller. But *Humphry Clinker* (1771) is incomparably better, and stands comparison with the work of Smollett's great predecessors. In it, he combines the ironic range of Fielding with Richardson's epistolary method and unbroken illusion of probability. Smollett orders his characters' correspondence very differently, however, in that he gives only one side of their exchanges. This brilliant device engages the reader more actively in constructing the story: one must compare the diverse travel accounts and draw one's own conclusions. Smollett's travel action allows for satire on a wide range of topics; although it never becomes a mere vehicle or pretext. On the contrary, one can feel that *Humfrey Clinker* exists in large part for the sake of its characters. (It was the first novel to do so.) A stereotype of the author (crude, irascible Scot) has tended to impede appreciation of the delicate stylistic adjustments of his masterpiece – not to speak of its intricate structural organization.

Laurence Sterne's seminal *Tristram Shandy* (1760–7) initiated a new form, the work-in-progress fiction or POIOUMENON. This is less concerned to imitate an action performed by characters than to follow the thought of a single character writing about it. To make this fertile new departure (which was anticipated only by fumbling experiments), Sterne in effect inflated the authorial element of the Fieldingesque novel until it filled the entire work – and in the process fictionalized the author. For he denied that continuous fiction of the sort derived from classical epic could achieve anything like an adequate representation of life. Where would one begin? Instead, *Tristram Shandy* is all gothic digression, and digression within digression: when the 'cause and crotchet' of an impulse has been set forth at chapter length, 'when that's done, 'twill be time to return back to the parlour fire-side, where we left my uncle Toby in the middle of his sentence'. Sterne needed a digressive method if he was to render the truth of individual experience by following out trains of thought; since these were now believed to work through associations or 'chains of ideas'. But this was no reductionist programme. Lockeian theory, far from dispelling the mind's mysterious unsearchability, added further complication, such as the symbolic displacement underlying Uncle Toby's obsessional model-making, or the multiple time-schemes that the Shandy family variously inhabit.

Sterne's insight into these problems of representation seems at times congenially modern; particularly when it finds expression in devices of self-reference – passages left blank for one's participation, or diagrams of his own digressions. He may seem almost anachronistic – until one reflects that every age contains much the same literary potentialities, but differently accommodated, developed, emphasized. In Sterne's time there was already a taste for fragmentary disorder in art. Besides, he only pretended to throw over the literary rules. Actually his work obeys quite rigorous decorums – not only a rule of maximum outward disorder, but also a hidden pattern of esoteric ideas:

> I write a careless kind of a civil, nonsensical, good humoured *Shandean* book, which will do all your hearts good –
> – And all your heads too, – provided you understand it.
>
> (VI.xvii)

The kernel of *Tristram Shandy* is a vision of creaturely being. Its realism lies in representing not a completed world (*natura naturata*), but rather a process (*natura naturans*) – the process of creation, of growth, of the author's imagination of his own world, with all its emergent contingencies, idiosyncratic perspectives and alternations of cosmic and local scale. The action is nothing less than creation itself – making a child, a microcosmic model, an individual, an autobiography – so that its completion must always recede before fresh interruptions of life. With its ever degenerating, ever renewed narrative, *Tristram Shandy* recalls at times *The Faerie Queene*. Like Spenser's poem, it communicates a sharp impression of life's underlying nature (the subject, *au fond*, that all Sterne's characters meditate). He himself finds it ironic or sadly comic, an affair of unnecessary wounds, voluntary miseries, absurdities, miniature magnificences. And his response to it is eloquence – a marvellously fluent rhetorical display of wit that half satirizes man's grandiose erudition and explanatory pretensions, half uses the learning to relish his oddity. He shows the breakdown of enlightened attempts to organize life, when history extends itself and breaks in (like the new-fangled window sash that circumcises Tristram). But against historical or clock time – the enemy of human volition – he asserts a sublime interconnectedness. Each alone is impotent to grasp this. Yet it will empower any who begins 'with writing the first sentence – and trusting to Almighty God for the second'. Sterne's psychological amusements, his recurrent themes of impotence, displacement, disproportion, obsessive 'hobby-horses' – even his desire to surprise – are complemented by a certain seriousness. The fundamental disproportions are religious: that men should intellectualize about God, for example, or practise sophisticated siege warfare against their fellow creatures.

The combination of fluent learned wit with an abruptly digressive method came (through Rabelais) from the Menippean tradition. But Sterne's further addition of suspended narrative was a happy new invention. It quickened the novel with spontaneous inner life, and for the first time made possible sympathy with several characters at once. Whose sympathies are not divided, when Walter in full flow has to manoeuvre Toby past words that must trigger his *idée fixe?*

The tenderness, almost compassion, that suffuses *Tristram Shandy* and *A Sentimental Journey* (1768) was congenial to the generous Enlightenment warmth of the 1770s, and exerted much diffused influence. Sterne had no immediate formal successors, however; although there is much benevolent sentiment in works like Oliver Goldsmith's *The Vicar of Wakefield* (1766), Henry Brooke's *The Fool of Quality* (1766) and (closest) Henry Mackenzie's *The Man of Feeling* (1771). Similar emotions were also an ingredient of the gothic romance. But a very different genre was to have a more profound effect on fiction than even the literature of sensibility: namely, the NOVEL OF DOCTRINE. During the century's last three decades many of these semifictional exemplary (didactic) novels appeared, setting out social views of an Enlightenment or Rousseauesque tendency. Most – like those of Mrs Elizabeth Inchbald, Robert Bage and William Godwin – are pretty cold fare. They now interest chiefly when they verge on the NOVEL OF MANNERS by going into social behaviour in more than usual detail. Then, indeed, they show themselves a model for Jane Austen's exemplary characters and firmly thematic moral structure.

But one novelist of doctrine, Maria Edgeworth (1767–1849), stands out. The historical importance of Edgeworth's novels is beyond question. Historians point to her structural innovation in *Castle Rackrent* (1800), whereby a family's fortunes are traced through several generations from an observer–narrator's point of view (the faithful retainer Thady). As a regional novel, moreover – it is set in Ireland – it opened the way to distanced representation of an entire society: to Scott, in fact, and the historical novel. But an even larger claim could be made for Edgeworth's later novels, such as *Patronage* (1814), which is equally path-cleaving if not so completely successful. Here we meet, almost fully formed, the novel with a thesis. Edgeworth carries out rigorous analysis of different types of patronage in every walk of life; working through ingenious and ever more telling variations, until it seems she must condemn the whole system. From this conclusion, however, she draws back, with an effect of enhanced subtlety. The plot is well diversified, combining 'great and little events'. A reformer's concern and human interest in 'underplots of life' are linked by trains of causation that make everything depend, say, on a caramel. For pages at a time Edgeworth reads like Austen; even showing a similar acuity of moral observation. But then her values will become too explicit; or her exemplary programme call for too frequent changes of characters; or her fiction collapse into essay (for there are far too many ideas for fully narrative realization). She has a flawless ear for speech; so that she is at her best in the brilliant dialogue, which manifests a scintillating intellect with startlingly wide interests. In *Belinda* (1801), smoother but less intense, Edgeworth attempted the difficult subject of match-making – one that was to be returned to by many later novelists, notably Austen (*Emma*) and Trollope (*The Way We Live Now*).

For a time Edgeworth enjoyed an international reputation that extended as far as Russia. Although she may never recover such a standing, she surely merits far more attention than fashion currently concedes her. It was from the exemplary novel that later genres derived the thematic concerns now taken for granted. And of all early exemplary novels, Edgeworth's are the most intelligently interesting.

9
Romanticism and Poetry

T HE late eighteenth-century novel generated little new development, and was effectively displaced in the last decade by gothic
romance. This revival of romance can be seen as part of a retrospective movement gathering strength throughout the century's latter
half.

THE POPULAR POET

In various ways, interest turned to earlier literary forms and modes of
feeling, as if to gather resources for some large change of sensibility.
Some have regarded this as a counterstatement to established culture –
an attempt to move outside classical tradition. But it could as well be
seen as expressing Enlightenment openness: the drive to investigate
national origins would naturally improve familiarity with the medieval,
'gothic' past. A signal achievement in that direction was Thomas
Warton's unfinished *The History of English Poetry* (1774–81). Warton not
only invented the idea of literary history but actually implemented it, so
far as medieval and Tudor literature was concerned – periods generally
unknown in his time.

Enthusiasm for the past was far from being limited by ignorance of
history: it extended freely to spurious antiquities. A warmly contested
issue was the authenticity of James Macpherson's translations of celtic
epics purportedly by Ossian, a poet of the third century (*Fragments of
Ancient Poetry*, 1760; *Fingal*, 1762). Hugh Blair believed, Dr Johnson
doubted. But it is difficult now to imagine how anyone can have thought
of Macpherson's solemn cadences as deriving from an original other
than the Authorized Version. Gray's Norse translations and Welsh
imitations reflected a similar interest in early minstrelsy, as did his 'The
Bard' (wr. 1757). And much pleasure was taken in the fake medieval
'Rowley' poems of Thomas Chatterton (1752–70), 'the marvellous boy'

(as Wordsworth called him), whom neglect nevertheless drove to suicide at eighteen. Chatterton could be vague as to period (his poetry has Elizabethan as well as fifteenth-century features); but so keen was his enthusiasm, and so great his ability to evoke historical distance, that he did much to intensify the mood of medieval romance:

> Liste! now the thunder's rattling clymmynge [noisy] sound
> Cheves [moves] slowlie on, and then embollen [swollen] clangs,
> Shakes the hie spyre, and losst, dispended, drown'd,
> Still on the gallard [frighted] eare of terroure hanges;
> The windes are up; the lofty elmen swanges;
> Again the levynne and the thunder poures,
> And the full cloudes are braste [burst] attenes [at once] in stonen showers.
> ('An Excelente Balade of Charitie' st.6)

In this period the very word 'romantic' became a term of praise, implying imaginative appeal.

Meanwhile scholarly folklorists – still working largely from written sources, however – were collecting and popularizing antiquities; among them Bishop Thomas Percy (*Reliques of Ancient English Poetry*, 1765) and Sir Walter Scott (*Border Minstrelsy*, 1802–3). Nevertheless, any departure from classicism was still potential or preliminary: the ballad, after all, had already (thanks to Addison) received approval from the Augustans.

In Scotland, Allan Ramsay's *The Ever Green, Being a Collection of Scots Poems, Wrote by the Ingenious before 1600* (1724), amateurish as it was, restored the Makars to the canon; while in the same year his *The Tea Table Miscellany* began a revival of song writing in the vernacular. And there were other similar efforts. The romanticized primitivism of the late Enlightenment encouraged a taste for the vernacular simplicities of untutored geniuses wherever they might be found. – Or invented: Robert Burns (1759–96) confessed himself to be not really an untutored ploughman – that was 'a part of the machinery . . . of his poetical character'. In fact he had some education and much knowledge of literature. His own poems were not originary: he acknowledged debts to Robert Fergusson (1750–74); and his language combined a Scots diction very like Ramsay's with the syntax common to Scots and southern English. What distinguishes his best poetry is warmth and depth of feeling. He shares the Enlightenment's breadth of sympathy, with its radical meritocratic intensity; as in 'Song – For aa that and aa that':

> Then let us pray that come it may,
> As come it will for aa that,

That Sense and Worth, owre aa the earth
   Shall bear the gree [win first place], and aa that.
     For aa that, and aa that,
   It's coming yet for aa that,
That Man to Man the warld owre,
   Shall brothers be for aa that.

He is stronger still in tender love songs like 'The Bonny Wee Thing', 'Mary Morrison' and 'Ae Fond Kiss':

   Ae fond kiss, and then we sever;
   Ae fareweel, and then for ever!
   Deep in heart-wrung tears I'll pledge thee,
   Warring sighs and groans I'll wage thee.

The passionate expression of a song like this is not the whole of its art. Much of the pleasure comes from exquisite adaptations of rhythm and sense to the pattern of a previously existing tune. It is, in fact, art song.

   Sometimes, as in 'John Anderson my Jo', there was even an earlier (perhaps bawdy) version of the words, from which Burns could take a line or two, purifying the sentiments:

   John Anderson my jo [lover], John,
     We clamb the hill the gither;
   And mony a canty [lively] day, John,
     We've had wi ane anither:
   Now we maun [must] totter down, John,
     And hand in hand we'll go;
   And sleep the gither at the foot,
     John Anderson my jo.

This is only a part of Burns's range: there are also drinking songs and patriotic songs and elegiac songs on places, besides other subjects, all confidently handled with a sure touch. He already included songs in the Kilmarnock (1786) and Edinburgh (1787) editions of his *Poems, Chiefly in the Scottish Dialect*. But in the later years of his short life he devoted himself primarily to writing songs and collecting them for Johnson's *The Scots Musical Museum* (1787–1803) and Thomson's *A Select Collection of Original Scottish Airs* (1793–1825). Burns was the greatest poet to be involved in collection, and in him vernacular traditions of song writing attained new heights of elegant art song. He consequently occupies a special place in the distinguished line of Scottish lyric poets running from Dunbar through Fergusson to Soutar and the early MacDiarmid. Although Burns had no immediate successors of comparable worth, he was able to transmit the art to an even more songful century.

Burns's reputation by no means rests exclusively on his lyric achievement. His satire is as fine; and 'Holy Willie's Prayer', by internalizing
that genre, can even be said to have given it a strategic new direction.
His moral poems, like 'To a Mouse', have an endearing humanity and
largeness of sentiment. And the best of his tales are marvellously judged
– especially 'Tam O'Shanter', whose supernatural terrors are so well
distanced by framing ironies that a modern reader cannot help looking
(in vain) for multiple narrators.

LITERATURE AND NATURE

The new warmth of feeling was a strong vector of change; and so was the
taste for folk songs and ballads surviving from an earlier condition of
society. Yet another – perhaps the most effective of all – worked through
nature poetry. Augustan writers had been fond of invoking nature as a
value. But nature has many meanings; and the ones that classicists
invoked tended to be preconceived, abstract, philosophical, static. Now
other senses came to the fore: not only new abstractions, but also
psychological nature; scientific; even the concrete nature of geographical exploration. These interacted throughout the Romantic
movement: nature was still the watchword, but in a very different,
altogether more organic way.

Nature for Pope was a composition of balanced opposites, much like
a painting. And in *The Landscape* (1794), Richard Payne could still speak
of joining landscape's 'various parts in harmony . . . With art clande-
stine, and concealed design'. But in *The Seasons* (1726–30) the Scottish
poet James Thomson looks at nature in a very different way: with the
informed eye of the scientific enthusiast. Thomson observes acutely. He
describes for the first time in detail many natural phenomena, such as
an electric storm; invents many picturesque scenes that have been
imitated ever since (like the robin coming into the house for crumbs
in *Winter*); and brings into poetry many fresh particulars –

> The Daisy, Primrose, Violet darkly blue,
> And Polyanthus of unnumber'd Dyes;
> The yellow Wall-Flower, stained with iron Brown . . .
>
> (*Spring* 531–3)

> Indistinct on Earth
> Seen through the turbid Air, beyond the Life,
> Objects appear; and, wildered, o'er the Waste
> The Shepherd stalks gigantic.
>
> (*Autumn* 724–7)

Yet his description is never merely literal, but always expressive of scientific or philosophical ideas. (In the last quotation the idea is refraction.) Even his poetic diction sometimes has a basis in contemporary science – as is true of periphrases like 'scaly breed'. Somewhat less successful is his blank verse. His imitations of Milton's rhythmic patterns resemble couplet variations: systematic in their controlled minutiae, they achieve distinctive effects. But they lack emotional pressure, and can easily seem diffuse. Nevertheless Thomson was once 'the most popular of all our poets' and enjoyed an international reputation that extended as far as Russia. Dr Johnson judged him to be entitled to the highest praise for his originality in a new kind (a new subgenre of georgic?): 'he thinks in a peculiar train, and he thinks always as a man of genius.'

Mention of Thomson's scientific interests prompts a side glance here at the natural history that began to influence literature about this time. For more than a century, feeling for nature was sustained by a constant flow of information from enthusiastic naturalists, many of them amateurs. Of these, the earliest still readable with pleasure is Gilbert White, whose *Natural History of Selbourne* (1789) in effect comprises a series of letters to friends about remarkable or puzzling natural phenomena – largely ornithological. White had a keen mind, and was a good empirical investigator, capable of carrying out thorough experiments. He had also a great affection for his subject, as every detail shows:

> the feeble little golden-crowned wren, that shadow of a bird, braves our severest frosts without availing himself of houses or villages . . . The blue titmouse, or nun, is a great frequenter of houses, and a general devourer. Besides insects, it is very fond of flesh; for it frequently picks bones on dunghills: it is a vast admirer of suet, and haunts butchers' shops. When a boy, I have known twenty in a morning caught with snap mousetraps, baited with tallow or suet.
>
> (Letter xli)

Observation so affectionate gives much delight – especially when it is combined with rigorous thought capable of arriving, through long trains of reasoning, at conclusions at first quite unforeseen.

The letter vehicle could also be used in the travel reports abounding in a great period of exploration. It was the age of Anson and Cook in the Pacific, of Bruce and Mungo Park in Africa. Most of the travel accounts were subliterary, but they could nevertheless be vivid; and they excited the Romantic imagination. Several of the travel writers offered idyllic descriptions – of paradises peopled by noble savages, of alluring freedom from civilization and its constraints. The idea of innocence was thoughtfully developed by the American quaker William Bartram, whose *Travels* (Philadelphia, 1791; London, 1792) describe botanic excursions in the Deep South, including encounters with alligators in Florida. Bartram is one of the first to express love for wild nature – a theme that will recur in American literature, for example in Parkman and Thoreau. Bartram's style may be rather too purply-adjectival; yet his endless landscape imagery – the ruggednesses and continually luxuriant vegetation – remain compelling. Descriptions like that of the sunfish are unforgettable –

> the whole fish is of a pale gold (or burnished brass) colour, darker on the back and upper sides; the scales are of a proportionable size, regularly placed, and every where variably powdered with red, russet, silver, blue, and green specks, so laid on the scales as to appear like real dust or opaque bodies . . .
>
> (Pt II, ch.5)

– and so, as the author of 'Kubla Khan' discovered, is that of

> the inchanting and amazing crystal fountain, which incessantly threw up, from dark, rocky caverns below, tons of water every minute, forming a bason, capacious enough for large shallops to ride in, and a creek of four or five feet depth of water, and near twenty yards over, which meanders six miles through green meadows, pouring its limpid waters into the great Lake George, where they seem to remain pure and unmixed.
>
> (Pt II, ch.5)

It is not easy, now, to grasp how much this emotion was effectually unprecedented.

Until the seventeenth century at least, rough nature was generally thought repulsive, even horrible. Only by very gradual change, with wider settlement and growth of town populations, did a new sensibility begin to find expression in voluntary travel into wild regions. A famous early instance was Horace Walpole. On 28 September 1739 he wrote to his friend Richard West:

> But the road, West, the road! winding round a prodigious mountain, and surrounded with others, all shagged with hanging woods, obscured with pines or lost in clouds! Below, a torrent breaking though cliffs, and tumbling through fragments of rocks! Sheets of cascades forcing their silver speed down channeled precipices, and hasting into the roughened river at the bottom! Now and then an old foot-bridge, with a broken rail,

a leaning cross, a cottage, or the ruin of an hermitage! This sounds too bombast and too romantic to one that has not seen it, too cold for one that has.

West replied: 'Your description of the Alps made me shudder . . .'. British theorizing about the experience of the sublime went back to Shaftesbury (who took it from the ancient rhetorician Longinus); but it received its first full development from Edmund Burke (1729–97). The Irish writer, although he argues without real clarity, is more than a fine contender or mere persuasive expositor. If he cannot claim rigour as a thinker, he is nevertheless adventurously original in exploring the sublime. He develops an interesting contrast between the sublime and the beautiful (qualities previously confused), and sees that their emotional sources are opposite too:

> For sublime objects are vast in their dimensions, beautiful ones comparatively small. Beauty should be smooth and polished; the great, rugged and negligent . . . Beauty should not be obscure; the great ought to be dark and gloomy. Beauty should be light and delicate; and great ought to be solid and even massive. They are indeed ideas of a very different nature, one being founded on pain, the other on pleasure . . .
>
> (*A Philosophical Inquiry* (1757) iii.27)

Burke lacks historical perspective (he has little sense of differing period styles); but he registers suggestive insights. He has grasped that terror, darkness, solitude and the infinite, when they are felt in safety, can all give delight.

This was the very element of irrationality excluded from the neoclassical ideal of beauty. That had been based on human proportions; but the sublime belongs to an altogether different, non-human (or nonindividual) scale. It is the larger world to which Beattie's enthusiast responds:

> And oft the craggy cliff he loved to climb,
> When all in mist the world below was lost.
> What dreadful pleasure! there to stand sublime,
> Like shipwrecked mariner on desert coast,
> And view the enormous waste of vapour, tossed
> In billows, lengthening to th'horizon round,
> Now scooped in gulfs, with mountains now embossed!
> And hear the voice of mirth and song rebound,
> Flocks, herds, and waterfalls, along the hoar profound!
>
> (*The Minstrel* (1771) i.21)

The feeling is strong, if not very powerfully realized. Emotional enthusiasm, indeed, is a characteristic of the period that calls for careful attention. Similarly with its focus on the poet's own feelings – the narcissistic concentration on purely internal, solitary experience. Both characteristics appear (as we saw) in Cowper and Collins. And they already combine in Joseph Warton's 'Ode to Fancy' (1746), where he rejects the idea that he should ever write without Fancy's 'powerful aid'. The poetry Warton wanted (this cannot have endeared him to Johnson) was private and emotional – 'Like lightning, let his mighty verse/ The bosom's inmost foldings pierce'. He might have been prophesying the advent of Wordsworth.

Warton's disgust with frigid artificiality was not the only negative note in late eighteenth-century literature. With greater force of social consciousness George Crabbe (1754–1832) flouted convention by choosing sordidly realistic subjects. He wrote a kind of anti-pastoral, substituting weeds for the customary flowers, laborious misery for the expected idyll. The wretches inhabiting *The Village* (1783) drag out a dismal existence,

> Where the thin harvest waves its withered ears;
> Rank weeds, that every art and care defy,
> Reign o'er the land, and rob the blighted rye:
> There thistles stretch their prickly arms afar,
> And to the ragged infant threaten war;
> There poppies nodding, mock the hope of toil;
> There the blue bugloss paints the sterile soil;
> Hardy and high, above the slender sheaf,
> The slimy mallow waves her silky leaf . . .
>   (*The Village* i)

But Crabbe's strong feelings at first leave him no leisure to arrive at a style distinct from that of the literature he rejects. He still uses old patterns of diction and couplet structure; although he sometimes achieves with them effects of sombre power.

It was only in his later work, after the earlier phase of the Romantic movement, that he was to achieve a fully original integration of ideas and their embodiment. Then, in tales like that of the outcast murderer Peter Grimes, he would introduce a new kind of landscape of the mind, subjective in a way that foreshadowed the Victorian novelists and poets:

> There anchoring, Peter chose from man to hide,
> There hang his head, and view the lazy tide
> In its hot slimy channel slowly glide;

Where the small eels that left the deeper way
For the warm shore, within the shallows play;
Where gaping muscles, left upon the mud,
Slope their slow passage to the fallen flood; –
Here dull and hopeless he'd lie down and trace
How sidelong crabs had scrawl'd their crooked race; . . .
(*The Borough* (1810) Letter xxii)

All the factors I have mentioned – internal orientation, intensification of feeling, revaluation of nature, the sublime, the vogue of travel, and the rest – united in the great shift of sensibility known as the ROMANTIC REVIVAL. European Romanticism is often presented as overturning the static, frigid order that preceded it; and so far as Germany is concerned, and the movement of Goethe, Novalis and the Schlegels, that may largely be accurate. But in Britain, where Romanticism began, almost the reverse is the case. The more dynamic Enlightenment was a fertile reorganization from which Romanticism emerged as a natural development as much as a counterstatement. At first the British movement had little of the morbidity of the Continental; so that it appeared more of a renaissance or revival. Yet the Romantic revival ultimately rejected classicism with its imitative procedures, in preference for expression privileging the imagination. And it revalued nature in a manner that had no precedent. The poet's vision was reconciled with an outer world informed with a spirit greater than his own. This living universe rediscovered, in part, the *animus mundi* of Renaissance Platonism. But the abandonment of reason as the arbiter of how inner and outer reality corresponded was a new departure fraught with large consequences.

WILLIAM WORDSWORTH

The first obviously innovative production of the Romantic poets was *Lyrical Ballads* (1798), the result of a collaboration of William Wordsworth (1770–1850) and Samuel Taylor Coleridge (1772–1834). To an age given to discussing Rousseau and the Noble Savage, there was nothing affronting about serious tales of rustics; and the ballad, as we have seen, already counted as a reputable form. But these poems came with a distinctly provocative manifesto. They were 'written chiefly with a view to ascertain how far the language of conversation in the middle and lower classes of society is adapted to the purposes of poetic pleasure'. In actuality their diction is fairly low; although they are not unfurnished with poetical ornaments like inversion and rhyme. The 'experiment' is a very mixed success, resulting in banality and even in

bathos as well as in some fine poems. But in his tender report of an idiot
boy's experience of owls and moonlight, Wordsworth makes beautiful
sense of the irrational: 'The cocks did crow to-whoo, to-whoo,/ And the
sun did shine so cold.' At its best, *Lyrical Ballads* gives earnest of a return
to 'the real language of men in a state of vivid sensation' (the revised
formulation of 1800). And it has the compassion for the poor and
wretched that characterizes much of Wordsworth's best work.

Poems on such social topics were not new – indeed, an earlier fashion
for them was being driven out by counter-revolutionary sentiment.
Nevertheless, Wordsworth could be said to have entered more seriously
into humble and childish passions than was common. Again, it is
claimed that he was the first to question the language to be used in
poetry – something that has remained problematic ever since. But it
would be truer to say that in this regard he revived Tudor and
Restoration concern.

At Alfoxden with Coleridge in 1798 and during the following year in
lonely isolation with his sister Dorothy at Goslar in Germany,
Wordsworth was already writing *The Prelude*. Nothing shows the
exploratory innovation of this masterpiece better than the experimental
method of its composition. At first Wordsworth meant it as apprenticeship for *The Recluse*, a long blank-verse poem of which it would form
part. But *The Prelude* expanded into two-book and five-book versions,
until with the transfer of *Recluse* material a thirteen-book *Prelude* was
drafted (1805), still without publication. Only after forty years of
laborious and brilliant revision did Wordsworth at last publish the
fourteen-book *Prelude* of 1850. Of *The Recluse*, however, only one part
was published in his lifetime: *The Excursion* (1814). How different from
the compositional method of the neoclassical poets, who were accustomed to construct their poems on a rhetorical armature, projecting an
outline of the divisions that made it possible to plan specific numbers of
lines in each. Wordsworth, by contrast, works through successive drafts
of quite different dimensions, as if he were writing exploratory prose.
His arduously minute revisions may seem to run counter to his own
idea of good poetry as 'the spontaneous overflow of powerful feelings'.
But the contradiction is only apparent: 'spontaneous' has changed in
meaning, and what he meant was '*voluntary* overflow'.

The originality of *The Prelude* has to do with its autobiographical
concentration, the entire subject being the poet's own mental development. Locally Wordsworth made use of Cowper, or Beattie, or the Latin
scientific poet Lucretius, and in his elevated language had learnt
something from Milton, the most personal of epicists. But he had little

poetic precedent for extended autobiography that went behind mature adult consciousness into the earlier experiences on which personality was based. Wordsworth's material is highly internalized, since it depends altogether on recollection; and this has a comprehensive effect on his semi-epic form. Instead of an opening invocation of afflatus, there is simply joy at an ordinary breeze, and 'rigorous inquisition' of his natural gifts and suitability for the proposed work: instead of a Miltonic catalogue of subjects rejected, he considers alternatives in terms of his own preoccupations: and instead of the inspiring Aganippe (or Siloa), he turns to natural rivers that influenced his childhood.

The thrust of *The Prelude* is not outward towards the world, but retrospective, into the earlier experience that poets had previously taken for granted. Wordsworth aims to trace his spiritual development in terms of relationships with nature. Accordingly he presents two sorts of poetry. The first is a series of memories of early experiences, some of them visionary: skating in the Lake District; vacations from Cambridge; travel in the Alps; alienation from London; the 'bliss' of France after the Revolution and before its betrayal; and subsequent horrors. Second, there is a matching series of meditations – interpreting the memories, speculating about nature's influence – conceived in language that rises to lofty heights of abstraction. Nature becomes again a living force, in a way not felt since the seventeenth century (although the symbolism is now more individual). It is an 'infinitude', a 'presence', a 'spirit'. Wordsworth's reverence for the transcendental in nature amounts to a religion: at least, he accords his experience of nature a religious value.

These two types of writing alternate more or less regularly; so that the structure of *The Prelude* seems to follow a psychological pattern of association – a key idea in contemporary metaphysics. But this should not be pressed in a reductionist way: to Wordsworth, the imagination was much more actively complex than that would suggest.

It is easy to prefer the memorial parts with their clear vivid narration. (They are indeed the parts to start with on a first approach.) In the account of birdnesting, when the boy hangs

> almost (so it seemed)
> Suspended by the blast that blew amain,
> Shouldering the naked crag,
> (Book i(1850) 333–5)

the precise line breaks throw stress on 'Shouldering' and 'Suspended', and enact the suspension. Many know the stripped nature of mountain tops, and have heard the wind's 'strange utterance': these verses make one feel them afresh. The interpretation that follows seems at first less convincing, with its talk of

> a dark
> Inscrutable workmanship that reconciles
> Discordant elements, makes them cling together
> In one society.
>
>   (Book i(1850) 341–4)

But this is not merely an alternative, inferior style. The labouring reflection is meant to encourage generalization of the anecdotal experience, so that it may repeat its influence. Wordsworth believed that such memories or 'spots of time' have enduring significance, and sustain subsequent life. By reviving them, he hopes to enable them to work as correlates of new experience. Thus, the memory of inglorious birdnesting and nature's consequent 'not ignoble' challenge implicitly relates to the meditation – and to the whole presentation of the poem's challenge in Book I. 'Discordant elements', mean and noble purposes, 'cling together' like the boy to the crag.

The memories serve as correlates of the abstract meditations in countless ways. An extreme instance is the recollection of ascending Snowdon on a misty night. A shepherd's dog makes a find (a familiar metaphor of poetic invention); and the pattern of dog *versus* hedgehog finds repetition in the poet's combat with his earthy nature during his struggle to ascend, 'as if in opposition set/ Against an enemy'. Then the epiphany:

> as I looked up,
> The Moon hung naked in a firmament
> Of azure without cloud, and at my feet
> Rested a silent sea of hoary mist.
> A hundred hills their dusky backs upheaved
> All over this still ocean; and beyond,
> Far, far beyond, the solid vapours stretched,
> In headlands, tongues, and promontory shapes, . . .
>
>   (Book xiv (1850) 39–46)

In this obscuring 'ocean' is a fixed abysm through which mounts the single voice of innumerable streams of inspiration – the roar of torrents below. For Beattie it would have been sufficient to describe such a scene; but Wordsworth must now explore its content. It is 'the type/ Of a majestic intellect', 'the emblem of a mind' that broods on infinity. The consequent meditation challenges one to ponder an unusually profound conception of human creation.

Opinion is divided whether *The Prelude* of 1805 or of 1850 should be preferred: whether the revisions are artistic improvements or churchmanly falsifications of experience. In fact the earlier version's meditations are, for all their Platonism, less irreconcilable with Christianity than has often been argued. The revisions generally tighten the blank verse, remove banalities and make the diction more particularized ('lurcher' for 'cur' is a typical change). On the other hand, 1850 can sometimes lack immediacy. The differences are usually exaggerated. In both versions the language – abstract in diction but vigorously concrete in operation – represents a triumph of the exploratory imagination as it pushes back the bounds of inarticulacy.

Wordsworth succeeds by his unremitting adherence to truth. In this respect, as in some others, he has the greatness to span two ages. His conscious introspection, his sense of his own experience as typical, his broad sympathies: all are of the Enlightenment. But his deeper investigation of what Keats called the 'egotistical sublime', like his feeling for transcendental nature, belongs with the incoming century – and reaches forward to influence Emerson and Thoreau and Wallace Stevens. So far as his attention to epiphanies of insight is concerned, indeed, Wordsworth may be called the first modern poet.

Besides *The Prelude*, he wrote, mostly in the decade immediately following 1798, a number of similar but shorter poems such as 'Lines Composed a Few Miles Above Tintern Abbey' (included in *Lyrical Ballads*) and 'Resolution and Independence'. Yet he was also responsible for the totally different Lucy poems, short intense lyrics; for some great sonnets; and, in later life, for a considerable heap of very dull verse.

SAMUEL TAYLOR COLERIDGE

Romanticism's intense interest in personality shows in the vast quantity of journals, notebooks, letters and memoranda that have survived from the period. No previous generation of writers left anything like this wealth of material. For the first time the biographical context of literature becomes fully detailed. It gives a strong (and partly valid) impression that the Romantics lived their poetry continuously: that it arose from habitual imaginative excitement. The *Journals* of Dorothy Wordsworth are full of materials for poems (some of them actually written by her brother William); and so are Coleridge's notebooks:

> Water and Windmills: Greenness, Islets Green,
> Willows whose trunks beside the Shadows stood

Of their own higher half, and willowy Swamps,
Farm-houses that at anchor seemed and on the inland sky
The fly-transfixing Spires –
Water, wide water, greeness and green banks
And water seen . . .

                                        (*Notebook* 40, folio 27)

. . . . es of biographical information undeniably put interpretation
on a new footing. But they can be an embarrassment; and earlier this
century their dazzlement distorted the course of criticism in a disastrous
way. Knowing about the fine shades of a poet's character, or details of
the genesis of his poetry, can be something of a distraction. A critic may
not find it of much use to know that Wordsworth loved his wife
passionately or that his political judgement was much consulted. Still
less, that Coleridge suffered morbid guilt or that he was a drug addict, a
liar and a voluble talker given to sustaining endless monologues.

It is not difficult to relate 'Kubla Khan' (1816) to Coleridge's biographical circumstances. He goes out of his way to make the opium
connection himself, supplying a prose preface to explain that he had
taken an 'anodyne' when he fell asleep reading in Purchas's travels
about the tyrant Kubla:

> In Xanadu did Kubla Khan
> A stately pleasure-dome decree:
> Where Alph, the sacred river, ran
> Through caverns measureless to man
> Down to a sunless sea.

But that does not take one far. It is more helpful to join Livingston
Lowes (*The Road to Xanadu*) in tracing probable associations with the
images. But at some stage one has to work out their arrangement in
similar or contrasting pairs. How has Coleridge related dream and
vision, symphony and song, Kubla's dome and the poet's? The pleasure
palace that the tyrant built by enclosing 'twice five miles of fertile
ground' is measured, but the palace of art or 'dome in air' that the
dangerous poet wishes to raise draws on a less circumscribed vision, and
responds to a world of Romantic chasms and lovers, where the river of
inspired life runs partly underground through an infinitude of
'measureless' caverns. In short, the images relate as symbols of
contrasted ways of life. Coleridge guardedly offered 'Kubla Khan' as a
curiosity of dream composition; but many see it now as the quintessential Romantic poem. Here is dependence on Romantic literary

material; exploration of dreams; hints of an earthly paradise; and magic powers of the poet set apart from society. Above all, here is an apparently irrational sequence. The poem's order is not that of prose logic: its fragmentary nature interrupts ordinary reality in such a way as to make the relation of real and imaginary worlds problematic. The appearance of fragmentary incompletion – and even the publication of actual fragments – was a feature of late eighteenth-century and Romantic poetry.

'The Rime of the Ancient Mariner', Coleridge's most important contribution to *Lyrical Ballads*, has also a complex symbolism, although it appears a simple ballad with a narrative sequence. The consequences of killing the albatross are magical, as in a supernatural ballad. But beneath the irrational story is a symbolic enactment – almost an allegory – of the stages of regeneration. Much of its interest lies in the extremely implicit nature of its deeply felt action, in which narrator, glossator and interpreting wedding-guest have each their role.

Coleridge was versatile in the invention of new genres, and it is in quite a different one, the so-called conversation poem, that, beginning with 'The Aeolian Harp' (1796), he made his main contribution to poetry. In effect these poems, 'This Lime-tree Bower My Prison' (1797), 'Dejection' (1802) and the rest, are interior monologues – a natural form, perhaps, for Coleridge the exterior monologuist and notebook writer. They express what seem actual trains of thought: not indeed whole streams of consciousness, but the more active operations of a 'self-watching, subtilizing mind' proceeding partly by steps of reason or association, partly by imaginative leaps. The best of them succeed in conveying the mobile life of the mind – often, as in 'This Lime-tree Bower', by alternately expanding and contracting the scope, now to take in a panoramic view of absent friends and the vistas they see, now to focus on the solitary poet's feelings.

In 'Frost at Midnight' (1798) the alternations are temporal; jumping from adult meditation to memories of childhood, or from the present infant by the poet's side –

> Whose gentle breathings, heard in this deep calm,
> Fill up the interspersèd vacancies
> And momentary pauses of the thought! . . .

– to the future, when the grown-up will 'learn far other lore'. Yet for all its immediacy, the poem is shapely: it works in an orderly way through the seasons and ages of life before returning to winter and 'the secret ministry of frost'. As often, Coleridge introduces a correlate of poetic thought, here the film fluttering near the low fire, whose motion in the stillness gives it 'sympathies' with the poet –

> Making it a companionable form,
> Whose puny flaps and freaks the idling Spirit
> By its own moods interprets, every where
> Echo or mirror seeking of itself,
> And makes a toy of Thought.

It is worth reiterating that the correlates of subjectivity are discovered in the course of meditation, rather than being intellectually antecedent. The ash film was not an established symbol. Coleridge's poem has in fact something of the shape of speculative thought. Its starting point, at least, is within the poet's own personality – an 'egotistic' location that Coleridge boldly defended. Yet he can talk about himself without being egotistic in a bad sense; since, as Hazlitt argued, 'in him the individual is always merged in the abstract and the general'. The main thrust of Coleridge's monologues is towards an enhanced self-consciousness. And the same applies (such is his historical importance) to a large part of poetry since.

Coleridge has great significance as a thinker. In a way that Wordsworth could never have done, he constructed from first principles (although not without plagiarizing from contemporary German works) a complete Romantic philosophy – a mode if not exactly a system of thought. This he achieved simultaneously with copious journalistic writing, not only for his own papers *The Watchman* (1796) and *The Friend* (1809–10), but also for other organs. Desultory and incomplete his output may be; it nevertheless implies a consistent political philosophy, besides containing a great many profound ideas.

Coleridge's most impressive prose work, the *Biographia Literaria* (1817), is sometimes called disordered; but that view misapprehends the order aimed at. One of its underlying ideas, which has pervasively influenced subsequent Romanticism, is that of literature's organic unity: a unity not mechanical, not like the narrowly rational pre-ordained unity of the neoclassicists, but emergent, akin to nature's living coherence in the progression of development. Hence the autobiographical, chronological order of *Biographia Literaria*, which constructs a philosophy step by step by assimilating interactions with Southey, Wordsworth and others. Coleridge's defence of his own ideas – as well as the philosophical chapters v–ix, xii–xiii tracing his development away from materialism towards transcendentalism – belong to the same plan. So, obviously, does his exhaustive disengagement from the ideas of Wordsworth, whom he keeps returning to, and from whose Preface to *Lyrical Ballads* Coleridge's second volume of the *Biographia* constitutes an extended dissent. (There is to be no easily categorized school of Lake poets.) Add the strand of religious interest, and the complexity of a growing personality begins to emerge.

Coleridge's whole approach to literature relies on his concept of the creative imagination as an agency of change, of growth. For this reason (and because he had himself been an associationist) it is vital to him to distinguish imagination from any mere 'fancy' or associative ingenuity subordinated to mechanistic psychological laws:

> The poet, described in *ideal* perfection, brings the whole soul of man into activity, with the subordination of its faculties to each other, according to their relative worth and dignity. He diffuses a tone, and spirit of unity, that blends, and (as it were) *fuses*, each into each, by that synthetic and magical power, to which we [*sc*. I] have exclusively appropriated the name of imagination. This power, first put in action by the will and understanding, and retained under their irremissive, though gentle and unnoticed, control . . . reveals itself in the balance or reconciliation of opposite or discordant qualities . . .
>
> (*Biographia Literaria* xiv)

The ideal poet must have a fully active consciousness.

IMAGINATION AND VISION

Of all the British Romantic writers, Coleridge did most to work out the central doctrine of imagination theoretically. His strategy was to distinguish it sharply from fancy, its own more trivial aspect. Fancy receives its materials from mechanical associations of ideas: 'a mode of Memory emancipated from the order of time and space' – 'no other counters to play with, but fixities and definites'. But the imagination is far more active and powerful. The primary imagination, indeed, is nothing less than the 'Agent of all human Perception'. The secondary imagination ('differing only in *degree*, and in the *mode* of its operation')

> dissolves, diffuses, dissipates, in order to re-create; or where this process is rendered impossible, yet still at all events it struggles to idealize and to unify. It is essentially *vital*, even as all objects (*as* objects) are essentially fixed and dead.
>
> (*Biographia Literaria* xiii)

Introduction of this concept makes a watershed in English literature, separating all before it from much that is to follow. For, if the imagination's processes are on the same footing with those of nature, then

purely imaginary subjects may have an equal value. Imaginative
processes may even be thought autonomous – without need for
continual validation in terms of *mimesis*, or imitation of the external
world.

In his commitment to the creative imagination, Coleridge (and the
same is true, later, of Shelley) was profoundly serious. It took him far
beyond enthusiasm. He tackled the problems of the new ideas radically,
returning to first principles, and bringing all philosophy to bear, in a
way that contrasts strikingly with Akenside's or Beattie's (or, earlier,
with Pope's) shallowness of thought. From this lucubration he came to
reject the Enlightenment account of human nature as inadequate, and
returned to orthodox Christianity. Like Wordsworth he retreated (or
progressed) from a temporarily radical posture. Merely political
solutions came to seem to him superficial. He reacted strongly against
the French atheistic radicalism of the 1790s; but this reaction was not
solely political. Indeed, he himself was later to become an apostle of
liberalism. The drift of his own polemic has been described as internalizing – moving the sphere of significance from event to thought. There is
something in this; yet his religious thinking conspicuously engaged with
politics and education, and in these areas exerted an influence on the
Christian socialist F. D. Maurice.

However that may be, the 'younger Romantics' – Shelley, Byron and
the unpolitical Keats – were a good deal more liberal or radical, like
their friends Peacock, Leigh Hunt and Hazlitt, or the older visionary
Blake. Their readership was correspondingly more select. They too
applied the Coleridgean doctrine of imagination to subjects from
nature. But, more characteristically, they turned it to visionary subjects
– visions that, however cloudy and sweeping, were distinctly political in
implication. Perhaps for that reason, they often used mythological
disguise. The mythology, of course, need not be classical or traditional.
They would invert the values of familiar myths, or (taking a suggestion
from the northern gods of Gray's Norse imitations) introduce new
pantheons altogether. The invented legendary world of *Gebir* (1798), an
epic of pace-setting difficulty by the republican Walter Savage Landor,
belongs to this tendency. All the mythologizing had a profound effect on
poetry; making possible new freedoms of narrative, countenancing new
depths of obscurity. Yet it should not be thought of merely as an
unfortunate tactic dictated by prudence. For it came to be a valuable
mode of intuitive reasoning.

The vision of William Blake (1757–1827) was a transfigured view of
the present world that resulted from a life-long attempt to unthink the

assumptions of corrupt conventional wisdom by systematically avoiding reason in its accepted form. To begin with, Blake hardly rejected the poetic conventions of his time. *Songs of Innocence* (1789) are pastoral poems within the tradition of Isaac Watts's *Divine Songs for Children* (1715); although they have certain strangenesses, certain sad ironies, which are taken up in corresponding *Songs of Experience* (1794). These are bitter outcries against a city capable of the enslavement of children – a city given over to loveless religious hypocrisy. The songs of the two series pair in various ways: sometimes they have similar subjects, as with the two chimney sweeper poems; sometimes they are in contrast, as when 'The Lamb' is answered by 'The Tiger.' But *Experience* should not be assumed to disprove *Innocence* (in some ways the opposite happens); still less to join with it in making an easy antithesis. The reader is involved in a more difficult heuristic process – searching for a meaning that will combine both truths. This may free one from 'the mind-forged manacles' that sound, for example, in every voice in 'London'. Blake's metaphors are anticonceptual; even if they seem at first to be familiar enough –

> O rose, thou art sick:
> The invisible worm
> That flies in the night,
> In the howling storm,
>
> Has found out thy bed
> Of crimson joy;
> And his dark secret love
> Does thy life destroy.
> ('The Sick Rose', *Songs of Experience*)

However one identifies the worm that causes loveless marriage, the poem's lyric force recalls the power of Jacobean, even Shakespearean song. Both song series were accompanied by engravings and interlinear ornament in the manner of gothic manuscript illumination. Blake was a very considerable visual artist, and most of his subsequent volumes were to be multimedia works, executed with a brilliance that puts them in a category almost peculiar to themselves.

Everything in *Innocence* and *Experience* relates – although not always obviously – to Blake's individual vision. He cannot say 'Am not I/ A fly like thee' without continuing 'Or art not thou/ A man like me'; for the eternal man contains all forms of life. This visionary coherence becomes apparent in *The Marriage of Heaven and Hell* (1790), an amalgam of

Biblical vision, Swedenborgian parody and invented proverbs. Structurally inchoate though it may be, it offers a useful introduction to Blake's thought, which is less a system than a way of life. The 'Proverbs of Hell' in *The Marriage* are in effect epigrams – a form he always used with strange power. They develop the principles of the preceding section: 'Without contraries is no progression'; 'Good is the passive that obeys reason: Evil is the active springing from energy' (note the mimetic animation of 'springing', by contrast with 'is'). Blake's originality lies in determination to keep both contraries – until doing so threatens to become itself part of a system without contraries. Thus 'The tigers of wrath are wiser than the horses of instruction'. Interpreting such a proverb calls for a wisdom it has not always received. ('Horses' is probably chosen less with reference to docility than in allusion to Chiro, the rational centaur–instructor of heroes.) In 'Enough, or too much!' the first element abbreviates the ancient aphorism 'Nothing too much', and must therefore be offset by its contrary 'too much'. (After all, as another of the proverbs has it, 'The road of excess leads to the palace of wisdom'.) In such ways, Blake's tiniest details relate to his largest visions. It is a strength, as well as a weakness.

The bulk of Blake's output is in the form of prophetic books such as *Vala, or the Four Zoas* (?1797–1800 with later revisions), *Milton* (?1800–9) and *Jerusalem* (?1804–20). These are long illustrated poems, loosely structured after the Biblical apocalyptic visions, and similarly disturbed by abrupt transitions. They teem with lists of unfamiliar names, made the more obscure by seeming to be confused with familiar British or Hebrew names of the present or the ancient past. Obscure mythology had been acceptable since Ossian; but Blake's conglomerated pantheon was altogether more impenetrable. His popularity is consequently a remarkable phenomenon, only explicable in terms of widespread misreading (as when 'And did those feet in ancient time' is vaguely referred to Christ), together with the British fondness for defiant anarchy. Not that Blake's obscurities defy interpretation. We can learn that Albion's timelessness as an eternal vision warrants incorporating ancient British embodiments, topicalities and anticipations of its future in the New Jerusalem. We can learn to decode the invented myths – like that of Los the creative spirit – and the vatic utterances ('Reuben is Merlin/ Exploring the three states of Ulro'). The problem is rather that all this learning one has to do seems disproportionate. In the end the ideas arrived at turn out disappointingly seldom to be realized more than perfunctorily.

Perhaps because he had no public, Blake had little sense of his readers – of how much of his private mythology they might take in. Indeed, he had not constructed the mythology for them, but to cope with his own inner conflicts. It was necessary; since existing systems of reason and abstract morality were the cause of guilt:

> O Divine Spirit, sustain me on thy wings,
> That I may awake Albion from his long & cold repose!
> For Bacon & Newton, sheathed in dismal steel, their terrors hang
> Like iron scourges over Albion; reasonings like vast serpents
> Enfold around my limbs, bruising my minute articulations.
>
> (*Jerusalem* I.xv.9–13)

Blake's preferred antisystem is profoundly irrational; yet it drives ideas to ferociously logical conclusions. Perpetual forgiveness provides its basis; yet it sustains private hatreds with a paranoid intensity. Its world attempts integration, yet writes its contradictions so large that perhaps only such an age as our own would regard it as anything but mad. By a final paradox, the solitary Wordsworth became a public poet, whereas Blake, whose every word took society into account, became isolated from it.

What calls for notice here is the powerful example of autonomous creation set by Blake's prophetic books. Their sole authority was the imagination. Visionary poetry, after them, need not be mimetic – it need not pursue validation in detailed correspondence with the external world. Their very scale won freedoms of visionary expansiveness. And in their lyric parts – as in the great short lyrics – Blake achieved a compression almost unknown for more than a century. By eliding rational connections and depending on an underlying POETIC SYNTAX of articulation through imagery, Blake recovered the possibility of lyric intensity.

SHELLEY AND KEATS

Percy Bysshe Shelley (1792–1822) turned away from Coleridge's German Romanticism, and like others of his poetic generation re-affirmed Mediterranean values. Classical imagery – Greek, now, rather than Roman – was a vital element of the visionary world. But if Shelley warmed to an ideal Grecian past, that by no means made him neo-classicist. His work has little in it of the eighteenth century. Indeed, in the way it develops an abstract argument through concrete detail, it has more in common with modernism. And his personifications are not

rhetorical in the Augustan manner. They recall rather Spenser's visions;
seeming to issue alive from the depths of experience.

Shelley's major work, *Prometheus Unbound* (1820), is a mythological
drama with an enlarged Greek pantheon. Its traditional gods, however,
are much revalued: a tyrant Jupiter embodies the powers of the present
dispensation; while Demogorgon (an obscure deity of chaotic potentiality in Spenser) becomes a central figure standing for something like
historical necessity. There are definite political contents; although the
action goes deeper, to evoke 'beautiful idealisms of moral excellence'
(Preface) and profound changes of the soul whereby it gains freedom to
love. As often in Romantic narrative, a turning point (here Prometheus'
refusal to curse) comes with abandonment of struggle. It is hard to say
which passages are finest: perhaps, for psychological penetration and
lyric power, Asia's descent to the depths of reappraisal, or the final
ecstatic vision of a renewed cosmos. *Prometheus Unbound* is the greatest
long poem after *The Prelude*, and can offer strange beauties far beyond
Wordsworth−

> The Magus Zoraster, my dead child,
> Met his own image walking in the garden.
> That apparition, sole of men, he saw.
>   (i.192−4)

A historically significant feature is that Shelley follows Blake in giving
songs and other lyric forms a main function in what must count as a
philosophic if not an epic poem. This exaltation of lyric will have a
considerable influence on Victorian literature.

Unlike Coleridge, Shelley preferred ostensibly classical genres such
as ode and elegy; although he handled them in new ways. *Adonais*
(1821), long as its meditations on death may be, remains an enlarged
elegy. And 'Ode to the West Wind' (1820) is what its label promises,
despite its freight of natural history. Shelley's imagery often draws on
contemporary science − notably, studies of electrical phenomena − in a
way very different from the Lakists'. Here, the phenomenon is meteorological:

> Thou on whose stream, mid the steep sky's commotion,
> Loose clouds like earth's decaying leaves are shed,
> Shook from the tangled boughs of Heaven and Ocean,
>
> Angels of rain and lightning: there are spread
> On the blue surface of thine aëry surge,
> Like the bright hair uplifted from the head

> Of some fierce Maenad, even from the dim verge
> Of the horizon to the zenith's height,
> The locks of the approaching storm. Thou dirge . . .
> ('Ode to the West Wind')

F. R. Leavis criticizes Shelley's style for its unpremeditated, self-propagating vagueness: 'the "boughs", it is plain, have grown out of the "leaves" in the preceding line, and we are not to ask what the tree is'. But if one were to ask, Shelley could answer, that the invisible tree is evaporation (from 'Ocean' to 'Heaven'), which produces storm clouds ('tangled boughs'); while the leaves blown off are loose clouds separated from the main mass and foretokening storm. The west wind itself is a wind of change. But in spite of the compass direction it need not quite be identified with the American revolution. Similarly the submarine foliage pales with fear not only in topical allegory, but as a deeper symbol of upheaval. As a poem of idealistic hope and oblation to change, 'Ode to the West Wind' has no close rival.

For a corrective to these gravities, it is a good idea to turn to *The Witch of Atlas* (1824), where Shelley's almost unparalleled poetic skills work on a subject of delicate lightness. It is an EPYLLION, or miniature epic, yet it treats nothing at all, or else its own inventive powers. (The witch is an enchantress of the imagination, possessed of intellectual beauty.) If the poem takes up the burden of 'Kubla Khan', it is with a readier ease, reaching a more effortless length — sending its magic boat not only through Coleridge's caverns and 'deep romantic chasm' but out the other side:

> And down the streams which clove those mountains vast,
> > Around their inland islets, and amid
> The panther-peopled forests, whose shade cast
> > Darkness and odours, and a pleasure hid
> In melancholy gloom, the pinnace passed;
> > By many a star-surrounded pyramid
> Of icy crag cleaving the purple sky,
> And caverns yawning round unfathomably.
> > (*The Witch of Atlas* 425–32)

Shelley's fluent visions are highly unusual – and unusually delightful – in that he bodies them forth in crisply specific detail. *The Witch of Atlas* carries self-involvement to a new extreme; yet it seldom gives the impression of being vague or incompletely imagined. What does it all mean? From a narrowly rational standpoint, it is as obscure as John Ashbery's self-referring compositions. But there is this great difference,

that Shelley conceives all in terms of imaginable landscape and
narrative. We now may ponder why his boat of the imagination
belonged originally to Venus; but in the nineteenth century many
would simply follow the story, approaching implicit answers to such
questions only at a subliminal level.

Shelley's visions have been disparaged as too remotely incorporeal.
This criticism betrays a failure to meet the challenge of his learned
subtlety. But it is true that identifiable natural scenes are absent from
his poetry. And he introduces observed details only to lead on to
scientific laws (more real to him than defective institutions), which in
turn he uses to illustrate the human predicament:

> He will watch from dawn to gloom
> The lake-reflected sun illume
> The yellow bees in the ivy-bloom,
> Nor heed nor see, what things they be;
> But from these create he can
> Forms more real than living man,
> Nurslings of immortality!
> (*Prometheus Unbound* i.743–9)

The image of upward reflected light may be hard to apply; yet it is
anything but vague or impalpable.

In feeding on 'the aereal kisses that haunt thought's wildernesses'
Shelley sometimes turns from matters of common interpersonal
concern, to take a solitary path. Mary Shelley's objection that *The Witch
of Atlas* contained no human interest might, with qualification, be
extended to other of his poems. But it would be wrong to call his woes
private or narcissistic: they are those of any prophet.

The visionary poetry of John Keats (1795–1821) also makes extensive
use of Greek mythological materials. The mythology fails to convince in
Endymion: A Poetic Romance (1818), an immature dream-vision tracing a
poet's wanderings through a vague yet sensuously classical realm,
where the ideal can only be achieved by seeking unselfishly. Despite
savage reviews and deteriorating health, however, Keats's sensibility
passed through an astonishing process of self-education which had
made possible the mature odes before his early death from tuberculosis.
'Ode to Psyche' (wr. April 1814) shows one line of development, the
internalizing of myth. The poet is now to be 'priest' of the psyche. 'Ode
on a Grecian Urn' (May 1819) relates the world of imagination to
mutable reality by means far more implicit: the urn itself symbolizes
art; but its image of a citadel-emptying procession going to sacrifice has

a depth less easily fathomed. It has to do with the conducing of purely natural things to a sacred conclusion. The urn may be said to consecrate nature.

Images like those in 'Ode on a Grecian Urn' are the outcome of Keats's long meditation on visual art – not on single works only but on the ethos of ancient paganism as evoked by such diverse sources as Claude's paintings and the Elgin marbles. This method of inducing mood doubtless accentuates the images' static, charged quality. Strongly tactile and visual, they give the impression of freezing moments or attitudes. Consider from this viewpoint

> She cannot fade, though thou hast not thy bliss,
>   For ever wilt thou love, and she be fair!
>   *   *   *   *
> More happy love, more happy, happy love!
>   For ever warm and still to be enjoyed, . . .

– or, in 'Ode to a Nightingale', the arrest of the 'beaker full of the warm South' (Virgil's *aestivo . . . vitro*?), in which the 'beaded bubbles winking at the brim' remain unburst. Such moments are more languorous, and yet also more desperate, than Wordsworth's epiphanous 'spots of time'. Keats had to hold, fix, preserve the instant in unspoilt perfection, as if movement or development would lose all to mutability. His mysticism of frozen moments was to have authority for Tennyson and the pre-Raphaelites – as it still has for some poets today. And, more generally, his pictorial qualities appealed strongly to almost all the Victorians.

Keats's odes, which are among the finest short poems of the century, show their greatness in a complete assimilation of language and thought. Everything in them is proportioned, integrated, transformed; until the smallest suggestion carries meaning. More controversial is Keats's incomplete blank-verse epic *Hyperion. A Fragment* (1820). It is sometimes said to betray the stultifying effect of its Miltonic model – an influence Keats tried to resist in a new attempt *The Fall of Hyperion* (wr. 1819). But if the poem fails, it is for deeper reasons. Keats's sublimely simple Grecian gods aim at an impossibility: a fully experienced vision that evokes mood, yet effaces the poet. Grand impersonality is achieved in *Hyperion* at the cost of lifelessness; and in *The Fall of Hyperion* the poet has to reappear. Mythology, it seems, has become inescapably psychological.

Keats's best realized vision is the gothic one of *The Eve of St Agnes* (1820, wr. 1819), a narrative poem in Spenserian stanzas. Influenced as it is by recent works of Scott, Mrs Radcliffe and the Coleridge of

Christabel, its atmosphere escapes from the more primitive medievalism of Gray, or of romance writers like Clara Reeve. Keats brilliantly embodies his vision in vividly sensuous yet economical details, focused on psychological moments, but also dilated to explore mood. All is based on the gothic romance opposition between love and family hatred; between erotic warmth and the cold of ascetic or unfeeling morality (a cold echoed by that of nature). But Keats's intensity is new; as is the subtlety of texture, which holds gorgeousness in restraint:

> A casement high and triple-arched there was,
> All garlanded with carven imag'ries
> Of fruits, and flowers, and bunches of knot-grass,
> And diamonded with panes of quaint device,
> Innumerable of stains and splendid dyes,
> As are the tiger-moth's deep-damasked wings;
> And in the midst, mong thousand heraldries,
> And twilight saints, and dim emblazonings,
> A shielded scutcheon blushed with blood of queens and kings.
>
> (lines 208–16)

Here the sensuous observation is acute, but Keats never allows description to become voluptuous: intricate architectural forms control the colours; precision ('knot-grass'; 'deep-damasked') vouches for pictorial objectivity; and when the focus softens to 'dim emblazonings', this is countered by 'saints' and the virginal 'blushed'. The technical application is extraordinary. The diction – optimally compressed, verbal rather than nominal – suggests a Shakespearean or Miltonic model. And the narrative organization is equally impressive; as when images of enclosure are used to heighten a sense of the dangerously unguarded sanctum – of Madeline's coolly withheld accessibility. The mature Keats has been said to retain some of his early 'vulgarity'; but this poem at least is a masterpiece of tact. Here his NEGATIVE CAPABILITY – capacity to enter into 'selfless sympathy' without impatiently reaching after certainty of meaning – has enabled him to achieve one of the finest poems about sexual surrender in our literature. If mankind is really divine, it seems, the small or oblique subject can acquire a new significance.

ROMANTIC IMAGERY

Romantic writers gave a new emphasis to IMAGERY. Imagery had always been an element in literature: the representation of ideas or feelings through things had always been available as an auxiliary device. But it now became a main articulating connection. This is very noticeable in Romantic nature poetry – in contrast to that of the Enlightenment, where emotions find direct distinct expression, and imagery has a quite subsidiary function.

In Romantic poetry imagination was at last free to combine with natural appearances. Its operation on phenomena of nature, its resonances, now gave whole poems their structure. No longer was it a matter of stating and then illustrating natural analogies. Now, the analogies were to be discovered through the imaginative process itself: 'organic' structure was the aim and the criterion. Often the imagination would dwell on landscape, pursuing fugitive latent meanings – as in Wordsworth's meditation on the Simplon Pass, with its 'immeasurable height/ Of woods decaying, never to be decayed', and its raving torrents, its images of 'tumult and peace':

> The unfettered clouds and region of the Heavens,
> Tumult and peace, the darkness and the light –
> Were all like workings of one mind, the features
> Of the same face, blossoms upon one tree;
> Characters of the great Apocalypse . . .
>   (*The Prelude* (1850) vi.634–8)

Here, unchanging landscape features are internalized, becoming images of enduring peace that transcend or assimilate the tumult. Before the analogy emerges as explicit statement (of a sort the later Romantics will avoid) it has been fully explored in anthropomorphisms like 'Black drizzling crags that spake'; so that the boldness of 'features/ Of the same face' is arrived at naturally.

In such meditations, meanings should emerge spontaneously. They must therefore emerge by way of 'natural' metaphors. That is to say, the vehicles and tenors of the metaphors ('torrents': 'tumult') must seem naturally alike. There is no place for wittily disjunctive comparisons in the Metaphysical manner. With the Romantics, the personifications of earlier poetry descend into nature itself: the same landscape provides both objects of meditation and images of discourse.

Keats's 'To Autumn' (wr. 1819), the last of his major odes, offers a good example of the imagination's interaction with nature. Here the personification is not principally traditional, however closely Keats has studied visual representations of autumn in the mirror of art. It is a spirit raised from elusive intimations of the moment of the season:

> Who hath not seen thee oft amid thy store?
> Sometimes whoever seeks abroad may find

> Thee sitting careless on a granary floor,
>   Thy hair soft-lifted by the winnowing wind;
> Or on a half-reap'd furrow sound asleep,
>   Drowsed with the fume of poppies, while thy hook
>   Spares the next swath and all its twinèd flowers:
> And sometimes like a gleaner thou dost keep
>   Steady thy laden head across a brook;
>   Or by a cider-press, with patient look,
>   Thou watchest the last oozings hours by hours.

Instead of generalizing personification there is meditation on arrested poses or details — details in which nature seems invested with mysterious significance: the 'half-reap'd furrow'; 'the last oozings'. Imagination finds the human and the natural profoundly intertwined. Nature is a reaper too, so that the wind is 'winnowing' even when it gently lifts the hair. In brooding on such images Keats discovers not only reluctance to move on to the completed harvest of death, but also the season's own 'careless' posture towards time. In a dying season it is possible to 'keep/ Steady' and glean, even as the swallows twitter for departure. Images of transience and renewal, like the swallows and 'full-grown lambs' of the following stanza, look both forward and back; so that the ode seems to sum up the human experience of time.

This method of meditating sympathetically with nature was continued by later Romantics; but not without criticism. Keats's poetry — for example his image of a wave 'Down whose green back the short-lived foam, all hoar,/ Bursts gradual, with wayward indolence' — provided texts for Ruskin's censure of the PATHETIC FALLACY in portrayal of nature. Ruskin understood that strong feeling may genuinely attribute human qualities to nature; but 'the pathetic fallacy is powerful only so far as it is pathetic [passionate], feeble so far as it is fallacious' — inferior, therefore, to truthful portrayal of the facts. 'And there is no greater baseness in literature than the habit of using these metaphorical expressions in cold blood.' Ruskin could see the beauty of such 'fallacious' passages; unlike those who now reject the so-called organicist myth. It may be doubted, however, that any fallacy was involved. Far from intending 'true' description of physical nature, the Romantics were bent on exploring their own internal states.

They pressed that exploration especially by contemplating images — often fully developed images on a large scale. (This could lead, although not through any necessary connection, to poetic imagery of a visual, even pictorial kind, as in Keats.) Imagery became strategically central as it had not been since the seventeenth century. Study of that period, indeed, was one of the Romantics' main stimuli, in their attempt to escape the Enlightenment. Now, however, imagery was not to be confined, as in the Renaissance, within a tight logical net. Set free to range with the imagination, it was to be only lightly reined in by poetical judgement or vigilance of introspection. Poems came to follow the sequence of fantasy rather than of argument. Add to this the Romantics' deliberate irrationality (for they all reacted more or less strongly against the 'Newtonian' overemphasis of reason), and it will not be surprising if their imagery does not always seem very coherent. The images themselves, moreover, are often difficult; especially where they refer to dark places of the psyche. When unconventional emotions were to be expressed, obscure fantasy was a common resort. Nevertheless, Romantic images obey a poetic logic, which can to some extent be understood, particularly in terms of anti-Enlightenment ideology.

Romantic images are often developed so elaborately that they become big with significance – the abstract significance, in fact, of SYMBOLS. In certain instances, they stand out as foregrounded ICONIC objects, which may be crucial to interpretation of the work they appear in – like Keats's Grecian urn, or the *A* in *The Scarlet Letter*, or the picture in *The Picture of Dorian Gray*. Where the Augustans neglected imagery but concentrated on a small number of genres, the Romantics diversified genres but focused their effort on a very few images. Throughout the century the commonest subjects of meditation were found in the same group of major symbols: the sea and the desert, the voyage, the mirror, the palace of art. Certain of the symbols, like the magic boat, the Romantics largely invented; for others they went back beyond the Enlightenment to Spenser or to Biblical typology or to the ancients. Probably all the main symbols relate fairly directly to arche-types of the unconscious – as is obviously true of the *femme fatale* in Keats's 'La Belle Dame sans Merci'. It need hardly be said that this was little recognized at the time. Indeed, a characteristic of Romantic symbolism of the irrational was that it could be 'innocent' through being split off from consciousness. Even in the late Victorian period, when some of the symbols had become familiar enough to be well understood, the reason could always repudiate them in case of embarrassment. By 'understood', I do not mean to suggest that the symbols had fixed meanings. Much of their point lay in the possibility of metamorphosis issuing in the fresh statements of individual writers. Tennyson's palace of art is not the same as Keats's temple of Moneta or Coleridge's pleasure dome. Keats was the first to carve out a separate kingdom of art, albeit a socially conscious one.

Nevertheless, Romantic treatments of the major symbols have also something in common. As W. H. Auden traces in *The Enchafèd Flood*, the sea had anciently symbolized passion and disorder, potentiality and chaos: the ship of state ventured on it only in time of crisis. It was viewed very differently by the Romantics. They regarded voyaging (and, what is more, voyaging to unknown destinations) as the normal condition of man, his search for identity. Like Byron's Childe Harold, 'Where rolled the ocean, thereon was his home . . .' Anyone of sensibility now chose the deeper life of the sea rather than the trivial life of the shore. This remains true, however much motivations during the voyage vary, from the Ancient Mariner's alienation to the more communal enterprise of Tennyson's Ulysses, who 'seek[s] a newer world' with a crew 'sitting well in order'. These symbols will continue valid throughout the century: one thinks of Arnold 'in the sea of life enisled', an 'unplumbed, salt, estranging sea' almost divinized in its mysterious, pitiless impenetrability; or sailing as a

> pale master on his spar-strewn deck
> With anguished face and flying hair
> Grasping the rudder hard,
> Still bent to make some port he knows not where,
> Still standing for some false, impossible shore.
> ('A Summer Night' (1852) 65–9)

– or of Swinburne in 'A Channel Passage', with the 'steam-souled ship' fighting the waves in 'glad loud strife'. The island, again, may symbolize isolation or earthly paradise; but in either case it is an opposite of the city; just as the sea is, in its potentiality, and the desert, in its punishment or purgation. As for the ship, it stands for the microcosmic human society, or for a differentiated group; although belonging to the ship's company may be almost inevitable, as in Melville's *Moby Dick*, or very difficult, as in his *Israel Potter*.

The magically impelled boat seems a distinct symbol from the ship, even if the two are combined in 'The Ancient Mariner'. It was first launched by Robert Southey, in *Thalaba* (1801), as a typical Romantic reworking of a Spenserian image – the effortless boat of Phaedria or Idleness. It reappeared, again isolated by moonlight, in the 'elfin pinnace' of *The Prelude* i. And it was further developed in Southey's *Kehama* (1810). But only in Shelley was the symbol's full potential released. In *Alastor* (1816) 'the little shallop' takes the wandering poet from 'the lone Chorasmian shore' through engulfing caverns on a long voyage 'led/ By love, or dream, or god, or mightier Death'. In *The Witch of Atlas* (wr. 1820) Shelley more reflectively gave the boat a myth of origin, tracing it to an earlier erotic vehicle (libido?) and making the witch of imagination provide its motive power through the fabricated life of Hermaphroditus. In it she flies throughout nature and dream, everywhere building tabernacles of art in cosmic idealizations. To Shelley the soul-boat is poetry's vehicle for the imagination on an inner voyage of rebirth.

Other Romantic images derived from sublime nature. Images of light and dark, such as Turner was rendering in paint, expanded the mind; while a bottomless chasm opened beneath. (The concept of infinity was now at last being assimilated by laymen.) Coleridge's 'caverns measureless to man' and Shelley's 'caverns yawning round unfathomably' belong to the same tendency. Neither is like Shakespeare's 'antres vast'; although (as Blake's 'unfathomed caverns of my ear' show) the anatomical component of the symbol remains operative. It would be facile to seize on the psychological regression implied by fantasy journeys through anthropomorphic caverns. For the regression is here often *pour mieux sauter*, and the journey – often continued beyond the cavern – takes the soul on to rebirth.

Similarly with the images of fatal horrors, which may imply much more than the notorious 'death wish'. The Romantics transplanted the ghastly vegetation of Spenser's garden of Proserpina, and poisonous vapours drift through the gardens of Shelley's 'The Sensitive Plant' and Hawthorne's 'Rappacini's Daughter' (1846). Such symbols have to do not merely with external nature, but with a darker side of man, that the conscious aspiration of Romanticism tended to overlook. They are the means of a more profound inquiry, like certain other symbols: images of death associated with beauty, of discontinuous identity, of trances, dreams and hypnotic states. The Romantics' morbidity – their preoccupation with death – has been the subject of much critical interpretation (some of it brilliant, like Mario Praz's *The Romantic Agony*). It cannot concern us here, beyond its part in moulding literary forms. Suffice it that fashion, influence and imitation were at work, in addition to pessimistic disillusionment. A fatal ideological vacuum awaited freethinkers who lacked an adequate moral alternative to churchmanship.

The Romantics liked to call their poems dreams. And resemblances to dream can in fact be found throughout their works – strikingly, as we have seen, in the reliance on images as the primary means of expression. Some would add the further resemblance that the poems are like dreams highly PLURALISTIC, or ambiguous to the interpreter. Certainly

Romantic poems are often many-faceted enough to have prompted divergent interpretations. But literary ambiguities are to my mind different from those of dreams, in that they are more subject to choice. The poet's formative genius organizes them, even if this process is unconscious. Moreover, Romantic images of the dream type are liable to be qualified by intermingled images of a more conscious, typological variety. The meaning of TYPOLOGICAL figures, such as Melville's Ishmael or Keats's Ruth, was tightly controlled by a series of familiar correspondences between passages of the Bible or of other literature.

THE IMAGE OF THE POET

Of all the images, the most significant for subsequent literature is that of the poet. Idealized poets figure prominently in Romantic poetry, and come to have marked family resemblances, so that they amount to a new symbolic type. The Romantic poet is an alienated outsider like the Ancient Mariner, 'alone, alone, all, all alone'. But despite his emphatic loneliness he is an expressive being, and cultivates his self-absorbed sensitivity openly. Indeed, he positively revels in it. There has been reaction against this narcissistic individualism in our own period; but who can deny that it was a fruitful narcissism? Its obverse, however (and the obverse of an associated political idealism), was a deeply pessimistic 'dejection'. This could take extreme forms, such as nihilism or satanism: postures that fitted well enough with Romantic rebellion against late Augustan conventionality – or with the wish *épater les bourgeois*.

These features of the poet's image were generally symbolic, but one actual poet at least embodied them all in real life: George Gordon, Lord Byron (1788–1824). Byron's debauched life led to effective exile; here was an Ishmael with a vengeance. His exotic life of travel, some of it beyond Europe; his uninhibited self-expression; his defiance of scandal: all these stimulated a personal cult. And this cult persisted throughout the century, authorizing much bohemian conduct and even a little wildness. Farouche extremities of feeling became habitual to the artistic nature – to 'genius'. One thinks of such later instances as Dante Gabriel Rossetti, who buried his poems in his wife's coffin and then had them retrieved in a nocturnal exhumation.

Unlike some Romantics, Byron acted out the poet's role to the full – to such an extent that it could be called his life's work. He projected his image throughout the theatre of Europe; cultivating it rather more than

his poetry. In consequence his letters shine amongst the most brilliant
in our literature. But his earlier poems – such as *Childe Harold's
Pilgrimage* (1812; 1816; 1818) – are too much conceived in terms of self-
projection. They are satanic self-portraits, and achieve little artistic distance from a tortured life. Southey's description – 'literature of Satan' –
implies a limiting judgement. Byron himself described *Manfred* (1817),
another such portrait, as 'of a very wild, metaphysical, and inexplicable
kind' and as a 'piece of fantasy'. Such poems succeeded once, through
participation in a vogue, and by the interest of their variety. But, apart
from some good phrases with an Augustan flavour, the language is trite:
the poetic work of embodiment in form has hardly begun. It is not even
clear when Byron has a serious aim. The underlying intention may
sometimes have less to do with emancipation of feeling than with a
search for effects sensational enough to sell.

Byron's romances – *The Giaour* (1813), *The Corsair* (1814) and *Lara*
(1814) – represent little improvement. They exploit Scott's repertoire of
romance forms, while accentuating the sombre element already
present in *Marmion* (1808). But Byron lacks Scott's narrative creativity,
and – apart from an occasional exact word – his felicity in adjusting
texture to narrative content. In most of Byron's work linguistic
structures are unsatisfactorily loose – a besetting fault, to a lesser
degree, of all the Romantics. This is true even of Shelley and Keats, in
their longer poems, as comparing their blank verse with Shakespeare's
or Milton's makes plain. In Byron, infrequency of stylistic events
becomes positively unacceptable. His incurably fluent style (at an
opposite extreme from that of Keats) almost justifies the modern notion
of the unpremeditating Romantic poet. Byron's romances have been
popular with the lay public, perhaps, just because their sensational
stories are relatively uncomplicated by poetic craftsmanship. In the
same way, they used to be popular on the Continent because they were
translatable.

It is another matter with *Don Juan* (1819–24). Here Byron at last finds
a stanza that suits him (*ottava rima – ababab cc*), and a style, consistently
low, that makes sense of his enjambement and looseness of texture and
miscellaneous subjects – shaving, for example:

> A daily plague, which in the aggregate
>   May average on the whole with parturition,
> But as to women, who can penetrate
>   The real sufferings of their she condition?
> Man's very sympathy with their estate
>   Has much of selfishness and more suspicion.

Their love, their virtue, beauty, education,
But form good housekeepers, to breed a nation.

(xiv.24)

Now all is unified by the persona of the incorrigibly digressive, worldly-wise (and sometimes truly wise) narrator. The imagined poet–hero has matured in realism – has learnt, indeed, to be unheroic, to resist high ideals. His romanticism has been tamed to a dull despair, mitigated by delusory hopes and escapes. But there is also a new urbanity, which it seems can encompass any external experience – even cannibalism after the shipwreck in Canto ii. Autobiographical experience has become correspondingly distanced. The resulting stance is receptively agnostic: 'I know nought. Nothing I deny,/ Admit, reject, contemn . . . ' (xiv.7). Byron will not omit what is nethermost, but will keep opposites in play with a persistence reminiscent of Blake's. 'The world is all before me' is not allowed to stand without the continuation 'or behind' (xiv.9). Under the uppermost narrative incidents and reflections sound undertones, 'mystic diapasons', a buried stream (to change the metaphor) of dream situations and wish fulfilments.

How is one to assess the Romantic phase? There can be no doubt that it vastly enlarged literary understanding of the human psyche. And it increased the range of feelings that could be taken seriously – although Augustan literature was by no means so limited in this regard as some have asserted. On the other hand, the Romantics' explorations of sensibility could be premature, unwise, even morbid. Arguably they scattered seeds of decadence. And their association of eroticism with death and horror is of very dubious value; even if their linking of pleasure and pain has come to seem less unnatural. With the Romantics' enlargement of the poetic domain, expressive power increased immensely. This must surely be admirable. How noble to pursue expression of emotions that were elusive, neglected, unsanctioned, or, indeed, previously unconscious. Equally creative was the introduction of organic form – structure deriving from the nature of contents, rather than imposed rationally. Paradoxically, the Romantics' artistry seems nevertheless more questionable. Doubtless their attention often focused on large-scale images rather than on verbal structures. And their stress on genius must also be held responsible. A Keats might improvise complexities of texture exquisitely corresponding to shades of emotion. But in the absence of an adequate rhetorical tradition, the general level of literary craft declined.

It is difficult to assess the movement objectively, since it still continues today. In our own composition, for example, the organic method remains dominant. And in any case it is hard to be just, when Romantic literature so often fails to sustain its quality. Even the best writers descend from touchstones of greatness to slovenlinesses such as no Augustan writer would have allowed to pass. Yet at their finest moments, it must be conceded, the Romantics blaze with a glory hardly equalled by any generation before or since. Think of the publications of one great year, 1820: Shelley's *Prometheus Unbound*; Keats's 'La Belle Dame sans Merci', *Lamia*, *Isabella*, *The Eve of St Agnes* and *Hyperion*; Crabbe's *Collected Works*; Clare's *Poems, Descriptive of Rural Life*; Lamb's *Essays of Elia*; Scott's *The Monastery* and *The Abbot*; Maturin's *Melmoth*; Irving's *The Sketch Book*; Galt's *Ayrshire Legatees* – to name only some of the most eminent. It must have been bliss in that dawn, too, to be alive.

IO

Transformations of Prose

LAMB, Hazlitt and De Quincey were contemporaries of the Romantic poets, but did not realize their potential until the 1820s or later, so that Romantic prose constituted a distinct phase. Yet the essayists set a very similar course to the poets'. And their innovations were equally radical, if not more so. The poets had been able to build on Cowper, Thomson and other predecessors; but the self-expressive essayists had to reject Johnson's impersonality, and even the very rhetoric of the entire Johnsonian school (save perhaps for Burke). That rhetoric had been based on emphatic parallels, or bifurcations invented for the sake of apparent parallelism, as in the passage that closes Johnson's second *Rambler* essay: 'Some are too indolent to read any thing, till its reputation is established; others too envious to promote that fame, which gives them pain by its increase . . .'. Such a style offered an enjoyably artificial framework of predictable syntax, capable of sustaining generality and abstraction. But the Romantics had almost the opposite aim of particularity, of naturalness. And they shunned the very appearance of abstract argument (even if, like Hazlitt and the Shelley of *The Defence of Poetry*, they were themselves quite at home with abstractions). De Quincey ridiculed Johnsonian sentence structure; seconding the rhetorician Whately when he compared Johnson's needlessly inflated clauses to false handles or keyholes added to furniture for mere symmetry. Johnson's bad influence was supposed to have produced 'the lifeless mechanism of a style bookish and artificial.'

THE ROMANTIC ESSAYISTS

William Hazlitt (1778–1830), although he secretly imitated Johnson in many things, was as careful as De Quincey to avoid anything like Johnsonian parallelism. This he contrived in two ways. First, like

Peacock, he shortened his period; practising the terse abbreviated balance of what Coleridge called the 'Anglo-Gallican style'. Hazlitt wanted his words to exert their force functionally:

> It is not pomp or pretension, but the adaptation of the expression to the idea that clenches a writer's meaning. – as it is not the size or glossiness of the materials, but their being fitted each to its place, that gives strength to the arch . . . I hate any thing that occupies more space than it is worth.
> (*Table-Talk* (1821–4), Essay xxiv, 'On Familiar Style')

Secondly, when he had to develop antitheses, he used Drydenesque informality to sink or break the parallels into irregularity. Or else he would stay for as long as possible on one side of the antithesis, rather than make frequent contrasts back and forth, so that momentum might build up unretarded by changes of direction.

What generates momentum in Hazlitt is direct expression of opinion: he drops the Augustan essayist's mask, and increasingly, indeed, any editorial persona. His opinions are not even argued for, but simply put out one after another with a tremendous ferocious gusto. But they are opinions worth having. For example, on literature, to which he came late from philosophy and biographical labour, Hazlitt is always worth attending to. Adopting the approach of Johnson's *Lives*, but omitting the biography, he focuses criticism on the writer in a way now taken for granted. Despite his revolutionary convictions, moreover, he extends sympathy to a wide variety of writing – virtually everything except, notably, medieval literature and Metaphysical poetry – with a justice that has proved of lasting value to literary historians. When he discusses a political adversary such as Wordsworth, his own opinions, far from biasing the assessment, seem rather to put him on his mettle, to quicken his sense of fairness. He must still be read on the novelists, on *Hudibras*, on Burns and – his greatest leap of sympathy – on Jacobean drama.

Hazlitt's essays show his philosophical competence in many ways – in reach, in subtlety of distinctions, in readiness to entertain diverse views – or to introduce controversy, with a robustness quite foreign to Lamb. He chooses an oblique informal method not because he is incapable of formality but because he thinks it his best way to open up ideas:

> I had remarked that when I had written or thought upon a particular topic, and afterwards had occasion to speak of it with a friend, the conversation generally took a much wider range, and branched off into a number of indirect and collateral questions, which were not strictly connected with the original view of the subject, but which often threw a

curious and striking light upon it ... it therefore occurred to me as
possible ... after stating and enforcing some leading idea, to follow it by
such observations and reflections as would probably suggest themselves
in discussing the same question in company with others.

('Advertisement' to *Table Talk*, 1821)

Conversational discontinuities allow him to essay further-reaching
connections. The resulting tone is natural, direct, open; although when
an elusive topic requires it, or a peroration, Hazlitt can rise to impressive
imagery; as witness his famous description of Coleridge's mind in terms
of nuances of atmospheric change around a mouldering tower. The
Coleridge essay is one of a portrait type that Hazlitt made his own: a
development by enlargement of the seventeenth-century Theophrastan
character. Another type treats an abstract topic – as old as Montaigne,
this, but given a new turn by Hazlitt in essays like 'On the Fear of
Death', by mingling the testimony of the ages with the present's
confessional immediacy. In several of his finest successes, 'On Going a
Journey' for example, he accentuates this autobiographical element so
much that he arrives at a new essay type altogether.

But his most fertile invention was the large scale digression – as in
'The Indian Jugglers', where the ostensible subject, skill versus art, is
abandoned for another one altogether: greatness. Hazlitt never fears
turning aside from the subject, because he has always his eye steadily on
the theme, and the truth. He sticks to that, even when it seems incorrect
to do so. This makes him a bold writer: no essayist is more invigorating
to read, or fuller of the gusto he admired in others. Hazlitt could have
brought the essay into the nineteenth century single-handed.

All the same, he was in many ways (not all political) a child of the
Enlightenment. By contrast, Charles Lamb (1775–1834) seems the most
thoroughly Romantic of the essayists. As Wordsworth and Coleridge in
poetry, so he in prose strove to trace the stream of consciousness
through its divagating associations. He, too, in his less philosophical
way, pursued throughout *The Essays of Elia* (1820–3) organic expression
of mind. It is this that underlies his abrupt darting or wandering
changes of direction ('wide of my subject'), as it does his sudden
compressed allusions – often momentarily obscure, especially when
combined with the opaque periphrasis he is fond of – 'less timed and
tuned to the occasion, methinks, than the noise of those better befitting
organs would be, which children hear tales of, at Hog's Norton'. Such
assumptions of understanding are pleasantly intimate; but the intimacy
can be too informal, too confessional, too hard to follow. As Carlyle puts

it, 'His speech wriggles hither and thither with an incessant painful fluctuation.' There has to be a meeting of minds with Lamb, because his style is not apt to the subject matter, only to the expressing sensibility. His effort goes into making a style just to his mind. In this he has little of Hazlitt's normal stance, or sense of balance. Lamb is odd in his quaint, unidiomatic diction; odd in his proportions (think of the series of direct addresses and allusions that give 'All Fools' Day' its formal quiddity). He early published an imitation of Burton; and almost throughout his work he tried for stylistic singularities reminiscent of Browne or Sterne. One type is the thought that surprises by sudden penetration, like his reason for not saying grace before a good meal – 'to be thankful for what we grasp exceeding our proportion is to add hypocrisy to injustice'.

Some suppose Lamb's essays to be very limited; since they are familiar not only in style but in avoidance of public, philosophical and didactic topics – indeed, of all large disturbing questions. But in practice the limitation is not crippling. True, Lamb shied away from modern developments, and dwelt imaginatively in the historical past, or in that of his own memories; but he was not alone in this. Indeed, in such essays as 'The South-Sea House', 'My First Play' and 'Witches and Other Night-Fears', he was a representative figure, making of the past a nostalgic pastoral of innocence. Besides, it is not altogether a cosy retreat either 'The night-time solitude, and the dark, were my hell'. Lamb had experience in plenty to draw on, of coping with appalling personal problems. In literature, similarly, although his taste was confined to 'belles lettres' (as the central genres were now called), it must be acknowledged sound and discriminating His sensitive response to Jacobean drama did much to make it accessible to the general public.

So much in *The Essays of Elia* depends on personality that it may come as a surprise to discover that Elia is not quite to be identified with Lamb. His essays have more art than appears; although it can sometimes be traced through the working up of topics from his fine letters to Coleridge and others (a correspondence that gives an incomparably intimate view of the literary scene). Lamb's style is sometimes perverse – outrageously overstuffed with quotations, for example. All the same, it hardly deserves to be neglected as it has been, by critics heedless of style altogether.

We have seen something of local discontinuities in Lamb (whose favourite punctuation is the dash), and of Hazlitt winding his way into the real subject of 'The Indian Jugglers' (greatness of imagination) through a long digression. More clearly than either of them, Thomas De Quincey (1785–1859), an authoritative critic of prose, saw what 'organic' development of the digression might mean; even if in practice he only intermittently succeeded in achieving it. De Quincey was one of the few writers of the period with an adequate understanding of rhetoric; and this enabled him to make discriminating use of the seventeenth-century stylists, as well as of Sterne. He carried Hazlitt's device of narration much further: in *The Confessions of an English Opium-Eater* (1821), indeed, he moved over from picaresque essay almost to intellectualized romance. At the same time, he conceived his essays as complete wholes; aiming, far more than Hazlitt, at formal continuity.

This leads to strange experimental syntax, such as the long loosely-structured sentence with floating or sideways-darting phrases; while on a larger scale apparent digression follows planned digression, until at last the structural principle stands revealed as digressiveness itself. Thus the Second Section of 'The English Mail Coach' (1849; 1854) begins with a short essay on the horror of sudden death, passes into narrative of a night journey to Westmoreland, breaks off for a disquisition on methods of staking claims, and returns to recognize the Cyclopean coachman (with asides about philology, *The Arabian Nights* and earlier journeys) and to speculate why he is so far north:

> Meantime, what are we stopping for? Surely we have now waited long enough. Oh, this procrastinating mail, and this procrastinating post-office! Can't they take a lesson upon that subject from *me*? Some people have called *me* procrastinating. Yet you are witness, reader, that I was here kept waiting for the post-office.

The train of thought matters less than the train of implicit connections. Throughout the digressions, for example, associations of death uneasily recur; as when we hear of trespassers being kicked – 'or decapitated'. The method allows anything whatsoever to be brought in that De Quincey feels requisite; so that he is able to arrange long sequences of imagery with subliminal continuities which lead into the vision of horror, and then on, tumultuously, through the 'Dream-Fugue', to the final extraordinary Shelleyan vision of cosmic victory.

Looked at broadly, the Romantic essay can be seen to have roots in seventeenth-century georgic as well as essay. In particular, it developed two features of georgic: the local expressive decorum and the lofty digression. Digression accorded well, as we have seen, with the new essay's dependence on non-logical connections such as imagery sequences. And so far as local decorum was concerned, the essay gave it a new form, far reaching in its consequences. It adjusted style so as to express not subject matter but the writer's individuality. 'They call this', writes Lamb, 'an age of personality.'

Personal styles abound in nineteenth-century literature: the profusion of letters, journals and memoirs, many of them highly individual, never ceases to astonish. Lockhart's great life of Scott (1837–8) claims attention here for its clear easy informality. And Lord Cockburn's *Memorials* (1856) is another late fruit of the Scottish Enlightenment; although its astringent style cannot restrain mordant pungencies such as the notorious remark on Edinburgh's council chamber: 'Within this Pandemonium sat the town-council, omnipotent, corrupt, impenetrable ... Silent, powerful, submissive, mysterious, and irresponsible, they might have been sitting in Venice.' The century's biographical achievements include also such impressive works as Elizabeth Gaskell's *Life of Charlotte Bronte* (1857), John Forster's *Life of Dickens* (1872) and Mark Pattison's *Memoirs* (1885). But almost all of these are marred by a tendency to idealize their subjects, the outstanding exception being Edmund Gosse's *Father and Son* (1907; written much earlier).

So far as diaries go, the period opened with James Woodforde's rumbustious *The Diary of a Country Parson* (1758–1802) and Elizabeth Wynne's surprisingly outspoken *Diaries* (1789–1820). It continued with many others. I have mentioned Dorothy Wordsworth's *Journals*; and there followed more continuous sketches such as Henry David Thoreau's deeply meditative *Walden* (1854) and Nathaniel Hawthorne's posthumous *American Notebooks* (1868), which hover absorbingly on the edge of connected essay or narrative. Among letter writers, Byron luxuriated in the most personal epistolary style of our literature, and the most brilliant (if not exactly the best). Lamb's quaint sweet letters, too, speak the man. But it is perhaps the letters of Edward Fitzgerald (1809–83), the translator of Omar Khayyam, that now give the most delight of any: astonishingly varied, they sparkle with life and fun.

With so many personal styles, one might expect a general abundance of good prose. But this is not the case. In fact, early Victorian prose deteriorated badly enough to disturb critics such as De Quincey. Certain causes of the decline are obvious. The Romantic cult of the natural militated against any cultivating of fine style – even against rhetoric itself. Poetry had received a new theory of organic expressivism; but literary prose, which lacked 'primitive' sanction, instead received neglect. Or else it was written like poetry, organically. Unfortunately, organic expression is hard to arrive at, let alone sustain; and prose needs a set style. Conceived of as expressive effusion, organic prose tended to take the form (or formlessness) of prose loosened in decorum and even in syntax, with frequent dashes or ellipses leaving the reader to guess. Moreover, as the novel established itself and the reading public grew, 'informality' increased; so that the very taste for fine prose dulled. The sense of style height deadened, for example, until sublimity became a matter of mere inflation. Simplicity (which needs to be cultivated) was lost, while urgency came to be manufactured by mechanical antitheses, earnest distortions, heavy reiterations. All this may be related to solemn Victorian philistinism. But it cannot be denied, either, that the Romantic essayists, however good they were to read, made bad models. One begins to feel that the late Victorian opposition of fine style to 'self style' might have been put more strongly still: that personal style and good style were incompatible.

Against the odds, however, several remarkable figures of the early Victorian period achieved prose so memorable that it would not be perverse to represent the age as one of great prose writers at least. Of these, Thomas Carlyle (1795–1881) presents the most extreme case of personalism. He wrote a prose indefensible in its mannerism (some would say, oddity), yet carried it off by sheer greatness. His urgent seriousness was beyond all ordinary art. Not that he lacked art: he designed his prose consistently to express an individual vision. Rather was he above it, outraging it passionately in the struggles of a personal drama that can still challenge strong responses.

Carlyle's best prose comes in works of his early maturity, especially *The French Revolution* (1837) and *Sartor Resartus*, although the later journalism continues to touch the nerve of the age. His *Life of John Sterling* (1851) has unforgettable portraits of Coleridge and other writers, and fine descriptions like that of London:

> under olive-tinted haze, the illimitable limitary ocean of London, with its domes and steeples definite in the sun, big Paul's and the many memories attached to it hanging high over all.
>
> (chapter viii)

But *The French Revolution* is Carlyle's masterpiece. It makes history as vividly detailed as a novel. And indeed he partly fictionalizes it with an intrusively rhetorical style that often leaves narrative to the reader to define: 'Laugh, black Royalists: yet be it in your sleeve only; lest Patriotism notice, and waxing frantic, lower the Lanterne!' Carlyle's favourite procedure is not by logical steps, but by gestures to the large-scale images he develops. So 'all France is ruffled, – roughened up (metaphorically speaking) into one enormous, desperate-minded, red guggling Turkey Cock!' And when the king takes to flight Carlyle imagines the news carried in plain 'leathern diligences' throughout the country; not only ruffling France's feathers but energizing her on a universal scale that warrants contrast with the steady constellations. All participates in a cosmic drama of allusion relating everything to everything else. Nothing, therefore, is neutral. Carlyle is always reacting passionately. He demands why he himself was not present, Thor's hammer in hand, to defend the Princess de Lamballe; he exclaims at the royal folly of fleeing in a conspicuously new berline (we are to remember the efficient plain leather diligences).

Much of Carlyle's feeling goes into charged words or phrases, repeated until they acquire the force of refrains – like the bizarre epithet 'seagreen' applied to Robespierre, which culminates in the prediction 'O seagreen Incorruptible, thou shalt see!' This is an odd sentence; and there are others odder still; for Carlyle's largeness in its rapid passage takes in many such incidental gothic grotesqueries. In the same category may seem to fall his coinages, many of them plural abstract nouns ('Chartisms'; 'unutterabilities'). But these are often thematic, belonging to the metaphysical drama enacted throughout Carlyle's works, which sets pluralisms, evil or worldly – 'our lovings and our sufferings, and confused toilings' – against the single divine fact. Other distortions result from extreme syntactic inversion ('The man from whom you take his Life, to him can the whole combined world do *more*'), characteristically attempting to enforce emphasis on more words than the language will suffer to bear it. Energy almost becomes Carlyle's god. He finds it (and this is a great strength) everywhere – even in the revolution: 'here is the miracle. Out of that putrescent rubbish of Scepticism, Sensualism, Sentimentalism, hollow Machiavellism, such a Faith has verily risen; flaming in the heart of a People.'

In Carlyle's later work, this optimistic biolatry ceases. Indeed, the *Latter-Day Pamphlets* (1850) are notorious for pessimistic racism. They have been defended for their value as fiction – for the personas generated in them. But it is better to admit that Carlyle got some things wrong. Even so, there is nothing wrong with his seriousness, nor his fearless exploration of the irrational. Carlyle's penetration, psychological as well as intellectual, is prophetic: one has often to concede his relevance, even when he is least congenial.

The age was one of sharp crisis, calling for the advice of heroes of the mind – advice to be expressed, necessarily, in an authentic, spoken, conversational way. From among much controversial prose, John Henry Newman's *The Idea of a University* (1852), *Apologia Pro Vita Sua* (1864) and *The Grammar of Assent* (1870) – all written after his conversion to Roman Catholicism – stand out for their lucid yet subtle style, personal yet free from oracular oddity like Carlyle's. Newman in fact greatly disliked such abrupt jerkiness, and aimed at a prose that would be continuously smooth. The result shows the usual mid-Victorian faults, particularly excessive repetition and parallelism. But it does so to a minor extent only. Newman's style comes close enough to conversational informality for the man to speak through; its personal coloration communicates an unostentatious, pleasant good nature. By power of mind he succeeds in unfolding contents easily: 'building up ideas' in accordance with 'the providential system of the world', in which every apparent argument against him turns out to be really, if unobviously, a point on his side. To these ends Newman uses imagery sparingly but with an effectiveness that recalls Bacon:

> Thirty years ago, education was relied upon: ten years ago there was a hope that wars would cease forever, under the influence of commercial enterprise and the reign of the useful and fine arts; but will anyone venture to say that there is anything anywhere on this earth, which will afford a fulcrum for us, whereby to keep the earth from moving onwards?
>
> (*Apologia Pro Vita Sua* ch.5)

Whatever your views, you can enjoy the brilliance of such tactics. But beware: no just reader can totally reject Newman's position for long, he is so reasonable.

Another of those sages who loom grandly over the Victorian scene is the American Ralph Waldo Emerson (1803–82), prophet of change and priest of large tendency. Emerson's prose has a considerable range. He can write like an essayist of Montaigne's or Bacon's stamp, as he does in *English Traits* (1856), delivering sharp general observations in rhythms well varied for emphasis, although too short. But his main strength (and the source of his considerable influence) shows in the high evolutionistic–Platonic speculations of such philosophical essays and lectures as 'The Over-Soul' (1841, revised 1847) and *The Natural History of Intellect* (1893), as well as in more accessible pieces such as 'Self-Reliance'. Here the short declarative sentences have a *raison d'être* in profound matter or surprising thoughts that require intervals for reflection:

> To believe your own thought, to believe that what is true for you in your private heart is true for all men, – that is genius. Speak your latent

conviction, and it shall be the universal sense; for the inmost in due time becomes the outmost, – and our first thought is rendered back to us by the trumpets of the Last Judgment ... In every work of genius we recognize our own rejected thoughts: they come back to us with a certain alienated majesty. Great works of art have no more affecting lesson for us than this.

('Self-Reliance', *Essays*, 1841, 1847)

Throughout, Emerson's writing is informed by a vision which, although it changes with his maturing thought, has impressive consistency. The transcendentalist stance is always there – 'Our being is descending into us from we know not whence'. Nowadays Emerson's large intuitions seem less commanding. Yet in their candour they have a bold immediacy, and they can seem (for what that is worth) utterly modern. Emerson delivers independent impressions of mind: declarations of truth rather than exhortations.

With Matthew Arnold (1822–88) began the diversion of energy into literary criticism that was increasingly to affect literature. The defects of Arnold's criticism now seem so considerable that it could easily be described in negative terms. He had few ideas about rhetoric, none about genre – and false ideas about literary form, which he fatally confused with content. His limited notion of prose contrasted it far too sharply with poetry. And we should not like now to test for literary greatness, as he did, with the 'touchstones' of short passages or even phrases. Yet he had certain ideas about the role of criticism that have proved of lasting value: notably the idea of it as 'the free play of the mind upon all subjects ... without which a nation's spirit ... must, in the long run, die of inanition'. In essays such as 'The Function of Criticism at the Present Time' (1865) he staked out a ground-plot of criticism that located it above politics and other practical concerns. Criticism tries 'to know the best that is known and thought in the world, irrespectively of practice, politics, and everything of the kind'. Criticism, in fact, is concerned with no lesser conflict than that between 'Culture and Anarchy' (the title of another of his works). Or, criticism defines intellectual moments.

All this Arnold expressed in a controversial style modelled on those of Carlyle and Newman. He combined Carlyle's abruptnesses with Newman's conversational parentheses, personal tone and occasional sharpness (often achieved by HYPERBATON, or unusual word order – 'for now many years'. It is the tone of much modern criticism: confident, superior, ironic. Arnold's prose can have the sort of vagueness that gives liberal humanism at times a bad name ('society was, in the fullest measure, permeated by fresh thought'). It can be overinsistent in repeating phrases too frequently, especially when they are long. And its loose argument can degenerate into mere positivistic assertion. But at its best it will brilliantly combine opposing qualities – subdued diction with a striking idea, perhaps, or suave movement with the sudden trip of a provocation – in such a way as to produce subtly cogent effects: 'For this [middle] class we have a designation which now has become pretty well known, and which we may as well still keep for them, the designation of Philistines.'

For the most part, however, early Victorian prose declined from the standards of Johnson and Burke. Perhaps this was partly due to overproduction: Macaulay had not time to pace out his paragraphs like Gibbon. Be that as it may, the works of most of the greatest Victorians – even of Carlyle and Dickens – fall often into overwriting or grotesquery. And with Macaulay, the very passages rightly used to advance his claims as a historian are, for all their vigour, lurid, overspecific and grossly inflated. Prose kinds were not indeed expected to vie with poetry: poetry, as even Arnold still assumed, was the exclusive medium for 'genius'. Only gradually did the finest literary discrimination come to be extended to prose writing, and to its then wider range of subject matter. And this was achieved not through any further refinement of personal styles but by pursuing a more conscious, lyric adjustment of words to thought.

LYRIC PROSE: RUSKIN TO STEVENSON

John Ruskin (1819–1900) was a great natural writer, who might have been expected to become, as he did, a fine stylist of personality. Yet through out-and-out mastery of his medium he also transcended personal style, and achieved a lyric prose that has never been surpassed, unless perhaps by Henry James himself. (By LYRIC PROSE is meant prose that not only communicates ideas but expresses them formally.) Ruskin's chief gift was exactitude of visual observation: he saw in minute detail, with a preternatural, photographic clarity. And everything he describes is similarly clear-cut and well-defined, as if taken in a long, wide-angled exposure. It was a Victorian mode of vision, dependent on a keenly inquiring interest in God's handiwork such as one finds in many contemporaries – in the Kingsley of *Glaucus* (1855), for example. This passion for detail possessed Ruskin to a quite extraordinary degree, however. It may seem at its most extreme in his botanic or meteorological studies. But his account of San Marco in Venice is also comparatively detailed:

> beyond those troops of ordered arches there rises a vision out of the earth, and all the great square seems to have opened from it in a kind of awe, that we may see it far away; – a multitude of pillars and white domes, clustered into a long low pyramid of coloured light; a treasure-heap, it seems, partly of gold, and partly of opal and mother-of-pearl, hollowed beneath into five great vaulted porches, ceiled with fair mosaic, and beset with sculpture of alabaster, clear as amber and delicate as ivory, – sculpture fantastic and involved, of palm leaves and lilies, and grapes and pomegranates, and birds clinging and fluttering among the branches, all twined together into an endless network of buds and plumes; and, in the midst of it, the solemn forms of angels, sceptred, and robed to the feet, and leaning to each other across the gates, their figures indistinct among the gleaming of the golden ground through the leaves beside them, interrupted and dim, like the morning light as it faded back among the branches of Eden, when first its gates were angel-guarded long ago . . . as if in ecstacy, the crests of the arches break into a marble foam, and toss themselves far into the blue sky in flashes and wreaths of sculptured spray, as if the breakers on the Lido shore had been frost-bound before they fell, and the sea-nymphs had inlaid them with coral and amethyst.
>
> (*The Stones of Venice* II.ii.14)

If such passages are gemlike, Ruskin's *oeuvre* is as full of gems as the *pala d'oro* itself. Much of his work amounts to description – but description so authoritatively analytic that it makes the works of nature or of man unfold before the mind's eye; coexisting simultaneously, delightfully, in a wealth of particulars. In *The Stones of Venice* (1851, 1853), the city seems to be built in one's presence – not sequentially, in narrative, but visibly, in a complete description that takes in natural context, historical connections and moral as well as aesthetic values. For Ruskin was a critic of society as well as of art.

He was in fact the finest British art critic of his time. And when he engaged with literature, he showed himself its greatest explanatory critic too; in that endeavour he surpassed even Coleridge. To a feeling for words and especially for rhythms (probably owing much to early maternal instruction in the Bible), Ruskin added a cultivated sensitivity to prose in its larger movements.

His own mastery of prose (for he could do anything with it) enabled him continually to vary his style with content across a very wide range, from the grand panoramas of *The Stones of Venice* to the close political logic of *Unto this Last* (1862) and the vivid yet calm memoirs of *Praeterita*

(1885–9), which themselves span childish 'watercress life' and exotic intellectual experiences, all lucidly proportioned. So responsively did Ruskin practise this accommodation of style to subject that something miraculous happened, and the threshold of lyric prose had been crossed. (He may have been aware of this, for he more than once used 'lyric' in the sense 'expressive of feelings' – already close to Walter Pater's 'expression, the finer accommodation of speech to that vision within'.) Ruskin's truth to his feelings for nature gives great pleasure; as in the famous description of the Rhone –

> Fifteen feet thick, of not flowing, but flying water; not water, neither, – melted glacier, rather, one should call it; the force of the ice is with it, and the wreathing of the clouds, the gladness of the sky, and the continuance of Time.
>
> Waves of clear sea are, indeed, lovely to watch, but they are always coming or gone, never in any taken shape to be seen for a second. But here was one mighty wave that was always itself, and every fluted swirl of it, constant as the wreathing of a shell. No wasting away of the fallen foam, no pause for gathering of power, no helpless ebb of discouraged recoil; but alike through bright day and lulling night, the never-pausing plunge, and never-fading flash, and never-hushing whisper, and, while the sun was up, the ever-answering glow of unearthly aquamarine, ultramarine, violet-blue, gentian-blue, peacock-blue, river-of-paradise blue, glass of a painted window melted in the sun, and the witch of the Alps flinging the spun tresses of it for ever from her snow.
>
> (*Praeterita* II.v)

The visual details, copious as the river itself, are delightful; but how much more so the transcriptions of emotion – the sense of nature's continuity, of its continual inexhaustibility: of the inexhaustible variety of blues, for example, which can be matched only by the 'improvising' coinage 'river-of-paradise blue'.

On a larger scale, Ruskin's prose is expressive in a deeper sense, communicating something of his profoundly split vision of life. For his vision of blessedness and nightmare ugliness (as in 'The Two Boyhoods') partakes of his intermittent madness.

Ruskin's lyric practice was complemented with theoretical formulation in the criticism of Walter Pater (1839–94). And it was Pater's subtle influence, as much as anything, that formed the *fin-de-siècle* ideal of superfine, exquisite, even sometimes *raffiné* prose. The strategic work here was his great essay 'Style' (in *Appreciations*, 1889), a discriminating exploration of the nature of imaginative prose – the privileged medium, he advises, of an age too chaotically various for poetry. Prose is fine art in proportion as the writer aims at 'the transcribing, not of the world, not of mere fact, but of his sense of it'. Scrupulous truth to impression matters above all: 'all beauty is in the long run only *fineness* of truth, or what we call expression, the finer accommodation of speech to that vision within'. Pater's was an austere art, which excised all 'surplusage' – anything (even a potentially distracting allusion) not necessarily part of the work's anticipated shape. From one viewpoint this doctrine returned to the Renaissance ideal of formal decorum. But, from another, it had already something of modernism, particularly in the elusive idea of an all-important 'structure . . . that architectural conception of work, which foresees the end in the beginning'. This architecture is nevertheless such as to involve many expressive 'irregularities, surprises, and afterthoughts'. In a sense Pater was moved by a gothic ideal of literary, as of visual art.

Paradoxically, the restraint of Pater's style promotes a more intimate revelation: of fleeting, private and occasionally disconcerting feelings. He cultivates his impressions intensely – 'To burn always with this hard, gemlike flame, to maintain this ecstasy, is success in life.' Sometimes he will use a mask of fictionalized history, as in *Imaginary Portraits* (1887); sometimes, as in his art criticism, the impresssions will be directly aesthetic. Yet they are also a great deal more. Here is a part of what George Saintsbury called Pater's 'purple panel' – a description of the ideals embodied in the Mona Lisa –

> She is older than the rocks among which she sits; like the vampire, she has been dead many times, and learned the secrets of the grave; and has been a diver in deep seas, and keeps their fallen day about her; and trafficked for strange webs with Eastern merchants: and, as Leda, was the mother of Helen of Troy, and, as Saint Anne, the mother of Mary; and all this has been to her but as the sound of lyres and flutes, and lives only in the delicacy with which it has moulded the changing lineaments, and tinged the eyelids and the hands.
>
> ('Leonardo da Vinci', *The Renaissance*, 1873)

Notice the fine shading whereby the specific, immediately intelligible art-historical points – about the Leda and St Anne types – emerge from a more obscure passage ('keeps their fallen day about her'), which appropriately follows the unconscious implications of 'diver in deep seas'. This was prose of a radically new kind. It explored imaginative reaches not by the use of reason alone but also by formal means: by amplifying impressions stylistically.

Pater deployed the gothic features of his style with restraint. But restrospective medievalism could also take a broader, more obtrusive shape, notably in writers who departed from the language of their own time in favour of some special diction. In this way William Morris (1834–96) gave preference to sturdy simple Saxon words; basing the rhetoric of his 'Wardour Street' English on medieval or Tudor models:

> Yea, forsooth, once again I saw as of old, the great treading down the little, and the strong beating down the weak, and cruel men fearing not, and kind men daring not, and wise men caring not; and the saints in heaven forbearing and yet bidding me not to forbear . . .
>
> (*A Dream of John Ball*, 1888)

In fantasies like this, as in romances like *The Wood Beyond the World* (1894) and *The Sundering Flood* (1898; wr. 1896), Morris found inspiration in the language of a heroic (and pre-capitalist) Middle Ages, a 'free society'; although he produced something curiously different from original medieval styles. Elsewhere, as in *News from Nowhere* (1890), he tried for a timeless prose, which in the event turned out somewhat bodiless – while still superior to that of most utopian fiction. By contrast, Charles Doughty's *Travels in Arabia Deserta* (1888) achieved greatness precisely through a style that seems timeless. But in fact its language is retrospective (albeit more subtly), in keeping with the heroic content. The *Travels in Arabia* towers above almost all other travel books in our literature.

Pater's influential ideals – and his French models – were in large part shared by Robert Louis Stevenson (1850–94). Stevenson may have been less of a theorist, but he was a much greater writer, and a superior, more flexible stylist. He came closer than any other to reconciling the incompatibilities of personal style and fine style. His own is unique, inimitable, the man himself – but also exemplarily fine. He appears in these pages as an artist of narrative; yet all his prose – not least his essays – attained the high point of style. For those sensitive to rhythm and texture, Stevenson is possibly the most pleasurable of all Victorian writers. At the same time, he has the compressed content that often accompanies brilliance. His rapid thought penetrates like lightning, melting the marrow without printing the skin – 'Marriage is a step so grave and decisive that it attracts light-headed, variable men by its very awfulness.' Stevenson's prose might be said to be as well written as good poetry.

The century's end saw a reaction against fine style. Indeed, Stevenson himself came to dislike 'alembicated' or overrefined smoothness, and in his last works aimed at 'more and more naked writing'. All the same, it would be a mistake to see this next phase in terms only of reaction. The aestheticism of Pater and Stevenson persisted as a distinct strand in modernism – as can be seen plainly enough in the ideas that Stevenson and Henry James shared in their correspondence. Far from the current notion of a crisis in the later nineteenth century, style then reached a new concentration, as well as a new delicacy of finesse. In the work of Ruskin and Pater, Stevenson and James, prose recovered its earlier greatness, its high, committed art.

II

Victorian Poetry

T HE transition from Romantic to Victorian in poetry is said to be clearly distinct. Certainly the premature deaths of Keats (1821), Shelley (1822) and Byron (1824) interrupted development abruptly enough. But one should remember that Wordsworth's *The Prelude* only appeared in 1850, and that an extensive critical interest in Wordsworth continued throughout the Victorian period – a fact not unconnected with the voluminous output of introspection in plain colloquial language. And in another direction, the fashion for Scott continued to influence poetic diction, giving it a more and more pronounced archaic flavour. Scott lived until 1832, and even after that there were eleven separate editions of his *Poetical Works*, besides many editions of the more popular individual poems. Then, there were poets whose work overlapped the division between periods: notably Walter Savage Landor (1775–1864) and John Clare (1793–1864), together with minor figures like Ebenezer Elliott (1781–1849), an elegist of resonant intensity. In short, there were many continuities. While Victorian poetry turned to more public types of verse, at the same time it continued Romantic. Two Romantic inheritances came to be of particular importance: the use of retrospective forms (as in medievalizing poetic diction); and the freely inventive transformation of genres.

LYRIC TRANSFORMATIONS

Apart from Wordsworth, Clare was the most impressive poet continuing in an older style. Too much attention has been paid to his madness, and the oddities of his peasant life: he is a considerable figure, now so much imitated as to deserve a place in our main tradition. In his later work particularly, he shares the Romantics' interest in resonances of inner and outer experience – as when the Burthorp oak makes him feel 'that earth's grandeur should decay'. (His sense of landscape, of his own roots in it, makes him often attack the evils of enclosure.) To this Romantic nature poetry he adds detail – sometimes minute, for 'every trifle will his eye detain' – until his pages teem with sensory particulars, with facts in a more Victorian manner ('columbines stone blue or deep night brown'). Selective quotation could make Clare seem a mere observer – and it is a limitation of the earlier poems that he sees too many things. But he is also an unusually bookish poet, drawing on the linguistic resources of a wide range of previous literature: not only Augustan literature (as used to be said) but earlier periods too, 'What ere wi time has sanction found'. His literary diction – mainly but not entirely in the pastoral and georgic traditions – enriched Victorian poetic language as Scott's relatively crude and repetitive fustian could hardly do.

Clare's most sustained achievement, *The Shepherd's Calendar* (1827), is, in spite of its name, a georgic calendar, of labours as much as contemplative pleasures. Its simple rambling description seems loosely connected on a random basis, but is in fact subtly composed. Multiply articulated, by associative linkages as well as oblique, sly implications, it builds up considerable compression – as when, just after rude jokes embarrassing the maidens, we hear of 'the stacks swelled bellying round'. Or, to take a simpler instance:

> The owlet leaves his ivy tree
> Into its hive slow sails the bee
> The mower seeks his cloaths and hides
> His scythe home bent wi weary strides
> And oer his shoulder swings his bag
> Bearing in hand his empty cag [keg]
> ('July' 495–500)

Here the sense of satisfaction with the harmonious closure of the July day comes partly from the fitness of the counterpointed movements of owlet and bee, or of the similar movements of the swinging bag and the no longer swinging scythe (which passes its traditional epithet 'bent' to the mower himself). In consequence of its unobtrusive art, as much as of its rich observation, *The Shepherd's Calendar* is probably the most enjoyable long poem of the century. But I should not give the impression that Clare was a nature poet only: his *oeuvre* is resourcefully varied, while everywhere showing that a hold on objects can be combined with the purest lyric forms.

Throughout the century, intense creative energy went into modulations of genres. Among these, none were so prominent as mixtures of

lyric or of elegy. These two genres came to be so highly regarded that
they tended to overflow into many other kinds. Even the hyperclassical
Walter Savage Landor (1775–1864) – who liked marmoreal solidity of
form, and preferred 'fixed' genres – learnt to modulate his odes or
epigrams into lyric and elegy. He might take his starting point from the
'sweet' tender epigrams of the Greek Anthology (currently sharing in
the Hellenic vogue). But then he would introduce verbal repetitions
more characteristic of elegy. Or elegiac self-realization would swamp
the neat epigrammatic closure:

> Our youth was happy: why repine
> That, like the Year's, Life's days decline?
> 'Tis well to mingle with the mould
> When we ourselves alike are cold,
> And when the only tears we shed
> Are of the dying on the dead.
>
> (*Last Fruit* (1853) clii)

Several Victorian poets practised a similar elegiac modulation of
epigram, and, taken up by Hardy and Yeats, it was to form our own
century's taste for short poems. (We expect these to have the interior
vision of elegy, but the simple diction of epigram.) Landor not only gave
epigram back its classic structured finality; he also made it carry new
weight of emotional reticence. But in general he badly overestimated
how far it was possible to ignore the Romantic movement. And he
lacked supportive traditions for his efforts. When one turns to longer
poems, it is hard to give the solitary Landor his due, so many are his
failures of judgement and tone, so many the flashes of greatness. Lamb
was not very unfair to *Gebir* (1798) when he spoke of 'lucid intervals'. Yet
Landor's epics and Greek idylls merit rather more than being remembered as narrative models for Tennyson. The chief point made
against Landor is only that he was out of phase with his contemporaries.

To understand Victorian poetic development, one must first grasp
how far it was dominated by the lyric and elegiac modes. This shows
itself in countless ways, not least in the proportions of the period's
anthologies. Palgrave's *The Golden Treasury of Songs and Lyrics* (1861), the
preeminent anthology, consists almost exclusively of short lyric or
elegiac poems.

Most obviously, lyric could take the form of actual songs. In these the
density of semantic content, or thought, was at a minimum; whereas
non-syntactic or musical structures came into their own. It was not a
great period for songs (nothing like the Elizabethan); yet art song

flourished, and many items still in the repertoire were written then, such as 'Believe me, if All those Endearing Young Charms', 'Oft in the Stilly Night' and ''Tis the Last Rose of Summer' – all by Thomas Moore (1779–1852). The urge towards lyric also underlay the great interest still taken in lyrical narratives – not just in the many ballad collections, from Scott's (1802–3), Peter Buchan's (1825) and William Motherwell's (1827) to Francis James Child's (1882–98), but in imitations or adaptations, from Scott's to de la Mare's. But examples are almost misleading, the lyric modulation was so pervasive. Throughout the period, attenuation of thought and accentuation of melodiousness set distinctive proportions for the poetic medium.

The lyric taste showed up markedly in translation, where the brilliant achievement of Edward Fitzgerald (1809–83) provides an outstanding example. A Suffolk poet and friend of Tennyson's, Fitzgerald is now known (apart from his letters) for one work, the *Rubaiyat* of Omar Khayyam (1859). The Persian poet's *Rubaiyat* (irregular quatrains) express a sceptical epicureanism congenial to his adaptor – who at times seems more an eighteenth-century or *fin-de-siècle* aesthete than a mid-Victorian. Indeed, the work's acceptance, let alone its eventual success is perhaps only explained by its classic status. Fitzgerald secures the simple intelligibility lyric needs by keeping to a monotone of moral ideas. Each quatrain is a variation on one of only two or three themes:

> 'Tis all a Chequer-board of Nights and Days
> Where Destiny with Men for Pieces plays:
>   Hither and thither moves, and mates, and slays,
> And one by one back in the Closet lays.
>
>   *   *   *
>
> The Moving Finger writes; and, having writ,
> Moves on: nor all thy Piety nor Wit
>   Shall lure it back to cancel half a Line,
> Nor all thy Tears wash out a Word of it.
>   (1859 edition, sts 49, 51)

This makes possible economy of implication, besides a subtle rhythmic variety that stands out when one compares the first with the fourth (1879) edition, or either with casual misquotations. About half Omar's quatrains are translated, the rest loosely adapted, and all rearranged. Fitzgerald freely 'mash[ed]' the original quatrains (as he said in a letter) and 'ingeniously tesselated' them into the pattern of a day's course. But on the whole he was faithful to the spirit of Omar's work. Cumulatively, the variation form gives a sense of inevitability; and so do the carefully screened diction and the simple emphatic rhyme – which (as Fitzgerald said of another poem) 'strikes a more Lyric Chord'. Nevertheless he uses the lyricism (and even, in an unexpectedly modern way, uses Omar's ideas) to express disillusionment with his own age.

Fitzgerald's diction is for the most part timeless; although one notices Biblical turns, besides archaisms (such as ''tis' and 'slays' in the quotation above). In other Victorian poets, above all the influential Tennyson, the diction often seems more obviously retrospective, if not specifically medieval – more so than in Scott or Keats (whose example played its part, however). Since Wordsworth, the idea of agreeing a conventional poetic diction had been scouted: poets were expected to open up new resources by exploratory reading. And in practice Victorian poets continued to explore widely – none more widely than Tennyson. Yet they may strike one as having agreed too readily that poetic language should be archaistic.

The antiquarian now replaced the primitive. Poets cultivated a retrospective art, in which medieval or Tudor words, idioms and literary echoes took their places beside already assimilated classicisms. How poetic to prefer older forms still just current, like 'thou' and 'kith' and 'twain'; to revive obsolete ones like 'rathe' (early) and 'saving' (unless) and 'puissance' (power); or to cultivate medieval phrases like 'by main might'! (It seems not to have been considered that selecting such words gave them a quite unmedieval prominence.) Perhaps to compensate for the impoverishment of rhetoric, or for the growing ugliness of cities, it was a tendency of nineteenth-century poets – although not one without countertendencies – to assemble words with literary associations and construct with them an exclusively 'poetic' language. Poets such as Rossetti actually collected arcane words of this sort for future use.

Such poetic diction is often jeered at nowadays; so that it presents obstacles to one's appreciation of Victorian poetry. Approached sympathetically, however, it can be seen as having offered a valuable poetic resource. For example, freedom of word order made possible many effects ruled out by our own more fixed (but equally conventional) order. Victorian poets can be regarded as returning to their cultural inheritance in order to draw strength from it to meet new challenges. They aimed at a diction that might transform contents. And at their best they achieved a lyrical medium that seemed capable of dissolving the difficulties of any matter – however much choice of subject might in practice be restricted. Inevitably, perhaps, they paid a heavy price for this diction in diffuseness, imprecision and (at worst) unresponsive deadness.

Alfred Tennyson (1809–92) gained recognition in his own time as the greatest living poet: a reputation easily justified in terms of accomplishment. Tennyson stood in the line of Spenser, Milton and Keats, and brilliantly reaffirmed their tradition of rich texturing. He was a master, qualified to rival them in devising lyrical structures accommodating form to sense. A famous example is 'The Lotos-Eaters' (1832):

> Music that gentlier on the spirit lies,
> Than tired eyelids upon tired eyes.
>
> (lines 50–1)

Here the ASSONANCE or euphoniously repeated vowel sounds combines with a pattern of lengthened stressed syllables and very light subsidiary stresses, in a manner highly appropriate to the idea of somnolent fatigue. (Tennyson himself commented that 'tired' is 'neither monosyllabic nor disyllabic but a dreamy child of the two.') A similar example is from *The Princess* (1847):

> Myriads of rivulets hurrying through the lawn,
> The moan of doves in immemorial elms,
> And murmuring of innumerable bees.
>
> (vii.205–7)

– where rhythms simulate the streams' multiplicity or rapidity, while consonantal patterns match the sounds of doves and bees. And subtler textures than these were at Tennyson's command – textures comparable with Keats's finest; as in 'Tears, idle tears', where he gives elusive emotions precisely elusive form. Tennyson's lyrics are among the greatest of the century. Yet (unlike Keats) he could also write effective narrative.

The *Idylls* (1859), his longest work, is retrospective medievalism of a sort that has long been out of favour. It is not of course historical medievalism (although Tennyson knew something of early polyphonic romance): its values are subtly, and sometimes not so subtly, Victorian. The Middle Ages functioned for Tennyson as an ideally faithful yet deeply flawed society, in which, for example, honour symbolized modern respectable virtue. As the contemporary frame of his *Morte d'Arthur* (1842) shows, his loading of the old tales with contemporary morality was anything but inadvertent. Yet it did not prevent the slow lyricized narrative from working effectively. Compared with Scott's, the story is easy to follow, lucid, visually distinct. And the similes are neatly contrived as an indirect means of smuggling in sensuous description. True, the dialogue is fustian; but then all Victorian poets – even

Browning – found direct speech difficult, and tended to overelevate it with archaism. A more serious problem is that the *Idylls* go too far in the direction of prose organization – towards continuity, dilution and repetition. In this they are like many of Tennyson's narratives (and he is often, perhaps too often, telling a story): they try too hard to compete with the novel in readability. Nevertheless, it seems at times that Tennyson can do anything in poetry. If philosophical thought is an exception, we may think it more than made up for by his mythological strength.

On looking more closely, however, one notices that Tennyson's narrative concentrates either on description or on lyrical evocation of mood. He is best at evocation of a single mood through many variations – especially a mood of resignation with an elegiac tinge. Even in an early poem like 'Mariana' (1830), everything in the 'dreamy house' and the symbolic landscape of depression around it confirms, with a powerful cumulative effect, the heavy atmosphere of neglect. The moss-crusted flower-plots, the 'rusted nails', the 'blackened waters' of the sluice, the 'level waste', the 'wild winds' shaking the poplar: all these are trivial in themselves, but all reinforce the mood of a woman with no love to look forward to –

> She only said, 'My life is dreary,
> He cometh not,' she said;
> She said, 'I am aweary, aweary,
> I would that I were dead!'

Much depends on harmony of detail, and on the recurrence of aspects until they come to acquire subjective value. Already this is almost the world of the symbolist poets.

Tennyson's mood poems are unlike those of earlier Romantics. For one thing, his dramatic or narrative frames license a new extremity. Mood is not merely expressed but wallowed in. Yet it is often a pessimism of Tennyson's own: he was inclined to be passive – fascinated by gloomy inevitabilities that could only be endured. Needless to say, for all the antique frames and disguises of his retrospective art, he addressed a common modern predicament. But his was not the ordinary Victorian adjustment, manic defences well to the fore. Tennyson came to terms with his depressive feelings. And in one instance, *Maud* (1855), he expressed 'abnormal' emotions in imagery of new psychological intensity.

Tennyson distrusted high claims for art's autonomy – as his agonizing in 'The Palace of Art' shows. On the other hand, he felt the claims of society keenly; so that when he roused himself from moods and dreams he tended to speak in too representative or 'BARDIC' a voice. A fine exception is 'Ulysses' (1842, wr. 1833). Some see this poem as dramatic – less in Tennyson's voice than in that of an unrealistic aspirer to adventure, whose comrades are long gone. But the myth is deeper. Ulysses indeed shares his last quest with dead companions. With them he may 'see the great Achilles':

> Death closes all: but something ere the end,
> Some work of noble note, may yet be done,
> Not unbecoming men that strove with Gods.

Tennyson's representative voice is more confident than Wordsworth's in expressing resolution. And when he subsumes generalized communal experience – as with the feminist and socialist ideas in his medley *The Princess* (1847) – he not only assumes rhetorical command, but can also show real honesty, if not a great deal of penetration.

Tennyson's greatest work is *In Memoriam A. H. H.* (1850), a sequence of short, intensely personal elegies occasioned by the death in 1833 of his friend Arthur Hallam. They are in quatrains rhyming *abba*, a minor-key Renaissance stanza Tennyson thought he had invented. He keeps up their 'sad mechanic exercise' (v) with a persistence born of his temperamental passivity – his endurance of helplessness. The earlier of the elegies follow every turn of grief and despair, from childish feelings of loss to intellectual doubts – 'Is this the end? Is this the end?' (xii). The voice of nihilism (compare 'The Two Voices') is strong. The later elegies generalize Hallam, however, identifying him more calmly with familiar images of nature: there is 'No gray old grange, or lonely fold,/ Or low morass and whispering reed' (c) but he dies in them again as they pass from the mind. Hallam's 'all-subtilizing intellect' (lxxxv) justifies extending the poem to take in issues raised by contemporary science – 'seeming-random forms' (cxviii). Opinion has divided between views of *In Memoriam* as a religious poem and as a poem of doubt. But its strength lies in being both: 'There lives more faith in honest doubt . . .' (xcvi).

Characteristically, Tennyson's thought found the 'strange diagonal' or creative vector of opposing pressures. He had deepest hopes of a reconciliation of religion with science, and under their joint influence he moved, in the course of *In Memoriam*'s sequence, by steps not always clear, from thinking of death as unjustly outraged prayer (vi) to the idea of 'those we call the dead' as a higher form of life. In others of his poems Tennyson could be facile (as the popular level of his poetry invited); but here his struggle with 'matter-moulded forms of speech' (xcv) impresses by its commitment. *In Memoriam* is our most profound lyric–elegiac consideration of death; and many have drawn support from its purging ritual of renewal – 'Ring out the grief that saps the mind' (cvi). It is also rare among Tennyson's poems in not seeming to lack thematic unity.

Victorian retrospection became an explicit programme for the pre-Raphaelite movement in literature and art. This elevated the Middle Ages, with their scrupulous detail and 'strict adherence to nature', as a model of true creativity. Dante Gabriel Rossetti (1828–82), the movement's central figure, was both poet and painter (more eminently the latter), and some of his poems belong to double art works, like 'The Blessed Damozel' (1850). Rossetti's dreaminess seems less embodied than Tennyson's, being loosely compounded of Keatsian aspiration, Petrarchan trance and vague ideas of medieval Platonism. The medievalism is primarily aesthetic – indeed decorative, and given to unrelated details:

> 'We two,' she said, 'will seek the groves
>   Where the lady Mary is,
> With her five handmaidens, whose names
>   Are five sweet symphonies,
> Cecily, Gertrude, Magdalen,
> Margaret and Rosalys.
>   ('The Blessed Damozel' xviii)

Some will dislike this lush evasive religiosity; and it is certainly very different from Coventry Patmore's downright theology of sex. But the poem – and Rossetti's poetry generally – should not be dismissed as diffuse adolescent fantasizing. He had the passion to aspire energetically towards deeper values than his society's. Unfortunately, his ill-conceived theories abounded in contradictions – like the notion of treating Romantic subjects literalistically.

Rossetti's pre-Raphaelite realism succeeds locally with modern subjects – as in 'Jenny', a morally dubious yet touching reverie about a prostitute; or 'A Trip to Paris and Belgium', one of the earliest poems on rail travel. The non-narrative sonnet sequence *The House of Life* (completed 1881) contrasts strikingly with Meredith's autobiographical sequence: its structures are better formed and its words better chosen. Yet its thought remains imperfectly realized; like all the pre-Raphaelites, Rossetti gives only the feeling of exactness. His best effects are momentary, even fugitive – 'the desultory feet of Death' (lxv); 'cold commemorative eyes' (xcvii). And, far more than Tennyson, he suffers from weak thematic grip.

Last Romantic as he was, Algernon Charles Swinburne (1837–1909) learnt from the craft of Tennyson and the aestheticism of Rossetti as well as from the fastidious classicism of Shelley. And in a distinctly un-Victorian way he made use of European writers (Mazzini, Hugo, Baudelaire), and even exerted influence in the other direction. But he subdued all his borrowings to a characteristic sameness that has rather unfairly been condemned as impervious. Swinburne dominated the later nineteenth century, a period of post-Tennysonian minor poets; and today his work still seems an egregious phenomenon. It carried Victorian lyricism to such a point of elaborate textural and rhythmic and metrical structuring that at times one can hardly read through to meaning: 'the low last edge of the long lone land'; 'the bliss-bringing bulk of a balm-breathing baby'. Lyricism could go no further in that direction. Technically, Swinburne has remained a landmark – and a quarry. (His metres are extraordinarily varied.) Moreover, his success led to changes in the sort of meaning expected from poetry. For Swinburne's is a poetry of words. Objects in it find expression in the most general terms, so that they blur into soft focus; while local progressions of thought often remain unclear, even though repetitive.

But Swinburne's diffuseness is, as T. S. Eliot said, 'one of his glories'. It allows emotion to expand to infinities of amplified mood; as when 'A Forsaken Garden' extends to 'weeds that grew green from the graves of its roses' – roses that are not only dead but 'lie dead'. Words in Swinburne seem to generate their own meaning by some fluent proliferation. In 'The dream foregone and the deed forborne' ('The Triumph of Time', ii), it is hard to resist the suspicion that 'forborne' resulted from superficial formal pressures, rather than from a train of thought or feeling. One even begins to think of affinities with subjectless postmodern poets. But Swinburne's poetry is deceptive. He may be immature, but his larger content goes far beyond pagan sadness, vague seasonality and world sickness. Read him in quantity, and you will find that his fantasizing meditation on literary structures arrives gradually at collective, deeply impersonal contents. Only locally does his exploitation of aura demand surrender of the logical faculty. And even his local procedures can often be defended rationally. In the *Atalanta in Calydon* chorus stanza that Eliot objected to –

> Time with a gift of tears;
> Grief with a glass that ran . . .

– the interchange of Time's and Grief's attributes is no casual vagueness. It amplifies the inherent grievousness of temporality: time gives cause for tears to run as well as sand.

The work of Gerard Manley Hopkins (1844–89) pushed lyricism to a limit that was also a threshold – sometimes to greater things, sometimes to incoherent obscurity. To juxtapose Hopkins with Swinburne may seem strange, since it is customary to treat the former almost as a modernist poet. Unpublished in his lifetime, Hopkins was not fully presented to the public by his friend Robert Bridges until 1918. Yet some of Hopkins's poetry goes back to the 1860s; and he invites comparison with his contemporary in view of his rich assonantal patterning – as in the sonnet on 'Duns Scotus's Oxford': 'Cuckoo-echoing, bell-swarmed, lark-charmed, rook-racked, river-rounded'. Hopkins even takes his place as a Victorian retrospective artist (baroque retrospective, perhaps, relating to that other intellectual lyricist, Richard Crashaw).

An intense Roman Catholic belief, characterized by mysticism of an 'inscape' or individuality of creatures, informs every detail of Hopkins's work:

> Glory be to God for dappled things –
>   For skies of couple-colour as a brinded cow;
>   For rose-moles all in stipple upon trout that swim;
> Fresh-firecoal chestnut-falls; finches' wings;
>   Landscape plotted and pieced – fold, fallow, and plough;
>   And áll trádes, their gear and tackle and trim.
>   ('Pied Beauty', wr.1877)

Often it is as if the intensity of vision makes Hopkins try to say everything at once, until his syntax becomes compressed to the point of obscurity and resistance – or of charge and illumination. The happier result just eventuates in 'his riding / Of the rolling level underneath him steady air' ('The Windhover'). Here 'level' seems at first a noun ('riding the level underneath him'); but then 'underneath-him-steady' turns out to be a sort of composite adjective, qualifying 'air' – one of the series that begins with 'rolling level'. 'To what serves Mortal Beauty' offers many instances of a similar extreme ellipsis. In such ways Hopkins reacts powerfully against Victorian diffuseness. His thick verbal impasto is quite unlike Swinburne's in one respect: namely, in demanding maximum attention to each word in its semantic distinctness. He was an excellent classical scholar, and had a deep knowledge of the character and inheritance of words. This led him to revive Old English forms – not just accentual metres (his 'sprung rhythm'), but semantic forms too. Thus his poetic syntax will often give an idiomatic impression; except that the idiom is invented, as in 'speaks and spells' or 'Keeps grace' ('As Kingfishers Catch Fire'; compare the usage 'keeps faith').

In striving to combine direct intensity with lyric transformation Hopkins sometimes fell into strident oddity. And unfortunately he was comparatively insensitive in imagining readers' probable responses – a shortcoming that isolation in a religious order did nothing to mitigate. Indeed, he actually opted for idiosyncrasy. More reading of the best models of diction, he said, would only 'refine my singularity'. This choice at once made his originality possible, and his place in literature problematic. Nevertheless, however eccentric he may have been to the main course of development, there can be no doubt that his free-footed accentual rhythms profoundly influenced T. S. Eliot and others. And he made other contributions, such as an enlarged sonnet form of real use. Hopkins's main interest has been found in subtly sensuous images on the very edge of intelligibility – ideal for explication. But above all, his poems have strong individuality as aesthetically structured objects. They are built to last.

DIFFERENT VOICES

Towards the end of poetry's openly Romantic phase, it began to lose itself in a labyrinth of conflicting directions. There were insuperable obstacles, it seemed, to interpreting in social terms the psychic material released to consciousness by the Romantics. These were now criticized for lack of thought; by which was sometimes meant lack of political opinions. As we have seen, the insights of Romanticism were partly assimilated – in a sense most Victorian poetry was Romantic. But they were also partly suppressed, the Victorians preferring to approach the contents of the 'undersoul' less directly. Official doctrines of poetry's moral elevation increasingly drove real expression out of the literary mainstream: not only into the satiric subculture, but into humorous or even nonsense verse, like that of Thomas Hood (1799–1845), Edward Lear (1812–88) or Lewis Carroll (C. L. Dodgson, 1832–98). Nonsense verse can be seen as representing an extreme of the lyric tendency discussed earlier.

But there was another movement, and eventually another tradition, which took up Wordsworth's extension of colloquial diction to poetry – something now taken for granted – and gradually succeeded in carrying it further. The extension was not easy. When Arthur Clough wrote 'we have something new to say, but do not know how to say it', he diagnosed the acute difficulty of finding an authentic voice for poetry under modern conditions. In the event, many different ways of saying new things were found – perhaps too many for the wellbeing of the art. New colloquialized topics proliferated, and so did generic improvizations enlarging and legitimizing the freedoms Byron had snatched.

Typical of this line of development is the novel in verse, with its highly colloquial diction and a style loose-textured for fast reading. Here Browning is anticipated by his wife Elizabeth Barrett Browning (1806–61) in *Aurora Leigh* (1857), an accessible achievement, yet one only now beginning to win just appreciation. Elizabeth Browning inherits Wordsworth's egotistical conception of epic, with the individual soul at its world's centre; but for nature she substitutes love. And she domesticates (or trivializes) the form, moving it in a decidedly novelistic direction. It would be easy to criticize her for prattling – for a fatal fluency that condemns her to the surface of things. But in fact she is also 'bold to leap a height': she locates a whole range of uncharted experiences, and finds ways of talking about them that will be invaluable to others besides her husband. His rhetoric she can anticipate as well as echo:

> We shape a figure of our fantasy,
> Call nothing something, and run after it
> And lose it, lose ourselves too in the search,
> Till clash against us comes a somebody . . .
> (*Aurora Leigh* vi)

Robert Browning (1812–89) did more than any other Victorian to modernize poetry; later, indeed, he was to represent a point of departure for the modernist movement. He perpetually experimented and innovated, although sometimes in a reckless, slapdash, heavy-handed way. And his content is characterized by what Walter Bagehot described as 'a taste for ugly reality': the mean landscape of '"Childe Roland to the Dark Tower Came"', for example, is like an industrial wasteland. Browning favours novel images, such as the newfangled match in 'Meeting at Night' (1845); and piquant ones, from exotic life or (realistic) visual art. Perhaps his most radical innovation – which seemed grotesque to some of his contemporaries – is the use of a compacted colloquial language as staple diction for all subjects. The results are extremely readable: only the early, analytic Browning, as in *Sordello* (1840), can be called obscure. His loose-textured narratives and reflections found, in fact, a large, semi-educated public; so that they were only ever difficult in a very relative sense. Browning's public has to be kept in mind when assessing his innovations in the direction of deceptive obliquity. Thus, he invented a type of poem (later popular with the Georgians) which has a simple direct surface meaning, but also contains digressions or apparently gratuitous elements, tangentially related to the rest. 'How It Strikes a Contemporary' (1855) is an example, where the details of the poet's idling may seem merely to illustrate his personality –

> the ferrel of his stick
> Trying the mortar's temper 'tween the chinks
> Of some new shop a-building, French and fine
> (lines 20–2)

– until one sees that they signify poetry's investigation of the social fabric.

Browning's chief contribution is the dramatic monologue, a genre limited to the simulated speech or writing of a dramatic character – often one who communicates his garrulous thoughts during a time of crisis. The antecedents of the Browningesque monologue include not only Landor's *Imaginary Conversations* (1824–9) but also Donne's *Satires* (Browning was unusual for his time in admiring Donne). Its own influence was prodigious, and may be suspected even in the Jamesian novel. The monologues of Browning's *Men and Women* (1855) are often in a blank verse which, while well adjusted to character, generally follows colloquial rhythms. But if retrospective art does not much appear in the language, it is very evident in the situations. Many of these are historical; several being junctures when old beliefs are degenerating ('Fra Lippo Lippi'; 'The Bishop Orders his Tomb at St Praxed's Church') or when new belief is emerging ('Cleon'; 'An Epistle Containing the Strange Medical Experience of Karshish, the Arab Physician').

Browning's concern with faith and doubt finds most direct expression in 'Bishop Blougram's Apology', the reflections of a conforming sceptic. Here such devices as the leisurely simile of life's passenger with his cultural luggage tend to identify the poet (and perhaps the reader) with the practical bishop. After all, if we jettison belief 'Where's / The gain? how can we guard our unbelief, / Make it bear fruit to us?' Browning has been criticized for not making his own position distinct by censuring the bishop. Santayana condemns 'the arrest of [Browning's] dramatic art at soliloquy'. But the charge of ventriloquism is a philosopher's objection – an attempt to pin down the poet's doctrine in a way alien to literature. True, Browning himself provoked the criticism by insisting that his poems were 'though often Lyric in expression, always Dramatic in principle, and so many utterances of so many imaginary persons, not mine'. Nevertheless, his imaginary persons were invariably similes for parts of himself, with his ideas, his concerns, his passions.

To condemn Browning for not speaking out (as he condemned himself) is to miss what was his greatest achievement: namely, poetry that concealed the poet within deliberately ambiguous situations, and so forced the reader to respond on his own – poetry that made way, in fact, for Henry James and modernist fiction. A fairer charge against Browning might be that he did not always cover his traces scrupulously enough. Although he took in life's multitudinousness with the apparent gusto of a Victorian tourist, he was anything but bluffly optimistic: his neogothic décor seems often to half-conceal revealing fears.

In one view, Browning's dramatic monologue was the vehicle for a vision of transcendental truth fractionally embodied in individual crises. From this standpoint the genre reached its most ambitious development in *The Ring and the Book* (1868), a verse novel based on a late seventeenth-century murder trial. Here monologues are multiplied until no fewer than twelve offset (or undercut) one another. The result has been seen as a great epic – and would be a sharply appropriate one for an age that worshipped fact, since it uncovers the sordid means by which facts come to be modified. But the poem is so extended that it has to be judged as a verse novel; and as such, in spite of some detective-story interest, it fails to come alive. Broad tracts of it seem laboured, devoid both of narrative realization and literary event. Moreover, the increased objectivity of cancelled relativities is gained at the expense of the empathy that is Browning's greatest strength. Nevertheless, *The Ring and the Book* has had formal influence on novelists as different as Virginia Woolf (*The Waves*) and William Faulkner (*The Sound and the Fury*).

Arthur Hugh Clough (1819–61) was more radically discontented with his age than Browning; yet he found ways of speaking out about a great many issues. He was an Oxford don until he resigned his fellowship because of doubts, and his poetry gives the sense of a keen intelligence, in touch with intellectual as well as social trends, and prompt to take sceptical progressive stances towards them. *Amours de Voyage* (1858) is a semi-autobiographical epistolary novel in classical hexameters and elegiacs, set in Rome during the French seige of 1849. The quick light play of Clough's intelligence dances throughout – as in Claude's smart delivery (note the telling line-break):

Rome disappoints me much; I hardly as yet understand, but
Rubbishy seems the word that most exactly would suit it.

(i.19–20)

The poem's scepticism is certainly carried to extreme lengths:

So I have seen a man killed! An experience that, among others!
Yes, I suppose I have; although I can hardly be certain . . .

(ii.162–3)

All the same, disproportionate stress on the earlier cantos has obscured
an underlying quest for reality.

In some ways a greater achievement, and the one that brought
Clough voguish success, is *The Bothie of Toper-na-Fuosich* (1848), revised
as *The Bothie of Tober-na-Vuolich* (the first title was indecent). This
novelistic treatment of an Oxford reading party in the Scottish
Highlands (which were just being opened up to visitors) finds opportunities for fun as well as for intellectual tourism. The poem is subtitled 'A
Long-Vacation Pastoral'; but in fact the georgic mode declares itself
everywhere – in its mock epic treatment of feasting and costume and
highland games, its full landscape descriptions, its detailed explanations
of undergraduate tasks and opinions. Unlike Longfellow's hexameters,
where accentual rhythm and quantitative metre monotonously coin-
cide, Clough's allow counterpointing variation; although for comic purposes he can on occasion use broad effects, as in the laborious spondees
of 'Walked up perpendicular hills, and also down them' (iii, 121). As for
his deliciously fastidious diction, it ranges with impressive ease from
classical mock epic elevation, through technicalities, or post-Romantic
descriptive language warm with erotic implication, to extravagant novelistic slang (some of it invented).

These language games, like the conventional generic forms, serve to
mask Clough's outspoken expressions on sensitive political issues such
as the game laws or landlord absenteeism – or on the 'woman question'.
Nevertheless, debate is well subordinated to narrative, especially to the
cross-class romance of the radical Philip Hewson. His story finds in the
end an idealistic solution; although only by resorting to emigration. *The
Bothie* is a marvellously orchestrated poem. Beneath its clever, charming surface Clough pursues much deeper concerns, notably in his
investigation of young love:

She paused, but quickly continued,
Smiling almost fiercely, continued, looking upward.
You are too strong, you see, Mr.Philip! just like the sea there,

> Which *will* come, through the straits and all between the mountains,
> Forcing its great strong tide into every nook and inlet,
> Getting far in, up the quiet stream of sweet inland water . . .
>
> (vii. 122–27)

This delicately interrogative account would be remarkable in any age.

Clough's friend Matthew Arnold (1822–88) shared many things with him: classical tastes, difficulties of belief, the influence of Thomas Arnold. Arnold had less success in finding an individual style; perhaps because his diction was unconsidered to the point of vagueness. Sincerity of convictions combined unhappily with overemphasis on content to make his expression too explicit. Still, his impersonal tone could be very effective when it summed up the feelings of his age. It does so in 'Stanzas from the Grande Chartreuse' (1855) and 'Dover Beach' (1867), on the decline of faith. Arnold's authoritative moralizing was to influence an important line of disillusioned or sceptical poets – Swinburne, Meredith, Hardy, de la Mare, T. S. Eliot. The dull style of 'Dover Beach' – the pale epithets and careless, unemphatic phrasing ('the moon lies fair'; 'sweet is the night-air') – reflects almost a deficient interest in words. Yet the action of the sea on the pebbles becomes an eloquent symbol for the erosion of faith:

> But now I only hear
> Its melancholy, long, withdrawing roar,
> Retreating, to the breath
> Of the night-wind, down the vast edges drear
> And naked shingles of the world.

It was not entirely Arnold's fault that the poetic language had deteriorated, so that even his allusions lost themselves in privacy. He has sometimes been disparaged as narrowly academic; but this is at best a half truth. His intellect made him respected as a European thinker, and enabled him to range far more widely than almost any of his contemporaries.

For much of his life Arnold had a disappointing lack of success: professional duties limited his *oeuvre* and made it uneven. He attempted long poems, several with an alienated protagonist; but these are failures except for a few passages, particularly in 'Empedocles on Etna' (1852). Clough was probably right in thinking Arnold's best poem to be 'The Scholar–Gipsy' (1853); although even here prosy explicitness breaks in, in the passage on 'this strange disease of modern life' (l. 203). Glanvill's gipsy story had rich associations for Arnold; so that its reapplication generates a subtle criticism of Victorian society, almost in mythic form –

and further distanced (a favourite device of his) by the coda with its simile of a symbolic Tyrian trader. In this and in certain other of his poems, Arnold used varied line lengths, and so helped to give renewed currency to a vitally important lyric resource.

The deficiencies of Victorian poetic language were most of all limiting to religious poets. As we have seen, Hopkins felt the diffuseness and deadness of contemporary poetic words keenly enough to make a decisive break with the whole recent tradition. But others made no such isolating break – certainly not Coventry Patmore (1823–96), the great poet of domestic love. Patmore has enjoyed something of a European reputation; yet he is still not fully rehabilitated in his own country, even if one critic has compared him with Donne. The comparison is not quite vacuous; for Patmore thought intensely, even mystically, about erotic experience. All the same, mention of Metaphysical poetry reminds one how far poetic language had deteriorated. Patmore's is diluted almost to flatness with narrative or prosy explanation. *The Angel in the House* (1854, 1856) and *To the Unknown Eros* (1877), which often appeal to different readers, should both be tried. The former has an unusual alternation of preludes and narrative sections, borrowed from George Wither (1588–1667). In *To the Unknown Eros,* poems such as 'The Toys' and 'If I Were Dead', rough though they are, communicate their being deeply felt; and they have rhythms better conveyed, at least, than those of Patmore's correspondent Hopkins.

There was nothing innovative, either, in the diction of Christina Rossetti (1830–94), a pre-Raphaelite, although one with far purer delicacy of feeling than her brother Dante Gabriel. Hers is an authentic voice, honestly natural enough for deep confessional intimacy, as she shares the monotonous pathos of depression. The clear structure of such fine sonnets as 'Remember' and 'Rest' make painfully evident, however, the weaknesses of Victorian thought-forms – 'Until the morning of Eternity / Her rest shall not begin nor end, but be . . .'. Nor will the diction or rhetoric bear close examination. One notices lack of economy even in a successful poem like 'Uphill' ('Will the day's journey take the whole long day?'); and there is overreliance on figures of repetition, not only for elegiac effect but also – as in the anaphoras of 'A Birthday' – for explanatory accommodation of readers orientated to prose.

There was far more formal achievement in the 1,000 or so brief intense lyrics of the New England poet Emily Dickinson (1830–86). Dickinson lived a narrow, retired life of extreme moods, yet kept detached from them. She sometimes succeeded in breaking through to

the self within the self by sheer violence – by ferocious sceptical
persistence of thought. For her little allegories, like her simple diction,
are masks. They cover cool paradoxes, or idiosyncratic ideas expressed
with Blakeian economy. Dickinson gave the lyric epigram a compression quite uncharacteristic of the period; although she was able to do so,
one notes, only by extremities of ELLIPSIS – incomplete chains of
discourse, helped out by a private system of rhetorical punctuation. Her
poems were published only posthumously:

> This is my letter to the World
> That never wrote to Me –
> The simple News that Nature told –
> With tender Majesty
>
> Her Message is committed
> To Hands I cannot see –
> For love of Her – Sweet – countrymen –
> Judge tenderly – of Me

Another American poet, Walt Whitman (1819–92), calls for notice; not
only because he manifested characteristics of his age in an extreme
form, but because he had British admirers from the 1870s on, and was
to be an important model in our own century. Whitman read some
literature, including Greek; he had worked as a teacher. But he was
much more of a journalist, mixing with ordinary people in a way
unusual for Victorian men of letters. His great *Leaves of Grass* (1855,
1856, 1860) is an assertion of total freedom by a mythic figure – a
representative now of democratic average man, now of the Romantic
Goethean or Carlylean superman. Its new beginning seems to set
literary conventions boldly aside. But are they exchanged for simple
spontaneity – or for unrestrained torrents of verbiage in crude
anaphoric sequences, an image per line? Neither impression is entirely
just. For example, 'Song of Myself' makes extensive (although very free)
use of Hesiodic conventions. And on the other hand, roughnesses and
lapses into prose are undeniably there, yet somehow hardly matter. To
object to them would be, as Whitman himself puts it, to 'conceive too
much of articulation'. For he takes Victorian sententiousness to its
logical extreme, and opts for content all the way. He utters his thoughts
in a direct, unmediated, unformalized way, as the urgency of his
doctrine of new life dictates. And this works – at least to the extent that
we find his vision of universal sympathy exhilarating. If it is bad poetry,
or not poetry, *che importa?* Besides, Whitman's artlessness concealed art.
And he succeeded in introducing a larger rhythmic unit, modelled on

patterns from the Authorized Version, that foreshadowed the phrasal unit of some modern free verse.

Whitman was a metrical innovator, then. And in genre, too, his poetry gives a sense of profound renewal – of conventions relaxed, thresholds crossed, outworn structures broken. His vaunt in 'Shut Not Your Doors' has largely been justified by history:

Shut not your doors to me proud libraries,
For that which was lacking on all your well-fill'd shelves, yet needed most, I
　bring,
Forth from the war emerging, a book I have made,
The words of my book nothing, the drift of it every thing,
A book separate, not link'd with the rest nor felt by the intellect,
But you ye untold latencies will thrill to every page.

It is perhaps only after many readings that one comes to recognize (as D. H. Lawrence did) the portentousness of Whitman's 'empty Allness', or to see that his diffuse style correlates only too well with the loose thought behind such conceptions as 'sympathy'.

Whitmanesque 'spontaneity' and prolixity were to continue ever-green in American literature – one thinks of writers as diverse as Pound, Kerouac and Creeley. And in such poems as 'Crossing Brooklyn Ferry' and 'When Lilacs Last in the Dooryard Bloom'd' Whitman not only proposed many of the topics of modern poetry, but sounded the tone of urgent attack often now taken for granted as poetic.

During the later nineteenth century the diction of poetry underwent a profound change, which to our own age has seemed entirely for the better. Earlier, the literary language (shaped in the Enlightenment to rational ends) had become for poets an object almost of distrust. The Romantics and their early Victorian successors even avoided trying to formulate their trans-rational contents precisely; and relied instead on expression through multiple attempts – sketches or aggregations of details. It was a method that inevitably resulted in diffuseness. Precise denotation came to be considered less important than suggestive connotation, especially in the sanctified words of poetic diction – that 'band of words' which Francis Thompson (1859–1907) derided as 'the Praetorian cohorts of poetry'. This special diction had its uses; but it brought the risk of clashes with other words of a less poetic register – and so led to periphrases such as Tennyson's 'the knightly growth that fringed his lips'. The search for new subjects (poetic or unpoetic), and new diction to go with them, generated a great variety of minor poetry. From this *embarras* of miscellaneous *richesses* may be selected for mention John de Tabley (1835–95); the novelist George Meredith (1828–1909) – especially the sixteen-line sonnets of *Modern Love* (1862); and John Davidson (1857–1909). Davidson ranged from Pre-Raphaelite anthology pieces to Kiplingesque ballads and extraordinary experimental poems with scientific imagery and 'unpoetic' diction – as in 'The Crystal Palace' (1908):

> So sublime! Like some
> Immense crustacean's gannoid skeleton,
> Unearthed, and cleansed, and polished!
> (lines 16–18)

His work would later provide models for MacDiarmid. Meanwhile, however, greater changes impended than these experiments could effect.

The language itself began to alter. It became more concise, less conducive to separation of thought from feeling. There was, in fact, a new precision of language. This is very evident in the ballad-like epigrams of A. E. Housman (1859–1936). His emotional range may not be very wide, but he sustains a marvellously accurate tone of concentrated irony or (more often) of moving pathos:

> By brooks too broad for leaping
> The lightfoot boys are laid;
> The rose-lipt girls are sleeping
> In fields where roses fade.
> (*A Shropshire Lad* (1896) liv)

The diction of poetry was now much less exclusively based on poetic words. Poets were beginning to open up the broader register of modern poetic language, with its abrupt shifts, its unpredictability, its freshness – although also, unfortunately, its loss of weight. In their use of demotic language, Rudyard Kipling's (1865–1936) strongly effective ballads, left-handed by-works though they may be, contrast significantly with the retrospective ballads of Rossetti or Morris.

Linguistic change, rather than poetic fashion, appears to have moulded the diction of even the best poetry of the turn of the century. The theory that modernism was a response to a crisis in Victorian literature gets little support from the poetry of Thomas Hardy (1840–1928), which was not difficult, or intellectual, or novel – which was still in fact Victorian – yet whose language has continued to seem vigorous and newly rewarding. It is noteworthy, however, that many of Hardy's strengths were provincial; as if metropolitan culture had indeed become debilitated enough for him to return to Dorset roots for rejuvenation. Thus he would turn to dialect, or country subjects; or would take up ballad forms (interpreting them with a more inward tact than Kipling's), and use them in curious, offbeat ways, to poignant effect – as in 'Drummer Hodge' or 'The Newcomer's Wife'. Hardy's metrical variety, in itself phenomenal, was extended by free recourse to local gothic irregularities; so that he avoided any constraint of metre, and could realize Pater's ideal of making every detail expressive. The rhythmic variations in his greatest poems, such as 'After a Journey', repay the most minute study. Consider 'And the cave just under, with a voice still so hollow', or 'Trust me, I mind not, though Life lours'.

For all its high esteem, Hardy's poetry has not been much imitated directly (one exception is Philip Larkin). A reason for this may lie in his idiosyncrasies. The language of integrity involved him in odd simplicities, even prosaic banalities: 'Where you will next be there's no knowing'; 'The smile on your mouth was the deadest thing'. Hardy was able to mix these with poetic diction – 'Yes: I have re-entered your olden haunts at last'; 'I shall go where went I then' – in such a way that the resultant switches and clumsinesses somehow vouch for the hesitant sincere effect. He put together an attractively pragmatic style, and one that by its eclectic freedom pointed a possible way forward. Miraculously expressive though it is, Hardy's poetry at its best suggests not only a personal 'voice', but also an anonymous presence:

> It filled but a minute. But was there ever
>   A time of such quality, since or before,
> In that hill's story? To one mind never,
>   Though it has been climbed, foot-swift, foot-sore,
>   By thousands more.
>
> Primaeval rocks form the road's steep border,
>   And much have they faced there, first and last,
> Of the transitory in Earth's long order;
>   But what they record in colour and cast
>   Is – that we two passed.
>
> ('At Castle Boterel')

There is a certain impersonality, too, in the way Hardy the modernist questions ideas of his time; staunchly refusing, for example, to idealize life's cruel hardness, or death's. His attitude to ultimate questions is many-sided. It almost encourages the idea that he seeks truth by offsetting or even rebutting his own expressions.

Perhaps with this in mind Hardy took up, in his fine elegiac 'Poems of 1912–13', the genre of Tennyson's *In Memoriam*. This he developed in the direction of the connected sequence – arguably the most significant poetic form of the twentieth century. By abandoning narrative progression the sequence allows steps that need not be validated in terms of individual biography; to say nothing of encouraging bolder leaps of the imagination. Throughout 'Poems of 1912–13' Hardy applies his novelistic powers to great effect, both in the architectonics (we are reminded he began as an architect) and in following up unexpected viewpoints with consistency of imagination. In their increasing compression, however, his spare lines are far from novelistic; they show how far the language of late Victorian poetry was already moving away from diffuse, low-pressure discursiveness. Hardy now seems the last great writer to communicate responses to life more or less directly, in ways intelligible to the ordinary reader. His work has cardinal value, not only as achieving great eloquence of the heart but as offering our nearest access to the simplicities of Victorian poetry.

12

Nineteenth-Century Fiction

EXCEPT for Sterne and Richardson, the eighteenth-century novelists tended at first to observe action from a certain distance. In this respect the GOTHIC NOVEL, a new form of romance, made a great change. It was psychologically orientated, and sometimes treated emotions quite minutely – or, at least, a particular range of them. The gothic novel was a tale of terrors – especially the fear that rational individuality would be overwhelmed, whether by rape or death or the supernatural. Usually it was set in antique or uncultivated environments (wild forests, ancient castles, labyrinthine passages, ruined graveyards), among circumstances of torture or unquiet death. From Sade onwards, commentators have tried to connect the genre with the atrocities of the French Revolution; but it began much earlier, in Britain, and had to do, rather, with the excitements of gothic irrationality, the cult of ruins and the fantasies their contemplation encouraged. Indeed, its imagery harked back further still, to the neogothic of Jacobean tragedy, Shakespeare and, above all, Spenser. *The Faerie Queene* offered great store of horrors, monsters, ruined castles, 'shadowy shapes' and 'visions old' (the phrases are Collins's in his 'Ode to Fear'), the very features to which gothic novel readers thrilled.

GOTHIC NOVELS

The gothic novel began with *The Castle of Otranto* (1765), by the great connoisseur and letter writer Horace Walpole. At first Walpole pretended it to be a translation from a sixteenth-century Italian print of a medieval romance, but subsequently presented it as an original work – an attempt to release the 'great resources of fancy' in the novel (dammed up by involvement with ordinary triviality) by opening it to 'imagination and improbability'. And in fact *The Castle of Otranto* has little period flavour: its action, as in many later gothic novels, seems to take place in a limbo of the imagination. Walpole provides vaguely gothic décor, however, and a few (unexplained) sensational events, such as the materialization of a gigantic helmet heavy enough to crush fatally. None of this arouses much terror: there is more sense of indulging a literary mood – of the exercise of taste. A taste for gothic ornament had never entirely disappeared in the eighteenth century (as witness Vauxhall Gardens, or Hawksmoor's 1716–33 All Souls quadrangle at Oxford); so that when Walpole invented the gothic novel, and rebuilt his own house Strawberry Hill in the gothic style (1753, 1773), he could set a fashion rather than merely seem eccentric.

Nevertheless impulses deeper, if less conscious, than those of taste were involved in *The Castle of Otranto*. Its superhuman armour derived from Piranesi's *Carceri* etchings, those morbid fantasies of overwhelming restrictions and imprisoning infinities. And significantly Walpole began composition – as Coleridge and Mary Shelley were to do – at the prompting of a dream. Walpole's is an extraordinary case: the author of a relatively pallid work, he as it were fantasized his way, by mere submission to mood, into a place in literary history. He may be said to have assembled the gothic romance's repertoire; although without doing much to exploit it.

A greater generator of the gothic novel was Mrs Ann Radcliffe (1764–1823). Her masterpiece, *Mysteries of Udolpho* (1794), is a classic account of feminine terror and related emotions. It makes a girl's bereavement, subsequent dependence and imprisonment among banditti the occasion for an extended study of the shades of terror (rather than horror): from fear and awe of death, through grief, pain of separation from a lover, fear of abandonment, fear of rape, fear of the dark, fear of the supernatural and terror of the mysterious, to terror at the very landscape –

> she saw only images of gloomy grandeur, or of dreadful sublimity, around her; other images, equally gloomy and equally terrible, gleamed on her imagination.
>
> (II.v)

It is often said that Radcliffe's romances are distinguished by the scrupulosity whereby she introduces novelistic detail to explain each supernatural event rationally. Even the veiled 'picture' that causes Emily to faint, although it is long left mysterious with powerful effect, at last undergoes mere description. But to emphasize Radcliffe's rationality is misleading, since her abnormal focus on dark emotions itself receives no adequate explanation. Perhaps only a psychological interpretation, taking into account Emily's sexual inexperience, could explain the mixed character of her feelings, 'now agitated with fear, and now with admiration'.

The coherence of Radcliffe's miscellaneous repertoire of features depended on current aesthetic theories such as those of Edmund Burke. As we have seen, Burke treated the ideal of the sublime as distinct from that of beauty – as founded not on pleasure but on pain. Wonder at nature's sublimities began now to supplement the wonders of personal emotion that characterized earlier romance. Indeed, Radcliffe's most obvious originality lay in her endless digressions into description of Salvator Rosa-like panoramas. She established wild landscape as a standard feature of romance; even if, as she wrote, the full terror of landscape ('beauty sleeping in the lap of horror') was already fading.

> Emily, often as she travelled among the clouds, watched in silent awe their billowy surges rolling below; sometimes, wholly closing upon the scene, they appeared like a world of chaos, and, at others, spreading thinly, they opened and admitted partial catches of the landscape – the torrent, whose astounding roar had never failed, rumbling down the rocky chasm, huge cliffs white with snow, or the dark summits of the pine forests, that stretched mid-way down the mountains.
>
> (II. i)

Such digressions gave (and still give) a very special pleasure to lovers of landscape. But they are also part of an interlaced structure that keeps delaying the action and distancing it into perspective. A taste for medieval romance underlies Radcliffe's fondness for returning to scenes after a long interval, in a way that makes for elegiac retrospection.

A great many other gothic novels soon appeared. From being a minor strain until about 1790, during the next three decades the genre became dominant, and enjoyed a popularity that contrasts with the relatively limited appeal of the Fieldingesque novel. Hundreds of gothic romances were published, some of them (like Matthew Lewis's) translations or imitations of German originals. But in most instances their quality is too low for literary interest. Some have pressed the claims of *Melmoth the Wanderer* (1820), by the Irishman Charles Maturin, but its inflated language has a fatal vagueness: everything in it is 'inexpressible', little expressed. Nevertheless the period was one in which lurid inventions and atrocious writing could succeed; and Maturin had some prestige (shared with Walpole, Radcliffe, Clara Reeve, 'Monk' Lewis and such German writers as E. T. A. Hoffmann) for the later masters Poe and Hawthorne.

A conspicuous innovation was that the gothic protagonist might now be 'evil'. The villain–hero's diabolism had a primarily symbolic force, however: it need no longer imply spiritual wickedness. Indeed, throughout nineteenth-century romance the powers of darkness often stand for powers of the unconscious; while the forbidden merely signifies what is currently unconventional. The symbolism of the capacious gothic genre has still to be fully explored: but it probably contains several distinct strands, corresponding to depression and guilt at the dwindling of religious belief; guilt at 'the haughtiness of the noblesse' (Radcliffe); fascination with old emotions proscribed during the rationalism of the Enlightenment; and a sense of the oppressiveness of confining social conventions.

SCOTT AND THE HISTORICAL ROMANCE

Sir Walter Scott (1771–1832) had made his reputation with historical verse romances like *The Lay of the Last Minstrel* (1805) and *Marmion* (1808) before he wrote any novels. And it was in verse that he first sounded the note of romance with a full resonance, evoking the magic of distant strangeness. What made this possible seems to have been that Scott was inward with the past, in ways inaccessible to his predecessors. He had access to Scottish oral tradition – to ballads and personal reports that made the past alive for him. He also had an encyclopedic knowledge of history (extending even to miscellaneous antiquarian objects, which he collected), and a formidable memory for what he knew.

With these strengths Scott was able to body forth the past credibly. A reader of *Marmion* follows the characters in entering and leaving castles with authentic procedures; journeying by sea along the Scottish coast, past vistas of unruined medieval places, to a convent under stern discipline; stopping at a hostelry with a representatively varied company; or meeting a herald with appropriate protocol. Such scenes are now taken for granted. But it was Scott, a fine historian, who first imagined them – and who thus intensified the retrospective value of romance by restoring the historical specifics omitted by Walpole and Reeve.

Meanwhile, Scott's introductions to the Cantos of *Marmion* subtly conjured the mood of romance from modern landscapes, and so added solidity of temporal perspective. (The introductions should be read by anyone interested in the Victorian picturesque.) Mood is important in *Marmion* itself; yet the energy also bustles, making everything coruscate with movement:

> Day set on Norham's castled steep,
> And Tweed's fair river, broad and deep,
>   And Cheviot's mountains lone:
> The battled towers, the donjon keep,
> The loophole grates, where captives weep,
> The flanking walls that round it sweep,
>   In yellow lustre shone.
> The warriors on the turrets high,
> Moving athwart the evening sky,
>   Seem'd forms of giant height:
> Their armour, as it caught the rays,
> Flash'd back again the western blaze,
>   In lines of dazzling light.
>
> (*Marmion* I.i)

Scott developed his narrative powers in the verse romances; and their influence on taste make them historically important. But as poetry they are not on the highest plane. The verse at best is adequate – enlivened only on occasion by orchestration of texture or local adjustment of rhythm to sense.

Greatness, however, is unquestionably an attribute of Scott's Waverley novels, beginning with *Waverley* itself (1814). The 'Postscript, which should have been a Preface' pretends that the novel emulates Maria Edgeworth's Irish tales; but the actual genre is very different, consisting in a highly original amalgam of history and romance. The narrator warns us from a Fieldingesque distance not to expect hippogriffs or Arabian Nights enchantments, only 'tolerable horses and a civil driver'. All the same – and in spite of the sharp sense of alterity (otherness), of a particular world 'sixty years since' – Scott's selection of events and frequent allusions to romance writers like Spenser make the work thrill with remoter associations of chivalric as well as Jacobite glamour. Even Waverley, ambivalent waverer as he is, seems 'like a knight of romance'.

The structure too is romance-like in its 'ambagitory' or 'circumbendibus' method, whereby narrative breaks off into descriptive digressions, to find echoes perhaps in the winding landscape:

> this narrow glen, at so short a distance, seemed to open into the land of romance. The rocks assumed a thousand peculiar and varied forms. In one place, a crag of huge size presented its gigantic bulk, as if to forbid the passenger's farther progress; and it was not until he approached its very base, that Waverley discerned the sudden and acute turn by which the pathway wheeled its course around this formidable obstacle.
>
> (*Waverley* I.xxii)

We have met these narrative discontinuities before, these descriptions of landscape or of iconic objects like the hall door of Tully-Veolan in *Waverley* or Oldbuck's tapestry in *The Antiquary*. And indeed Scott had studied Ann Radcliffe's romances carefully. He tried to make his own landscapes similarly picturesque; with such success that they were drawn by Turner and visited by countless tourists.

The discontinuities of romance gave Scott the 'arbitrary power' of selection that he needed in order to put together a consistent image of the past. But the Waverley novels have this difference that their narratives run on energetically, with a robust cheerfulness able to cope with anything – even with contrived plots. Scott makes his digressions contribute to the historical action; so that he sustains momentum, and keeps the *mise en scène* extraordinarily coherent. Everything fits into the period realization, apart from a certain 'necessary anachronism' whereby the characters retain modern interests and articulacy. These characters represent real social groups: in *Waverley* the two heroines correlate, like the contrasting landscapes, with Scotland's opposed cultures, highland and lowland. Scott's novels are thus inhabited by historical people in real contexts. In a way, his plots could be faulted as too coherent – too much under the historian's control – and thus too parsimonious in allowing the characters freedom for organic development.

Scott's great innovation was to realize in fiction a whole community in process of change. In this his work, for all its involvement with romance, belonged very much to the Enlightenment. The complete societies he represented include people of every rank – all treated with equal seriousness, all participating in political crises (the 1745 Jacobite rebellion in *Waverley*; the Porteous riots in *The Heart of Midlothian*). This was only possible because of Scott's broad sympathies, wide legal experience and social contacts ranging from royalty to humble drovers. His stories of reconciliation offer metaphors of an exceptionally wide political import; just as his reconstructions of the past have real value as history. Nevertheless, the Waverley novels are valuable less for their politics than their invention of fictive worlds teeming with vivid life, bustling with particulars, enthralling with plangent moods.

Scott wrote modestly about the popularity of his novels, with their 'hurried frankness of composition which pleases soldiers, sailors, and young people of bold and active disposition'; but in fact he enjoyed an unprecedented European vogue. (This had something to do with his stories' suitability for transposition as operas.) The earlier novels, particularly those with Scottish settings, merit success, even if Scott is insufficiently committed as an artist to achieve much stylistically. In this phase, he uses English for educated or aristocratic characters, and wonderfully authentic Scots for the other ranks. But the later novels, some of them set in the English Middle Ages, are more uncertain in diction, and abound with spurious Walpolean archaisms such as 'methinks' and 'God wot'. Indeed, they bear a heavy responsibility for their influence in establishing the style known as 'tushery'. For Scott's example dominated the emergent historical novel, as well as historical adventure stories like Charles Reade's *The Cloister and the Hearth* (1861); until Robert Louis Stevenson set a new standard with *Kidnapped* (1886) and *Catriona* (1893) – both of them returning to Scott's theme of reconciliation. The retrospective impulse in the nineteenth century created a huge demand for popular history and historical fiction. But it was difficult to emulate Scott; and the historical romances that came immediately after his were subliterary (G. P. R James, William Harrison Ainsworth). Even Charles Kingsley failed, with his *Hypatia* (1853), and George Eliot (Mary Ann Evans) with her laboured *Romola* (1862–3).

A luminous exception is William Makepeace Thackeray's *Henry Esmond* (1852), regarded by Trollope as the 'greatest novel in the English language'. Thackeray's eighteenth century is as unlike Scott's as may be. *Henry Esmond* has little to do with politics; being rather a history of small, or peripheral, things ('private affairs'): the return of a riderless horse, a celebration *after* the battle of Ramillies. Thackeray's narrative is much more discontinuous than Scott's; which he conceals by presenting it as the recollections of Esmond. This device makes possible an impressive structural and emotional unity. It also allows subtlety of perspectives: Esmond Senior's train of thought can be counterpointed with that of his younger self, whose story he tells in the first–third person, intimately yet at a distance; and either can be further modified by interpositions of the memoirs' family 'editor'. Steeped like Scott in the eighteenth century, Thackeray chose to simulate historical authenticity by a very different method, that of PASTICHE. Throughout he used a style imitated from authors of the period – a patchwork of old words, idioms and syntactic forms – such that cameos of historical figures like Addison and Steele could be slipped in without discordance. Trollope called the pastiche 'flawless', and so it must at one time have seemed. (After all, Thackeray's own style was based on that of the eighteenth century.) But on this point judgement has altered with temporal divergence. *Henry Esmond* has also suffered criticism on political grounds, apparently through a misunderstanding of its aims. These include comparison of historical periods, to assess the moral gains and losses brought about by change. In his objective way Thackeray shows the old high sentiments and 'passionate fidelity' to be accompanied by manners less than ideal. But the reader is not meant to approve either, merely because they are approved by Esmond. In fact, Thackeray himself thought of Esmond as a 'prig'. *Henry Esmond* is a remarkable novel – one of the most complex ever written.

THE PROBABLE NOVEL: AUSTEN TO MEREDITH

One of the most expressive of all genres is the PROBABLE or realistic novel. In this genre, Jane Austen (1775–1817) was the first to achieve the accomplishment of high art. From the various possibilities represented by Richardson, Fielding, Burney and Edgeworth, she selected so surely that she gave the novel its classic proportions. Not that Austen's six novels set a pattern for her immediate successors – they were intent on exploring in other directions. But in the longer term the Austenian proportions have come to be the ones considered normal.

Already, in Austen, actions of consistent probability are set more or less in the present: little happens that is not likely to occur in ordinary life. Her people resemble real contemporary people. With the exception of a few minor characters, like Mr Collins in *Pride and Prejudice* (1813), they never display the exaggeration of Fielding's or Smollett's 'originals' or eccentrics. From among all the ordinary possibilities, however, Austen selects – and in this differs both from Richardson and from the Victorian novelists – only so many details as she can organize morally in a way that is both pleasurable and economical. She keeps description of externals to a minimum; so that anything depicted at length, like Donwell Abbey in *Emma* (1816), stands out and assumes a symbolic value. Similarly, she presents the action from the moral standpoint of a single heroine – who is not, however, the narrator. Moral discrimination ('sense') and emotional response ('sensibility') are, indeed, the main activities of the protagonist, as of the involved reader. For an Elizabeth Bennet, life consists of character developments. These come about through moral blunders occasioned by her construction of private illusions, into which self-realization breaks:

> She grew absolutely ashamed of herself. – Of neither Darcy nor Wickham could she think, without feeling that she had been blind, partial, prejudiced, absurd.
> 'How despicably have I acted!' she cried. – 'I, who have prided myself on my discernment! . . .'
>
> (*Pride and Prejudice* II.xiii)

Such moral action is only sparingly interpreted by the author, whose explanations in any case are often disguised as half-reported thoughts of Elizabeth's, or masked by irony. Consequently values tend to be expressed through tone, or through equally implicit clarifying examples. These the plot brings to full lucidity, and they are clinched in the closure, for those who have not understood earlier, by firm apportionment of destinies. Much is conveyed simply by selection of narrative material. When conversation has a larger place than dancing at the Netherton ball, that proportion corresponds to Elizabeth's experience, and indicates her preference.

If Austen's novels do not fully anticipate the novel of realism, was this because of limited vision? Because she was blind to large features of the world outside her small circle? I hardly think so. After all, the events of Hartfield and of Highbury make up a life, too. Austen certainly focuses on a single class (the small gentry, with a few aristocrats thrown in); but selection is perfectly compatible with realism. And her modest scale and economical description should not be allowed to hide the fact that in Highbury she achieves realistic continuity of place. Austen was in her way a child of the Enlightenment: her fictional people inhabit credible topographical, historical and economic contexts, complete with financial arrangements and relations between classes. Servants have a small part in her novels – she deprecated ostentation – but are mentioned in passing, by name. In *Pride and Prejudice*, a conversation with Mrs Reynolds the Pemberton housekeeper even constitutes a turning point of the action. Moreover, Austen was more than usually sensitive to changes in the society of her time.

What makes her achievement partly retrospective is something quite different. It is the same quality that makes her novels seem perfect: namely, their pervasive moral structuring. This keeps her from giving character development its head. Just occasionally one glimpses further potentialities; as in the way that the brilliant style of *Pride and Prejudice* rises to Elizabeth's buoyant spirits

> She had dressed with more than usual care, and prepared in the highest spirits for the conquest of all that remained unsubdued of his heart, trusting that it was not more than might be won in the course of the evening.
>
> (I.xviii)

– or in the way Emma's point of view informs her half-reported speech. But even in *Emma* moral schemes control everything that happens. Its edifying pleasures depend on one's seeing such patterns as the gradation in Emma's errors, or the resemblance between Mr Elton's charade and Frank Churchill's anagram, or that between the instances of art – Harriet's portrait, Jane's piano, the Donwell landscape.

Emma tends to be preferred to Austen's other novels for its psychological interest, or the complex false trails of its plot – or because its didacticism is relaxed to the extent of allowing a few merely characteristic details. But a case could be made for *Persuasion* (1818), with its inventive symbolic geography and the deeper resolution of its closure.

Austen's is a perfect, classic art. She completely satisfies her reader intellectually. Yet it seems not intellectual application so much as sheer integrity that has arrived at her superconsistent moral structures. Their communication is wholly delightful; since Austen's imagination consistently finds fresh ways of presenting them. In some things – notably representation of character-revealing speech – she has never been surpassed.

The novel now took a very different turn, towards unselective realism. Here I am not thinking of Benjamin Disraeli's (1804–81) social novels, in spite of their sharply extended range of new political and other topics, including issues like that of the two nations. A novel such as *Coningsby* (1844) has little of realism, being dominated by abstract schemes. Realism came only with a changed attitude; and this awaited the impulse of Carlyle's ideas about immanence of the ideal in the real, or of Ruskin's subsequent advocacy of naturalism. For Ruskin, the ideal was to 'write the things *which thou hast seen*, and the things which *are*' – to represent things in all their particular weaknesses and imperfection. But even such ideas of realist art might not have been enough, without the congenial example of early works by Charles Dickens (1812–70).

In *Pickwick Papers* (1836–7), *Oliver Twist* (1837–8) and especially *Sketches by Boz* (1835–6), Dickens introduced more detail of external objects than had even been attempted in fiction. *Sketches by Boz* even has a prolonged description of old clothes, with speculations, only partly facetious, as to the wearers who produced their signs of wear. Previously, a subject so low would have warranted at most a perfunctory comic treatment. But with Dickens, things of all sorts – an entire material world – began to throng into the novel. They came, at first, hesitantly. In *Oliver Twist* it may be no more than is needed to specify a gesture and so sustain character in being. Mr Bumble will complacently inflict 'two open-handed slaps upon his laced waistcoat' (the choleric beadle is never far from physical violence); or an impressive hat will remind us from time to time of his self-importance. Dickens gradually arrived at a method whereby he explored personality indirectly through costume and belongings – and made these a subtle means of communicating his discoveries figuratively. Doubtless the method derived from the emblematic attributes of the old allegorists. But Dickens applied it in a more experimental way, and by the stage of *David Copperfield* (1849–50) he was finding room for less necessary things, like odours: a chariot on a fine day 'smelt . . . like a stable put under a cucumber-frame', and hotel corridors 'smelt as if they had been steeped for ages in a solution of soup and stables'. Such details are validated neither as moral symbol nor as implication of character. Ostensibly authenticating the 'autobiography', they have their true *raison d'être* simply in substantiating a plausible fictive world.

By an apparently opposite tendency, *David Copperfield* also carries further the assimilation of story to point of view. Here Dickens attempts nothing less than organic coherence – comprehensive shaping in accordance with his narrator's standpoint. Thus, he uses the distancing effect of memoir – with its long narrative perspective – to suggest the remoteness of early phases of Copperfield's life. These are nevertheless internally connected: 'This reminds me . . .'. The method was not easy; and there are inconsistencies. For example the innocent boy's view ('For my own part, I looked on Mr Jack Maldon as a modern Sindbad') tends to be abandoned for the adult's, sometimes with a not quite satisfactory attempt to imitate confusion: 'I cannot say of what it was expressive, I cannot even say of what it is expressive to me now, rising again before my older judgement.' All the same, Dickens achieves some development of viewpoint. And he has great success in shaping the narrative to express Copperfield's experience; as in the vague feverish account of his intoxication under the influence of Steerforth (Chapter xxiv).

David Copperfield appeared at the same time with *Pendennis* (1848–50); and from then on Dickens was increasingly challenged by Thackeray. As realism became more conscious, and as its exponents gained confidence from Continental examples like Balzac and Flaubert, they tended to turn away from Dickens. Thackeray had more obvious intelligence, more deliberate art; his sophisticated realism was inevitably the next development. Yet he shared Dickens's sentimentalism, as well as his relish for the details of imperfect life. Indeed, Thackeray's *Paris Sketch Book* (1840) and especially *The Book of Snobs* (1846–8) broke new ground in minute particularization. His novels have fewer long descriptive passages than Dickens's; their more classic art keeps detail in proportion. But Thackeray's brief descriptions are telling. He seems to find room for far more things than Dickens – and all of them eloquent

as to their owners' pretentions. Such is the 'chaste splendour' of Lady
Clavering's drawing rooms that

> the carpets were so magnificently fluffy that your foot made no more
> noise on them than your shadow: on their white ground bloomed roses
> and tulips as big as warming-pans: about the room were high chairs and
> low chairs, bandy-legged chairs, chairs so attentuated that it was a
> wonder any but a sylph could sit upon them, marqueterie-tables covered
> with marvellous gimcracks, china ornaments of all ages and countries,
> bronzes, gilt daggers, Books of Beauty, yataghans, Turkish papooshes
> and boxes of Parisian bon-bons. Wherever you sate down there were
> Dresden shepherds and shepherdesses convenient at your elbow; there
> were, moreover, light blue poodles and ducks and cocks and hens in
> porcelain; there were nymphs by Boucher, and shepherdesses by
> Greuze, very chaste indeed . . .
>
> > (*Pendennis* I.xxxvii, par.13)

Thackeray's material objects subtly adumbrate a specific social world,
and place his characters with devastating precision – as Lady Clavering
is placed (not to her disadvantage) by her discomfort in the room just
described. He gives a balanced picture of mid-century life, such as
Dickens hardly attempted. Their methods contrast strikingly –
Thackeray's accurate proportions and Dickens's exaggerated realization; realism of normality and realism of immediacy.

Thackeray's negligent art, which his contemporaries at first greatly
admired, poised Fielding's against Richardson's. Subtly ambiguous
and marvellously fluent, it was also, however, intermittently defective;
so that it suffered a reaction not altogether attributable to the offence
given by *Vanity Fair*. It is now inadequately appreciated, even by
sympathetic critics. Its ambiguities, some of them very brilliant, affect
much of the narrative. For example Pen, having spent a third of his
money on joining a club, calls on Major Pendennis and is relieved to
find him

> not yet returned to town. His apartments were blank. Brown Hollands
> covered his library-table, and bills and letters lay on the mantel-piece,
> grimly awaiting the return of their owner.
>
> > (*Pendennis* I.xxviii)

Grimness no doubt appertains to all bills, in the mind of a young man
so financially apprehensive as Pen; but one suspects it may just as well
characterize the Major's feelings about the debts of which he is the
'owner'. Thackeray's oblique narration allowed him endless probing

into unacknowledged motives, endless analysing of society's inconsistencies. Not infrequently the analysis went to reductive lengths, and
disturbed early readers by its cynicism. Anything can make an ironic
point in Thackeray: even his narrator's silences. So Miss Fotheringay's
worthless conversation is casually dismissed – 'need surely not be
reported'.

Thackeray extends his art into style, to a degree rare among novelists.
For example, his facility in pastiche and parody enable him to match
style to content in various ways. He can reproduce a letter of Miss
Fotheringay's without overdoing it, or contrive to introduce Captain
Costigan with the hint of an Irish bull – Costigan is not

> a very eligible companion for youth; but there are worse men, holding
> much better places in life, and more dishonest, who have never
> committed half so many rogueries as he . . .
>
> *(Pendennis* I.v, par.31)

Most remarkable of all the aptnesses must be his expressive shaping of
syntax. A good example is the long sentence describing vexations
occasioned by Pen's infatuation – 'While Mrs Pendennis is disquieting
herself about losing her son . . . – while the Major's great soul chafes . . .
– while Pen is tossing . . . – Mr Smirke has a private care . . .' (ch.xvi,
par.14) – where the syntactic suspensions not only simulate the
maternal 'anxious hold,' and mirror frustrated impatience, but have the
effect of keeping Mrs Pendennis and Mr Smirke apart, at sentence
length from one another. Other Victorian novelists used similar devices,
but none so frequently; it was from Thackeray that Henry James at first
learnt to shape his great mimetic style. Thackeray's example, indeed,
dominated the art in almost every way. George Eliot was not alone in
thinking him 'on the whole the most powerful of living novelists'.

Whether or not Dr Leavis was right in calling Thackeray 'a greater
Trollope', one cannot call Anthony Trollope (1815–82) a lesser
Thackeray – although he revered no one more. Trollope learnt from
Austen also (especially to select externals, and compose lucid thematic
structures). And he had qualities of his own. His particular note is to
concentrate on the agonizing of characters, as they try to extricate
themselves from the toils of social pressures – like the Warden between
the militants Grantly and Bold – or from conflicting demands of
conscience. Trollope's characters are intelligibly coherent like Austen's,
only more deeply shaded. They seem firmly planted, in a society
realized with unusual continuity. Trollope explores through an
extraordinarily wide social range; even if his main coverage is of

conservative gentry and those less privileged who nevertheless share their principles.

At first Trollope wrote about the rural south, in such novels of imaginary Barsetshire as *The Warden* (1855), *Barchester Towers* (1857) and (the most serious) *The Last Chronicle of Barset* (1867). Then increasingly he turned to the metropolitan world of politics and great houses, in such Palliser novels as *Can You Forgive Her?* (1864) and *The Prime Minister* (1876). Eventually he focused directly on the sordid London scene, in *The Way We Live Now* (1875). In both the former groups, Trollope made characters interact frequently and reappear throughout the series; so that he showed the possibilities of the ROMAN-FLEUVE, or sequence of semi-independent novels, better than Thackeray.

Trollope has a special way of taking you into his confidence about the story; sometimes directly revealing matters unknown to the characters themselves: 'Our story will perhaps best be told by communicating the letter to the reader before it was discussed with Lily.' This informal, deliberately awkward method, which acknowledges fictionality in a way Henry James greatly disliked, is often disparaged as a weakness. But it can be a strength. In *The Last Chronicle of Barset*, it frees readers from Crawley's tragic world where circumstances' necessity crushes, and coaxes them into the very different viewpoint of the novelist. In fact, Trollope's relaxed directness hides art while seeming not to. Art also underlies the many unobtrusive stylistic variations. And even where Trollope seems most loosely irrelevant – in tangential love plots or descriptive set-pieces – 'extraneous' material will often prove to be obliquely illustrative; as with the emblematic hunting scene in *Can You Forgive Her?*

Trollope is interested in his characters' complicated social code (which he sees as reconciling gentry and middle class values); but the existential struggles it occasions interest him even more. He makes characters like Crawley, Grantly as father, or Melmotte the Jewish financier undergo experiences that obviously elude the provisions of the code – which in any case he never allows to define individual interactions. Sharing his master's hatred of sham, Trollope uses Thackeray's attacks on the privileged, in order to generate dramatic conflicts. But he finds ways to do fuller justice to the gentry, by allowing them to answer for themselves. Often he tests social codes experimentally. Drama will arise, in a typical Trollopean family conflict, from an instance of upward mobility, or when a strong father like Wharton in *The Prime Minister* resists his daughter's wish to marry a Lopez, outside their class or race. Or someone will take a proud stand on principle, with consequences quite unforeseen. Ultimately, however, the code will be vindicated, even if also qualified. So it must be; since in Trollope's view it is based on moral principles derived from many Anglican centuries. Trollope is not perhaps very religious. But his intensely serious *The Last Chronicle of Barset* (in which even Mrs Proudie undergoes tragic modulation) at least shows him sensitive to the possibility of worldliness. Worldliness is here the subject of an authorial homily.

The Barsetshire novels may be too idyllic. Trollope at first underestimated the extent of economic change, and significantly ignored the industrial north. This changed dramatically in *The Way We Live Now*, with its exposure of the credit world, its pervasive symbols of financial dishonesty, its atmosphere of doom. Here the Tory squire, Carbury, is displaced; and his acceptance of personal change presages many others. There is no happy ending. But, for the most part, Trollope's calm is unruffled: a gentleman can always find the right decision. He sees as far as reflection discerns, and lacks the psychological insight to see further. All the same, his benevolence extends to an astonishing variety of characters. His fifty or so novels, many of them successful, represent a formidable *oeuvre*.

The work of George Meredith (1828–1909) intimated new directions for the novel: it would not be ridiculous to regard him as an early modernist, even if the modernists themselves largely rejected him. Few reputations have fluctuated more – from early recognition to neglect to overpraise (after *Diana of the Crossways*, 1885) to excessive reaction. This may have to do with his strenuous intellectuality and advanced views on a range of new topics. (A high level of abstraction allowed treatment of taboo matters; while his restless interests extended to such unlooked-for ideas as a post-industrial age.) Not all of these topics are very convincingly fictionalized. Nevertheless, Meredith's achievement endures. His feminism, which issued in credibly intelligent female characters, once seemed tendentious, but has now emerged as humane and reasonable. And his intellectuality – the 'brainstuff' that his formidable essayist–narrator adds to the mere 'drab' naturalism he distrusted – has come to contrast less sharply with the easier content of other novelists, as all, with the lapse of time, become more difficult. As the limitations of modernism itself appear, the relevance of Meredith returns.

Historically, Meredith's significance is great. He experimented with extended description as a language for psychological exploration: notably in the landscapes of *The Ordeal of Richard Feverel* (1859) and the view from the window in that great chapter of *The Egoist* (1879), 'Clara's Meditations' –

> After a fall of tears . . . she dressed herself, and sat by the window and watched the blackbird on the lawn as he hopped from shafts of dewy sunlight to the long-stretched dewy tree-shadows, considering in her mind that dark dews are more meaningful than bright, the beauty of the dews of woods more sweet than meadow-dews. It signified only that she was quieter. She had gone through her crisis in the anticipation of it. That is how quick natures will often be cold and hard, or not much moved, when the positive crisis arrives, and why it is that they are prepared for astonishing leaps over the gradations which should render their conduct comprehensible to us, if not excusable. She watched the blackbird throw up his head stiff, and peck to right and left, dangling the worm each side his orange beak. Speckle-breasted thrushes were at work, and a wagtail that ran as with Clara's own little steps. Thrush and blackbird flew to the nest. They had wings.
>
> (ch. xxi, par. 21)

E. M. Forster's criticism, that Meredith lacks tragic insight into the scenery of England, is beside the point. Meredith uses landscapes primarily to reflect his characters' deeper feelings; and his aims in this are exploration and resolution, not tragic absolutes. He frequently surprises by his penetration into unconscious contents, well before Freud. Thus, Clara suffers a psychogenic headache, and makes revelatory errors (several times confusing, or fearing to confuse, 'Oxford' and 'Whitford'); while Sir Willoughby is motivated by a profound fear for his infant self. Time and again Meredith succeeds in fixing fugitive states of mind with psychological precision – as when Rosamund in *Beauchamp's Career* (1876) 'detected herself running in and out of her nature to fortify it against accusations'. And at times he even anticipates the possibility of stream of consciousness narration.

Meredith's downfall, yet also his glory, lies in his opaque, magniloquent style. Even Henry James (grand master of difficulty) complained of its 'tortuosities'. A high style like James's own, or Conrad's, it constantly strains after impossibly rich effects, brilliantly conceived but irreconcilable: mimetic, ironic, generic. (Certain passages of *The Egoist* are consistently elegiac, others aphoristic.) One can never forget that Meredith was a poet. Yet he loved abstracts, and lavished elaborate extended metaphors on them, in sentences harder to construe than Latin. Small wonder that he came to be a high-brow novelist – an early instance of this possibility. He cared too little that his style could be so obtruse as to dissipate momentum.

Yet he succeeded locally in developing Thackeray's mimetic syntax: what has been taken for mere straining for emphasis can sometimes be organic form. Thus, a sentence repeatedly extended mimes the phased opening action of a telescope:

> A man, increasing in length like a telescope gradually reaching its end for observation, and coming to the height of a landmark, as if raised by ropes, was rising from the ground beside him.
>
> (*Beauchamp's Career* ch.xx)

Or an elusive predicate may disclose itself piecemeal, like the view – 'the prospect was partly visible, as the unknown country becomes by degrees to the traveller's optics on the dark hill-tops' – and turn out to have been there all the time ('visible').

These examples come from *Beauchamp's Career*, where Meredith achieves similar effects on a larger scale, by shaping the plot. Chapter xlvi offers a simple instance, when Tuckham's proposing marriage fails to be narrated in its chronological place; so that the reader shares with Beauchamp the stunning effect of Cecilia's refusal – 'it is too late'. Meredith can produce marvellous surprises; he can write comic scenes worthy of the author of *An Essay on Comedy* (1897); he can innovate technically (as in his interweaving of scraps of different conversations); and he can attempt everything at once, beyond the imagination of previous novelists. His decisive selection of 'internal history' almost arrives at the modernist novel of minimal plot. And in various ways he anticipates (of whom could one say as much?) both D. H. Lawrence and Henry James. Yet Meredith lacks measure; and sometimes only the saving grace of humour rescues him from ignominious failure. He offers ideas and glimpses of the complete novelist, but not the whole thing itself.

Meredith's style, fine though we must acclaim it to be, is too often overrefined, overblown, over the top. But then, style is not the strongest element of the novel generally. Dickens's style, although vivid, is often crude, repetitive, or unsatisfactory in rhythm. Trollope's is clean and lucid, yet its transparent colourlessness tends to be a little dull. George Eliot's can sometimes be great, but more often seems heavy and hard to read. In the end it is Thackeray's style that stands out. He may be guilty of ramshackle sentence structure; and his authorial comments may sometimes be pathetically weak; but at heart his style is the best of any Victorian novelist.

VARIOUS REALISMS

'Realism' is a slippery term, in this as in other spheres. Victorian novelists could attempt to carry it further in at least three distinct ways. Most obviously, they could aim at objective realism of content; offering fresh detail or addressing new areas of experience, so as to approach a fuller representation of life. They could take in, in their empirical way, such 'novel' matters as the conflict of faith and doubt, or any of a number of social aspects of more specialized interest. Thus, the novel became a chief source of society's dawning awareness of itself as an organism. No neglected topic seemed more shockingly real, in this sense, than the condition of the labouring class, which Dickens began to explore, almost like an anthropologist, in *Sketches by Boz* (1835–6) and *Oliver Twist* (1837–8). He made it a chief subject of *Hard Times* (1854), a work of strong conviction, which energetically expresses Carlylean anti-mechanism, yet signally fails to bring home the realities of Coketown's industrial scene with any immediacy.

So far at least as vivid realization was concerned, Elizabeth Gaskell (1810–65) succeeded in going much further. Her *North and South* (1855) puts the industrial north decisively on the literary map:

> For several miles before they reached Milton, they saw a deep lead-coloured cloud hanging over the horizon in the direction in which it lay ... Nearer to the town, the air had a faint taste and smell of smoke; perhaps, after all, more a loss of the fragrance of grass and herbage than any positive taste or smell. Quick they were whirled over long, straight, hopeless streets of regularly-built houses, all small and of brick. Here and there a great oblong many-windowed factory stood up, like a hen among her chickens, puffing out black 'unparliamentary' smoke.
>
> (ch.vii)

Even earlier, Gaskell's *Mary Barton* (1848), formed though it is within a romance matrix (with a plot from *The Heart of Midlothian*), already insists on its sordid *mise en scène*. It never flinches from remorseless portrayal of the details of injustice, poverty, class hatred and slum conditions. These it makes the setting for proletarian devotion:

> Heaps of ashes [i.e. faeces] were the stepping-stones, on which the passer-by, who cared in the least for cleanliness, took care not to put his foot ... The smell was so foetid as almost to knock the two men down. Quickly recovering themselves, as those inured to such things do, they began to penetrate the thick darkness of the place, and to see three or four little children rolling on the damp, nay wet, brick floor, through which the stagnant, filthy moisture of the street oozed up ...
>
> (ch. vi)

Paradoxically, Gaskell's determination to deliver the real facts at first restricts her realism; since her indignation leads her towards documentary – or breaks out of fiction altogether, into didactic exhortation: 'it is for you to judge'. Yet care for her characters establishes itself, in the end, and comes to matter more than facts about the other nation or vivid *reportage*, moving though these can be. Gaskell's forte is truth of feeling. This communicates itself not only in pathetic scenes (which convince even as one recognizes their designs on the emotions), but also in portrayals of general social conditions. She treats labour relations as having naturally an emotional dimension: an obvious thing to do, once she has done it.

But this is to move to a different realism – the realism of normality. That realism is better exemplified in *Wives and Daughters* (1866), Gaskell's finest novel. Here she achieves a fuller fictional realization by rendering life in its ordinary proportions, within a setting defined not only in terms of class, but of provinciality. It is the sort of realism in which Thackeray and (somewhat later) George Eliot reach the heights of greatness. Their expansive novels have room for slack intervals as well as packed variety. They present life in its quotidian measure, clarified by thematic patterns but undistorted by any exaggerated emphasis. Thackeray implies this conception of realism in his famous letter to David Masson in 1851; contrasting it with his rival's different conception. He quarrels with Dickens's

> *Art* in many respects: which I don't think represents Nature duly . . . The art of novels *is* to represent Nature: to convey as strongly as possible the sentiment of reality . . . In a drawing-room drama a coat is a coat, and a poker a poker; and must be nothing else according to my ethics, not an embroidered tunic, nor a great red-hot instrument like the Pantomime weapon.

Thackeray's approach by no means excludes symbolism, but tends to keep it unobtrusive; subordinating it to the ordinary consciousness of common everyday life.

No one will think Dickens devoid of realism: his mature work is profoundly true to life's pattern. But in the main he pursues the real by a third and quite different route, that of heightened feeling. He aims at realism of intensity rather than typicality, and concentrates on moments of strong passion, such as may open up the depths of experience. These significant moments tend to have symbolic value, like the discovery after the storm in *David Copperfield* of Ham's and Steerforth's bodies embracing in death. Eloquently yet indirectly, this moving image displays the insignificance of enmity, in the face of death. (Such a moment tends to blur moral discrimination; so that the wish to reconcile fidelity and promiscuity remains unexamined.) In Dickens's later work, he uses symbolism to expose underlying connections, and so to arrive at a coherent view of society's operations. This may involve exploring abnormal psychology through symptomatic objects (split personalities often appear in Dickens as individual equivalents of the social power structure). Or it may call on Allegory to disguise direct generalization.

No one could miss the allegory in *Our Mutual Friend* (1864–5); but it also abounds, although a little less obviously, in *Great Expectations* (1860–1), Dickens's greatest novel. When Pip discovers that his wealth has all along derived from Magwitch, allegory is giving him a chance to learn about the guilty origin of wealth in general – just as Estella's paternity should teach him about consciousness of rank. And Jaggers's Pilate-like handwashing, symptomatic though it may be of psychological traits, is as allegorical as anything in Spenser or Bunyan – whom Dickens's Moralities often resemble.

The tendency towards overt symbolism can also be seen in contemporaries of Dickens – particularly in novelists of emotional realism such as Charlotte and Emily Bronte. Theirs was a realism of passionate moments. So intense was it that it demanded expression through emblems of the heart: through the language, even, of dream.

Some may object that all this talk of realism assumes the novelists to be reporting on an objective 'real world'. And it must be admitted that Victorian reality was often by way of being a consensus – one that few would now wish to endorse. It has become usual to dwell on the gaps in the novelists' reality: on their conventions, their collusions of class, their conspiracies of silence. However morally edifying this emphasis may be, it has little value from a literary point of view. No one will understand the Victorian novelists who fails to do justice to their faithfulness in following every turn of life with the patience of a Constable or a Ruskin. Gaskell's slums, Dickens's prisons, Trollope's financiers: these were not the result only of following conventions, but of determined adherence to truth. Such efforts of realism might involve departing from the official consensus. Indeed, Trollope's *The Last Chronicle of Barset* calls in question the basis of Christian society itself. Besides, the 'classic realist novel' of the theorists has never actually existed. Even Trollope continually interrupts the flow of consistent fictional 'reality' – and means to do so.

MULTIPLOT NOVELS: DICKENS AND ELIOT

Comparison with Thackeray shows that Dickens was the less complete artist; so that his claim to be the greater seems to rest on such qualities as the energy of his symbolic realism. Yet on a broader view one can see that Dickens's art was creative enough to develop form after form subsequently found useful. Among these, the most significant is probably the MUTIPLOT NOVEL, the large expansive novel with several plots. The extraordinary device of telling several stories at once had precedents in Le Sage's picaresque, with its romance insets narrated by main-plot characters, and in Scott's historical romances, where doubling of heroes continued the breakup of classical unity. But Dickens was probably also led to multiply plots through the exigencies of serial publication. This called remorselessly for new material, and made it necessary in any case to evoke the fictive world afresh each month. Switching plots and characters challenged the same skills as picking up the threads of the monthly part or shaping it towards a memorable cadence. Perhaps the multiple plot novel was in part a solution of practical difficulties. In his 1837 Preface to *Pickwick Papers* Dickens protested that 'no artfully interwoven or ingeniously complicated plot' could be expected in the 'desultory' serial form. But in later prefaces he spoke more confidently of interweaving the different plot lines into tapestries with a 'whole pattern'.

In this idea of a holistic pattern lay a deeper origin of Dickens's multiplot genre. Like the medieval *romanciers* with their labyrinthine *entrelacements* he pursued a comprehensive image of life's mystery; juxtaposing, in his individual plots, complementary or even disparate facets. Henry James might call such novels 'large loose baggy monsters', and compare their unclassical form to that of a gothic building 'by no Vitruvian symmetry subdued'; nevertheless, like medieval romances they had their own poetic, based on multifarious connections. Thematic links between the plots are the most obvious of these. No one fails to notice that each plot in *Bleak House* (1852–3) has a detective exploring a mystery – a mystery of human nature withheld from most men. And in *Little Dorrit* (1855–7), who can miss the imprisoning appearances, the deceptions, the self-deceptions? Here, the connecting pattern is set out in an elaborate allegorical genealogy. Other links relate the individual Books of the novel – like the analogy between Dorrit's literal and metaphorical imprisonments. And coincidences, as in Blandois's recurrences, offer a further type of connection. Far from being mere defects of probability, these should be thought of as points of juncture, making allegorical statements. In the undervalued *Our Mutual Friend* (1864–5), plot links reach a peak of intricacy, with symbolism intensified to the excited state of allegorical romance. Nevertheless, the novel has also some of Dickens's best minor characters, and is far from lacking in specificity.

Such allegorical contents belong to a deeper level than the narrative; so that they may help to make sense of its apparent contradictions and irrelevances. In *Bleak House*, for example, Esther's story and that of the narrator are not irreconcilably plural. Their different perspectives contribute, rather, to a stereoscopic view more illuminating than either would have been on its own.

The student of Dickens may at first be surprised at how provisionally he planned – how much he could bring himself to alter at an advanced stage, sometimes in response to the reception of earlier numbers. Nevertheless the number plans show that he increasingly planned ahead (sometimes in new ways, like the one glimpsed in the self-instruction 'tone on'). Complex articulation had to be provided for, to communicate such ramifying world-visions as the universal prison of *Little Dorrit*, or the 'labyrinth of grandeur' – charitable and uncharitable – of *Bleak House*.

In this organizing, Dickens's generic model (apart from *The Arabian Nights*) was the romance. Its echoes sound in countless notes: in Radcliffean suspense (not originally a feature of novels); in delayed naming of characters; in confused relationships and their revelation; in spatial effects like the convergence of characters in *Little Dorrit*; in pathetic cadences like Lady Dedlock's withdrawal to die; and in descriptions of ancient places as focuses of symbolism. Jarndyce's neogothic establishment

> was one of those delightfully irregular houses where you go up and down steps out of one room into another, and where you come upon more rooms when you think you have seen all there are, and where there is a bountiful provision of little halls and passages, and where you find still older cottage-rooms in unexpected places, with lattice windows and green growth pressing through them.
>
> (*Bleak House* ch.vi)

Images of goodness and beauty are offset by ugly or horrible foils, just as in romances – but with the vast difference that Dickens relishes the ugliness.

He was not alone in this: a taste for the ugly characterized all the arts at mid-century. And this had a profound effect on the expansive novel, making it burgeon with local irrelevances. People, however meanly unpleasant, and places, however grim and sordid, came to be included for their own sake – simply for their vitality. Dickens took this realistic tendency very far: characters like the hyperbolical Boythorn, the combustible Krook, or Miss Flite the gentle lunatic are more alive than life itself.

Romance origins show up still more obviously in Emily Bronte's *Wuthering Heights* (1847). This may not seem a multiplot novel, since the two Catherines' stories follow one another in a single chronological sequence. But the narrations – Lockwood's, Nelly's and Zillah's – are interwoven into a complex fabric such that the two plots in fact develop concurrently, and analogously. The later plot, however, concerns experience lived at a more ordinary pitch: more refined, more restrained, more repressed. Catherine Heathcliff's cousins, one crude and the other weak, correspond only in a muted way to Catherine Earnshaw's loves, Heathcliff the child of dark nature and Edgar the responsible dutiful spouse. Both sets of values have their positives and negatives. Wuthering Heights, for all its fires of passion, is a prison to the second Catherine; just as the first Catherine feels a prisoner at civilized Thrushcross Grange (which has warm fires too). But the symbolism of such details as Catherine Earnshaw's lattice window proves to be elusive; apparently because Emily Bronte focuses exclusively on emotions. This enables her to express the passions of family life more intensely even than Dickens. However, she lacks his power to relate them directly to their social context: in *Wuthering Heights* the community dwindles to mere vestigial symbolisms, or becomes revealingly conspicuous by absence altogether.

Wilkie Collins's *The Woman in White* (1860) also combines romance with novel. Again, different chronological stages of one intricate plot are presented in stories of a minute though selective realism. And again a process of inquiry gradually disentangles the stages. But here melodrama is even more predominant. Gothic morbidity takes an overtly criminal shape, so that the inquiry eventually becomes a matter of external detection. Collins has nevertheless great suggestive power. In particular, his atmospheric, strongly visualized scenes can exert a haunting compulsion:

> As I walked down to the lake, I saw that the ground on its farther side was damp and marshy, overgrown with rank grass and dismal willows. The water, which was clear enough on the open sandy side, where the sun shone, looked black and poisonous opposite to me, where it lay deeper under the shade of the spongy banks and the rank overhanging thickets

and tangled trees. The frogs were croaking, and the rats were slipping in and out of the shadowy water, like live shadows themselves, as I got nearer to the marshy side of the lake. I saw here, lying half in and half out of the water, the rotten wreck of an old overturned boat, with a sickly spot of sunlight glimmering through a gap in the trees on its dry surface, and a snake basking in the midst of the spot, fantastically coiled, and treacherously still.

> (*The Women in White* Number xii)

Collins's sinister atmospheres have remained convincing in a way not generally the case. Despite some lack of economy, he has an impressive ability to orchestrate different elements, in such a way as to sustain deep psychological intensities. He well deserves his gradual revaluation.

In the greatest of all multiplot novels, *Middlemarch* (1871–2), George Eliot took the genre in a very different direction. Here the multiplicity has little to do with romance or allegory. It is a correlate, rather, of multiple centres of consciousness. 'Scenes which make vital changes in our neighbours' lot are but the background of our own.' *Middlemarch* has two main plots, because it has two main characters. And Eliot goes further still: 'Why always Dorothea?' she asks; and turns to Casaubon, who also has 'an intense consciousness'. This idea of multiple centres finds famous expression in her analogy of random scratches on a pier-glass, which seem concentric around any centre of illumination:

> It is demonstrable that the scratches are going everywhere impartially, and it is only your candle which produces the flattering illusion of a concentric arrangement, its light falling with an exclusive optical selection. These things are a parable. The scratches are events, and the candle is the egoism of any person now absent – of Miss Vincy, for example.
>
> (ch. xxvii)

For Eliot, multiplying perspectives means multiplying individual points of view – and consequential reciprocities – until an elaborate web of relationships results. The method is impressively objective but unwieldily cumbrous. Her expansive novel extends full treatment to dull minor characters like Mary Garth, some of them 'loobies' or clownish people, for whose inclusion the author apologizes in a tone embarrassing to her modern admirers. Nevertheless Eliot really is fond, like Dorothea, of 'ugly people': she delights in the 'truthfulness . . . in many Dutch paintings', and has a keen eye for 'that element of tragedy which lies in the very fact of frequency'.

This broad sympathy helps to make her one of our most exploratory novelists. She determinedly investigates the consequences of provinciality throughout many variations, such as Dorothea's limiting marriage choice; Lydgate's medical career (traced in careful detail); or the contrasting pushes of Ladislaw, who like many German Romantic painters escaped to metropolitan Rome. These explorations are interpreted in powerful authorial generalization; for Eliot is also one of the most intellectually ambitious of novelists. Instead of narrative links, she provides continuity in her authorial person, herself comparing the various plots and presenting them as graduated examples of the same life process. More implicit meaning is by no means lacking in the rich tapestry of *Middlemarch*. (It even has mythological strands, as when Ladislaw plays Bacchic sun god to Dorothea's Ariadne.) Nevertheless, one may well think that Eliot's authorial comments do too much for her reader – make too much overt.

Middlemarch tells so much about Dorothea that its reticence about her sexual experience has offended some. For example, only discreet imagery of a bird-soul 'fluttering in the swampy ground' indicates that Casaubon's inadequacy takes the form of prematurity (not impotence, as many assume). And Dorothea's sexual feelings for Ladislaw are almost entirely omitted. But this results from a limitation of Victorian society. So far as such limitations allow, Eliot observes with subtle penetration – most subtly of all, perhaps, in *Daniel Deronda* (1876). Here she achieves even more detailed realization, at the cost of a certain ponderousness in analysis. It seems she must log the most minute passages of feeling between Gwendolen and Grandcourt – 'character too is a process and an unfolding'. Certainly Grandcourt's languid self-containment invites prolonged analysis. And Eliot shares the Princess' scorn for 'cut and dried' talk about motives; so that she will sometimes alternate lines of speech with whole paragraphs of comment: 'the little pauses and refined drawlings with which this speech was uttered, gave time for Gwendolen to go through the dream of a life'.

The complicated thematic patterns of *Daniel Deronda* are matched by branching relationships of the sort that Mab rightly thinks 'something wonderful may be made of'. Many of these depend on a contrast between Gwendolen's self-seeking match and Deronda's selfless, originally compassionate, love for Mirah. But there are also many fleeting comparisons, of a more subjective nature; as when Gwendolen within a few moments sees Deronda first as in 'one group with' the displaced Mrs Glasher, and then as a judgemental arbiter like Klesmer. In this labyrinth of analogies the reader must depend heavily, again, on the author. And she, unfortunately, is not unbiased enough to refrain from attributing qualities (particularly to Mirah) without realizing them in narrative.

But at her best, Eliot often penetrated beyond moral analysis to deeper intuitions of great value. She showed how to take minor characters seriously. She carried authorial comment to a more demanding height than ever before. And altogether she did much to put the novel on a new intellectual footing.

OTHER NOVEL GENRES

The panoramic *Vanity Fair* (1847–8) might have been considered as a multiplot novel, interweaving the stories of Becky and Amelia. Thackeray the great remembrancer here multiplies plots in order to recapture experiences of varying degrees of innocence, which would otherwise be inaccessible to him. But *Vanity Fair* also belongs to a different genre, the POIOUMENON or self-begetting novel. This focuses on the author's dramatized persona as much as on the story. Indeed, the narrator of *Vanity Fair* might be called its principal character. He knows most of the others; although, as a character, his information cannot be depended on absolutely. He is always liable to intervene with unpredictable items of information, brutally settling doubtful points, perhaps, or else unsettling them, undermining authenticities – 'I have seen it, and can vouch' (that Dobbin's pinup is not like Amelia); 'it was at that very table years ago that the present writer had the pleasure of hearing the tale'. Thackeray flirts with the responsibilities of omniscience, even while his narrator flaunts a light untrustworthy indifference to facts. He will throw out crucial information *en passant*; allow us to think Dobbin engaged to Miss O'Dowd; conceal the slightest hint of Becky's marriage to Rawdon before its sudden disclosure; and let the reader judge her adulterous with Burjoice, only to add 'But there was nothing in the story'.

In *Vanity Fair*, many discontinuous episodes or brief insets, often ranged in contrasting pairs, demand to be ordered. One has to compose them into a complete narrative – and may be caught doing so prematurely. The author can always choose to disclose, from his omniscience, a further unsuspected irony; as in the famous closure of chapter xxxii: 'Amelia was praying for George, who was lying on his face, dead, with a bullet through his heart.' Thackeray leaves the contrasting careers of Becky and Amelia unconnected causally, and so makes them subject to 'arbitrary' decisions. How are we to think of them? The imagined reader 'with a pretty little handwriting' may find Amelia 'insipid' – an attitude dramatized when the Osborne sisters depreciate her too. But in her passivity Amelia may express disinclination to love seriously, just as Becky expresses active self-seeking. When at the end Amelia reveals that she has already written to Dobbin, Becky instantly exits: her striving is no longer necessary, her selfishness no longer appropriate.

No Victorian novel has been so generative of modern progeny as *Vanity Fair*. It has been widely emulated, and recognized to be a profound as well as a brilliant masterpiece. Nevertheless, its theme of a fundamental contrast between scheming and feeling may, in the end, be considered too vague, too facilely protean.

Thomas Carlyle (1795–1881) was Thackeray's immediate predecessor as charlatan–narrator. *Sartor Resartus* (1833–4) has been treated as autobiography; and beneath much swaddling it certainly hides an account of Carlyle's own conversion from scepticism ('the everlasting No') to a passionately theistic faith in man's duty to respond to the spiritual universe:

> Be no longer a chaos, but a world, or even worldkin. Produce! Produce! Were it but the pitifullest infinitesimal fraction of a product, produce it, in God's name! 'Tis the utmost thou hast in thee: out with it, then. Up, up! Whatsoever thy hand findeth to do, do it with thy whole might. Work while it is called Today; for the Night cometh, wherein no man can work.
>
> (Book II, ch.ix)

Nevertheless, *Sartor Resartus* addresses questions of human identity at large, not of personal history. And structurally it belongs to the genre of *Tristram Shandy* – a work Carlyle frequently alludes to. Its chief character is another author, Professor Diogenes Teufelsdröckh (God-born Devil's-dung), a stalking horse for Carlyle to hide behind as he shoots out wild conjectures or radical extremities, before moderating them in his capacity as narrator–editor.

'*Sartor Resartus*' means 'the tailor patched', the patches being a harlequin-garment of loose sheets – inset narratives; imaginary 'papers'; notes on this and that nonexistent book; Teufelsdröckh's biography; his loose papers and slips in paper bags; and above all his 'clothes-volume' setting out a philosophy of experience as the vesture of spiritual life. Multifarious fragmentary components like these typify the self-begetting novel. So do arbitrary schemes like the zodiacal classification used for Teufelsdröckh's paper slips. Any scheme will do as scaffolding, to help begin, to bridge the void, to construct thoughts about the unthinkable. For Carlyle attempts to penetrate to naked truths of man's place in history and the universe.

Any resemblance of *Sartor Resartus* to essays, or the essayistic novels of Peacock, is thus superficial. Carlyle has far more philosophic and prophetic models in mind, stylistic appearances sometimes to the contrary. His style, indeed, grotesquely mingles Sterne with the Authorized Version, manically inverted sublimity with maniacally self-referring irony. The irony serves as self-protection, like much of the satire and vilifying journalism that Carlyle aims at the nation's masochism. It is secondary to his determined effort to get beyond the 'clothes' of institutions – beyond the nation's psychological defences.

In this, despite self-deceptions of his own, Carlyle went further than most of his contemporaries. Stuffed with German ideas, ready to think about almost anything, Carlyle was a formidable figure. (His opinions can seem astonishingly timeless; partly because of the high level of generality on which he worked.) But even he could not know how much he achieved in *Sartor Resartus*. Long neglected (it remained unpublished in book form in Britain until 1838), it was to furnish modernism with a fictive model, as well as an authoritative text for the philosophy of realism.

Nathaniel Hawthorne's *The House of the Seven Gables* (1851) could also be seen as an early poioumenon. In it, Hawthorne follows Sterne in deliberately limiting his realism (in one direction) by intermingling it with much palaver about how the story should be told, or with interplay between its events and the fancies of the narrator. Thus he describes Hepzibah's and Clifford's flight as 'the flight of two owls', and later has the 'story now betake itself, like an owl, bewildered in the daylight, and hastening back to his hollow tree'. Similarly, the narrator has no sooner finished 'indulging our fancy in this freak [caprice]' of ancestral ghosts than Holgrave in the story also indulges the notion that 'the old Pyncheons were running riot in the lower rooms'. Indeed, the daguerreotypist (himself an 'artist') repeatedly serves as a surrogate of the novelist (himself an imitator of 'types'). In one sense *The House of the Seven Gables* simply dramatizes the writer's contemplation, as he looks, out of the natural house of seven ages, at an emergent world of new types. (The vantage point is a central 'arched window' poising Clifford's perspective against Phoebe's, the degenerating against the developing and vital.) This is all hindsight, however. What one now sees as self-begetting fiction Hawthorne himself would, like Henry James, have thought of as elegiac romance.

In the manner of a romance writer, Hawthorne works together

strands of the stories of its seven or so types – Phoebe's with Holgrave's, that of the ruined aristocratic Clifford with that of the humbled trader Hepzibah. Yet he does not so much interweave stories as move at will from one narrative scrap to another. This extremely selective discontinuity – he foccuses more arbitrarily even than Thackeray – will prove his most creative legacy to James and the modernists.

James does not indeed go the whole way with *The House of the Seven Gables*. He detects an unfulfilled expansiveness in the 'magnificent fragment', as well as a certain static quality. Its people are less characters than figures, or pictures: each is 'a charming piece of descriptive writing, rather than a dramatic exhibition'. One might add that, although Hawthorne's work is compelling, the worlds of implication surrounding its trivial events rather tend to indefiniteness. At times they mean little more than the 'something symbolic' projected in one of Hawthorne's notebook entries.

Hawthorne's *The Blithedale Romance* (1852) mingles romance with realistic material of a political nature; and so does Charlotte Bronte's *Shirley* (1849), with its portrayal of industrial unrest in Yorkshire and its bold expressions of feminism. Victorian literature was remarkably productive of such mixed genres. Romance could not only be combined with realism, but also modulated towards allegory – as in Meredith's glorious *Adventures of Harry Richmond* (1871). This traces its protagonist's development to mature identity through a symbolic BILDUNGSROMAN or narrative of upbringing. Similarly, Hawthorne's *The Scarlet Letter* (1850) is so thoroughly allegorical as almost to amount to a fable of guilt and blame. Such symbolic romances could take strangely obscure forms. For example James Hogg's powerful *Confessions of a Justified Sinner* (1824) has a narrative so schizophrenic that the objectivity of some of its events is still controversial. In these and kindred works the element of fantasy was pervasive. It was no coincidence that in the nineteenth century there also proliferated overt fantasies and fairy tales. In a work like Charles Kingsley's *Water Babies* (1863), the fantasy was explained or justified by didactic contents. But in George Macdonald's remarkable *Phantastes* (1858) and *Lilith* (1895), it took off into interior space. Using Hoffmann and Novalis as points of departure, Macdonald explored to astonishing psychological depths; anticipating now the typology of C. G. Jung, now the parables of the modernist Franz Kafka.

By contrast, the fiction of Thomas Love Peacock, from *Headlong Hall* (1816) to *Gryll Grange* (1860), mixed very sketchy romance with satire, taking a direction that would eventually lead to the essayistic novel of Aldous Huxley. Peacock's novels consist mostly of witty conversation;

the conversation mostly of satiric pastiche. This can be very funny – as when Mr Flosky (Coleridge) is asked for a plain answer:

> I never gave a plain answer to a question in my life . . . To say that I do not know, would be to say that I am ignorant of something; and God forbid, that a transcendental metaphysician, who has pure anticipated cognitions of every thing, and carries the whole science of geometry in his head without ever having looked into Euclid, should fall into so empirical an error as to declare himself ignorant of any thing . . .
>
> (*Nightmare Abbey* (1818) ch. viii)

Throughout the century, romance and novel made an axis. From the tensions between them, or from their intermediate amalgamation, many developments in fiction arose. And what developments the period saw! Probable realism, selective representation, thematic relation between multiple plots, the self-begetting novel, the symbolic romance: all these were additions (or readditions) to fiction in the nineteenth century.

THE SKETCH TO THE SHORT STORY

Another great innovation was the SHORT STORY – a development in which the influence and counterinfluence of American literature acted as stimuli. The short story had at least two origins, corresponding to its main types. One, which needs no explanation (and, indeed, eludes criticism) is ordinary storytelling. As Richard Steele said, 'a storyteller is born, as well as a poet'. Literary storytelling issued in the TALE, often set within a frame situation or narrative, and characterized by effects of temporal perspective, such as the sense of remoteness from which the narrator recalls events long past. The other type of story, less dominated by plot, originally took its departure from the semi-fictional essay. Addison's essays had sometimes built on a fable or anecdote; and in the hands of a Lamb or a De Quincey essay became evocative sketch or MEMOIR (account based on memory). Here the crucial innovation, neglected by historians, was to think of the SKETCH (descriptive study) as a suggestive fragment. From this followed the important idea of the resonant story.

Washington Irving's *Sketch Book* (1819–20) – particularly the sketches on English topics, with their leisurely development and neat, lucid style, may recall the Addisonian essay. But at times Irving has more evocative warmth. And a story like 'Rip van Winkle', told with sly ironies, achieves some resonance. Dickens's *Sketches by Boz* (1835–6), although they borrowed something from Irving, took a decisively different turn, which was long to determine the course of realism. They made a great impact. Offering an urban equivalent of Mary Russell Mitford's *Our Village* (1819, 1824), they surveyed the whole London scene, and brought to half the citizenry a revelation as to how the other half lived. Dickens's sketches may not be very smooth in style (despite occasional imitation of Addison); but they bounce energetically from one bold improvisation to another, in a way that holds the attention pleasurably. They live, above all, in their descriptive details. These reach an altogether new minuteness of visual characterization:

> It was quite a little feast; two ounces of seven-and-sixpenny green, and a quarter of a pound of the best fresh; and Mr Wilkins had brought a pint of shrimps, neatly folded up in a clean Belcher . . .

> two young men with very long hair, to which the sleet has communicated the appearance of crystallized rats' tails . . .

> the coachman . . . in a rough blue greatcoat, of which the buttons behind are so far apart, that you can't see them both at the same time.

Everything jostles for space with the next bit of information. The narration is vivid, and the description tells a story or makes a point, even when it fails to contribute to the unity of the whole. Without attempting history, Dickens nevertheless drew on his early experience with precision; the sketch was for him more than a way of working up material for novels.

John Earle's *Microcosmographie* (1628) and Thomas Fuller's *Worthies* (1662) had set precedents for linking 'characters' together in sets. In the nineteenth century, sketches were similarly linked to make an aggregate – a genre unlabelled then, but resembling what is now called WHOLE BOOK FICTION. In such a work the individual sketches share the same communal setting, and perhaps the same narrator; but hardly amount to a novel, since they are not dominated by a single action. The genre was dimly apprehended. Mary Russell Mitford wished for a novel without incident; and Galt regretted that his *Annals of the Parish* was received as a novel at all. (He meant it as a fictional memoir, or even, in an Enlightenment spirit, as 'a theoretical histor[y] of society', without plot and with only lightly sketched characters.) Mitford's *Our Village* (1819, 1824) has a Romantic narrator with intimate feelings for nature, who relishes her impressions of village life. She has an eye for wholesome 'Dutch' descriptive details. But she uses them to establish mood, or even to generate associations: in 'Frost and Thaw', the 'naked and colourless beauty' of frost-covered oaks occasions thoughts of death.

John Galt's *Annals of the Parish* (1821) has more narrative. He subdues his unified style, like everything else, to the artless viewpoint of a country minister close to his dotage but still capable of surprising shrewdness. Galt's own vision was international; when he renounces any sophisticated perspective on an issue like the American rebellion, he does so deliberately, for a sly purpose. Under such treatment, the most trivial matter, however pungent with locality, can achieve suggestive power, becoming 'a type and index to the rest of the world'. *The Provost* (1822) is almost as good as *Annals of the Parish:* Galt has rich resources of language, and is a much underestimated writer. These and certain other of his novels and stories sharing the same locality have been regarded as composing the first *roman-fleuve*.

Perhaps the finest memoir sketch collection is *Cranford* (1853), Gaskell's most finished work (unless one counts her short story 'Cousin Phyllis'). The parochial triviality of what passes for incidents at Cranford does not mean that perspective is lost; since the young narrator belongs not only to a different age group but to another town. Moreover, Gaskell comes to terms in *Cranford* with her own memories; so that the past constantly interplays with the present, giving point to description of manners and suggesting the nostalgic refreshment of country life. The spinsters of Cranford win sympathy as well as respect; their oddities and limitations arouse a little more pathos than amusement.

Another sketch collection − surely the most brilliant of all − is Thackeray's *The Book of Snobs* (1846, 1848). Here Thackeray adopts a consistently ironic mode, so that his observations amount to a satiric anatomy of philistinism and pretension and orgulous mediocrity, of every sort and in every walk of genteel Victorian life. The pleasure of *The Book of Snobs* derives partly from its style's perfect control − whether exercised in turns of bewilderingly subtle irony or in economical description. (Dickens might have taken a paragraph to describe what Thackeray gets into a phrase in 'the great banging, swinging cab'.) Partly, though, the pleasure lies in the work's sparkling scene. Thackeray's artist's eye takes it in whole:

> At six o'clock in the full season, when all the world is in St James's Street, and the carriages are cutting in and out among the cabs on the stand, and the tufted dandies are showing their listless faces out of 'White's', and you see respectable grey-headed gentlemen waggling their heads to each other through plate-glass windows of 'Arthur's': and the red-coats

wish to be Briareian, so as to hold all the gentlemen's horses; and that wonderful red-coated royal porter is sunning himself before Marlborough House; – at the noon of London time, you see a light-yellow carriage with black horses, and a coachman in a tight floss-silk wig . . .

(ch. xxxiv)

The Book of Snobs is a relatively neglected work that has long delighted all who know it.

Turning to the other type of story, the tale, one finds that Dickens's abundant short fiction, such as the various sets of Christmas stories, has also been passed over; apparently because it runs counter to the conventions of the modern short story. He contents himself with unhurried, uneconomical plot development, and (anathema to modernists) affects archaic chapter-divisions. But narrative in the oral tradition has its own rationale. And Dickens's chapters sometimes form groupings of great interest, in which story leads on to story in irresistible profusion. Or the tales may be presented, in the manner of framed collections, as 'branches' – like the three branches of *The Holly-Tree* (1855) or the branch lines of *Mugby Junction* (1866). Often a realistic frame-narrative envelops the miscellany of loosely connected stories (some of them perhaps by other writers). The genre has been connected with Dickens's favourite *Arabian Nights*. But its retrospective art also looks back, in an equally unclassical but more indigenous way, to the story collections of the Middle Ages, with their disregard of authorship.

In the Christmas stories Dickens explores in many directions. One of these is writing about writing. Many of the stories concern a writer, either directly or, periphrastically, in terms of his books or papers (mysteriously abandoned in *Somebody's Luggage*, 1862). In another direction, Dickens experiments with transitions and connections. The stories may connect with objects in previous stories ('His Boots'); be inset as vignettes; or interlace so intricately as to raise questions of fictive status. Similar experiments are attempted in sketches he contributed to *Household Words*, such as 'By Rail to Parnassus' (1855; Henry Morley collaborating) with its counterpoint of reading and travelling. Dickens's use of limited narrators leads to other ventures, such as the indirect reported speech of dramatic monologues like 'The Boots', Second Branch of *The Holly-Tree*:

> Where had he been in his time? he repeated, when I asked him the question. Lord, he had been everywhere! And what had he been? Bless you, he had been everything you could mention a'most!
>
> Seen a good deal? Why, of course he had. I should say so, he could assure me, if I only knew about a twentieth part of what had come in *his*

way. Why, it would be easier for him, he expected, to tell what he hadn't seen than what he had. Ah! A deal, it would.

But it would be wrong to see the Christmas stories only as experiments. Some are classics in their own right – notably 'The Signalman' (1866), a tale of the supernatural which is all the eerier for its up-to-date setting.

In his relaxed narration, Dickens resembles other Victorian short story writers, such as Mrs Gaskell or Wilkie Collins. Collins's pace is positively lingering. After gradually evoking mood he will eventually approach a dramatic incident, and focus it in striking visual images – like the silent cutting away of Franval's nightshirt in 'The Lady of Glenwith Grange'. More briskly introduced, such a scene would have been far less effective. Nowadays the anecdotal tale tends to be slighted; but it has its own qualities, which are distinct from those of the modern or unified short story. Besides, even on modern assumptions, this type of tale has the interest of underlying the perspectival narration pursued by Stevenson and Conrad.

The work of one practitioner of the expansive short story points forward in another way: Margaret Oliphant (1828–97). Although Oliphant was also a prolific novelist obliged to overproduce, she perfected a type of story less dependent on melodrama. Indeed, in certain of her extremely varied supernatural tales, such as 'The Secret Chamber' (1876) and 'Earthbound' (1880) – a ghost story interpretable in terms of sexual psychology – she looks forward to Henry James. At her quiet best, when she managed to avoid slackening of tension, she achieved a singleness of purpose, a freedom from plot and a consciousness of style that carried the expansive story to a new level.

Movements towards the unified short story began as early as the 1840s, with the work of Edgar Allan Poe (1809–49). Poe's authoritative stories, reinforced by his vehement theorizing, influenced every subsequent writer. He directed attention to the possibility of reading a short story 'at one sitting'. Everything in it should go to establish

> a certain unique or single *effect* to be wrought out . . . In the whole composition there should be no word written, of which the tendency, direct or indirect, is not to the one pre-established design.
> (Review of Hawthorne's *Twice Told Tales* in *Graham's Magazine*, May 1842)

In practice, this means simplifying plot to a single melodramatic line, neglecting character, concentrating on a protagonist's sensations in extreme circumstances and directing everything towards a strong closure.

Poe partly achieves momentum through simultaneity; as when, in 'The Cask of Amontillado' (1846), a descriptive datum, nitre on the walls, serves concurrently as the occasion for a feigned – and ominous – anxiety about Fortunato's health. Dramatic ironies like Montresor's mason's trowel abound; so that one is held in suspense as to whether the revenger will feel remorse, or go through with the revenge – or end in madness. The best effects are of a subtler order. What makes Montresor's hair stand on end is not only fear of Fortunato's going mad, but fear of his own madness – portended throughout by the story's manic tone. A final detail, the jingling of Fortunato's bells, recalls his foolishness, and resonates with Montresor's own more sinister madness.

So far as style is concerned, Poe's stories are not only meant to be read at a single sitting, but seem also written at one. (Only the callousness of foreigners to atrocious prose can explain his high reputation in France.) All the same, he impresses by his power to evoke the macabre. Story after inventive story achieves a unique 'effect': 'The Pit and the Pendulum' (1843); 'The Murders in the Rue Morgue' (1841); 'William Wilson' (1839); and 'The Fall of the House of Usher' (1839), with its unforgettable opening –

> During the whole of a dull, dark, and soundless day in the autumn of the year, when the clouds hung oppressively low in the heavens, I had been passing alone, on horseback . . .

– already containing the conclusion's storm. Some of Poe's stories suggest a *Blackwood's Magazine* tale of sensation that has been worked over for extra unity. But 'The Fall of the House of Usher' attempts something rather more complicated. Besides being a gothic novel in miniature, it has double closures (the Ushers' deaths; the splitting of the house) which invite reflection on their symbolic connection.

Poe's theory was based on the work of a more profound writer, Nathaniel Hawthorne (1804–64). And Hawthorne went further than Poe in unifying his stories through extreme selectivity. In one story, indeed, 'The White Old Maid' (1835), he selects so rigorously that one is left to surmise almost all the circumstances explaining the incident narrated. Even in 'My Kinsman, Major Molineux' (1832), one has to infer what the lady of the scarlet petticoat intends; why the rioters' ringleader has a party-coloured face; and why Robin joins in the laughter against his kinsman. Hawthorne is sometimes said to be ambiguous, to the extent of leaving the reader to make the meaning. And certainly in this story one experiences some of Robin's bewilderment. But in reality its pregnant gaps open up because the author has omitted all but the parts presenting his theme. These are enough to make clear that Robin undergoes initiation into a society no longer dominated by family connections – one where he learns to take protective coloration and become himself 'double-faced'.

Hawthorne's especial contribution to the genre was in the element of ideas. Not that his stories have detachable allegories: as one of his narrators says, when challenged for a moral, 'I can never separate the idea from the symbol in which it manifests itself'. But every detail in Hawthorne seems to issue from a continual revolving of the ideas suggested by his symbols.

This exploration became increasingly sceptical. At first, seeking an alternative to the inaccessible 'English' novel (which America lacked the social development to sustain), Hawthorne returned to the semi-fictional essay–sketch. This genre was hospitable to speculative trains of thought and even to transitions governed by ideas. His early work in it is grave yet lacking in intensity; and sometimes, as in 'The Ambitious Guest' (1835), the broadly allegorical narrative seems slight. But gradually the best stories – such as 'Egotism; or, The Bosom Serpent' (1843); 'The Birthmark' (1843); and 'Rappaccini's Daughter' (1844) – come to strike a fine balance between narrative and argument. These powerful stories brood on fundamental aspects of the human lot, like original sin; sometimes revaluing them (but never reductively) in terms of morbid psychology. They sometimes take up suggestions from Hoffmann or others; but always to make them more profound.

Hawthorne deals with individual experience as a 'type' of society's secret disquiets. Thus, in 'The Minister's Black Veil' (1836) he meditates on what it may be that separates men in their collusive privacies. Every incident touches on another aspect of this central emblem, the concealing veil, with its hint of some 'ambiguity of sin or sorrow.' Consider, for example, the cause of the minister's solitariness. The veil confessed that his persona concealed part of himself. This his fiancée (who intended to share his whole life) could not accept; and it so challenged the community that he became totally isolated. Hawthorne's ideas, deep as they are, have found aptly enigmatic embodiment, and spring to fresh life with each rereading.

The longer works of Herman Melville (1819–91), especially his great naive epic *Moby Dick* (1851), never found wholly appropriate forms. But in his shorter fiction, where he could learn both from Dickens and from Hawthorne, Melville achieved results not only compelling but shapely. He strenuously worked for effects of enigma; and these are still much analysed. That is notably true of 'Bartleby the Scrivener' (1853), which may be regarded as standing between Hawthorne's 'The Minister's Black Veil' and Kafka's 'The Hunger Artist', in a line of studies of sad isolation. (Melville was himself a depressive.) The individual Bartleby refuses a falsely communicative society: he 'prefers not' to communicate, and so effectually commits suicide by silence. Nevertheless his rejection of the impersonal social order, represented by his *alter ego* the lawyer, remains ambiguous. Was he depressed by the human condition, brought home to him by working in the dead letter office? Or by losing his job there? (Melville writes merely that 'he had been suddenly removed by a change in the administration'.) Ambiguity is throughout exuded from a certain unresolved vagueness of irony. Yet Melville, unlike Hawthorne, often steers towards a crude naive allegory, and may turn out ambiguous only because he is disinclined to analyse it and make it consistent. This may be said even of *Benito Cereno* (1856), a mysterious tale with a moral as cloudy as the atmosphere of the opening description. Melville's method is to leave the meaning undiscussed, beneath a beautiful, elaborate, highly wrought surface narrative:

> The sea, though undulated into long roods of swells, seemed fixed, and was sleeked at the surface like waved lead that has cooled and set in the smelter's mould.

This story's ambiguity lies in a relatively simple irony. The idealistic Captain Delano's illusions about the blacks are totally refuted – yet have saved his life. As for the allegory underlying this compelling surface irony, it remains undeveloped.

After Melville, the American short story continued to thrive, but on a lower plane. Bret Harte (1836–1902) favoured a type of frontier tale with a narrator distanced by education but still susceptible to sentimentality. Another genre of tale, concealing an oblique content behind the simplicities of a black narrator, Uncle Remus, was cultivated by Joel Chandler Harris (1848–1908). As for Ambrose Bierce (1842–?1914), he had both wit and art; but his Civil War stories, brilliant as they seem, are circumscribed by sardonic pessimism. His disgust with war predetermined macabre 'surprise' endings which, however effective, tend to be too predictably neat. The popular O. Henry (W. S. Porter)(1862–1910) accepted the limitations of coincidental symmetries and plot formulas dictated by magazine publication; although he contrived highly inventive variations. Finally, Stephen Crane (1871–1900) had great journalistic powers, and might have done much; but died young. Except for Robert Louis Stevenson (1850–94), there is no short story writer in English to compare with Maupassant or Chekhov, until one comes to Henry James.

The greatness of Stevenson has been obscured by reaction against his personality cult, as well as by the unusual nature of his *oeuvre*. For he avoided the novel, and took up light popular genres like the adventure. On these he lavished an artistry normally reserved for the highest kinds alone; so that his *Treasure Island* (1881–2) and *Kidnapped* (1886) have become classics, but classics disregarded, for the most part, by the academic establishment. Or else, as in *The Strange Case of Dr Jekyll and Mr Hyde* (1886) and *The Beach of Falesá* (1892), he devoted himself to the NOVELLA or long short story with several episodes – again a genre that has come to be neglected.

Nevertheless Stevenson was a narrative genius. His art included certain generalizable principles. He himself acknowledged that he pursued singleness by making every element work together to produce a living scene. (There is little mere description in his stories, for example.) This was to be a vital legacy to the age that followed. Something of his fascination can also be attributed to the atmospheric specificity of details like the clocks in 'Markheim' (1885), or the devil's appearing as a black in 'Thrawn Janet' (1881). The latter detail was not invented *ex nihilo*, but found in the course of research into seventeenth-century witchcraft; and similarly thorough preparation helped to give several of his stories their soundness and quiddity.

But such points hardly begin to sum Stevenson's narrative qualities. Far less can they be expressed in terms of prose style; although he is perhaps our finest narrative stylist (always excepting James). It might take one further to examine Stevenson's care to subordinate style to narration – a care not always evidenced by James or Conrad. Stevenson's art, in fact, is an art of pure narrative. He manages all other aspects (including plot), and shapes them plastically together, in accordance with the changing needs of the story itself. In 'Markheim', for example, the devil would be far less frightening if his entry were not preceded by unidentified steps on the stair – which in turn had been prepared for by detailed treatment of sounds. Art has gone before every minutest point. When to paint with broad strokes, when in miniature, when to be all fizzle and multiplicity, when slow and lyrical, when ordinary, when special in imitation of some turn of the story: all this and more Stevenson had learnt from Balzac, and above all from Flaubert. Following their examples assiduously, he took narrative in English to the height of art. At a critical historical juncture, he gave a decisive stimulus to the short story, a genre that became strategic for modernism.

13
Modernist Fiction

W HAT most critics call early modernist literature belongs in many
ways to a separate phase (1890–1910) as distinct from what
followed as from what preceded. Characterized by Pater's idea
of literary form as a detailed structure allowing no room for the casually
considered, it had a quite new concentration. This was the age of James
and Wilde and Yeats. They and their ablest contemporaries carried the
Victorians' lyric transformations further, and made more of their detail
expressively significant. But they did not depart from the broad
proportions of the genres, as they had been set in the period before.
Rather was their writing new – 'modernist' – in its formal compression,
its radical criticism of society and its comprehensive address to
tradition. Their Continental ideas about literary form, however, were to
lead on to still more thorough-going changes.

THE BEGINNINGS OF MODERNISM

Thomas Hardy (1840–1928), although a very great novelist, had little to
do with avant-garde movements, and was content to use traditional
genres without obvious change. His novels, all written before 1900, are
Victorian novels. But they make at least two fresh departures. First, they
set rural values against newer developments, chronicling changes with
an evident sympathy for the passing order. They express a deep sense of
loss – indeed, are set in a tragic mode to a quite un-Victorian extent.
Nature in them is a relentlessly determining order, trifled with at man's
peril.

In *Tess of the d'Urbervilles* (1891) Hardy offers a realization of rural
Wessex (Dorset) quite as full as George Eliot's of Middlemarch, yet
without her moral analysis of character. His people have few choices in
their helpless struggles with a tragic necessity. (He may have been
overvalued because his reaction against moral individualism is now

congenial.) Nature in *Tess* appears as a powerful presence, manifested by the strong physicality of fertile meadow and summer fogs (chapters xix and xx), as well as by the minutely detailed seasonal round of labours like milking. The mode in fact is sometimes as much georgic as tragic: Hardy's imagination is strongly visual, and his landscape descriptions reach the acme of satisfying richness. They are more sensuous than Meredith's, truer than Lawrence's. Nor is this description limited to PATHETIC FALLACIES, attributing characters' feelings to nature. Hardy's nature – like the indifferent sea of Stephen Crane's 'The Open Boat' (1898) – has its own disposition, conveyed at times in disturbing images:

> ... the whole field was in colour a desolate drab; it was a complexion without features, as if a face, from chin to brow, should be only an expanse of skin. The sky wore, in another colour, the same likeness; a white vacuity of countenance with the lineaments gone. So these two upper and nether visages confronted each other all day long, the white face looking down on the brown face, and the brown face looking up at the white face, without anything standing between them but the two girls crawling over the surface of the former like flies.
>
> (*Tess of the d'Urbervilles* ch. xliii)

Or a gap in the clouds will be 'a piece of day left behind by accident'.

Hardy's novels are poetic – and this is his second departure from the Victorian norm – to the extent that they incorporate description into their thematic structures. Their details are seldom merely realistic, but perform other functions simultaneously. So, in the Durnover section of Casterbridge,

> wheat-ricks overhung the old Roman street, and thrust their eaves against the church tower; green-thatched barns, with doorways as high as the gates of Solomon's temple, opened directly upon the main thoroughfare.
>
> (*The Mayor of Casterbridge* ch.xiv)

This is vivid enough, just as description; and at the same time it is continuing the topic of ancient survivals, hinting at the theme of justice, perhaps alluding to Solomon's wives and suggesting that some in Casterbridge make a religion ('temple') of their wealth. Such simultaneity, in which everything seems to be multiply connected and to contribute at the same time to a single aesthetic effect, gives the reader great pleasure. Hardy's style is sometimes flawed; but this hardly matters beside his inspired orchestration of disparities. In the combining of various elements the mind of an architect is wonderfully evident. Yet

Hardy's method, of simultaneity through concentration, was to become highly characteristic of modernism in general.

The novels of E. M. Forster (1879–1970), with their humanistic, omniscient narrators, are deliberately old-style works: solid and congenial – and too easily interpretable. *Howard's End* (1910) does not lack concentration. Everything in it is there for a reason – even Margaret's father's sword. Only, the reason is a little too evident; so that the thematic patterning comes to seem manipulative, verging on the allegorical. An interesting attempt has been made to draw modern complexities from *A Room with a View* (1908). But in the end perhaps only *A Passage to India* (1924), with its light delicate transcription of manners, escapes the charge – by now a grave one – of unambiguously overt symbolism. Nevertheless, although Forster was overrated in his own time, his quiet style has an undeniable appeal. In his Victorian way, he had a sharp eye for flaws in the Edwardian social fabric. And – what is rarer and of more permanent value – his novels and stories express an unwaveringly firm sense of the distinction between selfish and generous feeling.

At another extreme from Forster were a group of writers in whom conscious art issued in an over-refined style – George Moore (1852–1933), Oscar Wilde (1854–1900) and Max Beerbohm (1872–1956). Of these, Beerbohm is still enjoyable. His delicious *Zuleika Dobson* sustains its exquisite tonality through every verbal nuance; although it misses an answering content. Wilde was the most substantial, in spite of his paradoxical fireworks – 'vice and virtue are to the artist materials for an art'; 'when critics disagree the artist is in accord with himself'. Some of his provocative aesthetic doctrines (for example, that life imitates art) have become dogmas of our own age.

HENRY JAMES

In turning to the expatriate American Henry James (1843–1916) we approach a commanding figure capable of resuming the whole art of the novel – particularly of the line through Thackeray, George Eliot and Meredith – and of anticipating much of modernist and even neo-modernist art. He is the greatest novelist in the language, and one of our greatest writers of prose. In the course of a long and fascinating development he mastered the portrayal of a vast gallery of characters (although not that of a consentient woman). He learnt to subdue plot to his secret design – as witness the expressive turns of the conclusion of *The Spoils of Poynton*. And he became adept at realizing place (Oxford;

Paris; the Venice of *The Wings of the Dove*; the London of *The Golden Bowl*) – an element in his work that miraculously grew more convincing, as more sparing. It depended, like all his masterly description, on the precise observation (but also on the composition) of a visual artist. And the same strength underlay his firm architectural structures, with their intricate plans of framing arrangements – images and vistas, scenes and passages.

James's style seems effortless (except when the matter is inherently difficult); lucid; noticeably exact; inexhaustibly varied. It is a big style, however, and can make an obstacle for those not yet Jamesians. A style of precision, discrimination and fine qualification, it is a style of truth. Its concentrated simultaneity makes it unquestionably modernist; yet it may also be considered as a culmination of the lyric transformation traced in the last chapter.

In particular, mimetic effects of syntax, such as Thackeray occasionally hazarded and Meredith strained for, are generated by James (at least in his later phases) with a facility that has no parallel. From *The Spoils of Poynton* (1897) onwards, he moulds his syntax so that what it signifies grammatically is expressed also by its shape. To take a simple instance, in 'Everything at Poynton was in the style of Poynton' repetition simulates formally the extreme uniformity being described semantically. Similarly, in 'nothing but to hold', abbreviation of the usual 'nothing for it but to hold' amplifies the absence of recourse.

Such effects are carried furthest in *The Golden Bowl* (1905), James's most demanding work, beset with *doubles entendres* and ambiguous connections:

> But what had briefly checked his assent to any present, to any positive making of mystery – what had made him, while they stood at the top of the stairs, demur just long enough for her to notice it – was the sense of the resemblance of the little plan before him to occasions, of the past, from which he was quite disconnected, from which he could only desire to be.
>
> (Book I, Pt i, ch.5)

Here, the parenthesis itself demurs long enough for noticeability. And the last phrase of all, with its bare termination 'to be', confirms the renunciative simplicity of the Prince's desire to be 'disconnected' (the elided word); while at the same time ambiguities are opened up by the stress thrown on 'desire'. Much of the pleasure of James's style arises from the aptness of this extraordinary accompaniment of meaning. Yet, remarkable as it is, mimetic syntax counts as only one device. In imagery, texture and proportion, the style is almost equally formidable.

How was James to put his great style to use? Certainly not in the service of ideas: as T. S. Eliot said, 'he had a mind so fine that no idea could violate it'. James devoted his art to an interminable analysing, through fiction, of emergent forms of virtue. These he displayed through (or, more often, by contrast with) the morality and social manners of representative characters. Still, his work has several more specific subjects, such as the so-called 'international theme' of *The Europeans* (1879), *The Ambassadors* (1903) and many other stories, in which American and European 'types' – characters of increasingly subtle shading – interact so as to highlight fine moral discriminations. Another subject, the responsibility of the artist, appears in James's novels as early as *Roderick Hudson* (1876), and in many short stories, like 'The Lesson of the Master' and 'The Figure in the Carpet'. It is one subject of an obscure novel *The Sacred Fount* (1901), in which endless speculations about observed behaviour may stand for the imagination's continual enhancement and valuation of life. Sometimes, too, James will play off several subjects against one another like mutual symbols, as he does with love and death in *The Wings of the Dove* (1902).

Already in *Portrait of a Lady* (1881), art and love relate in this way – so consistently, indeed, that something approaching an allegory emerges. Thus, Isabel Archer (representing imaginative vision) could have found fulfilment with Caspar Goodwood (business activity) or Lord War-burton (political expression), but instead is united with Gilbert Osmond (stylish dilettantism: '"he's the incarnation of taste"'; '"I'm convention itself"'). A union of this 'sterile dilettante' with the smooth 'artist' Madam Merle has issued in the (brain-)child Pansy (*pensée*), whom Osmond sees as 'a precious work of art' and brings up in a restrictively conventional way. It is almost an allegory of how too much art and taste restricts creativity. But it gives a false impression to talk of patterns so schematic. In James, even moral distinctions – let alone abstract symbolisms – are mediated through tones of an experiencing sensibility. All is deeply implicit, only occasionally becoming luminous in an obvious way. What we are aware of – what the symbols illuminate – is the tragic spectacle of Isabel: the large-minded woman stifled by marriage to a tyrannical selfish husband, a small-minded, retentive coin-collector incapable of matching her warmth – a man who could only 'tap her imagination with his knuckle and make it ring'. Several of James's novels have elements referable in this way to writing, although not generally to the writing of the novel itself.

During his last phase James radically altered his fictive method, in such a way as to exclude authorial intervention. In fact he introduced two new methods, very different yet with results in common. One is the celebrated method of his greatest novels – *The Wings of the Dove* (1902), *The Ambassadors* (1903) and *The Golden Bowl* (1904) – where he goes further than Flaubert and presents the entire action from the point of view of characters, especially a sympathetic main character, whose sensibilities filter and colour it.

What *The Ambassadors* shows is mostly seen through the confusion of the protagonist, the mature, morally sensitive, yet innocent Strether. Peering through that medium the reader slowly grasps, or perhaps comically fails to grasp, life's secrets of giving. But Strether's expanding view is obviously not quite that of James himself, who was a good deal less innocent. The joke is on Strether, in fact, when he does more than justice to the effects of love on Chad. Yet his discovery of the intrigue – and of its deeper motives – marvellously renders the shifting perspectives of love. James allows characters the scope of self-consistent worlds: they freely occupy their own narrative centres. This generates a vivid realism that catches the very tone of life.

At times James switches, in effect, into STREAM OF CONSCIOUSNESS (his brother William's phrase, in a non-literary context), in which a character's thoughts and impressions are given *in extenso*, without external narrative or authorial comment. In *The Wings of the Dove*, when Milly Teale learns from her physician that she is mortal, she has to be alone in her vulnerability:

> No one in the world could have sufficiently entered into her state; no tie would have been close enough to enable a companion to walk beside her without some disparity. She literally felt, in this first flush, that her only company must be the human race at large, present all round her, but inspiringly impersonal, and that her only field must be, then and there, the grey immensity of London. Grey immensity had somehow of a sudden become her element; grey immensity was what her distinguished friend had, for the moment, furnished her world with and what the question of 'living', as he put it to her, living by option, by volition, inevitably took on for its immediate face ... she had been treated – hadn't she? – as if it were in her power to live; and yet one wasn't treated so – was one? – unless it had come up, quite as much, that one might die. The beauty of the bloom had gone from the small old sense of safety – that was distinct: she had left it behind her there for ever. But the beauty of the idea of a great adventure, a big dim experiment or struggle in which she might more responsibly than ever before take a hand, had been offered her instead.
>
> (Book V, ch.iv)

The words express or paraphrase Millie's thoughts; yet the style is James's. It is appropriate to her centre of consciousness, but in a specially direct way, in that its emphases can unambiguously show (rather than merely attempt to define) what the novelist thinks the character's experience inwardly to be. In this instance, the style brings out a certain generality of experience, a universality, that is not only Millie's thought, but also the quality James sees in it.

The second method James introduced, at first in *The Other House* (1896) and *The Awkward Age* (1899), was the dramatic. This gave dialogue in full, with minute notations of tone and gesture, but no further narration or author comment. James had serious ambitions as a dramatist, and he took endless trouble with these elaborately exquisite stage directions. Both methods, it will be noticed, had the momentous effect of eliminating (almost) the authorial role. This role had been growing more difficult and burdensome as psychoanalysis began to complicate the understanding of motive, and as gaps widened between official morality and aesthetic interests. Both methods, moreover, increased the appearance at least of ambiguity. James's tones of life, however easily they may escape moral categorization, remain intensely moral. His centres of consciousness are 'finely aware and richly responsible'. But when the reliability of the narrator is suspect, as notoriously in *The Turn of the Screw*, for example, intractable ambiguity can result.

Ambiguity also arises in James's fiction from its extreme selectivity. He selects in the interest of inwardness: expansive, even opulent as the late novels may be, they omit external detail to an unprecedented degree (justifying, to some, a charge of narrowness). In this, as in much else, James carries the novel back towards the romance, its genre of origin. By a device learnt from Hawthorne, he avoids telling his story directly. Instead he suggests it, by assuming the relationships and attitudes, the entire world, in which it must be taking place, for these to make sense. The reader's task is to piece together a story that squares with the characters' states of consciousness. The gradual apprehension of it, like their gradual arrival at thoughts, is the sense of life itself. James never altogether abandons omniscient narration (why should he?); but he avoids using it to make things unnaturally easy for readers.

One can see a model of the process (although a faulty one) in *The Golden Bowl*, in Fanny Assingham's labyrinthine imaginations of Maggie's story. It is only natural, since what we have to work on is so suggestive, and since James's treatment of subsidiary centres of consciousness is so generous, that different readers should arrive at distinct stories. Some see Charlotte and the Prince as becoming, in the end, the Ververs' victims, their possessions. But these terms seem too gross for the delicacies that the novel approaches; and, in any case, lovers commonly possess and are possessed. One issue may be whether Maggie and the Prince can learn generosities of love beyond their present conceptions, in time to save their relationship. The relationship itself, the flawed bowl of their marriage, is abundantly realized, in the nuances of its frail potentialities:

> 'It isn't a question of any beauty,' said Maggie; 'it's only a question of the quantity of truth.'
> 'Oh, the quantity of truth!' the Prince richly, though ambiguously, murmured.
> 'That's a thing by itself, yes. But there are also such things, all the same, as questions of good faith.'
> 'Of course there are!' the Prince hastened to reply. After which he brought up more slowly: 'If ever a man, since the beginning of time, acted in good faith –!' But he dropped it offering it simply for that.
> For that then, when it had had time somewhat to settle, like some handful of gold dust thrown into the air – for that then Maggie showed herself, as deeply and strangely taking it. 'I see.' And she even wished this form to be as complete as she could make it. 'I see.'
> The completeness, clearly, after an instant, had struck him as divine. 'Ah, my dear, my dear!' It was all he could say.
>
> (ch. xli)

If less ambivalence had been intended, it would not have been beyond the powers of 'the most intelligent man of his generation' (as T. S. Eliot called him), its greatest critic and its most conscious novelist. James's indirect method gives his reader the experience of gradual discovery (coinciding with the characters' own) of life's true alternatives. And through it he gets in so much of life that no one has had more influence on the modern novel.

CONRAD AND FORD

By the time James was making his most far-reaching innovations he had lost his public, so that at first they went almost unnoticed. The innovations in the more accessible work of Joseph Conrad (1857–1924) made a much greater impact. At first – in *Almayer's Folly* (1895) and *The Nigger of the Narcissus* (1897), Conrad was an impressionist, intent on communicating 'an impression conveyed through the senses' of life's 'enigmatical spectacle'. Like James he was steeped in the French tradition (in his case Hugo and Balzac, Flaubert and the realists). But, unlike James, he knew very little of English tradition, and thought nothing of overturning the regular chronological progression customary in Victorian fiction. In fact, he broke its smooth narrative surface up into fragments. These small sharp cubist 'retreating planes' constantly remind one that a 'method' is being practised – 'the way to do a thing that shall make it undergo most doing', as James put it.

Conrad's chosen method is one of plunge *in medias res* to establish a perspective (often the point of vantage comes just before a crisis); then of returns in fragmentary flashback; then of new plunges. *Lord Jim* (1900) opens with Jim as a water-clerk, but returns to episodes – themselves chopped up – of his early life. Next it carries his story up to the beginning of the Patna disaster, but then leaps to Jim's retrospective evidence at the Inquiry, and leaps again to a hypothetical narration by Marlow (long after Jim has ceased to be a water-clerk) formulating earlier 'inconclusive' cogitations over the Inquiry. And the parts between all these leaps are not so much ordered in narrative sequence as juxtaposed artistically. Conrad's method of time-shifts establishes control over every juxtaposition; making all belong to an overall composition like the simultaneously viewed parts of a cubist painting.

Such fragmentariness has been related to the impossibility of making sense of the modern world. But in Conrad almost the reverse is true; although the sense he made was highly sceptical, even nihilistic. (He believed that fidelity to the emotions of an 'epoch of one's existence' came nearer to authenticity than the 'permanent' truths of philosophy.) Conrad's time-shifts, far from confessing incoherence, serve an artistic purpose. They produce eloquently persuasive contiguities. So Brierly's suicide is recounted just before his severe opinion on Jim's 'cowardice', undercutting it and at the same time amplifying the courage needed to face the Inquiry.

Often, Conrad's juxtapositions explode the grandiosity of mythic pretences – romantic illusions in *Lord Jim*, mystifications of colonialism in the novella *The Heart of Darkness* (1902), revolutionary politics in *The Secret Agent* (1907). Most elaborately of all, in *Nostromo* (1904), the expected story – a confident unthinking plot of an emergent republic – is broken up piecemeal for a minute scrutiny that reduces and slows it to the paralysis of despair.

Such montage is only one of many ways in which Conrad made the genre more poetic. A poetic pattern or structure, deeply satisfying to discover, organizes the plan of each of his novels. Thus, the shifts of narration are not only designed to generate different viewpoints (although a shift from first-person to omniscient third person may be used to subversive effect). They can also make graded series; as when the narrations and inset narrations of narrations in *The Heart of Darkness* take one ever deeper into the Chinese box of dark truths of empire, so that the story-telling (in Conrad always marvellously realized and adjusted to the narrator) keeps in step with the underlying myth of the Dark Journey. Conrad's external stories – generally more striking than James's – have great poetic value; their events and physical properties accumulate deep personal meaning. Besides the treatments of colonization and revolution are other centres of concern, such as formation of the soul; personal development through disillusionment; ordeal by terror of emptiness (the Gulf in *Nostromo*); or the saving effect of duty. In relation to these, any element may furnish poetic symbols – not least the exotic landscapes, the awesome *verdures* that Conrad it seems can conjure at will.

Conrad seldom falls into casual pathetic fallacies about nature; instead, he constructs symbolisms consistently, gradually establishing them as focuses for allusion and contemplation. The jump from the Patna and the ideal soul-butterfly in *Lord Jim*; the silver in *Nostromo*; the ivory in *Heart of Darkness*: much of Conrad's meaning surrounds such symbols. (To Marlow, 'the meaning of an episode was not inside it like the kernel but outside, enveloping the tale which brought it out only as a glow brings out a haze'.) Even in that sombre masterpiece *Nostromo*, the narrative interlace is too intricate to issue in a single overt statement. Much of the significance is conveyed poetically, through such symbols as the loss of soul-treasure.

Finally, Conrad's style is poetic, too. It is sometimes so in the obvious sense of being 'opaque' or noticeable: now massively heroic, now sardonically puncturing. The descriptions can make scenes momentous, like Marlow's memory of his last sight of Jim:

> He was white from head to foot, and remained persistently visible with the stronghold of the night at his back, the sea at his feet, the opportunity by his side – still veiled. What do you say? Was it still veiled? I don't know. For me that white figure in the stillness of coast and sea seemed to stand at the heart of a vast enigma. The twilight was ebbing fast from the sky above his head, the strip of sand had sunk already under his feet, he himself appeared no bigger than a child – then only a speck, a tiny white speck, that seemed to catch all the light left in a darkened world . . . And, suddenly, I lost him . . .
>
> (*Lord Jim* ch.xxxv)

The masterly phrase 'the stronghold of the night at his back' simultaneously creates a strong visual effect and suggests a dark tower of evil forces, to which Jim is quixotically vulnerable. But the style more often works in a quieter, low-keyed way, whereby ordinary words become themselves resonant symbols, like the often-repeated phrase 'one of us' in *Lord Jim*.

Conrad's many-faceted novels may not match James's in refinement or precision of meaning; but they have far more sense of man's political destiny. They move through an enormous range externally – in geography and *mise en scène*. And they partly make up for what they lack of James's psychological range by their robust grasp of social issues. The comparison is inevitable, since, like James, Conrad wrote in a genre close to romance – not the old climactic quest-romance, but a demythologized 'romance of illusion'. This tends to conclude not with a rounded, but with a disturbing, closure. How authentic, how right, is Marlow's lie to the Intended at the end of *Heart of Darkness*? The disturbingly poised closure was one of Conrad's most valued legacies to modernism. It is justly valued; even if he sometimes used the device to escape responsibilities of choice.

The narrative fragmentation that Conrad agonized to invent was practised as a matter of course by his collaborator Ford Madox Ford (originally Hueffer: 1873–1939). Ford saw it as regularly replacing Victorian narrative methods. 'It became very early evident to us,' he wrote, 'that what was the matter with the Novel . . . was that it went straight forward.' His fragmentary method favoured the capture of fleeting unidentified 'impressions' of urban life. (Ford talked a good deal about impressionism, meaning by it something rather vaguer and less perceptual than the ideas of French Impressionism in the strict sense.) The method receives its fullest application in the Tietjens tetralogy – *Some Do Not* (1924); *No More Parades* (1925); *A Man Could Stand Up* (1926); *Last Post* (1928) – where the much-chopped-up story (its fragments sometimes smaller even than Conrad's) are woven around 'public events of a decade' such as the 1914–18 war and the Suffragette movement.

This fine sequence does everything one has a right to expect of fiction. It has well varied characters and great dramatic scenes and well-informed social background and memorable description, with many touching immediate impressions. It even has ideas. Its style is lucid, easy, perfectly judged. Moreover, it successfully combines traditional strengths with experiment – as in the extended passages in stream of consciousness format, or the brilliantly evocative Meredithian scraps of remembered conversations. And yet. There remains a serious reservation: a doubt as to whether Ford has quite succeeded in finding the 'pattern of the bewildering carpet' and giving it enough prominence to order the welter of impressions.

Ford's most perfect achievement lies elsewhere, in *The Good Soldier* (1915). Here the time shifts have a function, since they realize the involved narrator's leaps of memory. Point of view in this tragic tale is extraordinarily sustained, with a Jamesian unity of artistic purpose:

> She wanted, that is to say, to retain my respect for as long as she lived with me. I suppose, if she had persuaded Edward Ashburnham to bolt with her she would have let the whole thing go with a run. Or perhaps she would have tried to exact from me a new respect for the greatness of her passion on the lines of all for love and the world well lost. That would be just like Florence.
>
> (Pt III, Sect.i)

By any reasonable standard, Ford is a badly underestimated figure. At his best he rivals Conrad.

Whereas Ford is currently underrated, H. G. Wells (1866–1946) has been still more overrated. Indeed, were it not for his science fiction he would hardly merit mention here. For although he talked about the future a great deal, Wells was quite unable to move into it artistically. Like many of his contemporaries, he wrote sloppily. Even *Tono-Bungay* (1909), his energetic sketch of the Edwardian business world, can disgust by sheer incoherence. Wells's disregard for formal art matters least in his seminal works of science fiction – *The Time Machine* (1895); *The War of the Worlds* (1898). In this important but only semi-literary genre, verbal style at least, if not the literary medium in general, is a relatively subsidiary element.

There is no lack of art in the novels of Arnold Bennett (1867–1931), another figure at times overrated. *Riceyman Steps* (1923) has a fine-spun plot, with a covert symbolic mechanism besides, of minute, dispiritingly reductive, psychological causation. Bennett takes care to keep his great masses of symptomatic detail obviously subservient to the plot in every circumstance. His contract is fulfilled; but the trivialities interest only for the tiny fraction of a point they are put in to make. Bennett needs a great many details to show very little.

EXPERIMENTAL FICTION: JAMES JOYCE

Modernism's tendency to OPAQUE or noticeable style reached an early extreme in Gertrude Stein, an important eccentric whose contribution has even now not been assimilated. In a large *oeuvre* – readable popular works like *Three Lives* (1909) as well as more difficult ones like *The Making of Americans* (1911) and *Tender Buttons* (1914) – she experimented with language in new ways that added enormously to the writer's resources. *How to Write* (1927–31) deserves study by any would-be stylist. Stein's words are primarily used not as links completing a semantic chain of discourse, but as moveable things forming the playful arrangements – collocations repetitions and variations – of a poetic grammar. Self-reflexive arrangements are made, that release meaning unexpectedly from individual phrases. In a difficult passage in Stein it is of no use to read on, in the hope that the end of the sentence will bring illumination. Each phrase is to be felt for itself, as meaning what the whole work means in its simultaneity:

> How can there be a difference between twice once and twice twice once. Any little way to say she loves me.
> With within and mean, I mean I mean.
> What is the pleasure of their saving everything. Everything saving everything. I mean I mean. In between.
>
> ('With a Wife' (1927), in *Painted Lace*)

Here 'twice twice' conveys twiceness as well as saying 'twice' can. If it is not so economical, 'what is the pleasure of . . . saving' words? Similarly, 'I mean I mean' intensifies by repetition, but also puts 'I' 'in between' 'mean' and 'mean' – making it 'within' or internal to 'mean' – another 'little way to say' the inner sincerity of really meaning something. Such prose challenges exposition. And, at its best, it communicates the exhilaration of stylistic freedom. But her content is insufficiently compressed – or too determinedly diffused – to sustain interest; except in the more accessible criticism, such as 'Henry James' (*Four in America*, 1932–3). Stein's importance is undeniably great: in different ways the work of Cummings and Finlay and Joyce and Hemingway would have been unimaginable without its pioneering example.

James Joyce (1882–1941) is rare among experimentalists in having both creative and intellectual ability, great enough not only to justify his innovations but even to give them authority. Yet in his early stories experimentation makes little show; only after he left Ireland in search of artistic freedom (and so lost the direct relation to his readers that promoted lucidity), did he develop his brilliant cosmopolitan style. Modernism generally tended to be international; but in Joyce aspiration to an intellectual world-culture became a central motive.

From this high vantage Joyce saw beyond the limitations of the whole

tradition of the novel – its formal conventions and its customary moral
subject matter – so that he could not only treat additional topics in new
ways (like Conrad), but try to reshape fictional reality 'all round'.
Ulysses (1922) is a prodigious effort of realism – but realism meta-
morphosed. It is informed by a doctrine of 'epiphanies', or spiritual
manifestations, whereby the *quidditas* or 'thisness' of ordinary life may
be illuminated by some fleeting event ('a shout in the street'): a visionary
moment to be recorded as a self-contained artistic 'impression'. By
'ordinary life', Joyce meant very ordinary – not for him the refinements
of Jamesian sensibilities. He preferred to focus on the common or
garden Bloom, and to raise the magnifying power, in such a way as to
give (ostensibly without selection) many vulgar details previously
omitted from fiction – a riot of half-formulated thoughts and half-conscious impulses so multitudinous that the mere sketch of a single day's
non-events occupies a large book. Bloom lives vividly, above all in
stream of consciousness passages. These are formulated in a special
abbreviated summary way that allows much scope for ironies of implied
comment:

> And you a married man with a single girl! That's what they enjoy. Tak-
> ing a man from another woman. Or even hear of it. Different with me.
> Glad to get away from the man's wife. Eating off his cold plate. Chap in
> the Burton today spitting back gumchewed gristle. French letter still in
> my pocket book . . .

Instead of moral elevation, Joyce's characters are validated by their
mythic representativeness. This seems in general a poor exchange;
although it can have moving effects – as in the intellectual Stephen–
Telemachus's search for a father, and discovery of one in the ordinary
Bloom–Ulysses. In order to evoke the order of myth (and to escape the
bourgeois novel) *Ulysses* partly follows the conventions of Homeric epic,
besides alluding to other genres through a series of stylistic modulations. This method of pastiche (not parody) encourages the reader to
think in terms of literary composition rather than direct reflection of
reality. But, as the vitality of *Ulysses* shows, neither the dismantling of
the novel genre nor the disintegration of society is its main concern. It
teems with patterns – structural patterns and covert patterns listing
Bloomsday Dublin names and things – in such a way as to communicate order and completeness and unity. Its aim is almost anthrop-
ological: to realize a transcultural view of society, a vision of the human
city. It is, in fact, a poetic novel – unless one denies it the name of novel
altogether, and thinks of it as an early FABULATION (anti-novel or fable),

with antecedents in Rabelais and Cervantes and Nashe, *Tristram Shandy* and *Sartor Resartus*.

In *Finnegans Wake* (1939), Joyce is more arduously experimental: radically changing the scale of fiction, he extends its range to the cosmic in content, in form to the single word or even syllable. This is the work in which the very quintessence of modernist simultaneity may be found. It abandons narrative successiveness and continuous *mise en scène*; it subverts the Aristotelian sequence of beginning middle and end; and it frustrates even one's expectation of a connected chain of discourse within the sentence. Stylistically, it represents an extreme of expressionism pushed beyond grammar. Its opaque language demands attention, and forces its reader into a conscious intellectual participation very unlike the imaginative identification (or the passivity) usual with the traditional novel.

One's difficulty in *Finnegans Wake* is not lack of meaning, but excess of it. Instead of a primary sequence of discourse, several equally plausible connections will suggest themselves simultaneously, through resemblances (of rhythm or sound or structure) to various words or idioms or literary formulas. 'Passencore rearrived' will suggest 'passenger', but also Middle English 'passing' ('surpassing'), French 'pas encore' and (considering the amorous context) 'coeur'. In this way, composite invented words ramify out through multiplying roots, and allusions bring in, it seems, everything at once:

> Sir Tristram, violer d'amores, fr'over the short sea, had passencore rearrived from North Armorica on this side the scraggy isthmus of Europe Minor to wielderfight his penisolate war: nor had topsawyer's rocks by the stream Oconee exaggerated themselse to Laurens County's gorgios while they went doublin their mumper all the time: nor avoice from afire bellowsed mishe mishe to tauftauf thuartpeatrick: not yet, though venissoon after, had a kidscad buttended a bland old isaac: not yet, though all's fair in vanessy, were sosie sesthers wroth with twone nathandjoe. Rot a peck of pa's malt had Jhem or Shen brewed by arclight and rory end to the regginbrow was to be seen ringsome on the aquaface.

> *(Finnegans Wake* par. 2)

To indicate a few of the possibilities: there are suggestions of very soon/ venison, kidscut/kid skad (trick), butt/tended/upended, bland/blind, venery/Vanessa, two one/the one, Nathaniel/Nathan/nap hand/two in hand/Jonathan (the form in an earlier version). In a letter, Joyce explains that 'Parnell [called 'Butthead' as a boy] ousted Isaac Butt from leadership' and that 'Jonathan Swift's Stella and Vanessa had the same

Christian name Esther'. Although these names recur later, the effect is not of connected meaning, but of diffused meaningfulness – or perhaps of thought in the process of generating words in some super-concentrated pan-European language.

Joyce's associative allusions are not random; they develop thematic patterns, self-validated by reference to freely synthesized myths, classical and Biblical, Celtic and exotic. Nevertheless, for all its vigour, with all its playful fertility of invention, in spite of all its ideas, *Finnegans Wake* does not escape a certain static immobility. Since it has no progression or closure, one is free to begin where one likes; and perhaps at first it is best to dip at will, not aiming to comprehend, so much as to apprehend the play of sense. Approached in this way the play of 'meanings' is exhilarating for a time. But Joyce's relentless intellectualizing and minute arbitrary patterning – bizarrely offset though they are by ferocious scepticism – can easily disgust. *Finnegans Wake* is not satisfying or sustaining; nor is it meant to be. In the end, it must be judged a wrong turning for fiction: a work in which ideas about life have displaced life itself.

But if *Finnegans Wake* is a cult book, the cult is a large one, numbering among its devotees many serious students. From Joyce's experiments there followed a whole tradition of fabulations (antinovels) and METAFICTION, or self-conscious fiction, acknowledging its own artefactual nature. Joyce's influence on an international scale is undeniable; although one may recognize the fact with mixed enthusiasm. It has brought a welcome infusion of ideas. But it has also had the effect of sequestering much of modern literature in the academy. Joyce is a great writer; but he has not always proved a good model.

EXPERIMENTAL FICTION: WOOLF TO LEWIS

Virginia Woolf (1882–1941) lacked Joyce's large intellectuality; yet in her conception of the novel she intrepidly extended modernist freedoms. Standing partly in the tradition of George Eliot and Charlotte Bronte, she relied less than them on character or viewpoint as ordering principles. Thus in *To the Lighthouse* (1927) a crucial passage presents the 'experience' of an empty house. In fact Woolf's experiments pursued an overtly lyric form of novel. With this in view, she gradually developed a method (originally pioneered by Dickens) whereby stream of consciousness constituted almost the entire fiction – as in *Mrs Dalloway* (1925), where the slender narrative of such actions as a walk through London serves mainly to provide material, in the form of sensitive impressions, for association of ideas. In the more difficult *The Waves* (1931), even this amount of external narrative is set aside. Any scraps of story have now to be inferred from a set of co-conscious interior monologues – a cubist structure like that of William Faulkner's *The Sound and the Fury* (1929).

Woolf was a superb (if rather uneven) critic, well able to formulate what she was doing. She writes of consciousness as a stream of delicate transitory apprehensions, very different from what the tyrant plot insists on:

> The mind receives a myriad impressions – trivial, fantastic, evanescent, or engraved with the sharpness of steel. From all sides they come, an incessant shower of innumerable atoms; and as they fall, as they shape themselves into the life of Monday . . . the accent falls differently from of old . . . Life is not a series of gig-lamps symmetrically arranged; life is a luminous halo, a semi-transparent envelope surrounding us from the beginning of consciousness to the end.
>
> ('Modern Fiction', *The Common Reader*, 1925)

The stream of consciousness technique, as Woolf conceived it, turned out to involve interpenetrations of thoughts with external sense data – the beam of a lighthouse; the frill of a chair – in a way now taken for granted by novelists:

> It had seemed so safe, thinking of her . . . Suddenly, the empty drawing-room steps, the frill of the chair inside, the puppy tumbling on the terrace, the whole wave and whisper of the garden became like curves and arabesques flourishing round a centre of complete emptiness.
>
> (*To the Lighthouse* (1927), 'The Lighthouse' 5)

A myriad impressions are in this way composed into a satisfying poetic order, with extreme narrative economy and a style that is lucid if not very precise.

Dispraisers of Woolf's fiction regard her as naive – as too ignorant of other social classes to have written satisfactory novels. Certainly her psychological difficulties were so great that she could only write novels at all by a formidable effort of courage. But out of these very difficulties, perhaps, she won an artistic insight (which has little to do with class), 'that the precious stuff of which books are made lies all about one'. She saw how life might be represented in its contingencies and intensities, not by imposing on it the significant chronicle of plot, but by recreating its ordinary moments poetically. In this emphasis on moments of sublimity she exhibited, like Joyce, a Victorian or Romantic sensibility.

Independently, Dorothy Richardson (1872–1957) was also using the stream of consciousness method; although to laborious, unimaginative effect. But its most creative and powerful exponent, apart from Joyce, was the Mississipi novelist William Faulkner (1897–1962). In *As I Lay Dying* (1930) the method's constraints might seem to have narrowed the focus to the point of hypnotic monotony. But in reality the author's absence is exploited for a brilliantly sustained camped-up mock gothic effect. A still more remarkable achievement is *The Sound and the Fury* (1929). Here, no fewer than four discontinuous yet marvellously differentiated interior monologues open perspectives on the decline of the doomed Compson family, in such a way that the reader must extrapolate much of the story – events as well as larger situations. One of the monologues formulates the non-chronological memory of an idiot, Benjy:

> They came on. I opened the gate and they stopped, turning. I was trying to say, and I caught her, trying to say, and she screamed and I was trying to say and trying and the bright shapes began to stop and I tried to get out. I tried to get it off of my face, but the bright shapes were going again.
>
> (*The Sound and the Fury*, 'April 7, 1928')

At first the story can be locally ambiguous or obscure. Nevertheless it is so convincingly realized that it carries the reader on to learn the characters' narrative assumptions *en passant*. This success is partly due to the dependability of Faulkner's remarkable *mise en scène*, Yoknapatawpha County. This imaginary world might be compared with Hardy's Wessex, except that the Faulkner novels set in it interconnect much more, like *romans-fleuves*. Their symbolism, too, has a much more gothic cast. Yoknapatawpha's history is a gloomy one, of guilt and disgrace and death, the fall of old families and the rise of new. In Faulkner's vision values are tragically at loggerheads, good with good; while evil is bound up with innocence itself. Perhaps this finds reflection in his slightly overrich style, which is often characterized (although not so much in *The Sound and the Fury*) by long sentences prolonging the sense as if to hold simultaneous truths in suspension syntactically. Or he will unnecessarily add mention of opposites, like the later season in this description of Dilsey:

> The gown fell gauntly from her shoulders, across her fallen breasts, then tightened upon her paunch and fell again, ballooning a little above the nether garments which she would remove layer by layer as the spring accomplished and the warm days, in colour regal and moribund.
>
> (*The Sound and the Fury*, 'April 8, 1928')

Faulkner's style can irritate at first, but soon comes to be accepted, almost as a poetic diction.

Most of the experimental fiction so far considered might broadly be compared to impressionist or cubist art. But the work of Percy Wyndham Lewis (1884–1957), who totally rejected 'naturalistic' impressionism, has rather to be connected with the 'vorticism' that he himself practised as a painter. (The connection with vorticism or abstractionism is explicit in *Tarr* (1918).) Lewis's ambitious *The Human Age* (1955–6) includes a revision of *The Childermass* (1928), an enormous polemic–satiric vision of judgement, in a tradition descending through Jonson and Byron from ancient models. This is a work of large, sometimes startlingly Dantesque imagination; although it utterly lacks Dante's concentration and economy of detail. Lewis's ferocious satire seems to strike at random. No doubt it always serves some special idea; but that is to say little, for his independent thinking was confused, eccentric and extremist – besides being devoid of common sense. The characters' positions now seem chaotic:

> BAILIFF: 'We are not Greeks the Lord of Hosts be praised, we are Modern Men and proud of it – we of the jazz-age who have killed sexishness and enthroned sensible sex, who have liberated the working-mass and gutted every palace within sight making a prince of the mechanic with their spoils . . .'
>
> (*The Childermass*, 1928)

All the same, Lewis's satire is thought-provoking, even when his own thoughts are unimpressive. His style is uneven but bold and vivid in description. It is interesting, if not always wholly successful, in its experimental notation for dialogue: 'Imemer sight berternwot I was' (I'm a sight better than what I was'). Some have seen *The Human Age* as a neglected masterpiece.

In a history attending more to content, D. H. Lawrence (1885–1930) would claim a large place. Not only did he take himself very seriously as a moral sage and sex guru, but the great critic F. R. Leavis did so too; while legal proceedings against *The Rainbow* (1915) and *Lady Chatterley's Lover* (1928) further increased his focal standing. Lawrence certainly had intuitive penetration in treating unconscious motives; perhaps also in arriving at mysterious truths about men and (less often) women. But he was such an incoherent thinker that these intuitions seldom received analysis, or issued in believable characters. And his most successful novels are marred by prophetic intrusions of the novelist, either in his own person, or (what is almost worse) behind a bullhorn character-mask.

These intrusions are widely disliked – and not merely because Lawrence can be repellent personally (for he was one of the first to turn unpleasantness to literary account). The dislike arises because in the modernist, as distinct from the Victorian novel, there is a rule that, if writers are gods at all, they must be scrupulously hidden ones.

In this Lawrence reverted (or regressed) to the looser Victorian novel, with its authorial interventions. He rejected Jamesian art, as demanding too much constraint; by comparison, his own novels are crude, unformed, half-written. Niceties of narrative, description of the environment, moral discriminations, social manners: none of these matters to Lawrence, as he reaches out for life, which is to say primitive, even infantile, simplifications of it. Accordingly, when his novels are not tracts, they are poetic compositions. Things go in not because the story requires them but because they accord with Lawrence's immediate enthusiasm. Thus in *The Rainbow*, Lincoln cathedral primarily functions neither as a church nor an object of tourism. It is merely an occasion for Will Brangwen's feeling, which is so unmotivated as to be practically Lawrence's own. The feeling is a mysticism as sexual as it is religious:

> Then he pushed open the door, and the great, pillared gloom was before him, in which his soul shuddered and rose from her nest. His soul leapt, soared up into the great church. His body stood still, absorbed by the height. His soul leapt up into the gloom, into possession, it reeled, it swooned with a great escape, it quivered in the womb, in the hush and the gloom of fecundity, like seed of procreation in ecstasy.
>
> (ch. vii)

'Everything hangs together', but with a decorum, or unity, less of narrative or descriptive realism than of Lawrence's own vision. Henry James would have approached such an epiphany through character and event, tracing how it was arrived at. But Lawrence has little interest in character or individual moral development. He means the passage as an instance of a world of collective feeling we have lost: as a pattern of the experience he passionately advocates.

In effect, Lawrence tore up the novelist's contract with the judicious reader; replacing it by a liturgy for acolytes. Devotees were to receive his representations of life with as little critical discrimination as they might accord to religious or political writings. For the representations are not of life's surface appearances but of its putatively primitive 'heart' or 'roots'. Lawrence's secrets of Eros and Thanatos can be profound in their impression, particularly on the young. But to others, experience seems to teach that Lawrence's secrets are portentous clichés, or merely idiosyncratic notions. The repeated (and repetitive) accounts of coitus are a case in point. In a sense these serious, unpornographic confessions achieved a significant extension of literature's subject-matter. But although sexual intercourse can sensitively indicate character, the self it reflects is achieved through other, more diffused relations, which in Lawrence's fiction are absent, or at best sketched perfunctorily. Repetition substitutes, as an incoherent half-expression of experiences doubtless intense, but unshared.

Lawrence's attempts to explore the female psyche and to imagine women's erotic experience, however limited by his sexism, were extremely courageous. And historically they may turn out to have been of great value. His quest for a stance free from what he considered defects of civilized life has something of nobility. He hardly offers detailed role models; but the broad challenge his novels present can transform the reader incalculably. This, despite his avoidance of systematic, even of coherent, rationality.

If few indisputable claims can be made for the content of Lawrence's fiction, what of its art? One must concede at the outset that his engagement with literature, intensely serious as it was in moral ways, easily coexisted with what used to be called 'bad' writing. Lawrence sometimes wrote abominably. Indeed, he was a chief founding father of the growing school of deliberately unstylish writers, who hope to imitate him successfully at least in this. Even Lawrence's best novels – *Sons and Lovers* (1913) and *The Rainbow* (1915) – are badly written. Relatively effective passages can nevertheless be insufferably repetitive, laborious, heavy-handed, or vulgar:

> He had taken her at the roots of her darkness and shame – like a demon, laughing over the fountain of mystic corruption which was one of the sources of her being, laughing, shrugging, accepting, accepting finally. As for her, when would she so much go beyond herself as to accept him at the quick of death?
>
> (*Women in Love*, ch. xxiii)

Yet the best of the novels still hold attention, and give an impression of authentic attack. This elusive impression may in part have been achieved through Lawrence's practice of trying to discover himself afresh each time he wrote. The practice is not specially adapted to readers' pleasure; but can lead to exciting and surprising effects of transition or connection. Those who think of literature primarily as an arena of dangerous challenges met by the writer will be inclined to value

Lawrence highly. Time and again he exposes himself to the risks of a
genre not very often attempted in English literature, the 'work
impossible to write'. In such writing, the imminence of failure generates
a special excitement: how long will the author keep going? As we read
Lawrence's urgent novels, our hearts collectively go out to him, as to the
primal trapeze artist.

Lawrence pioneered the extension of representation to ranges of
emotional experience previously only half-conscious. His novels sometimes succeeded in breaking through to the intimate movement of life
(especially ungenteel or recrudescent life) as it is inwardly lived. That in
itself was a great achievement, from a historical point of view. As regards
art, however, Lawrence's best work is in his stories.

POPULAR MODERNISM

It is easy for literary history to slide into history of avant garde literature
– particularly when experimental writing has the calibre of Joyce's and
Woolf's. In fact, writing of other sorts abounded, even in the 1920s. Such
novelists as Elizabeth Bowen (1899–1973) and, in the United States,
Willa Cather (1873–1947) continued to produce more or less traditional
novels, complete with continuous narratives, plots and thematic
structures. And there were original developments of earlier forms, as
well as irregular works of genius, which, although they may represent
no trend, have remained the joy of readers: John Masefield's strange
yarn *Lost Endeavour* (1910); Walter de la Mare's symbolic autobiography *Memoirs of a Midget* (1921); T. F. Powys's sardonic allegory *Mr
Weston's Good Wine* (1928); Richard Hughes's *A High Wind in Jamaica*
(1929), with its child's eye view of pirates; and Djuna Barnes's *Nightwood*
(1936), with its splendid surrealist style. And on coming to the 1930s,
one finds that, so far as avant garde literature is concerned, *Finnegans
Wake* (1939) stands almost alone: the movement was away from the
experimental or the poetic.

Writers resumed continuous narration, external description and the
other old familiar novelistic conventions – unless perhaps there was now
a little more unconscious motivation, a little more real beastliness in the
bad characters. Serious novelists became markedly easier to read, and
so potentially more popular. Various reasons for this thirties reaction
have been advanced: change of fashion; loss of nerve (flinching from the
lonely avant garde mountain tops); disapproval of formal values by the
politically engaged. Perhaps experimental fiction was felt to be a wrong
turning because intelligible representation of society is an enduring

requirement. At any rate, the new phase – so called 'popular modernism' – was not modernist at all, on the surface. Its inheritance from modernism amounted to little more than a modicum of freedom in changing the proportions of the traditional novel repertoire.

The most obvious change of proportion, seen in many disparate writers, was to make character less prominent. In Scotland Lewis Grassic Gibbon's (James Leslie Mitchell's) *Scots Quair* (1932–4) and in America Dos Passos's *Manhattan Transfer* (1925) and *U. S. A.* (1938) attempted the 'collective novel'. All of these move their focus from the individual to the community, in such a way as to stereotype the characters and subject them to multitudinous incidents illustrative of social forces. Dos Passos used a discontinuous narrative – interweaving many lives of contrasted fortune – diversified with mildly experimental epigraphs, newspaper headlines, interior monologues and brief vignettes (some of them saturnine, most merely banal). His once influential novels are energetic with indignation; but their fragmentation and generalizing scale obscure the detail of social connections, so that they fail to persuade. From this point of view, Gibbon's trilogy is more successful, for it can often be moving.

Personality is reduced in a very different way in the many pungent novels of Ivy Compton-Burnett, such as *Brothers and Sisters* (1929) and *A Heritage and its History* (1959). They consist almost exclusively of dialogue, superficially resembling that of Greek tragedy. Compton-Burnett's notation of speech – sharp, epigrammatic, logic-chopping, whoever the speaker – gives great pleasure by its imperturbability in expressing a wide range of sentiments usually concealed – ferociously rapacious or otherwise startling. Neither decent appearance nor its formulation can be taken at face value – 'The smile seemed to relate to his own thoughts, and did so.' But the 'inside' the characters show is limited by melodramatic plots of incest, forgery and the like; so that potential tragedy generally comes out as black comedy. Nevertheless, if the right inferences are supplied, the comedy can acquire an Austenesque precision.

Henry Green (Henry Vincent Yorke) (1905–73) is a more complete novelist. He seems on the surface to unfold a realistic if minimal plot; but underneath he is an abstract, experimental artist, who might well have appeared in a previous section. Green uses plot as a mere pretext for language games that question ordinary formulations of reality. His banal diction and filmic narrative style conceal structures of clichés, images, repeated phrases, even of prepositions; so that such a phrase as 'drowning in his depth' may belong to an unobtrusive pattern of shallowness. Nevertheless, the prevailing flatness can also make occasional highlights of diction stand out with comic incongruity:

> 'Why if I had proof I'd choke the life out of 'er by poking a peacock down that great gullet she has.' Edith laughed. 'I would straight,' he assured her in a strong voice. 'And that's a death would be too good for the woman, the diabolical mason.'
>
> (Loving, 1945)

Obscure implications of the dialogue are subtly reinforced by narrative structures and lexical patterns. Green is a minor master, even if his lyrical method removes his novels far from ordinary reading. His characters are all pawns: he does not care about them and neither do we.

The recoil from experiment is much more pronounced in the novels of Anthony Powell (1905–), a cool ironist of considerable weight. From *Afternoon Men* (1931) to the Proustian sequence *A Dance to the Music of Time* (1951–75, including *The Acceptance World* (1955) and *Casanova's Chinese Restaurant*(1960)) – all of them leisurely, elaborate books replete with minute, pleasurably accurate details ('circumstantial things') contributing little but local colour; all of them expressed in a lucid but slightly cumbersome style – Powell has kept up a rich if selective sampling of social atmospheres, intended to arrive at 'the inner truth of the things observed'. But somehow the many careers and passionless assessments of obligations escape issuing in themes (which it may be Powell's sole modernism to omit). One learns a good deal about his characters, without their exhibiting development, or even – except for the ghastly Widmerpool – much vitality. Nevertheless Powell has had a great influence on the comic novel: one thinks, for example, of Kingsley Amis.

There is no lack of themes and judgements in Evelyn Waugh's (1903–66) inventive *oeuvre*. In such satiric novels as *Decline and Fall* (1928), each ridiculous event of the discontinuous narrative serves to make a thematic point. When the irrepressible Grimes is provided with a bottle and a pistol, if he takes the whisky but declines the gentleman's way out, this is to demonstrate rejection of the arbitrary code of honour. Most of the novel's subsidiary characters are caricatures, as is usual in Menippean satire; and the protagonist Paul has less personality than Voltaire's Candide. A more serious criticism might be that the satire is informed by little in the way of implied positive values – its impulse seeming to be something very like hatred of mankind. But this may be an unfair evasion of Waugh's challenging formal innovation. In modernist fashion, his neutral presentation elides the novelist, so that an apparent nihilism forces the reader to ask if there is anywhere to stand.

Concealment of the author has also given rise to problems of interpretation in several of the novels of Graham Greene (1904–). Throughout Greene's impressive *oeuvre* – more than twenty novels and 'entertainments', from *The Man Within* (1929) onward – a principal strength is his brilliant topical realism, comparable in the early phase with Dos Passos'. Yet this very realism is problematic, in that it seems not to issue from any discernible view of historical change. Or, to put it differently, in novels such as *Brighton Rock* (1938) and *The Heart of the Matter* (1948), the realism receives no identification in sociological or political terms. But, then, why should it? Sociological interpretation is not privileged; and we must accept that, for Greene, topicalities are particular instances of an unchanging predicament. His highly selective (yet persuasive) realism could be called visionary: Pinky's Brighton lies in the purlieus of hell, and Scobie's Africa has intimations of the same state. The external scene is characteristically sleazy and macabre:

> there was no change – the same hideous mauve silk cushions, the threads showing where the damp was rotting the covers: the tangerine curtains. Even the blue syphon of soda was in the same place: they had an eternal air like the furnishings of hell.
>
> (*The Heart of the Matter* Book II, Pt i, 2, iv)

Greene's version of the religious novel tends to disconcert critics. Victorian novelists of faith and doubt represented individual experience; but he thinks in terms of cultures of belief and unbelief – and with a gulf between, such as in *The End of the Affair* (1951) means the loss of Sarah. Greene's continuous narrative and readable style are alike pellucid; apparently justifying the idea that he has returned to the transparent, unambiguous, premodernist way of rendering reality. But this would ignore his modernist affiliations (particularly with his favourite Conrad). Faulkner's *The Sound and the Fury* may give different versions of the same action; but in *The End of the Affair* the version given by Sarah's diary actually subverts an earlier one. And this more than a decade before Fowles's The Collector (1963). Greene is a convincing realist, capable of moving by his stark perspectives on the human lot.

Meanwhile, in the United States, the prosperity of the twenties coincided with a burst of literary activity showing a new confidence and sense of national identity. Two impressive novelists, both of them readable and popular, confirmed the movement away from modernist difficulty: Ernest Hemingway (1898–1961) and F. Scott Fitzgerald

(1896–1940). Hemingway, a protégé of Gertrude Stein, wrote (as one might expect from that) with a pure style. But one might not expect it to issue in saving of words – in an economical style. This is seen at its best in *The Sun Also Rises* (1926; British title *Fiesta*), in *A Farewell to Arms* (1929) and in short stories like 'Fifty Grand'. Hemingway's topics – distinguishing the authentic; determining (like Ford) a viable code of behaviour – are few but important. His later work slackened, as he became content to find the authentic in laconic action.

As for Fitzgerald, in spite of a tragically small *oeuvre* (he was an alcoholic), it is not ridiculous to speak of him as the finest American novelist since James. As his notebooks help to show, he deliberately orchestrated the tiniest details – colours, single words – in such a way as to produce a consummate blending of content and form, at least in his two masterpieces *The Great Gatsby* (1925) and *Tender is the Night* (1934; 1951). Yet little of this appears on the surface. Indeed, Fitzgerald's example, like that of Henry Green, did much to move modern fiction towards concealed structure. In *The Great Gatsby*, the effacement of the author is itself concealed, by the use of a narrator, Nick Carroway. Nick is not obviously unreliable, but he is not to be trusted, either, as a SHIFTER-CHARACTER or author-surrogate always agreeing with Fitzgerald. Fitzgerald's oblique creations of mood and character are dazzling. Often he works them stylistically, by eager amplifications that risk preciousness or even silliness – as when Jordan moves 'as if she had first learned to walk upon golf courses on clear, crisp mornings'. But he does more; exploring in Gatsby nothing less than a national myth. Nick's despairing vision, which seems to close the book, figures Gatsby as hopelessly driven by the American dream of earthly fulfilment, 'the last and greatest of all human dreams':

> He had come a long way to this blue lawn, and his dream must have seemed so close that he could hardly fail to grasp it. He did not know that it was already behind him, somewhere back in that vast obscurity beyond the city, where the dark fields of the republic rolled on under the night.
>
> (*The Great Gatsby*, ch.ix)

SHORT FICTION

The MODERN SHORT STORY has generally been described as a well-defined, distinctively twentieth-century form, albeit influenced by Mérimée and Maupassant and Chekhov, and anticipated by Edgar Allen Poe and Robert Louis Stevenson. Poe had decreed that 'in the whole composition there should be no word ... not to the one pre-established design'; and the concentration of form in early modernism made it possible to carry out the prescient decree almost literally. The new genre was characterized by extreme unity, compressing a great many implications, in a poetic way, into the simultaneity of a single incident or perception.

All this is broadly true. But the short story was also influenced in other, and quite distinct, directions by such as Hawthorne, and the formally inventive Dickens of the Christmas stories. Around the turn of the century a writer could still take up any of a number of story types – by no means all of them closely unified – from the journalistic *reportage* of Stephen Crane (1871–1900), through the tightly economical yarn of W. W. Jacobs (1863–1943), to the formulaic story of O. Henry (W. S. Porter) (1862–1910) with its emphatic *coup de canon* ending. When one considers phases of development, it emerges that the unified story of Poe and Bierce did not lead on immediately to its modern culmination. Only gradually, and particularly after narrative had become less assertive, thanks to the example of James and Joyce – in fact, after the early modern phase of the novel – could the modern short story belatedly appear.

From this point of view it was Meredith's and James's stories that significantly broke new ground, followed by the *Yellow Book* stories of the nineties, by Kipling's later work, and by Joyce's *Dubliners* (1914). At that stage, a gulf between the popular and the literary story began to open. It has not closed – rather the reverse – so far as avant garde writing is concerned. But from the work of Katherine Mansfield (1888–1923) onward, there has otherwise been a distinct *rapprochement*, made possible by the late modernist concealment of complex structure under a readable surface. Subsequently the form has burgeoned creatively. It has become a major genre, capable not only of polymorphous invention but of intense feeling, profound introspection and subtle evocation of mood.

Henry James (1843–1916) published a large *oeuvre* of 112 tales, which in some opinions rival his novels in achievement. They often have similar subjects. Many of the early stories address the 'international theme' – perhaps studying some 'extraordinary American specimen' in Europe – and in several later ones, such as 'The Jolly Corner'(1908), it receives a profoundly personal development. Art's relation to society, or to reality, is the subject of many: notably 'The Lesson of the Master' (1888), 'The Aspern Papers' (1888) and 'The Figure in the Carpet' (1896). Such stories could certainly not be regarded as built around a

single incident. They are *nouvelles*, or novellas, or expansive long short
stories – roomy enough to realize social manners, and to develop a
graded series of incidents.

Their fictive method also resembles that of the novels – adjusted,
naturally, for the different scale. And their evocation of place is if
anything stronger: a Venice marvellously sketched, or, best of all, London, 'the huge oppressive amusing city that suggested everything, that
contained everything'. Descriptions are incomparably rich, reflecting
everywhere the sensitivities of the would-be visual artist. The greatest of
the stories have a more distinctly enigmatic, 'ambiguous' character than
most of the novels. Jamesians delight to excogitate in what sense there is
a figure in the carpet of 'The Figure in the Carpet' (1896), or what
exactly it was that happened in 'The Turn of the Screw' (1898). But they
agree at least as to the stories' subtlety, profundity and moral sensitivity.
Among James's many qualities none was of more moment for the short
story than his unswerving determination always to let readers see for
themselves – however much delay, circling and revisionary recursive-
ness it might take to put them in the position of being able to do so.

Rudyard Kipling (1865–1936) had a dazzling variety of short genres
at his command: fable, marvel, anecdote, science fiction, history, even
myth. But the one he most characteristically used, often in combination
with others, was the tale. In this ancient form the story may acquire
interest of perspective through being mediated by a fictional narrator,
who may in addition be set in a framing narrative. And in Kipling,
superb storyteller that he was, from the start the telling was more
important than the story told:

> '. . . It made me sick to look at it, for I'm clean-fleshed by nature. Chop
> me all over with a spade, an' I'd heal like turf. Then Mrs Marshall she set
> 'er own doctor at me. 'E said I ought to ha' come to him at first go-off,
> 'stead o' drawin' all manner o' dyed stockin's over it for months. 'E said
> I'd stood up too much to me work, for it was settin' very close atop of a
> big swelled vein, like, behither the small o' me ankle. "Slow come, slow
> go," 'e says. "Lay your leg up on high an' rest it," he says, "an' 'twill ease
> off. Don't let it close up too soon. You've got a very fine leg, Mrs
> Ashcroft," 'e says. An' he put wet dressin's on it.'
>
> ('The Wish House', in *Debits and Credits*, 1926)

If this speech imparts necessary information, it also – and much more –
embodies characterization and relished social coloration ('behither'),
while its submerged associations ('like turf'; 'on high') almost amount to
suggestions of dramatic irony, hinting that Mrs Ashcroft's 'fine leg' will
not be cured this side of death.

Kipling's earlier stories already show, in their use of dialect, this relative subordination of narrative – although they are marred by repetitiousness and journalistic crudity. When they succeed, it is partly because of his extraordinary empathy with all manner of men, regardless of colour or creed or class. (As his sympathies show, he was as little of an imperialist as Conrad.) Like other Edwardian short story writers, Kipling increasingly wrote about mysteries or 'rum' events: the preternatural, in one shape or another, was a staple topic of the genre. But he treated it in a distinctive, knowing way, which was related to his vision of inner circles or freemasonries – the ingroups responsible for civilization. (This theme dominates the collection *Debits and Credits*, 1926.) Kipling's vision finds natural expression in an allusive style, a feature that extends even to the accompanying epigraphs. His procedure becomes increasingly elliptic; he typically constructs a system of assumptions, such as to allow highly compressed internal allusion and symbolism. It is a method that has much influenced the subsequent development of the short story. Kipling's work is uneven; but it includes some of the greatest stories in the language, such as '"They"' (1904), 'Mary Postgate' (1917), 'The Wish House' (1924), 'On the Gate' (1926) and 'Dayspring Mishandled' (1932). Its authority, combined with Stevenson's, has made the tale fully available for the purposes of high art.

The short story is near enough to poetry for style generally to matter in it. Yet two writers – H. G. Wells (1866–1946) and the much greater D. H. Lawrence (1885–1930) – achieved success through sheer overall grip, despite their stylistic shortcomings. Lawrence's style is crudely repetitive; although those who like broad effects may think the repetitions well calculated in sum. More seriously, his stories often lapse into novelettish imagery: the characters experience emotions that go through them 'like a flame' or a 'hot flush'. But all this is of little account in face of Lawrence's psychological power. Whereas Kipling represented the outsides of characters – their words and actions – Lawrence opened their psychology; adumbrating deep instinctive feelings, human rather than individual. Such feelings might be apprehended only vaguely; but Lawrence set them down anyway, as instances of 'life'. It was a great thing to attempt. Even if the experience he summoned up did not always match the new psychoanalytic schemes, they remained of value nonetheless. For example 'The Woman Who Rode Away' – in which Lawrence attempts to recapture archaic attitudes towards life and death and their cosmic rhythm – is a profound story, even if it fails, perhaps, to support quite the argument intended.

From his earliest stories, Lawrence made sensuously vivid settings part of the total impression. In 'The Prussian Officer' (1914) the effect is one of repressed sexuality:

> The air was too scented, it gave no breath. All the lush green-stuff seemed to be issuing its sap, till the air was deathly, sickly with the smell of greenness. There was the perfume of clover, like pure honey and bees. Then there grew a faint acrid tang – they were near the beeches; and then a queer clattering noise, and a suffocating, hideous smell; they were passing a flock of sheep, a shepherd in a black smock, holding his crook. Why should the sheep huddle together under this fierce sun?

But the hypnotic concentration of all Lawrence's best stories comes from this integrity of purpose. He simply holds his focus, holds a single sustained focus. Often he explores relations between the sexes; and then his insights come as much from introspection (and generalization from his own experience) as from sensitivity to others.

With James Joyce's *Dubliners* (1914), the short story reached a consistently modernist phase. In 'The Dead' Joyce subdued narrative to the point of triviality, while creating one of the greatest stories in the language. 'Counterparts' has indeed a firm plot structure; but here the morality is made to depend heavily on analogies of unconscious motivation. Joyce is very abstemious, also, in his use of METALANGUAGE (author comment, or language attributable to the narrator). He prefers to convey his intention by ironies in the precisely observed dialogue. The particular misquotation in ' "As the poet says: *Great minds are very near to madness*," said Fogarty' speaks volumes about the community in which it could be made.

The modernist method was worked out more rigorously still by the New Zealand writer Katherine Mansfield (Kathleen Mansfield Beauchamp) (1888–1923). Mansfield's great reputation – formerly exaggerated and now under fashionable attack – is the first, in English literature, to rest entirely on short stories. Her New Zealand sketches – 'Prelude' (1917), 'The Voyage' (1921), 'At the Bay' (1921), 'The Garden Party' (1922) and the rest, with their atmospheric range and their brilliant evocation of childhood – have been seen, it is true, as chapters of an intended novel. But they are better appreciated as 'whole book fiction', like *Dubliners*. Mansfield dispenses with plot in the manner of the *Yellow Book* contributors of the nineties, and ultimately of Chekhov. But the best of her stories only ostensibly deal in external realism. Their true interest largely depends on a SUBTEXT or submerged sequence of imagery and suggestion, cued by repetitions and unexplained details in the surface action.

There could be no better example than 'Bliss' (1918; 1920). This much interpreted story repeatedly returns to a flowering pear tree, which relates to Bertha's late development, focuses her hysterical excitement and provides the story with whatever closure it has, after she discovers her husband's adultery with Miss Fulton:

> Miss Fulton held her hand a moment longer.
> 'Your lovely pear tree!' she murmured.
> And then she was gone, with Eddie following, like the black cat following the grey cat.
> 'I'll shut up shop,' said Harry, extravagantly cool and collected.
> 'Your lovely pear tree – pear tree – pear tree!'
> Bertha simply ran over to the long windows.
> 'Oh, what is going to happen now?' she cried.
> But the pear tree was as lovely as ever and as full of flower and as still.

Those who pursue ambiguities have wondered whether Bertha is left with lesbian, or voyeuristic, excitement. Such questions are natural, on a basis of novelistic assumptions. But Mansfield's more symbolist, more inward, art deals with 'moments' precipitating many feelings. Here the feelings suggest various irresponsibilities that stem from Bertha's splitting of experience between perfect tree and slinking cats. Mansfield might be criticized for leaving too much to the reader – unless one decides that for her stories no effort is too much. They are the most faultlessly written in the language. With Mansfield, the closure becomes enigmatically muted – less a *coup de canon* than a time bomb.

Unlike Joyce – whose stories, great as they are, tend to be overlit, with rational, cut-and-dried thematic structures – Walter de la Mare (1873–1956) was a connoisseur of darkness. At his best de la Mare achieved the strangest, most elusive effects of the period. His enormous *oeuvre* is absurdly undervalued; partly because its late Romantic, surreal material seems peripheral to modernism, partly because his escapism is misunderstood. In fact his 'escapes' from reality are metaphysical questionings of it, explorations of its shadowy edges – as in the period flavour of 'The Green Room' (1925; *On the Edge*, 1930), or the timelessness of 'The Vats' (*The Riddle*, 1923):

> ... I scanned their enormous sides, shaggy with tufts of a monstrous moss and scarred with yard-wide circumambulations of lichen. Gigantic grasses stooped their fatted seedpods from the least rough ledge. They might be walls of ice, so cold their aspect; or of a matter discoverable only in an alien planet.

Not that de la Mare was a great philosopher; but he was a genuine one, and audacious in giving his interest in preternatural experience its head. 'The Quincunx' (*A Beginning*, 1955) compares with Conrad's 'The Secret Sharer' in theme, and has more penetration of abnormal psychology.

Existential insights inform de la Mare's imaginary places and atmospheres (which are as memorable as most real ones), and charge a story like 'Seaton's Aunt' (*The Riddle*) with much of its force. Here the uncanny double ending may catch one out sharing the narrator's supernatural excuse for deficiencies of feeling. Such finessing on genre ('Seaton's Aunt' is far more than a ghost story) will be important in subsequent developments of the short story. De la Mare's is a poet's prose, whether rich in individual oddities and pleasurably varied textures, or restrained to transparency, with only occasional Stevensonian details like the boy's 'linnet legs' in 'An Ideal Craftsman' (*On the Edge*, 1930). Criticism has concentrated on de la Mare's more naturalistic (and less powerful) work; when it takes in the stranger stories, more justice may be done to his greatness. Meanwhile, he has no lack of readers.

In the United States, the short story was a more practised form (partly for reasons to do with marketing); and if this history were primarily concerned with American literature, many writers would clamour for attention, from Hemingway and Katherine Anne Porter and Faulkner and the uneven Fitzgerald, to the great contemporary Peter Taylor (1917–), whose work combines strengths of Jamesian delicacy, subtle Chekhovian restraint and deep Mansfieldian undercurrents. Faulkner had a formidable range, summing the history of his region in whole-books that contain such great stories as 'The Bear' (*Go Down, Moses*, 1942), with its long-suspended syntax holding the simultaneity of disparate truths in a single view, virtually in one passage, throughout a six-page sentence.

In the late modern phase of the short story, the most audacious American innovator was perhaps Eudora Welty (1909–), an admirer of Henry Green and a student of Hawthorne (as appears especially in historical pieces like 'First Love', 1943). Welty's stories are peopled with women who fantasize; with alienated eccentrics whose sanity one is not encouraged to question; and with children in whose world a sensuousness, usually repressed, is brilliantly recalled:

> Their toes exploded the dust that felt like the powder clerks pump into
> new kid gloves, as Jinny Love said twice. They were eye to eye with the
> finger-shaped leaves of the castor bean plants, put out like those gypsy

hands that part the curtains at the back of rolling wagons, and wrinkled and coated over like the fortune-teller's face.

('Moon Lake', 1949)

Much of Welty's fictional effort goes into a visionary overturning of literature's established mythologies of gender and political role (as in her valuation of the poor white). Sometimes her stories are mispitched; but often they succeed, and when they do they have a farouche, haunting power. She is at her best in a sort of dark purple poetic tragicomedy: in stories like 'June Recital' – or 'Moon Lake' (*The Golden Apples*, 1949), where an objection is felt to artificial respiration, as if it were public sexual intercourse. The subtext is explored more determinedly than in, say, Mansfield's stories. Welty's defect is the generous one of taking too many risks. To write what cannot be written is good, but sometimes results in what is not written well.

The short story was a chief triumph of the modernist movement. No other prose form – not even the novel – showed so much creative invention. Its variety astonishes; for (like poetry) it became diversified into a multitude of subgenres, which replaced such broad Victorian genres as the ghost story. Think of the range of stories, even within the individual *oeuvres* of Mansfield, de la Mare, A. E. Coppard (1878–1957), Elizabeth Bowen (1899–1973), V. S. Pritchett (1900–) and H. E. Bates (1905–). The short story was far more important in modernism than histories have generally indicated; and in postmodernist literature the genre was to play a greater part still.

At one extreme, the short story approached lyric poetry; at another it could be essayistic. The essay itself is often said to have died out in the twentieth century. That is as great nonsense as speaking of the death of the novel; but there are perhaps two grains of truth in it.

First, the informal familiar essay is now largely demoted to a journalistic status. It has been displaced in part by the fictional sketch, in part by the critical essay – both of which flourish. Critical essayists have indeed produced some of the best prose of the century. Some of this has been the work of writers whose achievement is thought of as being primarily in fiction. The Henry James of the Prefaces and *The Art of Fiction* (1884) and *Notes on Novelists* (1914) combines theoretic grasp with subtly persuasive tone; the D. H. Lawrence of *Studies in Classic American Literature* (1923) has penetration in getting to underlying issues; while the Virginia Woolf of *The Common Reader* (1925) – endlessly fresh, generally percipient – has to be saluted as an essayist of the great tradition. Others have done most of their best work in the essay form, like Max Beerbohm, Edmund Wilson, George Orwell, or

C. S. Lewis. Lewis's critical essays give the pleasure of surprising opinions cogently made good – the opinions of a mind that can make any matter (however abstruse) pellucidly simple. Sometimes he makes matters simpler than others think them to be; but who will say he has made them too simple?

Secondly, it is true that the digressive essay largely disappeared – a casualty, it seems, of modernism's classical tendency to unify. Even G. K. Chesterton tightened and sharpened the old obliquities into points of paradox, in such collections as *Heretics* (1905) and *The Glass Walking-Stick* (1955). But here there has been a further, postmodernist revolution. For in the avant garde prose pieces (stories? meditations?) of Guy Davenport and others, the digressive essay has returned in disguise. Anticipated by such works as Virginia Woolf's *A Room of One's Own* (1929), this tendency now owes much to the brilliant example of Jorge Luis Borges's stories. Nevertheless, it could also be seen as an oblique apotheosis of the essay.

14
Modernist Poetry and Drama

POETRY at the turn of the century can be thought of as still Tennysonian or pre-Raphaelite; and even some much more recent poetry has not entirely broken with late Romanticism. Like Hardy, W. B. Yeats (1865–1939) was to be a doyen of modernist poetry; yet his early work, right up to 1899, was mythological and vague – reminiscent of the pre-Raphaelites in its use of entrancing word-spells to work up a languorous, yearning mood:

> I will arise and go now, and go to Innisfree,
> And a small cabin build there, of clay and wattles made:
> Nine bean-rows will I have there, a hive for the honey-bee,
> And live alone in the bee-loud glade . . .
>
> I will arise and go now, for always night and day
> I hear lake water lapping with low sounds by the shore;
> While I stand on the roadway, or on the pavements grey,
> I hear it in the deep heart's core.
>
> ('The Lake Isle of Innisfree', 1890)

There is nothing modern about the repetitions and inversions here, nor the incantatory sound patterns, nor the drawn-out cadences ending the stanzas.

YEATS TO MACDIARMID

Ezra Pound and T. S. Eliot reacted violently against such Romantic dream worlds, as they did against Victorian poetic diction and conventions of metaphor. And Eliot was so impressive a critic that they were able to carry others with them; demolishing, for a time at least, some great reputations – Milton's and Tennyson's and Swinburne's – and brushing aside established traditionalists like Robert Bridges

('Rabbit Britches') without respect. The MODERNISTS (as the new school has since come to be called) preferred a more prosaic diction, colloquial and unliterary. In terms of genre, they turned away from the lyricism that had dominated much Victorian literature, and embraced the mode of epigram. Thus they seized freedom of subject matter – a freedom that had been desired by Pater, and that has since become increasingly distinctive of the century's poetry.

But in this movement Yeats himself was a mover: his changed style constituted one of the chief literary events of the prewar decade. He began to make claims about the relation of art to reality; to reject his own earlier languorousness; and to speak in a colder, angrier voice. Voice is a vital element in Yeats's poetry. For he dramatizes (and still mythologizes) the role of the poet; taking up now a bardic, now an alienated, stance, endlessly exhorting and quarrelling. 'We make out of the quarrel with others, rhetoric,' he said, 'but of the quarrel with ourselves, poetry.'

Yeats's bardic poems can sometimes seem pretentious. His humourless egotism betrays him into histrionics, or into too much talking – merely saying what he thinks (and in doing so, perhaps, giving away more than he means to). Yet, if the voice comes on too strong and mars some poems, others achieve greatness nevertheless. To select 'Among School Children' and 'Nineteen Hundred and Nineteen' and 'The Circus Animals' Desertion' is to omit dozens as good. This is true even of certain poems whose sense depends for its continuity on Yeats's notoriously eccentric visionary world system – like 'The Second Coming' or 'Sailing to Byzantium':

> O sages standing in God's holy fire
> As in the gold mosaic of a wall,
> Come from the holy fire, perne in a gyre,
> And be the singing-masters of my soul.
> Consume my heart away; sick with desire
> And fastened to a dying animal
> It knows not what it is; and gather me
> Into the artifice of eternity . . .
> ('Sailing to Byzantium', 1927)

Here 'perne in a gyre' is system terminology; yet the rhetoric almost carries one past its obscurity. And in Yeats's less hieratic poems, rhythm and movement are eloquent enough to override greater difficulties still. Some say that his seductive rhetoric hides defects of morality – as if by a cosmetic application. It might be replied that those who are morally imperfect need poems too. Besides, Yeats's rhetoric enables him to write many noble things that would otherwise be ineffable.

The poet's 'personal utterance', which in Yeats holds all together, is largely absent from the poetry of T. S. Eliot (1888–1965). As an American, Eliot found very hard the metrical refinements needed for poetry of voice; and in any case he preferred the irony of multiple personas, since they masked more ambiguously the personality he guarded. An exception is the Browningesque poem with which he made his debut, 'The Love Song of J. Alfred Prufrock' (1915), where the speaker's character explains away any uncolloquial extravagances of language. Almost all Eliot's later poems were much more difficult. The difficulty followed from concentration of form, and to some extent appeared in other writers of the time, such as Robert Bridges – as if they were obscurely epitomizing past culture in order to overreach it.

All the same, obscurity reached a formidable new pitch in Eliot's *The Waste Land* (1922), with its impossibly demanding allusions. Here the difficulty is of a new sort, arising from a discontinuity characteristic of modernism: an absence of transition between parts:

> O the moon shone bright on Mrs. Porter
> And on her daughter
> They wash their feet in soda water
> *Et O ces voix d'enfants, chantant dans la coupole!*
>
> Twit twit twit
> Jug jug jug jug jug jug
>
> So rudely forc'd.
> Tereu
>
> (lines 199–206)

Instead of the spoken voice's sequentiality in time, such poetry aims at a SPATIAL FORM, in which parts relate simultaneously as in visual art. What relates the pieces of Eliot's collage is not syntax but juxtaposition – an innovation pressed further by Pound's excisions from the manuscript. The juxtapositions are ordered intellectually, sometimes for satiric contrast of squalid modern sterility with earlier normality (as idealized in literature); sometimes so as to introduce a series of allusions to the remedial myths of the Waste Land and the Fisher King.

Occasionally a more elusive note is struck – as in the extraordinary passage in section v, beginning

> A woman drew her long black hair out tight
> And fiddled whisper music on those strings
> And bats with baby faces in the violet light

Whistled, and beat their wings
And crawled head downward down a blackened wall . . .
(lines 377–81)

in which Eliot reverts to SYMBOLISM or pure evocation, of a sort he had learnt from Mallarmé and other French *symbolistes*. Here communication matters less than fabricating an object for contemplation. *The Waste Land* is a work of historical importance, marking an epoch; nevertheless, only a few passages still give the impression of great poetry.

Every item in Eliot's small published *oeuvre* has its interest; and several – such as 'Gerontion' 'Marina' and 'The Journey of the Magi' – are memorable poems, enjoyable for their piquant combination of firm intellectual movement with specific, discontinuous images ('a watermill beating the darkness'; 'six hands at an open door dicing for pieces of silver'). But much of Eliot's reputation must rest on his long meditation on time, *Four Quartets* (1935–44), a poem of disputed stature.

The main problem seems to be that it is a Christian poem; which may be thought a narrow-minded objection. After all, Eliot understood better than Hopkins the requirements of apologetics in an age without faith in traditional religion. But *Four Quartets* has real flaws. Eliot had done graduate work on the philosopher F. H. Bradley, and was prepared to tackle metaphysical questions that the late Romantics had avoided (and that largely defeated de la Mare in his long poem *Winged Chariot*, 1951). In the process, a disproportionately developed intellect betrayed Eliot into some bald philosophizing ('Time present and time past / Are both perhaps present in time future') and some slack infill merely implementing the overall scheme. At its best, however, *Four Quartets* has the authority of a thinking mind – thinking impersonally rather than speaking – 'in the act of finding what will suffice'. Its difficulties are of the sort that draw one into inwardness. And for the most part it is wonderfully limpid; appealing to experience in a movingly simple way, yet not missing its complexity either:

Midwinter spring is its own season
Sempiternal though sodden towards sundown,
Suspended in time, between pole and tropic.
When the short day is brightest, with frost and fire,
The brief sun flames the ice, on pond and ditches,
In windless cold that is the heart's heat,
Reflecting in a watery mirror
A glare that is blindness in the early afternoon.
('Little Gidding' 1–8)

Four Quartets is perhaps the best long poem since Tennyson and Browning: it has the capacity to disclose new aspects with every reading.

The unquestionable centre of the modernist movement – friend and secretary of Yeats; friend of Eliot, T. E. Hulme, Wyndham Lewis, Henry James, Ford Madox Ford and William Carlos Williams; critic; collaborator; selfless impoverished patron – was Ezra Pound (1885–1972). Pound could be extremely persuasive (without him, indeed, Eliot's more traditional tendencies might well have triumphed), and had enough Whitmaniacal vitality to belong for a time to Lewis's 'Vorticist' cult of energy. He was well equipped to rally the new men for a radical 'modernization' of poetry. It now 'must be *as well written as prose*', and must discard literary diction, together with Victorian metrical conventions. This was no merely ignorant barbarity, for Pound could be a good critic and a fine craftsman – his earliest work had the late Victorian qualities in high measure. What Pound wanted was to increase intensity; as, for example, by LOGOPOEIA, a principle (based on Jamesian mimetic syntax) whereby words were in various ways to enact their meaning. But he was a confused thinker (not helped in that regard by Hulme's influence), and arrived at a false doctrine, which none the less was to be of great moment for subsequent literature.

This was the idea of discontinuity: of a 'lapsed grammar' suppressing syntax in the interest of intensity. The method appeared already in the famous HAIKU (Japanese seventeen syllable poem) 'In a Station of the Metro' (1913):

> The apparition of these faces in the crowd;
> Petals on a wet, black bough.

Here the juxtaposed images react on one another to suggest the likeness of people to brief flowers, and of diurnal emergence from the Underground to seasonal (and ghostly) emergence from death. In some ways this is in the manner of the IMAGIST poets (T. E. Hulme, 1883–1917; F. S. Flint, 1885–1960; Amy Lowell, 1874–1925), who organized their poems round images only. But its laconism is more extreme. All continuity of voice must be avoided as slackening tension – and as illusory; since mind itself, whether conceived in stream of consciousness or psychoanalytic terms, was discontinuous. While not silly – grammatical words can clog a poem – this theory badly underestimated the potential strength of syntax, and indeed its necessity for poetry.

Pound is most accessible in his earlier short poems, *Hugh Selwyn Mauberley* (1920) and 'Homage to Sextus Propertius' (1934, wr. 1917–18). In his major work, the unfinished *Cantos* (wr. from 1915; published in instalments, e.g. 1925, 1930, 1949 (*Pisan Cantos*), 1957, 1959, 1970), he often takes his method to absurd lengths, beyond any conceivable reader's capacity to follow. The difficulties multiply: elliptic authorial telegraphese; truncation of anecdotes; pastiche-translation of undistinguished, unpoetic authors (classical Chinese, Renaissance Italian, abstruse American); abbreviation of fragments from archives; allusion to unknown names; numbers; and ideograms – to say nothing of a substantial foreign language element. Some passages amount to marginalia on Chinese classics, or even on American histories, and can only make sense if they are read together with these absent texts. Governing all this miscellaneous material is a comprehensive cyclic theory of history, indebted to Spengler and possibly Yeats. (Like most of the modernists, Pound was profoundly orientated to the past – 'aware of the innumerable dead', as MacDiarmid expresses it.) The arrogance – indeed the madness – of his pseudohistory disguises the method's inherent impossibility and unhistoricality.

But the *Cantos* can be penetrating, even persuasive (as in the easy Usury Canto, xlv). And there are marvellously lucid lyrical passages, like parts of Canto xvii –

> Chrysophrase,
> And the water green clear, and blue clear;
> On, to the great cliffs of amber.

– where the logopoeia is pure joy. (The water's sound pattern mirrors the sky's and is repeated more densely in the cliff's: 'water . . . clear . . . clear . . . cliffs of amber'.) Such passages are thrown away among heaps of dross: the *Cantos* contain great poetry without being, in sum, an indisputably great poem. The beginning reader must either skip freely, or study with the help of academic commentary – a new possibility not intended by Pound.

The difficulty of Pound's poetry, together with the frequent changes of diction, makes his language very noticeable: opaque rather than transparent. Indeed this is generally true of the modernist poets, despite their avoidance of poetic words; and of none more than Hugh MacDiarmid (C. M. Grieve) (1892–1978). Even in fine short lyrics like 'The Watergaw [faint rainbow]' and 'The Eemis [balanced] Stane' (both in *Sangschaw*, 1925) the words have a hard functional compression that requires each to be weighed. MacDiarmid is sometimes said to write in dialect, or in vernacular Scots. But no one speaks his language, which is an artifical achievement – comparable in its way with that of *Finnegans Wake* – an amalgam of the old court Lallans of the Makars with standard Scots and obsolete dictionary words. His poems in English often have a similar opacity:

> All is lithogenesis – or lochia,
> Carpolite fruit of the forbidden tree,
> Stones blacker than any in the Caaba,
> Cream-coloured caen-stone, chatoyant pieces,
> Celadon and corbeau, bistre and beige,
> Glaucous, hoar, enfouldered, cyathiform,
> Making mere faculae of the sun and moon
> I study you glout and gloss, but have
> No cadrans to adjust you with, and turn again
> From optik to haptik and like a blind man run
> My fingers over you, arris by arris, burr by burr,
> Slickensides, truité, rugas, foveoles . . .
>
> ('On a Raised Beach' 1–12, *Stony Limits and
> Other Poems*, 1934; 1956)

There was nothing of symbolism in MacDiarmid's high-resolution materialistic vision of the world's dense, miraculous texture. It increasingly demanded expression in long, talkative 'wide-angle' poems about everything at once – the *Hymns to Lenin* (1931; 1935); 'The Kind of Poetry I Want' (1943); *In Memoriam James Joyce* (1955). Marred as these are by daunting polymath flourishes – 'even as we know / Schweitzer and Cappelletti on the Cimbric language' – they give a stronger sense of intellectual expansion and command than any other modernist long poems except those of Wallace Stevens:

> They are not endless these variations of form
> Though it is perhaps impossible to see them all.
> It is certainly impossible to conceive one that doesn't exist.
> But I keep trying in our forest to do both of these,
> And though it is a long time now since I saw a new one
> I am by no means weary yet of my concentration
> On phyllotaxis here in preference to all else,
> All else – but my sense of sny!
>
> The gold edging of a bough at sunset, its pantile way
> Forming a double curve, tegula and imbrex in one,
> Seems at times a movement on which I might be borne
> Happily to infinity . . .
>
> ('In Memoriam James Joyce', 1955)

MacDiarmid's pedantry and his inclusion of perishable unpoetic material have prompted diagnoses of 'undigestion'; in which he is no different from Pound. Like the 'Pound–Eliot *olla podrida* of tongues', his method is designed for ingestion, not poetic assimilation. (Sometimes all three poets make you wonder whether you are dealing with proud eagles or mere magpies.) But at least MacDiarmid's long poems achieve success more often than those of Pound's American emulators, William Carlos Williams's *Paterson* (1946–58) and Charles Olson's *The Maximus Poems* (1953–68), or than David Jones's more eccentric *The Anathemata* (1952).

MacDiarmid's work had a decisive effect on Scottish literature, uniting its lyrical and intellectual traditions, and turning what has come to be called the Scottish Renaissance in a modernist direction. Yet, although his boundless aspirations stirred many hearts, his poetic achievement proved hard to assess. For in his case, Britain's peripheral culture became more international, and 'higher', than most of its metropolitan culture. For decades criticism of MacDiarmid was obtusely provincial; and even now it only grudgingly recognizes his stature.

CONTINUATIONS AND RESUMPTIONS

Modernist poetic diction became established in a remarkably uniform and lasting way. Opacity of language was even to be found in light verse such as Edith Sitwell's in *Façade* (1922). In a line like 'Beelzebub called for his syllabub in the hotel in Hell', reading through the wordplay to the ideas is likely to miss the pleasure and the point. And after a partial reaction in the thirties towards comparative clarity, in the public poetry of W. H. Auden (1907–73), Stephen Spender (1909–) and C. Day Lewis (1904–72), opaque language returned with 'New Apocalyptic' poets like David Gascoyne (1916–) and George Barker (1913–), as well as with Dylan Thomas (1914–53).

Among the steps taken by Pound and Eliot to 'modernize' poetry, one of the most decisive was their countenancing of FREE VERSE or *vers libre*, a form of verse without metre. This derived from many sources, including Whitman and Mallarmé; it was by no means new as an occasional recourse. In effect, it gave up the subtleties of spoken rhythm counterpointed with metre, in exchange for a single rhythm. This cruder single rhythm was defined only by line length, line break and frequent use of repetitions or idioms predictable in rhythm. The formless flaccid verse that resulted on all sides appalled the openers of this metrical Pandora's box. By the twenties Pound (who had a good sense of rhythm) and Eliot (who at least kept a good pace) had largely reverted to irregular metrical rhythm. (Prosy lines in Pound's *Cantos*, supposed to show that he could get anything into poetry, in fact show that he could not.) The reaction was almost universal. After the thirties, however, free verse returned to favour, through the influence of William Carlos Williams (1883–1963) and the Black Mountain poets, especially Charles Olson (1910–70) and Robert Creeley (1926–).

Williams sometimes used the line break pause very intrusively, in order to get value from every word and in the (mistaken) hope of achieving 'thrust'. His much anthologized imagist poem 'The Red Wheelbarrow' is in these respects characteristic:

> so much depends
> upon
>
> a red wheel
> barrow
>
> glazed with rain
> water
>
> beside the white
> chickens.
> (*Spring and All*, 1923)

Apart from the stanzas' programmatic visual shape, the point lies in ambiguities forced by the line breaks. 'Much depends' physically, at first, on the 'wheel', and then, more abstractly, on the whole wheelbarrow; just as what falls as 'rain' after the line break becomes 'rainwater'. Williams had an inwardness with the rhythms of lively speech, as poems like 'Tract' show. But his disciples and successors cheapened the freedoms he had taken; coarsening his rhythmic verse into chopped-up prose. The vicious sequence *adjective / line break pause / noun* was soon commonplace – as one finds even in Creeley. Before long it became generally difficult to return to subtler rhythms; and now the old metrical skills are perhaps beyond recovery.

The suddenness with which international modernism was introduced into England (and the slowness of its acceptance) had much to do with the fact that many of the writers were not in fact English – James, Conrad, Ford and Mansfield in fiction; Yeats, Pound, Eliot, MacDiarmid and MacNeice in poetry; Shaw, Barrie, Synge, O'Casey, Bridie and Beckett in drama. Partly for the same reason, the modernists (especially Pound and MacDiarmid) could be said to have forced British poetry away from its 'natural', or at least indigenous, development.

The indigenous line was represented by the GEORGIANS — that is, in effect, the poets included in Edward Marsh's five anthologies (1912–22) during the reign of George V. These included Robert Graves, Walter de la Mare, Edward Thomas, Andrew Young, John Masefield and W. H. Davies, as well as the war poets Rupert Brooke, Wilfred Owen, Edmund Blunden and Siegfried Sassoon. Thomas's American friend Robert Frost is sometimes associated with the group (in so far as it was a group); but D. H. Lawrence, though he contributed, is not. The characteristic Georgian poem was oblique in movement, and comparatively unpretentious — even light — in tone. It continued the pre-Raphaelite pursuit of vague suggestion, but returned, for compensating precision, to the less arbitrary natural imagery of Romanticism. All this was rethought with a new economy. Thus, in 'The Flesh-Scraper', by the Herrick-like Andrew Young (1885–1971) –

> If I had sight enough
> Might I not find a fingerprint
> Left on this flint
> By Neolithic man or Kelt?
> So knapped to scrape a wild beast's pelt,
> The thumb below, fingers above,
> See, my hand fits it like a glove.

– much is left, typically, to the reader. One has to see for oneself how the hand fits and incorporates the guilty flint, just as the dissembling glove hides the fingerprint. One has to work out (it is never stated) the implication of primordial crime in a slight natural object. This strategy of indirection, which was adopted by poets as diverse as Robert Bridges and D. H. Lawrence, came to underlie many subsequent short lyrics and epigrams. It is one well adapted to give poetic pleasure.

Of the Georgian poets, de la Mare (1873–1956) is often underrated, or damned with patronizing praise as merely (merely!) our greatest children's poet. In fact he was one of the finest craftsmen in English literature, and used Romantic and folk material with a sharply new, metaphysical tonality. De la Mare is described as an 'escapist' poet; but this misrepresents his continual effort to show the 'reality' of scientific rationalism incomplete. Besides delicate lyrics like 'Old Shellover', 'Fare Well' and 'John Mouldy', he wrote strongly resonant (but still quiet) poems such as 'The Railway Junction', 'The Stranger' and 'The Song of the Mad Prince'. Remarkably often, he achieved unforgettably strange symbolic effects.

The best of the Georgians, had he lived, might well have been

Edward Thomas (1878–1917), a late developer who left some of the finest poems in the language – poems like 'The Chalk Pit', 'Lob', 'Swedes' and 'As the Team's Head-Brass'. Thomas usually describes a scene very fully, planning it in the minutest respects (despite the surface of casual sincerity), and realizing it with Keatsian textures and a logopoeia by no means inferior to Pound's. But he could also operate on a smaller scale, as in 'Thaw'(1916):

> Over the land freckled with snow half-thawed
> The speculating rooks at their nests cawed
> And saw from elm-tops, delicate as flower of grass,
> What we below could not see, Winter pass.

Here Thomas's meditations are so understated, so uninsistent, that you are won into forming his ideas as your own.

Edwardian and Georgian celebration of England has been so much in disrepute, and modernism so dominant, that for some time Georgian poetry itself has tended to be undervalued. But now there are signs of reestimation – not only as regards Thomas and de la Mare, but also Rupert Brooke (1887–1915). Brooke's various skills enabled him to make poems of very distinct individuality, which have proved their durability.

Robert Graves (1895–1985), like William Soutar in Scotland, toughened the diction of the Georgian poem, and did much to accomplish its development into the modern (or neo-Metaphysical) epigram and lyric, the standard short genres of the mid-twentieth century. A traditional poet using Romantic or folk material, Graves was nevertheless open to modernist influences (particularly that of his close friend, the American Laura Riding, an arguably greater poet than himself). He regularly worked out his metaphors in a logical, even Metaphysical, way. After his Georgian phase he kept developing in new directions; so that his work came to add up to a considerable, highly individual *oeuvre*. Although he had few immediate followers, his finely structured poems – as various as 'Outlaws', 'Pure Death', 'True Joy', 'Call it a Good Marriage' and 'Lollocks' – set benchmarks of long-term consequence for the craft of poetry.

If this history were not centred on British literature, it would now occupy itself with the Australian poet A. D. Hope (1907–), together with several Americans, accessible modernists of considerable weight: Robert Frost (1874–1963), who kept the possibility of narrative poetry alive; Marianne Moore (1887–1972), who wrote impressively precise SYLLABICS (verses based on syllable count, not metre), with flat, dry, prosaic rhythms; and above all the great Wallace Stevens (1879–1955), who resumed the tradition of the philosophical Romantics – giving it a sceptical bias certainly, yet all the same reviving eloquent poetry of large statement. As it is, we turn to Wystan H. Auden (1907–73).

Arguably the greatest poet since Tennyson, Auden is certainly like a great poet in declining to be easily placed. He seems indisputably modern in his colloquial diction; his images drawn from industry, flying and urban life; his Freudianism; and his fondness for reveries assessing current tendencies. Yet his poetry is not usually difficult or discontinuous, as one expects from a modernist. He has been seen as a late Romantic. And his generalizing diction and rational chains of discourse could be likened to their equivalents in eighteenth-century public or conversational poets. Think of 'Musée des Beaux Arts' (1938) – 'About suffering they were never wrong / The Old Masters . . .'; or 'The Capital' (1938) –

> . . . In unlighted streets you hide away the appalling;
> Factories where lives are made for a temporary use
> Like collars or chairs, rooms where the lonely are battered
> Slowly like pebbles into fortuitous shapes.

Yet Auden never gives the impression, as his contemporaries C. Day Lewis (1904–72) and Stephen Spender (1909–) sometimes do, of having introduced modern images in a merely deliberate or doctrinaire way. Auden actually *liked* industrial landscapes. He is said to have disowned both his own and his civilization's past – to have worked out his poems' wisdom afresh on each occasion.

But this, again, is only half the picture; for his versatile revamping of old forms, like his brilliant imitation of earlier writers (from Old English to de la Mare), brought literary tradition to bear none the less. This, in fact, gave Auden considerable historical importance. His authority was such as to make his work, as it were, a recycling plant, from which time-honoured genres and devices could be reissued, rendered viable once more. He even showed that traditional verse forms like villanelle, sestina and sonnet – given experimental modifications – need not mean old ideas. Modern incantations were possible.

Already as an undergraduate Auden was recognized by many as a major poet; no doubt partly because of his magisterial tone – a feature that continued in his later work (think of lines like 'Look, stranger, at this island now'; 'Our hunting fathers told the story'; 'Consider this and in our time'; 'O Love, the interest itself in thoughtless Heaven'). And the tone generally rings true: if Auden had not quite Eliot's intellect, he had a more comprehensive command as a poet. This extended over an astonishing range of forms and technical skills. Some have expressed scepticism, however, about how far Auden developed. There can be no doubt of his development up to the fertile period of *Look, Stranger!* (1936) and *Another Time* (1940), of the plays (written with Christopher Isherwood) (1904–86) and of *Letters from Iceland* (with Louis MacNeice): a time when he was publishing such poems as 'Lay Your Sleeping Head, My Love' and 'In Memory of W. B. Yeats'. After his move to the United States in 1939, however, Auden turned to longer poems, some of them commentaries on other literary works, like the brilliant *The Sea and the Mirror* (1945) and 'The Shield of Achilles' (1955). This phase has been seen as a decline, particularly by those who make the mistake of thinking Auden a political poet.

That Auden subsequently wrote many weak poems should not matter much: it is small-minded to prefer the tit's egg to the volcano, small perfection to wasteful greatness. And certainly he matured intellectually, in that his neutral urbanity grew more inclusive and less superficial. About his development in other respects, however, a question hangs. Attention needs to be given to the new emotional reaches that are finely explored in relatively late poems like 'In Praise of Limestone' (1951):

> If it form the one landscape that we, the inconstant ones,
>   Are consistently homesick for, this is chiefly
> Because it dissolves in water. Mark these rounded slopes
>   With their surface fragrance of thyme and, beneath,
> A secret system of caves and conduits . . .
>
> (lines 1–5)

Here landscape, human typology and natural setting are brought together to illuminate one another, in an easy yet satisfying way. But it is doubtful whether Auden's later work quite arrives at the increased depth of feeling and personal perspective hoped for from great poets in their last years. His is a flawed greatness: for all its craft, his poetry quite often fails to move the reader.

Some of Auden's main contributions were to the modern long poem on a conversational or meditative level, as in *The Age of Anxiety* (1947). This type of spoken reverie needs to be clearly distinguished from epic – the impossible great poem that Pound or Olson attempted, or Hart Crane in *The Bridge* (1930), or David Jones in *The Anathemata* (1952). Modern epics have all more or less failed to be readable, except for Basil Bunting's Poundian but lucid 'Chomei at Toyama' (1933) and his weighty, rugged-textured *Briggflatts* (1966). At a far remove from

Pound's or Jones's discontinuous, opaque, vast, mythic structures, the modern 'long poem' is of middle length only, and has a relatively unbroken, communicative flow. For models it reaches back before Whitman to Coleridge and Cowper, developing them in a way at once inward and ratiocinative; but perhaps its most seminal exemplars are the long poems of Yeats. Until recently it has not been a genre much practised in Britain, except by MacDiarmid. But in the United States, from the time of Wallace Stevens's 120-line 'Sunday Morning' (*Harmonium*, 1923), it came to be an indispensable part of the formal repertoire. Later Stevens examples like 'Notes Toward a Supreme Fiction' (*Transport to Summer* 1947) and 'The Auroras of Autumn' (1950) achieved profound philosophical effects. Stevens the sceptical myth-maker and cerebral Romantic – oddly assisted in this by the not particularly intellectual Auden – succeeded in giving the long poem a distinctly rational orientation.

A modernist specialty even more significant than the American long poem was the non-narrative SEQUENCE or cycle. Narrative sequences continued up to Meredith and in some degree even to Hardy. But in Hardy's elegiac 'Poems of 1912–13' and in Yeats's 'Nineteen Hundred and Nineteen' (1921), 'Meditations in Time of Civil War' (1921–2) and other sequences, a subtler relation obtains. It is one of recurrent imagery and themes, lexical echoes and varied tones – reminiscent, in fact, of Tennyson's *In Memoriam*. The items make fresh starts, and have each their own emotional climate. This kind of sequence soon lost its Victorian (or Tudor retrospective) affiliation. It attracted the major effort of several poets; becoming in effect a modern equivalent of epic (although smaller scale applications were also possible). *The Waste Land* could be considered a sequence of very dissimilar items; while *Four Quartets* is an excellent example, comprising formally balanced items in different tonalities. Pound's *Cantos*, multicentred and multitonal as they are, can be regarded similarly. And Williams's *Paterson* is so diverse – even chaotic – that it suggests sequence as much as unitary work.

A less ambiguous example is MacDiarmid's lyric sequence *A Drunk Man Looks at the Thistle* (1926), which as much as any work marked the efflorescence of the Scottish literary Renaissance. Other Scottish sequences followed, by Edwin Muir (1887–1959), Iain Crichton Smith (1928–), Edwin Morgan (1920–) and others. MacDiarmid's grittily brilliant work involves its visionary flights with the ideas of Continental poets like Blok (and with much more besides), yet succeeds in keeping up – perhaps even too remorselessly – a sustained purpose.

After the Second World War, the sequence became almost a dominant form, and was modified in a great variety of ways. One of its potentialities can be conveniently studied in Wallace Stevens's mini-sequence 'Thirteen Ways of Looking at a Blackbird' (1917), in *Harmonium* (1923):

I

Among twenty snowy mountains,
The only moving thing
Was the eye of the blackbird . . .

VIII

I know noble accents
And lucid, inescapable rhythms;
But I know, too,
That the blackbird is involved
In what I know . . .

Here Stevens successively delineates the blackbird through a series of very different perspectives, until it becomes a highly economical symbol. He arrives at complexity not only by syntactic means, but by juxtaposing images with very distinct implications. But if the sequence was sometimes tightly drawn together at a cerebral level like this, it could also be much more loosely related, like those in Yeats's *The Tower* (1928). A genre capable of great diversity and tonal surprise, it has organized some of the finest works of the century, such as Stevens's 'The Auroras of Autumn' (1948) and 'Credences of Summer' (1947), Geoffrey Hill's *Mercian Hymns* (1971) and John Montague's semi-narrative *The Rough Field 1961–1971* (1972).

MODERNIST DRAMA

After the decline of drama in the early eighteenth century and its temporary recovery in the time of Oliver Goldsmith (?1730–74), David Garrick (1717–79) and Richard Brinsley Sheridan (1751–1816), theatre flourished in the Victorian period – at least in the sense that it attracted mass audiences to farces and popular melodramas. Pantomime had its heyday; playing a vital part in keeping the myths of romance alive in the public mind. Victorian theatre offered little that could be called dramatic literature, however, until the 1880s.

Then two types of a more promising nature emerged, which have continued, with interruptions, ever since. The first, a drama of brilliant epigrammatic talk, took up certain possibilities of Restoration drama and added a touch of fantasy – as, very differently, in W. S. Gilbert's Savoy operettas (for example *The Mikado*, 1885), and Oscar Wilde's scintillating comedies of manners, especially *The Importance of Being Earnest* (1895). The other type – which became dominant and even rather tyrannical – was the play of naturalistic realism. This owed much to the powerful example of drama in Russia and Scandinavia (where indigenous theatrical tradition, always conservative, was happily absent altogether). By far the strongest influence was that of the great Ibsen, who was translated by William Archer. Archer's criticism instilled the notion of regarding the proscenium as if it were a missing fourth wall, or a window framing the slice of life on stage. Ibsen, with his social conscience and deep psychological symbolism, was at first a dangerous vortex of strong views. But eventually his method came to be followed even by the conservative Arthur Wing Pinero (1855–1934).

Pinero was a master of the WELL MADE PLAY – that is, the classically constructed play complete with thematic plot, revelations, reversals and emotional climaxes. Such plays are sometimes sneered at now by shallow praters. But Pinero's Jonsonian farces of character, like *The Magistrate* (1885), and even more his dramas or problem plays, like *The Second Mrs Tanqueray* (1893), have real substance, and can still give a deeply engaging dramatic experience. If the theatre has ceased to offer plays that are made so well, that is not a point in its favour. Other dramatists wrote well made plays of a not dissimilar kind: Henry Arthur Jones (1891–1929), the extremely interesting but uneven Harley Granville Barker (1877–1946) and the deserving, dull John Galsworthy (1869–1933) – who nevertheless had one prophetic oddity, that he left audiences to judge for themselves on the social issues he taught them about.

A strong challenge to naturalistic realism came from the Scottish playwright J. M. Barrie (1860–1937), in a series of London successes from 1894. Barrie has proved hard to assess: his plays call for robust emotional participation, and some have mistaken this warmth for sentimentality. But Barrie had quite unsentimental aims, and a method that entitles him to be considered an early modernist. For example his fantasies *Dear Brutus* (1917) and *Mary Rose* (1920), constructed as they are like well made plays, attempt realistic studies of the relation between wishes, fantasies, memories and reality (a hard field that will later need reworking by Harold Pinter). Earlier, in *The Admirable Crichton* (1902) and *What Every Woman Knows* (1908), matters of social structure – marital roles and egalitarian experiment – are treated in such a way that they can still engage the emotions. But the most interesting and least understood of Barrie's plays, only now beginning to be staged in a perceptive way, is *Peter Pan* (1904). This needs to be recognized as an early essay in EXPRESSIONISM, or non-naturalistic psychological realism. Barrie was well enough aware (better than some have supposed) what generational antagonisms this play projects, and what emotions of ageing. Also, what social implications. For the last speech of Hook the pirate of commerce, as he yields to the saurian emblem of time, is '*Floreat Etona*'. Barrie's tragedy was that he easily got away with anything audiences could treat as whimsy; so that critics have not troubled to probe more deeply.

The more obvious modernizer was George Bernard Shaw (1856–1950), professed disciple of Ibsen, fearless exponent of socialist views and scourge of the well made play. Yet Shaw's work, too, should be seen as Janus-faced. There was nothing new, and certainly nothing of modernism, in an obviously didactic stance; while his subversive wit was as entertaining – as little disturbing – as Wilde's. Shaw's modernism lay in the great innovation of introducing into England that alien genre, the drama of ideas. Interplay of ideas provides the rationale of much in his plots, his (relatively loose) construction, even his characters (who are never quite free to develop like people). But Shaw's intimate knowledge of the theatre, together with his fertile inventiveness, ensures that the ideas seldom overbear the entertainment or spoil the frequent surprises. Such ideas, one feels, are ideas in process of being worked out. In *Arms and the Man* (1894), *Man and Superman* (1905), *Major Barbara* (1905) and *Pygmalion* (1912) and the rest of his dazzlingly various successes – the score or so of his better plays – Shaw examines received prejudices in a centrifugal, apparently undetermined way; letting the dialogue (professedly modelled on Molière's) take its exploratory course, with an impromptu Peacockian brilliance that hardly ever fails to generate intellectual excitement. His characters, however, lack credible substance; as shows up perilously in his 'Russian' play *Heartbreak House* (wr. 1916). When Shaw's ambitious *St Joan* (1924) tries for emotional engagement, it partly fails.

If Shaw's plays were a little overestimated, this was perhaps to some degree because he made them ideal plays to read, by enhancing them with semi-narrative stage directions, often of an elaborate specificity – 'His collar, dyed Wotan blue . . .'. Such novelistic stage directions and prefaces are not so irrelevant as some have thought. They 'place' the characters within their social setting, in a way invaluable to empathizing actors. Thus Catherine Petkoff is 'a very splendid specimen of the wife of a mountain farmer'; and Liza Doolittle's hat is not just dirty, but 'has long been exposed to the dust and soot of London and has seldom if ever been brushed'. We are even told that Mrs Higgins 'was brought up on Morris and Burne Jones':

> There is a portrait of Mrs Higgins as she was when she defied fashion in her youth in one of the beautiful Rossettian costumes which, when caricatured by people who did not understand, led to the absurdities of popular estheticism in the eighteen-seventies.
>
> (*Pygmalion* Act III, first s.d.)

Besides, Shaw's stage directions were significant in other ways. By their means he established a quite new tightness of control over performance.

The creative ferment of the first decade or so of the century coincided with sweeping institutional changes. The most obvious was the founding of the Royal Court Theatre (1904), of the Abbey Theatre, Dublin (1904) and other repertory theatres. Another was the first replacement of actor–managers by directors: a change that was eventually to prove fatal to repertory and (with a few brilliant exceptions) disastrous to the theatre in general. After these changes, however, there seems to have been a distinct slackening of avant garde initiative.

English theatre had no emergent dramatist of the stature of the American Eugene O'Neill (1888–1953), whose somewhat cumbrous experiments have in consequence been overpraised. Indeed, there was actually a return to something very like the Victorian well made play, notably in the professionally varied *oeuvre* of Terence Rattigan (1911–77). About Rattigan's able work, opinions differ sharply. Plays like *The Browning Version* (1942) and *The Deep Blue Sea* (1952) continue to hold audiences, and sometimes to move them. They certainly show impressive technical skill; but it may be doubted whether they challenge on all the levels available to the dramatist. The depth of Noel Coward (1899–1973), on the contrary, is probably underrated – as if he were an inferior middlebrow Shaw without ideas or wit. Coward made his dialogue banal deliberately, in a modernizing release of comic speech from its literary corset, comparable to Pound's and Eliot's change in poetic diction. Characters in Coward find more distinctively theatrical means of expressing themselves than fancy words (sometimes, than words of any kind). *Private Lives* (1929) and other of his comedies may survive for their quintessential period flavour; and a play like *Design for Living* (1932) is by no means trivial, although it might be thought pernicious. A little later, J. B. Priestley (1894–1984) wrote on the nature of time (*Time and the Conways*, 1937) and other large subjects, but without precision of language or thought.

Non-illusionistic drama was kept alive by Scottish and Irish dramatists. It is usual to speak here of Sean O'Casey (1880–1964) as the most important figure. He was capable both of heightened realism, as in *The Shadow of a Gunman* (1922) or *Juno and the Paycock* (1924), and of non-realistic allegory. But his language, although at times extravagantly poetic, is uneconomical and lacking in sustained interest. O'Casey hated strongly enough to portray Irish life without idealizing it; but hated too much to see it straight. The Scottish dramatist James Bridie (O. H. Mavor, 1888–1951) has more range of topics and more invention. Plays like *A Sleeping Clergyman* (1933), *Mr Bolfry* (1943), *Daphne Laureola* (1949) and *The Baikie Charivari* (1952) easily escape from the limitations of naturalism, and open surprising Shavian perspectives on their subjects. But the comparison is disadvantageous, since he lacked Shaw's coherent views. Bridie's better claim rests simply on his enlargement of theatrical possibilities – or on his inspired unpredictability.

Another cross current in drama had its impulse in T. S. Eliot's principled endeavour to reintroduce literary, even poetic, language. His *Murder in the Cathedral* (1935) began a religious drama movement; and *The Family Reunion* (1939) might bear comparison with O'Neill's classical trilogy in its quest for a new dramatic language. After the great interruption of the Second World War, Eliot's later plays – like *The Cocktail Party* (1949) – bravely attempted tragicomedy, and even farce, in a verse indistinguishable from prose, unless by its faint elephantinity. Against the odds, Christopher Fry (1907–) had ephemeral success with out-and-out poetic drama. The gay Festival of Britain lyricism of *The Lady's Not for Burning* (1948) or *The Dark is Light Enough* (1954) will not bear study. But the fact that it worked for a time in the theatre shows the dissatisfaction with a realistic drama that had become stereotyped.

From the thirties to the early fifties, then, the development of drama was excursive or desultory. Two influential plays helped to change this in a decisive way. One of these, *Look Back in Anger* (1956) by John Osborne (1930–), now seems rather an oldfashioned realist play. But it was by a working-class playwright; and its long speeches of passionate diatribe expressed an impatience with prewar survivals that struck many resonances among the young. Its significance is that it opened drama once more to passionate expression – and not necessarily about political matters. This possibility was to be taken up in various ways by Harold Pinter, John Arden, Edward Bond and Ann Jellicoe; while a number of more or less working-class plays appeared, from Arnold Wesker, Henry Livings and others.

The second decisive play, Samuel Beckett's *Waiting for Godot* (1955, wr. in French 1949), was not at all realist or illusionistic. Indeed, it at first intrigued audiences by its general unintelligibility. But this apparent novelty covered a return (not very surprising in an Irishman) to medieval semi-allegorical Morality – to a drama orientated to death, as if that were life's central reality. *Waiting for Godot* avoids particular issues of morality or politics (except such very general aspects as are treated in Pozzo's oppression of Lucky). Its doctrine is existentialist philosophy: it is concerned solely with the fundamental human predicament, which it portrays as totally black, beyond human capacity to despair about adequately. To this starkly simple purpose, Beckett strips dramatic form to essentials (and in his later plays, as we shall see, will always have to go further in the same direction). The characters are undeveloped, the plot almost non-existent, the action discontinuous and mostly limited to basic patterns like music-hall routines. Even so, Beckett's enterprise, however serious, is self-falsifying. For every formal element in the play – the very zest of its language – relieves the blackness; as indeed art is compelled to do, in order that man may remain blind to it. After Beckett, black comedy with philosophical overtones became a fairly common form.

Both Beckett and Osborne may in themselves, perhaps, have been a little overrated; but it is undeniable that from them, in large part, has followed a whole 'new drama' – such as it is.

15
Postmodernism

THE end of the Second World War marked a new phase in literature. After the war, British writers (with occasional exceptions like MacDiarmid) shared a desire for change and a mood of reaction against political ideology – revulsion from fascism, disillusionment with communism. But only a few of them, such as Samuel Beckett and John Fowles (1926–), had any interest, at first, in the theoretically based innovations that were being made in Continental literatures, particularly French. Indeed, many English-speaking writers seemed to distrust radical changes of form as much as they distrusted large statements. They preferred minimal affirmations, often disguised, like those of Kingsley Amis (1922–), John Wain (1925–) Philip Larkin (1922–85), or Angus Wilson (1915–), under a cover of sardonic irony.

POSTMODERN VERSIONS OF REALITY

This split between 'advanced' and traditional writing had of course already existed in earlier modernism: Nabokov was hardly published in English until 1941, in Britain until 1957. But now the avant garde, although still separated from the public at large, drew increasing support from the young; and they began, at first in America, to build a larger following – without however increasing literature's total readership. The new avant garde literature (NEOMODERNIST or POSTMODERNIST) partly carried modernism further, partly reacted against it – for example against its ideology and its historical orientation. What it consistently pretended to be (and sometimes actually was) was *new*. Determinedly self-destructive, it attempted to cut off its branch of the past, by proposing entirely new methods, a fresh 'syllabus' or canon of authors (Nietzsche, Freud, Saussure, Proust) and a new register of allusions. (Postmodern writers like the American Thomas Pynchon (1937–) are more likely to allude to recent science and politics than to literature of the past.) Supporting all these innovations was a new aesthetic, based at first on existentialism, then on structuralist literary theory. And latterly, postmodern writing has been closely responsive to deconstruction.

These strains of thought have been uncongenial to most British writers, because of their extremity – whether the STRUCTURALIST extremity of denying the author's existence (concentrating on the relation between literary elements to the exclusion of their function), or DECONSTRUCTION's Nietszcheian scepticism about the possibility of meaning. In consequence, a certain insularity has characterized much postwar English fiction and poetry, for good or ill. Until recently, even the best English writers remained ignorant of the work of Nabokov, Barth and Pynchon, who were elsewhere seminal. Indeed for a time, from the late fifties to the early seventies, American fiction – like Scottish and Irish poetry – tended to overshadow English 'metropolitan' (but provincial) writing. Nevertheless, postmodernism in a broader sense eventually came to constitute a distinct period in English fiction too.

Distinguishing much postmodernist fiction was an awareness that simple realism leaves out a good deal, and presupposes countless assumptions about what constitutes the real. It reflected an awareness, in fact, that literary imitation is problematic. Individual character, for example, no longer seemed to motivate action adequately; so that it accordingly ceased to be the main focus, at least, of avant garde fiction. Recognizing all this, some novelists set out to 'damage' narrative illusion deliberately, by alienation devices. They might do so by making authorial intrusions like John Fowles's in *The French Lieutenant's Woman* (1969). Or they might introduce impossibilities into the narrative itself, like the seaboots in William Golding's *Pincher Martin* (1956), which force the reader beyond the story to its meanings. When Golding's novel first appeared, the implications of the boots were endlessly debated. Now readers take such damaged fiction in their stride, so pervasive has postmodernism's influence been.

Another possibility was to multiply versions of reality, as Lawrence Durrell did in *The Alexandria Quartet* (1957–60), or Fowles in *The Collector* (1963) and *The Magus* (1966, rev. 1977). The same idea underlay the alternative endings of *The French Lieutenant's Woman*, supposedly corresponding to different 'worlds'. This may not seem a very new device: it was already implicit in the double ending of Kipling's *The Light that Failed* (1891). But, even at their most experimental, the modernists took for granted the unitary seamlessness of a reality they were still content to imitate. And this the postmodernists refused to do.

Whatever their differences, they agreed in rejecting Ford Madox Ford's doctrine that 'the object of the novelist is to keep the reader oblivious to the fact that the author exists – even of the fact that he is reading a book'.

Traditional fiction nevertheless continued to develop strongly, if in a more expressionist way, in the work of such novelists as Graham Greene (1904–), Angus Wilson (1913–) and Iris Murdoch (1919–) – and for that matter in Fowles and Golding. Perhaps significantly, however, several of the finest of such novelists, including Patrick White (1912–) and V. S. Naipaul (1932–), worked within extra-European frames of reference, and to that extent may have seemed to escape the compromised ideological 'reality'. The most impressive *oeuvres* of the period, indeed, have been those of traditional novelists. No experimentalist has achieved more than Greene, or Naipaul with his masterly Conradian, and at times Jamesian, style. One might go so far as to speak of a continuing hunger for fiction of individual character. If this is not satisfied by traditional novels, it turns to biography (recently popular and of high quality), to journalistic documentary FACTION (the American Truman Capote (1924–84) is the most notable practitioner), or to novels with historical characters such as the Hitler of Beryl Bainbridge's *Young Adolf* (1978) or the Scott Fitzgerald and Ernest Hemingway of James Aldridge's *One Last Glimpse* (1977) – which however raise their own subtle questions about the boundary between fiction and reality.

When characters are comparatively undeveloped and the main emphasis falls on the story's meaning, the term FABULATION is sometimes used – a postmodernist way of saying 'fable'. Instead of having their structure based on character development, fabulations often depend on that of another literary work. This predecessor provides a subtext, or perhaps, rather, a myth to be 'demythologized' or subverted. Thus Golding's *Lord of the Flies* (1954) answers Ballantyne's *The Coral Island* (1858), just as his *Pincher Martin* (1956) takes its departure from Taffrail's *Pincher Martin* (1916). The same overtly acknowledged INTERTEXTUALITY, or dependence on another literary work, can be seen in short stories by the Argentinian Jorge Luis Borges (1899–), and by Davenport; in poetry such as Robert Lowell's *Imitations* (1961); and even in plays, for example Tom Stoppard's *Rosencrantz and Guildenstern Are Dead* (1967) and *Travesties* (1974). Borges, a dominating influence on the postmodernists, is one of the very few contemporaries who can unhesitatingly be described as a great writer.

Alternatively, fabulations may have a non-literary framework, like the 'nymphet' and butterfly hunt of Vladimir Nabokov's *Lolita* (1955), with its concealed philosophy of ideal form. A similar example is John

Barth's *The Sot-Weed Factor* (1960, rev. 1967), where a burlesque version
of colonial American history covers sceptical deconstruction of historio-
graphy. In another variant, a simpler genre like the adventure story or
explorer's tale can be made a vehicle – as in Saul Bellow's African tale
Henderson the Rain King (1959) and Paul Theroux's *The Mosquito Coast*
(1981). All these works, one notices, have something to say as well as to
tell: they are not so much imitations of life as narrative statements about
it. And indeed, when you think of such works as George Orwell's *Nineteen Eighty-Four* (1949), Anthony Burgess's *A Clockwork Orange* (1962)
and J. M. Coetzee's *Waiting for the Barbarians* (1980), it becomes noticeable how many of the period's strongest works are 'timeless' fables –
with timely if enigmatic messages for society. In this strategy, the postmodernists departed from the modernists, and returned to an older tradition: one going back to the Melville of *The Confidence Man* and the
Twain of *Huckleberry Finn*, and ultimately to Rabelais and More.

MINIMALISM

In the course of innovation, character was not the only feature under
threat. Progressively other elements could also be subtracted. For all the
modernist talk of a 'new culture', the postmodernists went far further
towards a radical restructuring of literature. Sometimes, indeed, they
removed so much as to reach MINIMALISM, in which the functioning of
remaining elements is enhanced by their iconic isolation, on a principle
of 'less means more'. Narrative was often reduced: already only implied
in late James and in Compton-Burnett, it was trivialized in *Ulysses* and
in the French *nouveau roman*. And Beckett steadily eliminated it from his
trilogy, *Molloy* (1955; in French 1951), *Malone Dies* (1956; in French
1951) and *The Unnameable* (1958; in French 1953). In plays like *Endgame*
(1958), Beckett reduces even the element of movement to a point at
which the slightest modification becomes portentous; while in short
prose pieces such as *Lessness* (1970; French 1969) he discards even
syntax.

   Some see minimalism in terms of 'minimal affirmation'; instancing
the poetry of Philip Larkin (1922–85) with its minimal differentiation
from prose and its cautious, highly sceptical positives –

> Hours giving evidence
> Or birth, advance
> On death equally slowly.
> And saying so to some

Means nothing; others it leaves
Nothing to be said.
('Nothing to be Said' 13–18)

(Notice, along one syntactic line, the telling omission of 'with' after 'leaves'.) Others see minimalism as avoidance of the unneccessary – of 'bourgeois' ornament. And others again find in minimalism's changing of proportions a wish to expose the processes of art, the frailty of linguistic imitation. This is surely true of some CONCRETE POETRY, in which a poet like Ian Hamilton Finlay (1925–) will take as material the written form of language, perhaps framing a poem out of the phonetic and typographic relations of 'star' and 'steer' – or even from the physical shape of an individual letter:

The Windmill's Poem
X

These are simple examples; but Finlay has composed some of the finest epigraphy since the Renaissance.

Doubtless minimalism means various things to different writers. With Beckett it seems a matter of concentrating austerely on the absurd essentials of existence – as if anything but silence in face of it is likely to smack of betrayal. But in Finlay, although austerity is by no means lacking, the minimal can be seen as a positive aesthetic ideal: 'small is beautiful'. It should be noted that minimalism is totally dependent on a continuing literature of 'normal' proportions – if only to provide the foil against which its own become noticeable.

A subtraction that sometimes makes postmodern literature difficult is that of rational sequence. This may take the form of an extreme digressiveness or irrelevance of parts (not postmodernism's only medieval-retrospective feature), which forces the reader of fiction like Donald Barthelme's (1931–) to suspend expectation of rational sequence. (The best reading strategy is to stay receptive to patterns of repetition, contrast and the like, without expecting direct clarification in terms of external reality.) Closely related is postmodernism's use of STOCHASTIC, aleatory or randomizing devices; as when William Burroughs (1914–) composes his narratively incoherent works by cutting up and shuffling the parts, or B. S. Johnson (1933–73) offers *The Unfortunates* (1969) as a set of cards to be shuffled by the reader himself. Or narrative and rational sequence may be replaced by rituals, like the sterile, absurdly logical permutations of possibilities in Beckett's *Watt* (1953).

Frequent interruptions of narrative sequence tend soon to result in a marked loss of interest. But in poetry, permutations and similar rituals have been more successful. The phonetic rule of Edwin Morgan's 'The Computer's First Christmas Card' is surprisingly productive:

> jolly merry
> holly berry
> jolly berry
> merry holly
> happy jolly
> jolly jelly
> jelly belly
> belly merry . . .
> (*The Second Life*, 1968)

INTERRUPTIONS OF ILLUSION

In many postmodernist works the sequence of ideas may seem a little surrealistic (although thoroughgoing surrealism based on dream processes has interested few British writers). There is likely, of course, to be some underlying order. But this may be so multiplied ('decentred') or so intricate – as for example in *Finnegans Wake* (1939) or Thomas Pynchon's *V* (1963) and *Gravity's Rainbow* (1973) – that it amounts to no order beyond that of the work itself. It would be as ridiculous to think of mastering *Finnegans Wake* as of understanding the world. Similarly, since almost anything can be compared to the letter V, its pattern is useless as a basis for ordering experience. Why this highly cerebral irrationality? Perhaps such writers wish to avoid being tamed by interpretation. Perhaps they are determined that their works will challenge – as extremely as a Rothko painting – a more direct response. A comparable revulsion from interpretation (at least in its traditional sense) can be seen in such criticism as Susan Sontag's *Against Interpretation*.

During the structuralist phase, the idea became current that works of the imagination might be self-validating, without mimetic relation to the world – an idea that drew support from scientific idealism, as well as from structuralism's own doctrine of the inaccessibility of reality. Such works are unlikely to last, however, unless their autonomy is qualified by mimetic content.

A frequent corollary of discontinuity has been fragmentation into small structural units. The epigrams of John Berryman's *Dream Songs* (1964–8), in eighteen lines, and those of Robert Lowell's *Notebook* (1969) and Edwin Morgan's *The New Divan* (1977), in fourteen lines or so, like the short prose pieces of Geoffrey Hill's *Mercian Hymns* (1971), allow any number of fresh starts or irrelevant transitions – and so escape expectations of an overall scheme. In case the sequence of *Notebook* should be thought imitative of the external world in any direct way, Lowell repeatedly changed it, first by revision and addition (1969, 1970), and then by comprehensive reordering in *History* (1973). Nevertheless, Lowell's individual epigrams often touch the nerve of individual experience. And Morgan's sequence evokes so intensely clear an emotional world that it even has a cumulative effect, like the sonnet sequences of an earlier period.

In much postmodernist writing, the parts tend to be related less by a larger syntax, or logical sequence, than by COLLAGE. This less explicit linkage of juxtaposition obviously continues a familiar feature of modernism – but with a difference. Whereas modernist collages explored metaphorical transitions, those of the postmodernists – like the urban fragments of Barthelme's *City Life* (1971) – appear to have an almost random sequence. (William Carlos Williams's *Paterson* (1953) was a transitional example.) In such works the logical and metaphorical connections ordering things in usual ways are removed, so as to make the reader see them afresh, as if an unideological vision were possible. Sometimes, a consistent overall pattern turns collage into mosaic, and a strong statement emerges. The result is likely to be a quasi-paranoid vision, often with an apocalyptic–satiric strain, as in Joseph Heller's *Catch-22* (1961) and Pynchon's *The Crying of Lot 49* (1966).

Such tendencies and devices have crystallized to shape several new genres. One broad grouping is the METAFICTION, or novel that exposes its own fictional illusion in some way – perhaps by taking up conventions only to discard them, perhaps by the use of an obviously naive narrator. In rejecting ordinary reality, the metafictions of the sixties and seventies for the most part reflected a somewhat paranoid alternative. But more recent practitioners have gained confidence, sometimes relaxing into the MAGIC REALIST or poetic novel (D. M. Thomas; Salman Rushdie; John Irving; Angela Carter). In this genre's kaleidoscopic variety, real places and historical events are often introduced, but all in a distorted or poetically moulded form. Typically, all such fabulators return to the loose, Dickensian form of the novel. They have a broad sweep, and open very large perspectives – resembling in this such Continental novelists as Bulgakov and Grass – in a way that contrasts sharply with the tight manner of the modernists.

It is also possible to see a narrower grouping, of POIOUMENA, or self-begetting novels. In this genre, the central strand of the action purports to be the work's own composition, although it is really 'about' something else – as Rushdie's *Midnight's Children* (1981) is about the composition of India after independence. Often the writing is a metaphor for constructing a world. The poioumenon has a long prehistory (hardly a tradition), going back through Beckett's trilogy and Carlyle's *Sartor Resartus* to Sterne's *Tristram Shandy*; but it is preeminently a postmodernist genre. After Nabokov's dazzling *Pale Fire* (1967), indeed, it became a dominant form: perhaps a quarter of the more ambitious novels of the seventies featured work in progress. Even the most considerable writers have felt obliged to attempt the genre, like Lessing in *The Golden Notebook* (1962, rev. 1972), Fowles in *Mantissa* (1982), and Golding in *Paper Men* (1983). Influenced more or less directly by literary theory, the poioumenon is calculated to offer opportunities to explore the boundaries of fiction and reality – the limits of narrative truth.

With this in view, such novelists interweave action with writing inextricably. In *Midnight's Children* the narrator's illness produces 'fabulism'; and in Frederick Busch's *Mutual Friend* (1978), narrated by Dolby, Dickens rubs shoulders not only with Wilkie Collins, but with characters from his own novels, in what purport to be their non-fictional guises. Authentic fragments of the ostensible work-in-progress may be inset. And Nabokov's *Pale Fire* presents a long inset poem with a pretended commentary, in such exquisite intertextual relation with the poem that it itself invites commentary, in a regress like that of Pope's *Dunciad* (to which the self-commentator alludes). Such self-reference, which is common in postmodernist fiction generally, becomes ubiquitous in the poioumenon. Confidential patter is likely to be kept up at each formal turn – 'I will not succumb to cracked digressions', says Rushdie's narrator. To some, the best in this kind will seem but shadows of shadows. Nevertheless, it has challenged resourcefulness in ways of hesitating between fictions, and has generated a brilliant rhetoric of uncertainty, exploiting ironies of the elusive distinction between a writer–narrator and a writer who narrates. A few poioumena, like Rushdie's, may even last.

Experimental metafiction has produced some bizarre styles, like Christine Brooke-Rose's with its unreadable assault course of self-referring devices. When the attention previously reserved for poetry is paid to prose, a formidable stylistic opacity can result. Most postmodernist fiction, however, has been much more transparent in style. One of the most interesting individual styles (although not so perfect as

Naipaul's) is that of the Australian Patrick White (1912–). White's prose is compulsively readable. Yet it has a rich opacity, an impasto arrived at by working in metaphors of memorial or unconscious material that have no direct relation to the literal situation – with consequent pressure on the syntax:

> Sometimes women, looking out from the cabins of trucks from beside their men, shared her lack of curiosity. The light was so fluid nobody lasted long enough. You would never have thought boys could kick a person to death, seeing their long soft hair floating behind their sports models.
>
> ('Five-Twenty' in *The Cockatoos*, 1974)

White's powerful landscapes are liable to make the poetic fallacy more valid than its rational alternative. Or he will lay submerged chains of discourse, perhaps linking different views, perhaps distinct stages of an action – as in 'The duck made straight for Glastonbury to stalk and hide in its wilderness'. Here 'stalk' (and therefore 'hide') belongs as much to hunter as to duck.

A feature of the seventies and eighties has been the emergence of feminist writing of a new type. This grouping may seem a rather arbitrary, external category, since the novel has always been a female domain. But it is argued that earlier forms of the novel, however largely invented by women, were nevertheless sexist in underlying assumptions. And certainly there is not a novelistic convention that the new feminists have omitted to rework: a processing from fresh perspectives that may have given the genre a new lease of life.

With Woolf and Welty somewhere behind it, the feminist movement has commanded high expectations. Admirable though many of its aims are, however, they have not issued in much considerable writing. The movement shows signs of declining into a minority cult devoted to a specialized genre bound by a very specific contract with its pre-determined readership. In feminist novels there is a tendency for the mask of fiction to drop, exposing furies that are not shown to be the characters'. Only a very few feminist writers rise above this level. It seems that a quick sense of injustice may not be a stance conducive to good writing. Perhaps literature calls for the deeper honesty of not knowing where justice lies unless exploration happens to reveal it. But then, literature itself seems to some a male concept.

Much feminist writing is deconstructive, in the sense that it exposes the sexist orientation of ostensibly neutral institutions and cultural forms. In this it has at least two distinct strategies. The first, a strategy of subversion, or reversal, or tat for tit, is evident in the work of Angela Carter (1940–). Carter's ferociously aggressive, highly inventive fictions, such as *Nights at the Circus* (1984), rewrite fairy tales and rework gothic romance motifs, so as almost to sketch out an inverted, alternative sexist culture. Carter has an economical style, crackling with intelligence:

> At that, she turned her immense eyes upon him, those eyes 'made for the stage' whose messages could be read from standing room in the gods. Night had darkened their colour; their irises were now purple, matching the Parma violets in front of her mirror, and the pupils had grown so fat on darkness that the entire dressing-room and all those within it could have vanished without trace inside those compelling voids. Walser felt the strangest sensation, as if these eyes of the *aerialiste* were a pair of sets of Chinese boxes, as if each one opened into a world into a world into a world, an infinite plurality of worlds, and these unguessable depths exercised the strongest possible attraction, so that he felt himself trembling as if he, too, stood on an unknown threshold.
>
> (ch. ii)

And Fay Weldon and Alice Thomas Ellis, too, have well-developed individual manners, together with the capacity nevertheless to surprise. But most users of this first strategy are too ideologically purposeful, too predictable, to have much literary interest.

Another strategy, which probably takes even more thinking out, is to assume the feminine viewpoint as normative, and proceed to ordinary realism. Although this can be seen in Margaret Drabble's Bennettian novels, a better example is the Canadian Margaret Atwood (1939–). Atwood's fiction, which has much more than productivity and hype to commend it, is marked by ardent intelligence. She seems ambitiously determined to leave no subject unattempted by her formidable talents; so that she understandably often gets out of her (considerable) depth. Like Lawrence in visionary assurance (especially in her fine story collection, *Dancing Girls*, where 'The Resplendent Quetzal' is almost an answer to 'The Woman Who Rode Away'), Atwood knows just what is wrong with contemporary society. This is much more than that it is run by men, however; she has too much self-knowledge for mere sexism. She is also quite unlike Lawrence in her detailed mimetic realism – a realism she carefully sustains even in the futuristic fable *Surfacing* (1972).

This realism makes for compulsive readability, but (given the curse of fluency) it unfortunately brings with it prolixity too. Novels like *Bodily Harm* (1981) have far too much incidental satire, too many atmospheric superficialities, too much topicality only partially in character. Journalism threatens. (The vitiating absence of economy brings to mind a similar feature in her formidable compatriot Robertson Davies: both write as if fiction still had the function of filling the time.) Structural ideas abound, but not the patience to implement them. If 'everything hangs together' in Atwood's fiction, it hangs loose to the point of slack punctuation. She is best at remembering childhood: an endeavour in which she writes more tentatively. Atwood is a poet, and her fiction very much a poet's fiction: strong in creativity but weak in sensing the proportions of prose. As Roy Campbell might have said, she uses the bloody horse all right, but where's the snaffle and the bit?

A writer who has been connected with deconstruction in quite another way is Muriel Spark (1918–), a much more accomplished artist. Spark's earlier novels, such as *The Ballad of Peckham Rye* (1960) and *The Prime of Miss Jean Brodie* (1961), belong to popular modernism. But in a novel like *The Abbess of Crewe* (1974), which is almost like a satiric flipside of Brian Moore's *Catholics*, we are dealing with fiction of a more complex simplicity. In this fable set in an ultramodern convent, events and style shimmer exquisitely between hypothesis and inevitability, representation and extrapolation: 'certainly Alexandra is to be Abbess of Crewe. And as surely, at this moment, the matter has been thrown into doubt by Sister Felicity's glamorous campaign'. Occasionally, the sequence will veer from narrative into an intertextual bricolage (miscellaneous assemblage) of Scripture, commentary, and jesuitical *realpolitik* application. Or the police will first appear in a prevenient metaphor, and then immediately after in 'actual' fact – as if anything can happen, when thought becomes act. All this could be given deconstructive interpretation. But just as relevant may be Spark's Scottish penchant for fantasy of a secretly amplifying sort. And behind the subtlety is a moral judgement as single as that, say, of Iris Murdoch.

Like Waugh, Spark practises extreme economy, as if discarding all but those parts of her narrative that happen to be interesting, formally or morally. Whenever Arnold Bennett details threaten, she breaks off. The reticent gaps make it often hard to pin down, if not in the end quite undecidable, how her story applies to actual social patterns and institutions. This may be considered a defect in her work. Not that it is evasive, but that in terms of proportion she needs rather more reference for satisfactory mimesis. Locally, however, Spark displays formidable powers of observation and realism:

> Gertrude, my devout logician, it is a question upon which I ponder greatly within the umbrageous garden of my thoughts, where you get your 'should nots' and your 'ought tos' from. They don't arise from the moral systems of the cannibal tribes of the Andes, nor the factions of the

deep Congo, nor from the hills of Asia, do they? It seems to me, Gertrude, my love, that your shoulds and your shouldn'ts have been established rather nearer home, let us say the continent of Europe, if you will forgive the expression.

(ch. v)

She is that rare sort of satirist (Waugh was such another) who identify social aberrations before these are generally recognized; so that her cutting satire at first gives as much interest as offence. It is nevertheless as deadly as a Gurkha's *kukri*.

POSTMODERN POETRY

It was in poetry, inevitably, that opacity was carried furthest. Here, at least, surrealism had something of an impact. Its dreamworld progressions – albeit combined with Christian and cosmic imagery – help to give Dylan Thomas's strange transitions their inevitability:

> Altarwise by owl-light in the half-way house
> The gentleman lay graveward with his furies;
> Abaddon in the hangnail cracked from Adam,
> And, from his fork, a dog among the fairies . . .
> ('Altarwise by Owl-Light'(1935), i)

Here there remains a modernist difficulty of obscure symbolic connections. But it is striking that Thomas's later poems, although they may seem to consist of clear, simple statements, say little about the world outside the poem. They nevertheless make sense of another sort; and everyone who cares for poetry will study such great lyrics (possessed of many traditional strengths) as 'Do Not Go Gentle into That Good Night', 'Fern Hill', 'Poem in October' and 'In the White Giant's Thigh'.

The forties and fifties were a poor period for British poetry, perhaps because of the absence of a generation of poets, lost in World War I. After the opaque poetry of the Apocalyptic group – George Barker, David Gascoyne and Norman MacCaig in his early manner – and Thomas's culminating *Collected Poems* of 1952, there was a sharp reaction to prosaic lucidity in the so-called 'Movement'. The Movement poets, such as Robert Conquest (1917–), Donald Davie (1922–) and the far more considerable Philip Larkin (1922–85)(the last despite Yeatsian beginnings) returned to what they saw as the true English tradition. They eschewed foreign entanglements, weak syntax and obvious difficulty. And they brought everyday life back into poetry – London and church-going and Whitsun weddings – as if they were confident that the problems of literature's relation to the world could be bypassed merely by taking up a no-nonsense stance. With them may be grouped the older John Betjeman (1906–84) and the younger Ted Hughes (1930–), although the latter's *Crow* (1970) took directness to a violent extreme. Larkin's poems are beautifully constructed (and to an extent this is also true of Betjeman's and others' in the group); which may help to make some of them last. But although Larkin stood firmly on Hardy's shoulders, he did not see much further.

There was much in the work of the school of Larkin that could have been better managed in prose, as prose had developed. Indeed, Sydney Goodsir Smith's Joycean prose extravaganza *Carotid Cornucopius* (1947) had more brilliant word play than most of the poetry of his time. He scorned the limitations of a period when anything that suggested literary diction was avoided, in the impossible pursuit of some 'writing degree zero' (Roland Barthes's phrase). The colloquial idiom of the school of Larkin almost invited poetry to be treated as informational: a tendency aggravated in the sixties, when the second wave of free verse brought in bad line breaks and rhythms like those of segmented prose. This was for poetry to be as well written as prose, with a vengeance.

The principal British poets of the sixties and seventies – Tomlinson, Porter, Morgan and Geoffrey Hill, and to some extent Sisson, MacCaig and Seamus Heaney – have escaped our besetting provinciality; but at the price of being distinctly more demanding. C. H. Sisson (1914–), a poet in the Hardy–Edward Thomas tradition, has latterly come to grips again with unsolved problems of modernism. MacCaig's Metaphysical epigrams enter into the process of perception itself. And Charles Tomlinson (1927–) similarly complicates the poet's reality with overlays of imagery. His landscapes are palimpsests of repeated construction – 'interrupted pastoral'; 'horizon . . . above horizon'; 'dense / With its own past' – where consciousness is 'feeling its way among . . . hesitant distinctions':

> The sky goes white. There is no bright alternation now
>   Of lit cloud on blue: the scene's finality
> Is robbed of a resonance. The day will end
>   In its misting-over, its blending of muffled tones,
> In a looking to nearnesses. A time
>   Of colourlessness prepares for a recomposing,
> As the prelude of quiet grows towards the true
>   Prelude in the body of the hall. Anew we see
> Nature as body and as building
>   To be filled, if not with sound, then with

> The thousand straying filamented ways
>   We travel it by, from the inch before us to the height
> Above, and back again . . .

('Movements' (1972) ii)

The Australian expatriate Peter Porter (1929–), by a different method, undermines the referential solidity of his images by admitting momentary trains of thought and feeling:

> The view from Patmos, the ghost inside
> the module! Living neither long enough
> nor so curtly brings us nominative snakes,
> time turned to blood upon the hour,
> fours and sevens when the Lamb lies down
> with Fury . . .

('Fast Forward' (1984))

In such poems, Porter interrupts the image sequence frequently (far more so than the modernists); so that his reader is obliged to give up facile interpretative construction and attend more closely.

Dylan Thomas's surrealist mantle seems to have been assumed by the potent psychoanalytic poet Peter Redgrove (1932–). But the Welshman's more significant influence may prove to have been an indirect one, on the American Ashbery. John Ashbery (1927–) enjoys an eminence almost like that of Wallace Stevens, in whose metaphysical tradition he stands, while carrying scepticism a good deal further. Such poems as 'Self-Portrait in a Convex Mirror' (1975) show Ashbery capable of eloquent meditations of great immediacy:

> The sample
> One sees is not to be taken as
> Merely that, but as everything as it
> May be imagined outside time – not as a gesture
> But as all, in the refined, assimilable state.
> But what is this universe the porch of
> As it veers in and out, back and forth,
> Refusing to surround us and still the only
> Thing we can see?

(lines 338–46)

Yet elsewhere he has chosen to exercise a freedom of transition that alienates many readers. In spite of his transparent (even commonplace) diction, he avoids external reference, with a consequent increase – a quantum jump, in fact – of difficulty. Like most other postmodern writers he is antisymbolist, rejecting metaphysical structures and reducing his symbols to temporary, relative, internally self-defined meanings.

But Ashbery also differs from the ambiguous modernists in not leaving one at liberty to extend his meanings into the external world in a freely polyvalent way. In fact, he intransigently bars free misinterpretation, either by writing about the process of composition itself, or else by breaks in syntax that hold the world in abeyance:

> Old-fashioned shadows hanging down, that difficulty in love too soon
> Some star or other went out, and you, thank you for your book and year
> Something happened in the garage and I owe it for the blood traffic
> Too low for nettles but it is exactly the way people think and feel . . .
>
> ('37 Haiku' in *A Wave*, 1984)

Continually frustrating readers' attempts to construct external worlds of their own, Ashbery insists that his poems be read as poems, not bits of novels. To get anywhere with them, one has to be receptive to *his* structures, *his* train of thought and feeling. With Ashbery, in this regard, may be grouped the British poets J. H. Prynne (1936–) and John Ash (1948–). If poetry were to continue on such a path, it would soon lack readers altogether. For there has to be a mimetic relation to some world (even if only an internal one) for poetry to have any interest.

But there are abundant signs of a more accessible style. (Poetry readings may have played a part in this.) Without any loss of interest in language, poetic style has now become transparent enough to make possible feeling elegy (Douglas Dunn; Peter Porter), narrative (Andrew Motion) and Irish fantasy (Paul Muldoon, Paul Durcan). In fact, it seems that the question of difficulty has altered. Some postmodern poets continue to practise a style as opaque as that of modernism; but many have found other ways to challenge or freshen their readers' world building – by involving them perhaps in problems of perception (Charles Tomlinson), perhaps of historical recollection (Geoffrey Hill). They can afford to have a clearer style, because the locus of difficulty has moved from diction and imagery, and is directly acknowledged to lie in ideology and reference. Of course, the various difficulties can coexist. Geoffrey Hill (1932–), who is the most complete poet of the period, stretches the reader's power to respond at every point.

THE NEW DRAMA

Drama has taken a similar course. There, too, noticeability of style has been a feature of the period. It is evident throughout Harold Pinter's obscure discontinuities and eloquent timed silences (acme of minimalism), as well as his delicious savouring of demotic speech, as in *The Caretaker* (1960). But it also shows in *tours de force* of dialect by John Arden (1930–) and even of *historical* dialect by Robert Maclellan (1907–1985), both with political point.

The literary development of drama, however, has been distorted by financial dearth, by lack of adequate theatres, by loss of dependable audiences, by the ephemeral influence of television and by the follies of directors' theatre. And the fifties divide between modernism and postmodernism seems in drama more marked. The 'theatre of the absurd' appears to have an obvious beginning with *Waiting for Godot* (1955), and an immediate continuation in N.F. Simpson's *A Resounding Tinkle* (1956). But Simpson can be seen as reenlivening a recessive native tradition of nonsense (Lewis Carroll, Edward Lear, the Goons). Moreover, Beckett himself is a large enough figure to span more than one style, and certainly too serious to accept the absurdity of man's condition without protest. (He is so evidently serious as effectually to disguise how little he says about the external world – except about our frailty, as in a radio play like *All that Fall*, 1957.) As we have seen, his drama revives the gothic Morality; anything further from the totally new could scarcely be imagined.

A distinct departure from Beckett's transitional style came with the thoroughgoing postmodernism of Harold Pinter (1930–), who although he began as an imitator of Beckett and Eugène Ionesco – with backward glances at the absurdist tradition of Jarry and the surrealists – has latterly come to occupy a role like Ashbery's in poetry, as doyen of the current style. Contrary to appearances, Pinter, again like Ashbery, pursues a meaning that is relatively univocal. Whereas audiences were free to interpret *Waiting for Godot* (even its broad allegory) as they pleased, Pinter's later plays, such as *The Homecoming* (1965) and *Old Times* (1971), make a more precise demand. His explorations of language and communication amount to realism, albeit a new realism on a more sceptical footing. Indeed, no dramatist since Jonson has observed speech so closely; and no one at all the meaningful proportions of its absence in silences.

In one way, the change of dramatic style has been particularly marked: in the proportions of dialogue and business. After modernism's lexical emphasis, postmodernist drama returned to an older and more central tradition, in which the verbal element was balanced more evenly by non-verbal action. This is true not only of Peter Shaffer (1926–) and Alan Ayckbourn (1939–) with their theatrical experimentation, but also of Edward Bond (1935–) and even of Tom Stoppard (1932–), despite his fondness for didactic speeches, as in *Travesties* (1974). (Ayckbourn's technical experiments – simultaneous actions, divided stages, plays viewed from behind – may at times be arid; but they have undeniably enlarged the repertoire of devices.) Many of the obscurities of postmodernist drama disappear if it is thought of as acting out feelings or ideas or clichés in literal fact, so as to preclude our habitual responses to them. All this is not to say that dramatic language has been neglected. Both Shaffer (for example in *Amadeus*, 1980) and Stoppard (in *Rosencrantz and Guildenstern Are Dead*, 1967) have combined brilliant verbal textures with spectacular action in an exciting way. The shift away from literariness has clearly proved invigorating and beneficial to the theatre. Whether it will lead to a dramatic literature of lasting value remains to be seen.

THE LARGER PROSPECT

From the essentially Edwardian position still occupied by many British readers, postmodernism may well seem the same as modernism, only more so. But from a more appropriate viewpoint it can be seen to have a distinct character of its own. As I have suggested, postmodernist writers tend not to have the symbolists' tolerance of polyvalent interpretation, but instead tend to devise interruptions that confront one more inescapably. Again, they have mostly abandoned modernism's easy dependence on the order of myth; although they may still have things to say about the larger world. Postmodernists can sometimes achieve a solider realism founded on epistemological immediacy. Another difference is that postmodernists are more given to brooding on 'the human condition' in a very general, transcultural way – which makes them prone to the escape of absurdism, or sometimes to what H. G. Wells called 'big thinks'. Several writers (Beckett and Hughes come to mind) have taken up very extreme stances, although one cannot yet be sure how central this is to postmodernism at large.

Throughout the period, literature has been increasingly influenced by literary criticism. This change perhaps began with T. S. Eliot's own critical activity: modernism went hand in hand with the criticism of congenially tough-minded Metaphysical poetry. But the tendency accelerated with the growing need for explication of difficult modernist authors like Joyce, with the development of graduate work in the modern field and with the founding of university posts for novelists and poets. In short, there is now an academic context for literature.

Joyce may not have anticipated the interpretation industry centred on *Finnegans Wake*; but subsequently many others have undoubtedly written in a way calculated to engage academic interpreters. In consequence, criticism has had a double, and perhaps an undue, influence. This shows, for example, in excessive ambiguity, the vice of mid-century poetry. Contemporary American New Criticism was a method specifically designed to generate multiple senses in the close reading of local opacities. And in Britain, despite the moral tradition represented by F. R. Leavis, it is William Empson's criticism, with its cult of ambiguity, that has had most impact on writers, particularly poets. Empson's influence, and that of academic structuralists, can be traced in a good many features of contemporary literature.

Some postmodernist writing is so dominated by theory that its forms do not even arise unpredictably from imitation of life. Instead they merely obey a programme of overturning realist expectations. Or else they display a narrowly intellectual ingenuity. There have been fears, indeed, that literature may split into two separate developments: one 'high', international, cerebral and difficult; the other 'low', insular, anti-academic and readable. But against that dark possibility the continuing popularity of several writers of the highest calibre – Golding, White, Naipaul, Pinter – counts as a ground for optimism.

This present work hardly encourages predictions about the future of literature. We can be fairly sure, indeed, that it will develop in surprising and disconcerting ways. It generally takes an unforeseen direction, so as to revalue just the elements of culture that are thought least of – perhaps obeying a law of compensation, or necessarily uttering the unspoken. However reasonable one's prediction, it is likely to be confuted by the writing that eventuates. The very cards in the generic pack are changing – and will change more with the introduction of new media. Nevertheless it is safe to forecast – because the change is already well advanced – that Commonwealth literature will be an increasingly significant part of the whole. The consequent diversification and enrichment of forms will surely be immense. Indeed, English literature, in the sense of literature of the English-speaking world, may be only beginning.

Suggestions for Further Reading

These suggestions for further reading are as far as possible arranged in order of difficulty and of generality. In each case, they begin with introductions to the literature of the period concerned, go on to more specialized topics, continue with editions and studies of individual writers, and end with anthologies. The last section consists of general items and books on topics unrestricted chronologically. Inevitably there are overlaps, so that it may be useful to consult neighbouring bibliographies besides the one immediately relevant.

The suggestions should be regarded as samples – there has been no attempt at completeness. In addition to recent publications, I have tried to include some classic items, which should be available in libraries, and from time to time in paperback editions. Unless otherwise stated, the books referred to are the first edition.

1 THE MIDDLE AGES

Lewis, C. S. *The Allegory of Love*. Oxford: Clarendon Press, 1936.
Lewis, C. S. *The Discarded Image*. Cambridge: CUP, 1964.
Alexander, Michael. *Old English Literature*. London: Macmillan, 1983.
Brewer, Derek. *English Gothic Literature*. London: Macmillan, 1983.
Burrow, J. A. *Medieval Writers and Their Work: Middle English Literature and Its Background, 1100–1500*. Oxford and New York: OUP, 1982.
Robertson, Durante Waite. *A Preface to Chaucer*. Princeton University Press; London: OUP, 1963.
Chaucer. *The Complete Works* (ed.) F. N. Robinson. London: OUP, 1957.
Howard, Donald R. *The Idea of the 'Canterbury Tales'*. Berkeley and London: University of California Press, 1976.
Gradon, Pamela. *Form and Style in Early English Literature*. London: Methuen, 1971.
Kolve, V. A. *Chaucer and the Imagery of Narrative: The First Five Canterbury Tales*. London: Edward Arnold, 1984.
Vinaver, Eugène. *The Rise of Romance*. Oxford: Clarendon Press, 1971.
Bevington, David (ed.). *Medieval Drama*. Boston: Houghton Mifflin, 1975.

Mitchell, Bruce and Robinson, Fred C. *A Guide to Old English*. Oxford: Basil Blackwell, 1964.

Happé, Peter (ed.). *English Mystery Plays: A Selection*. London: Penguin, 1975.

Burrow, J. A. (ed.). *English Verse 1300–1500*. London and New York: Longman, 1977.

Tuve, Rosemond. *Allegorical Imagery: Some Medieval Books and Their Posterity*. Princeton University Press, 1966.

Kermode, Frank and Hollander, John (gen. eds). *The Oxford Anthology of English Literature*. Vol. 1: The Middle Ages through the Eighteenth Century. New York: OUP, 1973.

2 RENAISSANCE PROSE AND VERSE

Spearing, A. C. *Medieval to Renaissance in English Poetry*. Cambridge: CUP, 1985.

Evans, Maurice. *English Poetry in the Sixteenth Century*. London: Hutchinson, 1955.

Stevens, John. *Music and Poetry in the Early Tudor Court*. London: Methuen, 1961.

Mason, Harold Andrew. *Humanism and Poetry in the Early Tudor Period*. London: Routledge & Kegan Paul, 1959.

Kinney, Arthur F. *Humanist Poetics: Thought, Rhetoric and Fiction in Sixteenth-century England*. Amherst, Mass.: University of Massachusetts Press, 1986.

Greene, Thomas M. *The Light in Troy: Imitation and Discovery in Renaissance Poetry*. New Haven and London: Yale University Press, 1982.

Ross, James Bruce and McLaughlin, Mary Martin (eds). *The Portable Renaissance Reader*. New York: Viking, 1953.

Lucie-Smith, Edward (ed. & intr.). *The Penguin Book of Elizabethan Verse*. London: Penguin, 1965.

3 ELIZABETHAN MANNERISM

Smith, Hallett. *Elizabethan Poetry. A Study in Conventions, Meaning and Expression*. Cambridge, Mass.: Harvard University Press, 1952.

Tuve, Rosemond. *Elizabethan and Metaphysical Imagery. Renaissance Poetic and Twentieth-century Critics*. University of Chicago Press, 1947.

Bush, Douglas. *Mythology and the Renaissance Tradition in English Poetry*. Minneapolis, Mich.: University of Minnesota Press, 1932.

Nohrnberg, James. *The Analogy of 'The Faerie Queene'*. Princeton University Press, 1976.

Spenser, Edmund. *The Faerie Queene* (ed.) A. C. Hamilton. Harlow: Longman, 1977.

Hamilton, A. C. *Sir Philip Sidney: A Study of His Life and Works*. Cambridge: CUP, 1977.

Wilson, Frank Percy. *Elizabethan and Jacobean*. Oxford: Clarendon Press, 1945.

Ault, Norman (ed.). *Elizabethan Lyrics*. London: Longmans, 1925.

Lucie-Smith, Edward (ed. & intr.). *The Penguin Book of Elizabethan Verse*. London: Penguin, 1965.

4 ELIZABETHAN AND JACOBEAN DRAMA

Evans, G. Blakemore (gen. ed.). *The Riverside Shakespeare*. Boston: Houghton Mifflin, 1974.

Colie, Rosalie Littel. *Shakespeare's Living Art*. Princeton University Press, 1974.

Clemen, Wolfgang H. *The Development of Shakespeare's Imagery*. London: Methuen, 1951.

Bradley, A. C. *Shakespearean Tragedy*. London: Macmillan, 1904.

Barton, Anne. *Ben Jonson, Dramatist*. Cambridge: CUP, 1984.

Bradbrook, Muriel Clara. *Themes and Conventions of Elizabethan Tragedy*. Cambridge: CUP, 1935.

Doran, Madeleine. *Endeavours of Art*. Madison, Wis.: University of Wisconsin Press, 1954.

Levin, Richard. *The Multiple Plot in English Renaissance Drama*. Chicago and London: University of Chicago Press, 1971.

Braden, Gordon. *Renaissance Tragedy and the Senecan Tradition*. New Haven, Conn. and London: Yale University Press, 1985.

Jones, Emrys L. *Scenic Form in Shakespeare*. Oxford: Clarendon Press, 1971.

Frye, Northrop. *A Natural Perspective*. New York and London: Columbia University Press, 1965.

Ornstein, Robert. *The Moral Vision of Jacobean Tragedy*. Madison, Wis.: University of Wisconsin Press, 1960.

Gomme, A. H. (ed.). *Jacobean Tragedies*. London: OUP, 1969.

5 THE EARLIER SEVENTEENTH CENTURY

Parfitt, George. *English Poetry of the Seventeenth Century*. London and New York: Longman, 1985.

Vickers, Brian. *Francis Bacon and Renaissance Prose*. Cambridge: CUP, 1968.

Williamson, George. *The Senecan Amble. A Study in Prose Form from Bacon to Collier*. London: Faber & Faber, 1951.

Colie, Rosalie Littel. *The Resource of Kind: Genre-Theory in the Renaissance*. Berkeley: University of California Press, 1973.

Peterson, Richard S. *Imitation and Praise in the Poems of Ben Jonson*. New Haven and London: Yale University Press, 1981.

Empson, Sir William. *Seven Types of Ambiguity*. London: Chatto, 1930.

Wilson, Frank Percy. *Seventeenth Century Prose. Five Lectures*. Cambridge: CUP; Berkeley and Los Angeles: University of California Press, 1960.

Witherspoon, A. M. and Warnke, F. J. *Seventeenth-Century Prose and Poetry*. San Diego and London: Harcourt Brace Jovanovich, 1963.

Grierson, Herbert J. C. (sel. & ed., with an essay). *Metaphysical Lyrics and Poems of the Seventeenth Century – Donne to Butler*. Oxford: Clarendon Press, 1921.

Gardner, Helen (ed.). *The Metaphysical Poets*. London: Penguin, 1957.

6 RESTORATION LITERATURE

Donaldson, Ian. *The World Upside-Down: Comedy from Jonson to Fielding*. Oxford: Clarendon Press, 1970.

Hume, R. D. *The Development of English Drama in the Late Seventeenth Century*. Oxford: Clarendon Press, 1976.

Wasserman, Earl R. *The Subtler Language. Critical Readings of Neoclassic and Romantic Poems*. Baltimore: Johns Hopkins Press, 1959.

Ricks, Christopher. *Milton's Grand Style*. Oxford: Clarendon Press, 1963.

Lewalski, Barbara Kiefer. *'Paradise Lost' and the Rhetoric of Literary Forms*. Princeton University Press, 1985.

Van Doren, Mark. *The Poetry of John Dryden*. Cambridge, Mass.: Gordon Fraser, 1931.

Miner, Earl. *Dryden's Poetry*. Bloomington, Ind. and London: Indiana University Press, 1967.

Love, Harold (ed. & intr.). *The Penguin Book of Restoration Verse*. London: Penguin, 1968.

7 AUGUSTAN CLASSICISM

Sutherland, James. *A Preface to Eighteenth Century Poetry*. Oxford: Clarendon Press, 1948.

Rogers, Pat. *The Augustan Vision*. London: Weidenfeld & Nicolson, 1974.

Erskine-Hill, Howard. *The Augustan Idea in English Literature*. London: Edward Arnold, 1983.

Brower, Reuben Arthur. *Alexander Pope: The Poetry of Allusion*. Oxford: Clarendon Press, 1959.

Chalker, John. *The English Georgic*. London: Routledge & Kegan Paul, 1969.

Highet, Gilbert. *The Anatomy of Satire*. Princeton University Press; London: OUP, 1962.

Quintana, Ricardo. *Swift: An Introduction*. London: OUP, 1955.

Lonsdale, Roger (ed.). *The New Oxford Book of Eighteenth Century Verse*. Oxford and New York: OUP, 1984.

Ross, Angus (ed.). *Selections from The Tatler and The Spectator*. London: Penguin, 1982.

8 LATER CLASSICISM AND THE ENLIGHTENMENT

Watt, Ian. *The Rise of the Novel. Studies in Defoe, Richardson and Fielding*. London: Chatto & Windus, 1957.

Krutch, Joseph Wood. *Samuel Johnson*. New York: Holt, 1944.

Wain, John. *Samuel Johnson*. London: Macmillan, 1974.

Wimsatt, William Kurtz. *The Prose Style of Samuel Johnson*. New Haven: Yale University Press, 1941.

Spacks, Patricia Meyer. *Poetry of Vision. Five Eighteenth-century Poets*. Cambridge, Mass.: Harvard University Press, 1967.

Paulson, Ronald. *Satire and the Novel in Eighteenth-Century England*. New Haven and London: Yale University Press, 1967.

Bate, Walter Jackson. *From Classic to Romantic*. Cambridge, Mass.: Harvard University Press, 1946.

Davie, Donald. *Purity of Diction in English Verse*. London: Chatto & Windus, 1952.

Macqueen, John. *The Enlightenment and Scottish Literature: Vol. 1: Progress and Poetry*. Edinburgh: Scottish Academic Press, 1982.

9 ROMANTICISM AND POETRY

Butler, Marilyn. *Romantics, Rebels and Reactionaries*. Oxford: OUP, 1981.

Praz, Mario. *The Romantic Agony* (tr. Angus Davidson). London: OUP, 1933.

Hough, Graham. *The Romantic Poets*. London: Hutchinson, 1953.

Abrams, M. H. *The Mirror and the Lamp: Romantic Theory and the Critical Tradition*. New York: OUP, 1953.

Frye, Northrop. *Fearful Symmetry. A Study of William Blake*. Princeton University Press, 1947.

Bush, Douglas. *Mythology and the Romantic Tradition in English Poetry*. Cambridge, Mass.: Harvard University Press, 1937.

Richards, I. A. *Coleridge on Imagination*. London: Kegan Paul, 1934.

Hartman, Geoffrey H. *Wordsworth's Poetry, 1787–1814*. New Haven and London: Yale University Press, 1964.

Auden, W. H. *The Enchafèd Flood*. New York: Random House, 1950; London: Faber, 1951.

Hugo, Howard E. *The Romantic Reader*. New York: Viking, 1957.

Kermode, J. Frank and Hollander, John (gen. eds). *The Oxford Anthology of English Literature: Vol. 2: 1800 to the Present*. London: OUP, 1973.

10 TRANSFORMATIONS OF PROSE

Stapleton, Laurence. *The Elected Circle*. Princeton University Press, 1973.

Holloway, John. *The Victorian Sage. Studies in Argument*. London: Macmillan, 1953.

Levine, George and Madden, William (eds). *The Art of Victorian Prose*. New York: OUP, 1968.

Hunt, John Dixon and Holland, Faith M. (eds). *The Ruskin Polygon. Essays on the Imagination of John Ruskin*. Manchester University Press, 1982.

Willey, Basil. *Nineteenth Century Studies*. London: Chatto & Windus, 1949.

Frank, Ellen Eve. *Literary Architecture*. Berkeley and London: University of California Press, 1979.

Read, Herbert. *English Prose Style*. London: G. Bell & Sons, 1928.

Buckler, William Earl (ed.). *Prose of the Victorian Period*. Cambridge, Mass.: Harvard University Press, 1958.

Jones, Edmund (ed.). *English Critical Essays: Nineteenth Century*. Rev. edn. OUP, 1971.

11 VICTORIAN POETRY

Richards, Bernard. *English Poetry of the Victorian Period 1830–1890*. London: Longman, 1988.

Johnson, E. D. H. *The Alien Vision of Victorian Poetry. Sources of the Poetic Imagination in Tennyson, Browning and Arnold*. Princeton University Press, 1952.

Ricks, Christopher B. *Tennyson*. London: Macmillan, 1972.

Buckley, J. H. *The Victorian Temper: A Study in Literary Culture*. London: Allen & Unwin, 1952.

Langbaum, Robert. *The Poetry of Experience*. London: Chatto & Windus, 1957.

Armstrong, Isobel (ed.). *The Major Victorian Poets: Reconsiderations*. London: Routledge & Kegan Paul, 1969.

Richards, Bernard G. (ed.). *Victorian Poetry 1830–1890*. London and New York: Longman, 1980.

Scott, Patrick (ed.). *Victorian Poetry 1830 to 1870*. London: Longman, 1971.

Macdonald, Dwight (ed.). *Parodies. An Anthology from Chaucer to Beerbohm – and After*. London: Faber, 1961.

Auden, W. H. (ed.). *Nineteenth Century British Minor Poets*. New York: Delacorte Press, 1966; London: Faber & Faber, 1967.

12 NINETEENTH-CENTURY FICTION

Leavis, F. R. *The Great Tradition. George Eliot, Henry James, Joseph Conrad*. London: Chatto & Windus: 1948.

Hardy, Barbara. *The Appropriate Form. An Essay on the Novel*. London: Athlone Press, 1964.

House, Humfry. *The Dickens World*. London: OUP, 1941.

Cecil, Lord David. *Early Victorian Novelists. Essays in Revaluation*. London: Constable, 1934.

Williams, Ioan. *The Realist Novel in England*. London: Macmillan, 1974; University of Pittsburgh Press, 1974.

Irwin, Michael. *Picturing: Description and Illusion in the Nineteenth-Century Novel*. London: Allen & Unwin.

Tillotson, Geoffrey. *A View of Victorian Literature*. Oxford: Clarendon Press, 1978.

Tillotson, Kathleen. *Novels of the Eighteen-Forties*. Oxford: Clarendon Press, 1954.

Calder, Jenni. *Women and Marriage in Victorian Fiction*. London: Thames & Hudson, 1976.

Hart, Francis Russell. *The Scottish Novel: A Critical Survey*. London: Murray; Cambridge, Mass.: Harvard University Press, 1978.

Manlove, C. N. *Modern Fantasy. Five Studies*. Cambridge: CUP, 1975.

13 MODERNIST FICTION

Levenson, Michael H. *A Genealogy of Modernism: A Study of English Literary Doctrine 1908–1922*. Cambridge: CUP, 1984.

Robson, William W. *Modern English Literature*. London: OUP, 1970.

Ellmann, Richard and Feidelson, Charles (eds). *The Modern Tradition. Backgrounds of Modern Literature*. New York: OUP, 1965.

Hynes, Samuel. *The Edwardian Turn of Mind*. Princeton University Press; London: OUP, 1968.

Jefferson, D. W. *Henry James and the Modern Reader*. Edinburgh and London: Oliver and Boyd, 1964.

Goldberg, Samuel Louis. *The Classical Temper. A Study of James Joyce's 'Ulysses'*. London: Chatto & Windus, 1961.

Litz, Arthur Walton. *The Art of James Joyce. Method and Design in 'Ulysses' and 'Finnegans Wake'*. London: OUP, 1961.

14 MODERNIST POETRY AND DRAMA

Hynes, Samuel. *The Auden Generation: Literature and Politics in England in the 1930s*. London: Bodley Head, 1976.

Ellmann, Richard. *Eminent Domain. Yeats among Wilde, Joyce, Pound, Eliot and Auden*. New York: OUP, 1967.

Wilson, Edmund. *Axel's Castle*. New York and London: Scribner's, 1931.

Perkins, David. *A History of Modern Poetry*. 2 vols. Cambridge, Mass.: Belknap Press of Harvard University Press, 1976–87.

Press, John (ed.) *A Map of Modern English Verse*. London: OUP, 1969.

Rosenthal, M. L. and Gall, Sally M. *The Modern Poetic Sequence: The Genius of Modern Poetry*. New York and Oxford: OUP, 1983.

Kermode, J. Frank. *Romantic Image*. London: Routledge & Kegan Paul, 1957.

Sisson, C. H. *English Poetry 1900–1950: An Assessment*. London: Hart-Davis, 1971.

Bentley, Eric. *Bernard Shaw*. Norfolk, Conn., 1947.

Roberts, Michael (ed.). *The Faber Book of Modern Verse* (1936). [Fourth edn., rev. Peter Porter. London: Faber, 1982.]

Larkin, Philip (ed.). *The Oxford Book of Twentieth-Century English Verse*. Oxford: Clarendon Press, 1973.

Bold, Alan (ed.). *Cambridge Book of English Verse 1939–1975*. Cambridge: CUP, 1976.

Allott, K. (ed.). *The Penguin Book of Contemporary Verse, 1918–60*. Rev. edn. London: Penguin, 1962.

Bentley, Eric (ed.). *The Modern Theatre*. 6 vols. New York: Doubleday, 1955–60.

15 POSTMODERNISM

Butler, Christopher. *After the Wake: An Essay on the Contemporary Avant-Garde*. Oxford: Clarendon Press, 1980.

Dodsworth, Martin (ed.). *The Survival of Poetry*. London: Faber & Faber, 1970.

Perloff, Marjorie. *The Poetics of Indeterminacy: Rimbaud to Cage*. Princeton University Press, 1981.

Esslin, Martin. *The Theatre of the Absurd*. London: Eyre & Spottiswode, 1962; rev. and enlarged, London: Penguin, 1968.

Kellman, Steven G. *The Self-Begetting Novel*. New York: Columbia University Press; London: Macmillan, 1980.

Waugh, Patricia. *Metafiction: The Theory and Practice of Self-Conscious Fiction*. London and New York: Methuen, 1984.

Lucie-Smith, Edward (ed.). *British Poetry since 1945*. London: Penguin, 1970.

Morrison, Blake and Motion, Andrew. *The Penguin Book of Contemporary British Poetry*. London: Penguin, 1982.

GENERAL

Among multivolume histories may be mentioned *The Oxford History of English Literature*, Oxford: Clarendon Press, 1945–; *The New Sphere History of Literature in the English Language*, 10 vols, London: Barrie & Jenkins in assoc. with Sphere Books, 1970–; *The New Pelican Guide to English Literature*, London, 1982; and *The Revels History of Drama in English*, London: Methuen, 1975–.

Robson, William Wallace. *A Prologue to English Literature*. London: Batsford, 1986.

Conrad, Peter. *The Everyman History of English Literature*. London: Dent, 1985.

Watson, Roderick. *The Literature of Scotland*. London: Macmillan, 1984.

Scholes, Robert and Kellogg, Robert. *The Nature of Narrative*. New York: OUP, 1966.

Nowottny, Winifred. *The Language Poets Use*. London: Athlone Press, 1962.

Kermode, J. Frank. *The Sense of an Ending. Studies in the Theory of Fiction*. New York: OUP, 1967.

Auden, W. H. *The Dyer's Hand and Other Essays*. New York: Random House, 1962; London: Faber & Faber, 1963.

Auerbach, Erich. *Mimesis* (tr. Willard R. Trask). Princeton University Press, 1953.

Booth, Wayne C. *The Rhetoric of Fiction*. Chicago and London: University of Chicago Press, 1961.

Empson, Sir William. *The Structure of Complex Words*. London: Chatto & Windus, 1951.

Frye, Northrop. *Anatomy of Criticism. Four Essays*. Princeton University Press, 1957.

Frye, Northrop. *The Secular Scripture: A Study of the Structure of Romance*. Cambridge, Mass. and London: Harvard University Press, 1976.

Bateson, F. W. *English Poetry and the English Language*. Oxford: Clarendon Press, 1934.

Eliot, T. S. *Selected Essays, 1917–1932*. London: Faber & Faber; New York: Harcourt Brace Jovanovitch, 1932.

Fletcher, Angus. *Allegory. The Theory of a Symbolic Mode*. Ithaca, N.Y.: Cornell University Press, 1964.

Woolf, Virginia. *Collected Essays*. 4 vols. London: Hogarth, 1966–67.

Brooks, Cleanth and Warren, Robert Penn. *Understanding Poetry. An Anthology for College Students*. 4th edn. New York: Holt, Rinehart & Winston, 1976.

Hough, Graham. *An Essay on Criticism*. London: Duckworth, 1966.

Lewis, C. S. *Studies in Words*. Cambridge. CUP, 1960.

Bloom, Harold. *The Anxiety of Influence*. New York: OUP, 1973.

Wellek, René and Warren, Austin. *Theory of Literature*. Third edn. New York: Harcourt Brace Jovanovitch, 1956.

Graff, Gerald. *Literature Against Itself: Literary Ideas in Modern Society*. Chicago and London: University of Chicago Press, 1979.

Lentricchia, Frank. *After the New Criticism*. London: Athlone Press; Chicago: University of Chicago Press, 1980.

Everett, Barbara. *Poets in Their Time: Essays on English Poetry from Donne to Larkin*. London: Faber & Faber, 1986.

Spacks, Patricia M. *The Female Imagination: A Literary and Psychological Investigation of Women's Writing*. New York: Knopf, 1975; London: Allen & Unwin, 1976.

Index

Figures in bold type refer to pages on which technical terms are defined or exemplified.